Prayer and communication ▼
"dearly departed" is an important
lives. Professors Plante and Schwartz, along with distinguished
colleagues from diverse scholarly disciplines, offer a contemporary
scientific, psychological, and theological foundation of this phenomenon that should educate and inspire readers looking for a serious
reflection on highly personal but often misunderstood part of life .

Rev. James Martin,
SJ, Editor at Large, America Media, and author of Learning to Pray:
A Guide for Everyone and My Life with the Saints

In *Human Interaction with the Divine, the Sacred, and the Deceased*,
Professors Thomas Plante and Gary Schwartz have assembled a
remarkable team of leading multidisciplinary scholars offering provocative, compelling, and evidence based reflections on communication with the divine and departed. They fearlessly attempt to address
a question on the minds of just about everyone for millennium, "Is
there consciousness after death and do the divine and departed hear
us?" The book is likely to become a classic in the field of science,
religion, and spirituality.

Harold G. Koenig,
M.D. Professor of Psychiatry & Behavioral Sciences and Director,
Center for Spirituality, Theology and Health, Duke University
Medical Center

The haunting refrain of the song *Immortality*: "we don't say goodbye"
has a telling immediacy for millions whose relationships were dis-
rupted as they mourn but remain in touch with deceased loved ones.
Making sense of the experience of communing with the departed
has been a dilemma for survivors and helping professionals. *Human
Interaction with the Divine, the Sacred, and the Deceased* is a bril-
liant, timely, and essential resource for solace and healing. Highly
recommended.

Len Sperry,
MD, PhD, author, Spirituality in Clinical Practice

Throughout history and in every culture, people have sought to connect with the divine and commune with departed loved ones. This
tour de force by Plante and Schwartz reveals the psychological and
spiritual gifts of these transpersonal experiences. This unique collection of essays offers us glimpses into the transformative potentials of
often fleeting encounters with the ineffable and points to their ability
to heal many a broken heart.

Marilyn Schlitz,
PhD, Author of Death Makes Life Possible

This is a fascinating, beautifully researched, insightful study of our yearning for contact with those we've lost and our quest for information on the afterlife. I learned a lot.

Ron Hansen is the Gerard Manley Hopkins,
SJ Professor in the Arts & Humanities at Santa Clara University and the author of Mariette in Ecstasy, Exiles, and most recently Hotly in Pursuit of the Real.

In *Human Interaction with the Divine, the Sacred, and the Deceased*, Thomas G. Plante and Gary E. Schwartz have brought together experts from a wide range of disciplines to address some of the most fundamental questions of human existence. This powerful, inspiring and important volume is one of the most comprehensive treatments to date of the afterlife, the nature of the divine, and communication with the dead. Believers and skeptics alike – and no matter where one falls on the religious/spiritual/agnostic/atheist spectrum – will benefit from the insights and findings contained in these chapters.

Valerie A. Abrahamsen,
ThD, author of Paranormal: A New Testament Scholar Looks at the Afterlife

Human Interaction with the Divine, the Sacred, and the Deceased

Human Interaction with the Divine, the Sacred, and the Deceased brings together cutting-edge empirical and theoretical contributions from scholars in fields including psychology, theology, ethics, neuroscience, medicine, and philosophy, to examine how and why humans engage in or even seek spiritual experiences and connection with the immaterial world.

In this richly interdisciplinary volume, Plante and Schwartz recognize human interaction with the divine and departed as a cross-cultural and historical universal phenomenon that continues to concern diverse disciplines. Accounting for variances in belief and human perception and use, the book is divided into four major sections: personal experience; theological consideration; medical, technological, and scientific considerations; and psychological considerations with chapters addressing phenomena including prayer, reincarnation, sensed presence, and divine revelations. Featuring scholars specializing in theology, psychology, medicine, neuroscience, and ethics, this book provides a thoughtful, compelling, evidence-based, and contemporary approach to gain a grounded perspective on current understandings of human interaction with the divine, the sacred, and the deceased.

Of interest to believers, questioners, and unbelievers alike, this volume will be key reading for researchers, scholars, and academics engaged in the fields of religion and psychology, social psychology, behavioral neuroscience, and health psychology. Readers with a broader interest in spiritualism, religious and nonreligious movements will also find the text of interest.

Thomas G. Plante is Professor of Psychology, and by courtesy, Religious Studies, at Santa Clara University. He is also Adjunct Clinical Professor of Psychiatry and Behavioral Sciences at Stanford University School of Medicine, the United States.

Gary E. Schwartz is Professor of Psychology, Medicine, Neurology, Psychiatry, and Surgery at the University of Arizona. He is also Director of the Laboratory for Advances in Consciousness and Health in the Department of Psychology at the University of Arizona, the United States.

Routledge Research in Psychology

This series offers an international forum for original and innovative research being conducted across the field of psychology. Titles in the series are empirically or theoretically informed and explore a range of dynamic and timely issues and emerging topics. The series is aimed at upper-level and post-graduate students, researchers, and research students, as well as academics and scholars.

Recent titles in the series include:

Declarative Mapping Sentences in Qualitative Research
Theoretical, Linguistic, and Applied Usages
Paul M. W. Hackett

Post-Capitalist Subjectivity in Literature and Anti-Psychiatry
Reconceptualizing the Self Beyond Capitalism
Hans Skott-Myhre

A Scientific Assessment of the Validity of Mystical Experiences
Understanding Altered Psychological and Neurophysiological States
Andrew C. Papanicolaou

The Relevance of Alan Watts in Contemporary Culture
Understanding Contributions and Controversies
Edited by Peter J. Columbus

Eastern European Perspectives on Emotional Intelligence
Current developments and research
Edited by Lada Kaliská and John Pellitteri

The Psychological Basis of Moral Judgments
Philosophical and Empirical Approaches to Moral Relativism
John J. Park

Developing a Model of Islamic Psychology and Psychotherapy
Islamic Theology and Contemporary Understandings of Psychology
Abdallah Rothman

Human Interaction with the Divine, the Sacred, and the Deceased
Psychological, Scientific, and Theological Perspectives
Edited by Thomas G. Plante and Gary E. Schwartz

For a complete list of titles in this series, please visit: https://www.routledge.com/Routledge-Research-in-Psychology/book-series/RRIP

Human Interaction with the Divine, the Sacred, and the Deceased

Psychological, Scientific, and Theological Perspectives

Edited by Thomas G. Plante and Gary E. Schwartz

 Routledge
Taylor & Francis Group

NEW YORK AND LONDON

First published 2022
by Routledge
605 Third Avenue, New York, NY 10158

and by Routledge
2 Park Square, Milton Park, Abingdon, Oxon, OX14 4RN

*Routledge is an imprint of the Taylor & Francis Group, an informa
business*

Library of Congress Cataloging-in-Publication Data
A catalog record for this title has been requested

ISBN: 978-0-367-61620-5 (hbk)
ISBN: 978-0-367-61621-2 (pbk)
ISBN: 978-1-003-10574-9 (ebk)

Typeset in Times New Roman
by KnowledgeWorks Global Ltd.

Contents

Acknowledgments

So many people other than the authors or editors help in the completion of a book project. Some contribute in a direct way while others help out in a more supportive role. We would like to acknowledge the assistance of the many people who worked to make this book project a reality.

First and foremost, we would like to thank the contributors to this volume. They include some of the leading scholars and thinkers in the field and have been a stellar team to provide the reader with state-of-the-art and evidence-based reflection and scholarship. Second, it is important to recognize the wonderful people at Routledge/Taylor& Francis who published this book. Most especially, many thanks to the editor, Elsbeth Wright for her efforts. Finally, we would like to thank our loved ones (For Tom this includes wife, Lori, and son, Zach, and for Gary, this includes wife, Rhonda) who are daily reminders that life is good and sacred and that we are blessed beyond words to have them in our lives.

Preface

Since the beginning of time, humans have wondered about what happens when we die and if we are still conscious after death. We have reflected upon the status of our deceased loved ones and speculated if they are in a better or worse place than when they were alive. We also have wondered about the gods or singular God as well as other sacred and divine spirits such as the saints and angels. People have been speculating about these matters for as long as human have walked the earth. Some have developed very thoughtful ways to think about these issues from various perspectives such as theology, science, technology, and psychology. During contemporary times, these experts have much more information and a rather sophisticated understanding of these questions. While we cannot answer these important questions with complete certainty, and may never be able to do so, we can certainly try.

The purpose of this book is to bring together some of the best minds on this topic in order to offer thoughtful and evidence-based reflections about communication with the divine, the sacred, and the departed. Contributors come from multiple academic and clinical disciplines including theologians and religious studies scholars, physicians, psychologists, social workers, and scientists, as well as from different cultural and religious backgrounds. This diversity provides a richness and multilayered approach to the book project. The topics and approaches presented are not exhaustive or encyclopedic but are an important sampling and representation of areas where various disciplines and informed perspectives weigh in on communication with the divine and departed. To our knowledge, this effort has never been made before in an edited academic book project.

This book is for believers, questioners, and open-minded unbelievers as well. It provides solid reasons and evidence to "to look from our lives" and envision a sacred big picture of life and the cosmos.

About the Editors

 **Thomas G. Plante, Ph.D., ABPP** is the Augustin Cardinal Bea, S.J., University Professor and Professor of Psychology and, by courtesy, Religious Studies, as well as Director of the Applied Spirituality Institute at Santa Clara University. He is also an Adjunct Clinical Professor of Psychiatry and Behavioral Sciences at Stanford University School of Medicine. He is a fellow of the American Psychological Association (APA) and the Society of Behavioral Medicine (SBM). He is the current editor of the APA journal *Spirituality in Clinical Practice*. He recently served as vice-chair of the National Review Board for the Protection of Children and Youth for the United States Conference of Catholic Bishops (USCCB) and was President of the Society for the Psychology of Religion and Spirituality (Division 36 of the APA). He has published over 200 professional journal articles and book chapters. Additionally, he has published 24 books. These include *Healing with Spiritual Practices: Proven Techniques for Disorders from Addictions and Anxiety to Cancer and Chronic Pain* (2018), *Graduating With Honor: Best Practices to Promote Ethics Development in College Students* (2017), *Do the Right Thing: Living Ethically in an Unethical World* (2004), *Sexual Abuse in the Catholic Church: A Decade of Crisis, 2002–2012* (2011), and *Spiritual Practices in Psychotherapy: Thirteen Tools for Enhancing Psychological Health* (2009). He has been featured in numerous media outlets, including *Time* magazine, *CNN, NBC Nightly News, The PBS News Hour, The New York Times, USA Today, The British Broadcasting Company,* and *The National Public Radio,* among many others. He has evaluated or treated more than a thousand priests and applicants to the priesthood and diaconate and has served as a consultant for a number of Roman Catholic and Episcopal Church dioceses and religious orders. *Time* magazine referred to him (April 1, 2002) as one of "three leading (American) Catholics."

Gary E. Schwartz, Ph.D., is a Professor of Psychology, Medicine, Neurology, Psychiatry, and Surgery, and director of the Laboratory for Advances in Consciousness and Health, at the University of Arizona. After receiving his Ph.D. at Harvard University in 1971, he served as an assistant professor in the Department of Psychology at Harvard. He moved to Yale University in 1976, where he was a professor of psychology and psychiatry, director of the Yale Psychophysiology Center, and codirector of the Yale Behavioral Medicine Clinic, before moving to Arizona in 1988. His research has spanned (and bridged) psychophysiology, health psychology, behavioral medicine, energy psychology, and spiritual psychology. He has published more than 450 papers, including 6 papers in the journal, *Science*. He has coedited 13 academic books including *Is Consciousness Primary* (Schwarz, Woollacott & Schwartz, 2020). He has authored 11 books for the general public including *The Afterlife Experiments* (2002), *The G.O.D. Experiments* (2006), *The Energy Healing Experiments* (2007), *The Sacred Promise* (2011), *Super Synchroncity* (2017), and *Extraordinary Claims Require Extraordinary Evidence* (2021). He was the founding president of the Academy for the Advancement of Postmaterialist Sciences (www.AAPSglobal.com).

About the Contributors

Amanda Alexander, Ph.D., completed her doctorate in Systematic Theology at Fordham University (2018), an M.Phil. at the University of Cambridge (2005), and a A.B. at Princeton *summa cum laude* in Religion (2004). Her dissertation, *Mystical Brain, Divine Consciousness: A Theological Appropriate of Cognitive Neuroscience* argues that what is often called mystical union is better understood as a mystical knowing-how that arises from the dialectic of the meditative practices of prayer and the prayer's own ontological participation in the divine act-of-being. She has taught at Fordham University, Franciscan Missionaries of Our Lady University, Santa Clara University, the Claremont School of Theology, and Loyola Marymount University.

Eben Alexander, M.D., is a former neurosurgeon who spent 15 years on the faculty of Harvard Medical School, thinking he had a reasonable idea of the relationship of consciousness to the brain. That all changed dramatically after a near-death experience due to a weeklong coma from a severe case of gram-negative bacterial meningoencephalitis in 2008 from which his doctors predicted no significant recovery. The extensive brain damage and resultant miraculous recovery to full function over two months changed his life completely, redirecting his focus to the deepest mechanisms of the nature of consciousness and healing. His books on his experience include *Proof of Heaven: A Neurosurgeon's Journey into the Afterlife, The Map of Heaven: How Science, Religion and Ordinary People are Proving the Afterlife*, and, most recently (coauthored with his life partner, Karen Newell, cofounder of Sacred Acoustics) *Living in a Mindful Universe: A Neurosurgeon's Journey into the Heart of Consciousness*.

Carrie York Al-Karam, Ph.D., is president of the Alkaram Institute, a nonprofit research and educational institute dedicated to advancing Islamic psychology to benefit society and improve lives. Her areas of interest include Islamic psychology, spiritually integrated psychotherapy, and virtue/character development from an Islamic perspective. She also has an interest in prayer and other spiritual healing methods.

She is an associate editor for a number of peer-reviewed journals including APA's *Spirituality in Clinical Practice* and the *Middle East Journal of Positive Psychology.* Her edited books are *Mental Health and Psychological Practice in the United Arab Emirates* (2015), *Islamically Integrated Psychotherapy: Uniting Faith and Professional Practice* (2018), a children's character development book called *Maya and the Seven Limbs* (2020), and a forthcoming textbook on Islamic psychology.

Hans-Ferdinand Angel, Ph.D., was trained in theology, ancient Latin philology, and history. He was Professor at the Technical University Dresden (1996–1997) and, since 1997, has been Full Professor of Catechetics and Religious Education at the Karl-Franzens University Graz. He was section editor (2008–2013) in the editorial board of the *Encyclopedia of Sciences and Religions* (Springer 2013). He is scientific director of the Credition Research Project at the Karl-Franzens University of Graz (Austria) [http://credition.uni-graz.at/de/] and was editor-in-chief of *Processes of Believing: The Acquisition, Maintenance, and Change in Creditions* (Springer 2017).

Hasan Awan, M.D., is a physician of internal medicine in private practice in Baltimore, MD. He also provides services at the Islamic Society of Baltimore Free Health Clinic. His range of studies under several Muslim scholars and imams over the last 20 years include elements of Islamic legal praxis, Quranic exegesis, Islamic theology, and especially the Islamic Hikma tradition (Islamic philosophy and Sufi metaphysics). He also has interests in alternative and holistic medicine and spiritual psychology and counseling. In addition to his role as a physician, he has also been serving the greater Baltimore Muslim community in various pastoral roles for over a decade.

Candy Gunther Brown, Ph.D., is Professor of Religious Studies at Indiana University. Brown is the author of *The Word in the World: Evangelical Writing, Publishing, and Reading in America, 1789–1880* (University of North Carolina Press, 2004); *Testing Prayer: Science and Healing* (Harvard University Press, 2012); *The Healing Gods: Complementary and Alternative Medicine in Christian America* (Oxford University Press, 2013); and *Debating Yoga and Mindfulness in Public Schools: Reforming Secular Education or Reestablishing Religion?* (University of North Carolina Press, 2019). She is the editor of *Global Pentecostal and Charismatic Healing* (Oxford University Press, 2011), and coeditor (with Mark Silk) of *The Future of Evangelicalism in America* (Columbia University Press, 2016).

Levi Checketts, Ph.D., is an adjunct professor of Religious Studies at Holy Names University and an assistant adjunct professor of Organizations and Responsible Business at St Mary's College of California. He serves as an English Ministry pastor at Jesus Love Korean United Methodist Church in Cupertino, CA and has been on the steering committee for AAR's Human Enhancement and Transhumanism interest group since 2018. He has presented work on theological ethical concerns of technology both in national and international venues, including the Society for Philosophy and Technology, the Society for Christian Ethics, and the Society for the Social Study of the Sciences (4S). His work is published in *Religions, Theology and Science* and *Dialogue: A Journal on Mormon Thought,* among other places. He is currently leading a program on Christian religious education on topics related to science and technology for young adult Asian American Christians in Silicon Valley through a UMC Discipleship Ministries grant, and has taught lay ministry courses on moral theology for the Roman Catholic Dioceses of San Jose and Monterey.

Larry Dossey, M.D., is an internal medicine physician, former Chief of Staff of Medical City Dallas Hospital, and former cochairman of the Panel on Mind/Body Interventions, National Center for Complementary and Alternative Medicine, National Institutes of Health. He is executive editor of the peer-reviewed journal *Explore: The Journal of Science and Healing.* He is the author of 13 books on the role of consciousness and spirituality in health, which have been translated into several languages. His most recent book is *One Mind: How Our Individual Mind Is Part of a Greater Consciousness and Why It Matters.* He lectures around the world.

Julie J. Exline, Ph.D., is a Professor in the Department of Psychological Sciences at Case Western Reserve University. She has a special interest in the struggles and challenges that people often experience around religion and spirituality, and she also studies the causes and consequences of supernatural attributions for events. She has served as PI on two projects from the John Templeton Foundation: one on religious/spiritual struggles and one on supernatural attributions. She is a licensed clinical psychologist in Ohio and has also been certified as a spiritual director through the Ignatian Spirituality Institute at John Carroll University. She is a past president of APA's Division 36 (Psychology of Religion and Spirituality).

Braden Molhoek is a Program Associate at the Center for Theology and the Natural Sciences and a Lecturer in Science, Technology, and Ethics at the Graduate Theological Union, and a Quarterly Lecturer in the School of Engineering at Santa Clara University. After double majoring in Genetics and Religion, Braden went on to pursue graduate work at the intersection of science and religion and ethics and technology. He received his Ph.D. from the Graduate Theological Union in 2016. His research interests, publications, and presentations cover topics including virtue ethics, gene editing, artificial intelligence, transhumanism, and ethical issues in higher education.

Kathleen C. Pait, M.A., is pursuing her Ph.D. in clinical psychology from Case Western Reserve University. In 2018, she received her Master's in psychology in education from the Spirituality Mind Body Institute at Columbia University Teachers College. While serving as Faculty-in-Residence at James Madison University, she taught several undergraduate courses including "Making Sense of Beliefs and Values: A Guided Tour for Global Citizens." Her research interests include spontaneous, organic, and synthetically induced transcendent and spiritual experiences. She is currently working on her second Master's degree investigating the therapeutic implications of After-Death Communication with a special focus on afterlife beliefs.

Raymond F. Paloutzian, Ph.D., is Professor Emeritus of Experimental and Social Psychology, edited *The International Journal for the Psychology of Religion* for 18 years. He taught at Westmont College, and was guest professor at Stanford University and Katholieke Universiteit Leuven. He authored *Invitation to the Psychology of Religion, 3rd ed.* (2017, Guilford), coedited *Forgiveness and Reconciliation* (2010, Springer), *Handbook of the Psychology of Religion and Spirituality, 2nd ed.* (2013, Guilford), *Processes of Believing: The Acquisition, Maintenance, and Change in Creditions* (2017, Springer), and *Assessing Spirituality in a Diverse World* (in review, Springer). Widely published, he gave invited talks on "The Psychology of Religion in Global Perspective" in various countries around the world.

Crystal L. Park, Ph.D., is Professor of Clinical Psychology at the University of Connecticut. Her research focuses on religious beliefs and religious coping, the phenomenon of stress-related growth, and the making of meaning in the context of traumatic events and life-threatening illnesses, particularly cancer and heart failure. She also studies integrative interventions and is currently PI or Co-PI of NIH- and foundation-funded studies of religious beliefs and stressful experiences and yoga for stress management. She co-authored *Empathic Counseling* and *Spirituality, Meaning, and Trauma* and co-edited *The Handbook of the Psychology of Religion and Spirituality* (first and second editions). She is editor of *Psychology of Religion and Spirituality*. At UConn, she maintains an active research lab of graduate and undergraduate students and teaches health psychology at both the graduate and undergraduate levels.

Patricia Pearson, M.Sc., is a journalist, author and grief counselor based in Toronto, Canada. Her most recent books are *Opening Heaven's Door*, an exploration of consciousness at end of life, and *Wish You Were Here*, an examination of traumatic grief and unsolved murder from Penguin Random House. She has written for the *New Yorker* and the *New York Times*, among dozens of other publications.

T. Anne Richards, M.A., is an interdisciplinary social scientist, retired from the University of California San Francisco and Berkeley where she was a research specialist conducting qualitative research in behavioral medicine and public health with a focus on spiritual aspects of caregiving, bereavement and recovery from grief. Ms. Richards has also developed programs through the Public Health Institute and Curry Senior Center aimed at reducing social isolation and loneliness among disenfranchised populations.

Paul J. Schutz, Ph.D., is Assistant Professor of Religious Studies at Santa Clara University. His research aims to reinvigorate the Christian theology of creation through engagement with contemporary science. His dissertation, on the writings of astronomer William Stoeger, SJ, proposes an "ecopolitical" theology oriented toward the flourishing of each creature. Recent publications include "En-Gendering Creation Anew: Rethinking Ecclesial Statements on Science, Gender, and Sexuality with William Stoeger, SJ" in *Horizons* (2021), two chapters in the *T&T Clark Handbook of Christian Theology and the Modern Sciences* (2020), "As Dewdrops on Indra's Web" in *All the Ends of the Earth: Challenge and Celebration of Global Catholicism* (2020), "Cultivating a 'Cosmic Perspective' in Theology: Reading William R. Stoeger with *Laudato Si*'" in *Theological Studies* (2019).

Rüdiger J. Seitz is a Professor of neurology at the Heinrich-Heine-University Düsseldorf and Honorary Professorial Fellow at the Florey Neuroscience Institutes, Melbourne, Australia. He has a degree in medicine with board qualification in neurology and post-doc specialization in clinical neurophysiology and functional neuroimaging. His scientific interest is in cognitive neuroscience including postlesional brain plasticity and control of human behavior. He pioneered international conferences on functional mapping of the human brain, has a broad publication record and was editor of the neuroscience section in *The Encyclopedia of Sciences and Religions* (Springer, New York, 2013) and coeditor of the book *Processing of Believing: the Acquisition, Maintenance, and Change in Creditions* (Springer, New York, 2017).

Catherine Wolff, M.A., M.S.W., M.P.M., is the former Director of the Arrupe Center for Community-Based Learning at Santa Clara University. She edited *Not Less Than Everything: Catholic Writers on Heroes of Conscience from Joan of Arc to Oscar Romero* (HarperCollins, 2013). Her book on the afterlife, *Beyond: How Humankind Thinks About Heaven*, will be published by Riverhead Books/Penguin Random House in May, 2021. She lives in Northern California with her husband Tobias Wolff, close to their three children and three grandchildren.

Introduction

Thomas G. Plante and Gary E. Schwartz

People across the globe have been trying to connect and communicate with the divine and with the deceased since the dawn of time. Prayers and rituals of various sorts, reflecting diverse faith traditions and cultures, have tried to not only interact with those who have passed on but have tried to influence the divine, the sacred (including angels and the saints), and the departed to act in ways that will benefit the living. Prayers for salvation, deliverance from troubles such as illness and traumas, as well as for insight, inspiration, wisdom, safety, security, and for basic needs are common. Experiences and desires for visitations from ghosts, angels, saints, deceased friends and relatives, and the divine are common too. There appears to be a longstanding, multicultural, multi-faith, and perhaps innate psychological desire to communicate with the gods and the departed to help better understand, manage, and cope with the various challenges of the living. In addition, clinically, those who are in grief, long to connect with loved ones who have passed on.

Perhaps just about everyone who is or has been alive has attempted, at one time or another, to pray to the divine for help. Additionally, likely everyone who is or was alive has also wondered about what happens when one dies and if consciousness continues after death. What happens when we die? Do we still think and feel things? Is it merely "lights out" as the saying goes? Do we go to heaven, purgatory, hell, somewhere else? Is there a God or higher power of some sort who hears us when we pray? Does some higher power hear us when we call out for help or when we ask for favors? These questions have been considered for millennia by just about everyone who has ever lived. Over the years, we have turned to established and perceived experts such as clerics, sages, philosophers, spiritualists, physicians, and others for answers or at least for informative speculations about these fundamental and universal questions. Prior to the Enlightenment, clerics were the go-to profession to consult about these matters in most parts of the world. Religious as well as spiritual leaders seemed to have the agreed-upon expertise to help answer or at least comment on these questions. Over time, and certainly after the scientific advancements of the twentieth century, in particular, many others including scientists, physicians, psychologists, and engineers have weighed in with thoughtful reflections and expertise while the influence of clerics has diminished as our society and culture have become more secular and empirically focused.

In contemporary times, during the late twentieth and early twenty-first centuries, controversy exists even in asking questions about the divine and departed. The influence of, and engagement with, organized religion in the western world has decreased dramatically over the past several decades as many countries have become more secular, and religious communities and traditions have become more marginalized. This is due to a confluence of reasons, but numerous religious organizational scandals have contributed a great deal to the receding influence of religion in western society. These scandals include the clerical sexual abuse crisis in the Roman Catholic Church, Islamic inspired terrorism, evangelical Christianity's relationship with the political right-wing and white supremacist ideologies, and religious and church-based financial shenanigans. The glaring hypocrisy of some religious leaders not practicing what they preach has also resulted in the loss of moral authority, and any authority and esteem in general, among many high profile religious leaders and clerics. These disturbing occurrences, and the press attention associated with them, have deeply tainted the veneer of moral authority and goodness that may have been associated with many religious groups and traditions. Scientific and secular ways of thinking have also marginalized questions of the afterlife and communication with the divine and departed as well. Many scientists, psychologists, and others, simply will not entertain these questions or concerns in a public forum and may even cast aspersions upon those who do.

Certainly, those of us who are interested in this area of inquiry or have published on this topic have raised a few eyebrows among colleagues in doing so. At least for the editors of this book, we took up this topic after, and not before, receiving tenure and full professor at our respective universities. Many colleagues may be concerned that they will not be taken seriously if they entertain and engage in topics such as communication with the divine and departed, at least in the social, natural, and clinical sciences. Yet these questions about the afterlife and communication with the divine and departed remain and are still very much in the hearts and minds of people across the globe. Those who work in many clinical fields such as medicine, nursing, social work, and clinical psychology find that their patients are often very much interested and engaged by these topics as well. Many of our patients care deeply and are plagued by these questions. How can we possibly ignore their concerns?

We believe that no thoughtful questions, addressed with state-of-the-art evidence and methodologies by scholars of goodwill, should be off-limits and so we have assembled a multidisciplinary team of scholars with unique expertise and qualifications to address the topic of human interaction with the divine, the sacred, and the deceased, examining psychological, scientific, and theological perspectives. To our knowledge, this gathering of experts from these diverse fields and perspectives offering thoughtful reflections regarding this important topic and then published in an academic professional outlet has never been done before. Therefore, we believe that this book project is groundbreaking.

We have divided the chapter contributions that follow, into four major sections with three to five chapters within each section. These sections include: (1) The personal experience; (2) theological consideration; (3) medical, technological, and scientific considerations; and finally (4) psychological considerations. The personal experience section offers chapters that well describe the actual experience of people communicating with the divine, the saints, and the departed to provide the reader with a more personal and lived experience of the phenomenon. Actual stories with real people, written and discussed in compelling ways, set the tone for the book and provide the reader with a firsthand experience of these issues. The theological consideration section tries to put these lived experiences into religious, spiritual, and theological context and ground the communication with the divine and departed experience within some of these great wisdom traditions. The medical, technological, and scientific consideration section examines these experiences through the lens of medicine, technology, and science, rooting the communication with the divine and departed phenomenon in evidence-based empirical research, clinical and medical best practices, and empirical data. Finally, the psychological considerations section turns to psychologists who interpret the communication with the divine and departed phenomenon through the lens of meaning making, cognitive processing and belief, attributions to understand the world, and ethical considerations.

Scholars who specialize in theology, psychology, medicine, neuroscience, and ethics are included in this volume thus providing a multidisciplinary, well-rounded, and grounded perspective on human interaction with the divine, the sacred, and the deceased. We come to these issues and questions from various informed academic and applied lenses along with diverse religious and spiritual backgrounds as well.

Although the jury is still out in terms of the answers to all, if not at least many, of our questions regarding human efforts to communicate with those who are beyond the realm of the living, these scholars together provide a very thoughtful, compelling, evidence-based, and contemporary approach. Their combined voices, hopefully, add much to our understanding of this critically important topic. While we all have more questions than answers perhaps, we can collectively move the ball forward in our understanding of this critically important topic in a thoughtful manner. We hope that the readers of this volume – believers, questioners, and unbelievers alike – will agree.

Part I

The Personal and Storied Experience of Divine and Departed Communication

1 Marginalizing the Sacred

The Clinical Contextualization of Sensed Presence Experiences

Patricia Pearson

In the late spring of 2015, my brother-in-law paid a visit to my sister's tomb, in an alpine meadow cemetery amid the Gatineau Hills of southern Quebec. My sister had been dead, at this point, for 7 years, and the pair had been separated as a couple for 12. Doug sat in the grass among planted geraniums for half an hour or so, musing about the rise and fall of their marriage. He told Katharine, or her tomb, that he was sorry for the part he had played in the dissolution. Then, plucking up and tossing a handful of grass, desultory, he began his 90-minute motorcycle drive back to Montreal.

> "The landscape is open there with a big wide sky, but it was overcast and had started to rain—just barely, but it made me a bit nervous," Doug later wrote to me. Even fit riders, as he surely was, begin to lose some confidence in their 50s. "It wasn't until I was maybe halfway home that I felt her presence."
>
> "The sense wasn't physical at first," he went on, "just this really nice, strong awareness of her. And then I had the distinct sensation of her arms around me, and her leaning in close against my back. It was tactile and fantastic. I felt warm. I was completely calm and happy, smiling from ear to ear. That hardly ever happens to me."
> His nervousness about the rain ebbed, and it occurred to him that Katharine was there to keep him safe on behalf of their two sons. She—her presence, her spirit—rode behind him for 20 minutes or so. "What I know is that it did not feel at all like a product of my imagination," he wrote. "It felt external to me. It felt *real*."

He wasn't prepared to name what the experience pointed to: that he was visited by my sister's ghost. Like other secular North Americans, he is aware we must uphold a certain paradigm and say "this cannot be." After all, Doug considers himself a rationalist: the son of an engineer, and himself an amateur astronomer. Nevertheless, the sensed presence mattered to him, deeply. "It was," he said, "a remarkable, indelible experience."

Sigmund Freud was the first to articulate the concept of "wishful psychosis" in grief, a notion of temporary madness featuring willfully conjured visions of the dead (Freud, 1917). A person who's lost someone might see the face of their beloved, or hear their voice, notice the smell of their pipe or perfume, or simply be struck by a feeling of their presence. This intimate and, for many, sacred experience has become a focus of interest in the grief literature. It appears to be far more common than previously realized: roughly 50 percent of the bereaved sense the presence of the deceased at some point, sometimes years after a death (Rees, 1971; Steffen & Coyle, 2012). Douglas Davies, an anthropologist at the University of Durham, United Kingdom, reported that approximately 35 percent of the people contacted for his 1995 survey of 1,603 people in 4 regions of the United Kingdom "had gained some such sense of the presence of the dead" (Davies, 1997, p. 171). Such ghostly apparitions were diagnosed as fanciful yearnings by Freud—they were pathological, a warning sign of some lingering dependency. In his 1917 essay "Mourning and Melancholia," he urged his patients toward grief recovery by "severing bonds" with the dead: move on, let go, lest sorrow bedevil and sink you. For decades, this became the counseling profession's modus operandi, with a sort of tacit agreement playing out between therapist and patient that what the latter sensed, no matter how comforting it might be or how real it may seem, dwelled in their head and would best be ignored and forgotten. When the physician W. D. Rees uncovered the prevalence rate of these hallucinations in a 1972 study of Welsh widows—about 50 percent—he also found that 3-quarters of them had never spoken of the experience before being asked in his survey. Unsurprisingly, these widows didn't wish to be pathologized. They also didn't want to move on (Rees, 1971).

In 1970, the English author Sylvia Townsend Warner, a frequent contributor of short stories to *The New Yorker*, had an unexpected visit from her dead lover, Valentine Ackland, lost the previous year to breast cancer. Roused one night at three a.m., Warner found, as she later wrote in her diary, that Valentine was presently beside her in their bed. "Not remembered," she clarified, "not evoked, not a sense of presence. *Actual.*" In the dark quiet of their British cottage, this "actual" Valentine, solid yet ephemeral, engaged in a reuniting embrace. Then she was gone. "I held her again," Warner noted with deep satisfaction. "It was. It is" (Law, 2016).

Ought anyone to have argued with her? Would a woman as fiercely intelligent as Townsend Warner have suffered the indignity of a therapist patronizing her by allowing her to have this imaginary friend whilst privately deeming it a grief hallucination? The perceptual phenomenon lays bare a metaphysical crisis at the heart of our common model of mourning. For there to be efficacy in recovery, these experiences must be respected as real. As counseling psychologist Edith Steffen of the University of

Roehampton, United Kingdom, notes, there is a "controversial reality status" at play that can erode the trusting relationship between therapist and bereaved person if not handled with care and nuance (Steffen, 2019, p. 166). The question that arises isn't whether or not these apparitions are real, so much as why the first impulse of many is to turn away from the sanctity of such experiences and dismiss them as false.

Familial and fraternal hauntings have long been central to the stories we tell, from Enkidu's ghost in *The Epic of Gilgamesh* and Odysseus conferring with his slain brother-in-arms Achilles to Banquo's discarnate presence in *Macbeth* and Heathcliffe's sorrowful Catherine. More recently, there's the grieving detective John River, who confers with his newly dead partner, Stevie, in the television series *River.*

In the nineteenth century, such fictive imaginings were often based on real losses, as infectious disease swept through families. Harriet Beecher Stowe, for example, watched her toddler Charlie die during a Cholera outbreak in Cincinnati during the summer of 1849. She began to read, as she described it, "of visions, of heavenly voices, of mysterious sympathies and transmissions of knowledge from heart to heart without the intervention of the senses, or what Quakers call being 'baptized into the spirit' of those who are distant." Her husband, the theologian Calvin Stowe, regularly perceived discarnates of one kind or another, according to the historian Harold Bush, and mused in a letter to a friend, "Is it absurd to believe that some peculiarity in the nervous system...may bring some men more than others into an almost abnormal contact with the spirit World?" (Bush, 2016).

In *Uncle Tom's Cabin*, Tom has a perception of his wife Eva's postmortem presence. As Beecher Stowe would later write, the dead "still may move about in our homes, shedding an atmosphere of purity and peace...We are compassed about by a cloud of witnesses, whose hearts throb in sympathy with every effort and struggle, and who thrill with joy at every success" (Stowe, 1896).

The first scientific survey that examined visions of the dead was conducted in the 1880s by some founding members of London's Society for Psychical Research (SPR). (Gurney, Myers, & Podmore, *Phantasms of the Living*, 1886.) Investigations into the unconscious mind were coming into vogue then, exploring the mysteries of hypnosis and the meanings of dreams. At the same time, cameras and telegraphs, with their disembodied voices and figures frozen in time, were upending what people thought possible. The SPR scholars, many of them scientists, were fascinated by the question of *how we know what we know.* One of these members was Alfred Russel Wallace, co-inventor of the theory of evolution, who disagreed with Darwin that natural selection explained consciousness. A brain could evolve and the transcendent mind could flow through it, like water filtering through a grate. Unlike Darwin's followers, he saw no inherent contradiction between the theory of natural selection and the prospect of transcendent consciousness. If mechanisms could be found for one, then perhaps they could be found for the other.

Another SPR member was Samuel Clemens, who went by the pen name Mark Twain. Clemens' interest stemmed in the year 1858, when he had had a vivid dream of his brother lying in a coffin. A few days earlier—and still unknown to Clemens at the time—that same brother had died in a steamboat explosion on the Mississippi River. When he went to see him, the body was laid out in the coffin in a manner that precisely matched the details of his dream (Blum, 2007). SPR member and Cambridge scholar Frederic Myers was intrigued by *telepathy*, a word that Myers cobbled together from Greek words for "distance" and "feeling."

An illustration of how these men were thinking can be found in the *Virginia Magazine of History and Biography* in 1903, where the profile of a local luminary from the eighteenth century makes reference to a family legend in which a relative saw "General Minor in the gallery upstairs— yet he was sure it was only his ghost," for the perception corresponded with the actual time and date of the general's sudden demise elsewhere in the state. About this, the biographer notes that,

> there was no ghost, nor was there anything supernatural in McFarland's vision. The art of photography and wireless telegraphy in the physical world prepares us to believe that on a mind peculiarly sensitive, impressions may be made by physical facts at a distance.
> (Barker, 1903, p. 437)

In other words, the men at the turn of the twentieth century who grew interested in investigating hallucinations, dreams, and synchronicities were as much influenced by scientific invention and the emerging field of psychology as by what we tend, retrospectively, to view as a faddish spiritualism. They were, after all, embedded in a world in which many folklores concerning visions and doppelgangers were still enfolded into human ways of knowing. These included Scotland's tradition of having "Second Sight" (Cohn, 1999) and Ireland's *TaiDhbHSe* (pronounced *taish*): "To see the double at night implies the death of the person seen," as explained by folklorist Lewis Spence (Spence, 1945). The Bretons called such portents *intersignes* (Badone, 1987), while elsewhere in France one spoke of the "revenant." Indeed, historically, great lengths were gone to in various cultures to keep wandering spirits becalmed or anchored, which implies a wide acceptance of such post-mortem sightings. As the French medievalist Claude Lecouteux notes, "The world was haunted, by the dead transformed into spirits passed on to another state, living another life in permanent conjunction with 'contemporary' humans and always capable of either giving them information or ceding to their imperious requests. The people of the Middle Ages had no fear of death: they dreaded the dead—some of the dead, in any case" (Lecouteux, 2009).

English historian William of Newburgh wrote in the 1190s, "one would not easily believe that corpses come out of their graves and wander around, animated by some evil spirit, to terrorize or harm the living, *unless there were many cases in our times*, supported by ample testimony [italics mine]".

In Europe, the Christian Church was uncomfortable with this lived reality of sensed presences because it didn't dovetail properly with Christian doctrine. How could Jesus be said to have miraculously arisen from the dead if that was, in fact, a fairly common occurrence? "Augustine posed the problem of perception," writes Lecouteux, referring to the influential fifth-century theologian. "Are these apparitions the creations of slumbering, somnolent or feverish men?" Upon reflection, Augustine decided that the apparitions were illusions or messages projected into the psyche by God: "It communicates to the dreamer that these dead bodies require burial," for instance, "and all without the knowledge of the former owners of these bodies" (Lecouteux, 2009). Pope Gregory the Great (540–604) pursued the quandary of apparitions down a path that would ultimately contribute to some degree to the establishment of Purgatory as a distinct location between Heaven and Hell, where restless souls awaited assignation. "Henceforth these individuals were regarded as imprisoned souls, or the damned. It was believed that the elect show themselves at times, but they are easily identified because they are radiant with happiness, and the clerics were incapable of confusing them with the sinners suffering the punishments of purgatory" (Ibid.).

Eventually, what seems to have happened is that the Christian Church reshaped revenants from guiding ancestors and the disoriented or vengeful dead into spiritually suspended beings who depended upon the living to pray for their passage to heaven. This reshaping enabled the Church to take control of pagan ancestor worship and bend its purposes to Christianity. Hence the monks of Cluny established November 1 as All Souls' Day, to incorporate the pagan feast of the dead. The irony of what the Church accomplished, though, is that it managed to take common and powerful experiences, each of which has its own context, as I will discuss—the guardian angel, the deathbed apparition, and the beloved deceased in our ongoing lives—and turn them into church-related set pieces that scientific inquiry, post-Darwin, swiftly turned its back upon.

The SPR was, for the above reasons, almost doomed from the start to be ridiculed. Nevertheless, their survey of non-pathological hallucinations in the British population became the first, and for many years the only, attempt to capture the prevalence of perceptions of the dead. Myers, along with his colleagues Edward Gurney and Frank Podmore, undertook a survey of British newspaper readers, putting out the question, "Have you ever, when awake, had the impression of seeing or hearing or being touched by anything which, so far as you could discover, was not due to any external cause?" They weren't sure what they would find, given the vagueness of the prompt. But, when the accounts came in, one surprise was the number of reports concerning family apparitions, rather than ghosts of the house-haunting variety. And given their preoccupation with the new concept of telepathy, the scholars decided to focus on cases where the death or danger had occurred either 12 hours before or after the percipient's experience of the hallucination. They clarified that, "no experiences of any sort—even though otherwise admissible as following within the 12 hours' limit—have been included in our telepathic evidence, if the fact of the death was already known to the percipient" (Gurney et al., 1886, p. 512).

They were able to identify and investigate 80 such cases with corroborated evidence, through written documentation or witnesses, that the hallucination corresponded with an unexpected death. An additional 17 cases corresponded with injury or illness. They clarified that, "no experiences of any sort...have been included in our telepathic evidence, if the fact of the death was already known to the percipient." It was a significantly easier investigation to conduct in that time when news of a death at sea or an illness abroad was slow to travel. Percipients had ample opportunities to make diary notations or discuss what they'd perceived with others before encountering the confirming fact.

A characteristic account in their collection, which, in 1886, they published in two volumes titled *Phantasms of the Living*, was provided by a Mr. Timothy Cooper, who described being busy at work when, "I was going down into the cellar to fetch butter for a customer, and as I was on the top step, I saw my father standing at the bottom of the cellar steps in his shirt and night-cap, and he seemed to walk into the cellar. I went down and fetched the butter and looked for my father, who was nowhere to be seen." At the time, his father was dying 250 miles away (Ibid., p. 40).

Wishing to expand upon this work, in 1889, the SPR recruited 410 volunteers to each ask at least 25 British adults, from various walks of life, the same question about spectral impressions. Ten percent replied that they had experienced the phenomenon. Five other countries participated in this Census of Hallucinations: the United States (organized by the "Father of American psychology" William James), France (overseen by psychologist Leon Marillier), Germany, Russia, and Brazil, culling 44,329 responses in total. Each survey reflected the results of the others, suggesting that 10–15 percent of otherwise healthy people experience sensory hallucinations at some point in their lives. It was the first social science data collected on this phenomenon. It was also the first international, albeit accidental, survey of grief hallucinations in general, which comprised a subset of the more "telepathic" category of response. "There was a cluster of cases, where the apparition was seen by the percipient at a time coinciding closely with the time of death," noted the scholar Henry Sidgwick in his report on their work in 1894 (Sidgwick et al., 1894).

The scholars theorized that perhaps humans could intuit a significant calamity occurring to those they loved, and then the unconscious mind projected this telepathic gleaning as some kind of confirmatory hallucination—a voice, for example, or a scent. Gurney speculated that we become aware of a crisis only unconsciously at first, and then gradually bring the idea to consciousness in some fashion, the way an alarm clock may ring in a dream. "There may be many other cases," he wrote, "where it never reaches the stage of even a conscious idea, never forces itself on the attention at all, and where, therefore, we never hear anything about it."

As William James later wrote: "we live sheltered, born with mental buffers to protect against such intrusions, to keep life from being too impossibly strange" (Blum, 2007, p. 224).

In fact, such an experience prompted Austrian scientist Hans Berger to invent the electroencephalogram (EEG), a few decades later. He created this now-common medical procedure in an attempt to track whether electrical currents in the brain might somehow have enabled his sister to "sense" the near-fatal collision he once had with a horse-drawn cannon, which had caused her to send an alarmed and unprompted telegram (Millett, 2001).

The Census of Hallucinations laid the groundwork for our subsequent understanding that hallucinations can be non-pathological. In reporting to the 1894 International Congress of Psychology, French researcher Marillier offered two conclusions: (1) there are indeed hallucinations in healthy subjects that differ from those in the mentally ill and (2) given the percentage of first-hand reports of coincident hallucinations, the probability of telepathy had to be admitted.

Reports of anomalous perception occurring when people are near death (or in danger) continue to be quite common. In a general population survey conducted in Germany, for example, such crisis impressions were identified as having occurred to 18.7 percent of respondents (Schmied-Knittel & Schetsche, 2005). In the United Kingdom, a five-year retrospective survey of hospice staff found that more than half of respondents were aware of coincidences, "usually reported by friends of family of the person who is dying, who say the dying person has visited them at the time of death" (Fenwick, Lovelace, & Brayne, p. 175). These synchronicities can serve as the first intimation that death has occurred. They may feature a brief visual hallucination, the hearing of a voice, a vivid—often repeating—dream, or the sudden onset of an urgent conviction that compels action, such as interrupting a trip and driving home or frantically making a phone call.

From a research perspective, it has been difficult to conceptualize these subjective experiences due to an unsettled vocabulary. The occurrences have been referred to, variously, as "crisis apparitions," (e.g. Evans, 2002), "telepathicimpressions" (Stevenson, 1970), "deathcoincidences" (Fenwick and Fenwick, 2008), "phantasms of the living" (Gurney et al., 1886), and "crisis ESP" (Schmied-Knittel & Schetsche, 2005). This author, in collaboration with Dr. Julie Beischel and Dr. Julia Mossbridge, recently conducted a literature review, and proposed the encapsulatory term of "crisis impression" (Pearson, Beischel, & Mossbridge, 2021) Sometimes, the phenomenon has been swept up into broader categories like "after-death communication" or, as I've noted, grief or "bereavement hallucinations." The semantics are for research purposes, though. To the grieving and to those in distress, it matters little *when* or *how* the event occurred, only that it did so.

H. D. Howells, the founding editor of the *Atlantic Monthly* magazine, defended grief hallucinations from an emerging class of skeptics after his 26-year-old daughter Winnie died. "I would have the bereaved trust their mystical experiences for much truth which they cannot affirm," he wrote in 1910's "A Counsel of Consolation." "They may be the kaleidoscopic adjustment of our jarred and shattered being; they may be prismal rays of celestial light: who shall say from knowledge?" (Howells, 1910).

But Howells' plea was cast aside. At this time, the fledgling field of psychology was attempting to establish itself as an objective science, and there was a desire among many to distance it from matters of inquiry that might be deemed mystical, irrational, or superstitious—anything that might offend the militant Darwinists of the era. The SPR hallucination surveys and much of their subsequent works were, therefore, largely ignored by the wider scientific world (Le Malefan & Sommer, 2015).

There were some exceptions. In 1924, physicist Sir William Barrett presented a collection of 57 accounts of *deathbed visions*, building on earlier work by James Hyslop (e.g. Alvarado, 2014) and Italian researcher Ernesto Bozzano (1923), to explore a related branch of anomalous experience. Dying people apparently perceived the deceased as well, an observation that has gained significant new attention in recent years. There are a mounting number of peer-reviewed studies of the visions and dreams of the dying in palliative settings (e.g. Kerr, 2014). Barrett became aware of such perceptions because of his wife, who was one of Europe's first female obstetricians, working in Edinburgh.

On January 12, 1924, Lady Florence Barrett attended the birth of a child in Dublin whose mother, Doris, now lay dying from complications and blood loss. "Suddenly," Lady Barrett later wrote,

> she looked eagerly towards one part of the room, a radiant smile illuminating her whole countenance. "Oh, lovely, lovely," she said. I asked, "What is lovely?" "What I *see*," she replied in low, intense tones. "What do you see?" "Lovely brightness—wonderful beings." It is difficult to describe the sense of reality conveyed by her intense absorption in the vision. Then—seeming to focus her attention more intently on one place for a moment—she exclaimed, "Why, it's father!

Oh, he's so glad I'm coming, he is so glad. It would be perfect if only W. (her husband) would come too." Briefly, Doris reflected to those in the room that she should, perhaps, stay for the baby's sake. But then she said, "I can't—I can't stay; if you could see what I do, you would know I can't stay."

At this point, Doris saw something that confused her: "He has Vida with him," she told Lady Barrett, referring to her sister, whose death three weeks earlier had been kept from her because of the pregnancy. "Vida is with him," she said wonderingly.

Hearing of this experience from Lady Barrett, Sir William Barrett solicited written accounts of Doris's apparent vision from his wife, an attendant nurse, resident medical officer Dr. Phillips, Matron Miriam Castle, and from Doris' mother, Mary Clark of Highbury, all of whom had been in the room. The descriptions corroborated one another, which prompted Sir Barrett to pursue other cases (Barrett, 1926, p. 24).

For the Western scientific establishment in general, however, ghostly visions became a laughing matter, a relic from humanity's naïve past. As we moved toward the medicalization of death and the pathologizing of sorrow, perceptions of the dying and the dead were disregarded and forgotten, except by all the people who continued to perceive them, creating a curious sort of spiritual underground that exists to this day.

With the rise of psychology as a discipline, grief therapy invariably evolved as a specialty, and Freud's "severing bonds" model took the form of advising the bereaved to make peace and let go. They would only "recover" from a loss by leaving the loved one behind and redirecting their emotional energy toward new relationships. In this context, ghostly presences, now dubbed grief hallucinations, were viewed as an obstacle to recovery, for they represented an unhealthy clinging to the past. A 1972 study of London widows undertaken by British psychiatrist Colin Murray Parkes led him to conclude that seeing or sensing their deceased partner—which they unexpectedly described to him—must pertain to a frustrated attempt to reaffirm a lost attachment. Parkes compared it to birds seeking out a forsaken nest. The hallucination was thus an ineffective coping mechanism and "may delay acceptance of the true situation" (Parkes & Brown, 1972).

Likewise, the psychiatrist Beverley Raphael dismissed grief hallucinations in her 1983 book *Anatomy of Bereavement* as common but unhelpful: "These perceptual misinterpretations reflect the intense longing and, like dreams are a source of a wish fulfillment," she wrote, echoing Freud (Raphael, 1983). The implication being that sensing the presence of the dead was infantile, like having an imaginary friend. As the psychologist Dennis Klass argued in the mid-90s, "the pathology of grief was associated with the stereotype of feminine behaviour"—dependent, irrational, wistful, hysterical. Klass himself disagreed, and proposed a new model of grief recovery in 1996 called "continuing bonds," which better accorded with the reality of most people's experience. "In the new model," Klass wrote, "the purpose of grief is the construction of a durable biography of both the dead person and the living person that enables the living to integrate the memory of the dead and their ongoing interactions with the dead into their lives" (Klass, 1996).

Klass and his colleagues had observed that North Americans themselves didn't experience their grief hallucinations or private conversations with their dead as an impediment to recovery. One study of widows in Boston found that all sensed their spouses, and none were swooning face-down on their beds. "The widows who continued to have vivid illusions of perceiving the deceased did not differ from other widows in the study in their acceptance of death, apparent self-esteem, or movement to building a new life," the researchers reported. "They also did not seem to be more isolated socially or to perceive themselves as more abandoned. They seemed rather to be better at this style of expressing grief, more accepting of it and more convinced of its meaning" (Klass, 1996, p. 194).

This accorded with the research of non-Westerners, many of whom have cultures that create space for ongoing engagement with ancestors. A study of Japanese widows, for example, found that their rituals of leaving food out and lighting candles for the present dead made them more psychologically resilient in grief than their American counterparts (Yamamoto, Okinogi, & Iwasaki, 1969). Similarly, American anthropologist Charles Emmons once conducted a study of ghost belief in Hong Kong. As one respondent told him, "I don't believe in just any ghost. But I believe in Grandma" (Emmons, 1982).

"New grief therapy techniques," psychologist Edith Steffen argues in the 2018 book *Continuing Bonds*, "draw on experiential connections with the deceased that appear to normalize and validate sense of presence and invite contact, even if only at a symbolic or imaginary level." In other words, like dreams, they can be brought into therapy without provoking an existential crisis in the therapist: "[Sense of presence experiences] can be a gateway toward accessing 'the back story' of the relationship which can be therapeutically supported with specific techniques such as letter-writing and dialoguing with the deceased" (Steffen & Hayes, 2018, p. 155).

The experience of sensed presences has by no means been confined to women, though widows tend to be the cohort most studied. The world wars are filled with reports of soldiers sensing or seeing newly dead comrades and siblings-in-arms. One such encounter was the subject of a memoir by the Canadian soldier William Bird, who was awoken at the front by his deceased younger brother, who urged him out of his tent and along a trench line moments before Bird's sleeping position was shelled (Cook, 2013).

This experience of a sensed presence was also encountered in the extreme environments that Europeans and Americans were newly exploring at the turn of the twentieth century. One particularly significant encounter was alluded to by the poet T. S. Eliot in *The Wasteland* in 1922: "Who is the third who walks always beside you? When I count, there are only you and I together/but when I look ahead up the white road/there is always another one walking beside you." Eliot was referencing the uncanny perceptions of explorer Ernest Shackleton, who traversed a mountainous stretch of Antarctica in 1916 after his expedition ship foundered in thick ice. He staggered along with 2 crew members for 50 kilometers in quest of rescue, and at some point in the harrowing trek, all 3 became aware of a presence, another companion, accompanying and guiding them. The presence—to Eliot the third man, although it was, in reality, a fourth—seemed to escort them safely to a Norwegian whaling station and then dematerialized.

None spoke about it during the journey itself, each presuming that he, alone, sensed the extra companion. Later, when Shackleton was asked about this, he refused to surrender what he felt was a sublime experience to scientific ridicule. "None of us care to speak about that," he said. "There are some things that never can be spoken of. Almost to hint about them comes perilously close to sacrilege" (Geiger, 2009). His reticence has been shared by the great many explorers, sailors, divers, and mountaineers who turn out to have experienced what later got dubbed "The Third Man" in the midst of duress and danger. In a manner that is strikingly similar to the perceptions of the bereaved, these companions have sometimes been visible, sometimes not, have sometimes been audible, often not, but always they have comforted in some ineffable way.

Early scientific explanations tended to focus less on the context—such as grief or terror—and more on the location. Soldiers were thought to be sleep-deprived in their trenches. Mountaineers were believed to be suffering the effects of altitude, lack of oxygen, and cold stress. Victims of shipwreck, who had plenty of heat and rich air, were assumed to have hallucinated due to sunstroke or dehydration. Polar explorers had been tricked into the illusion by monotony and sensory deprivation, a world of sunlit sameness—"the white road"—which prompts the brain to assemble absent imagery.

Meanwhile, men crossing the varied terrains of jungles and forests also encountered the Third Man. When Henry Stoker, cousin to the author of *Dracula*, and two fellow British sailors escaped a Turkish prison during the First World War, they wandered for days through the wilderness, and the presence kept pace. "We had all three been sensible of his presence throughout the most trying part of the night; we all three agreed that the moment he left us was when we had put the danger behind. I cannot exaggerate," Stoker later wrote, "how real his presence was, how content one felt – despite the mystery of it – that he should be there" (Geiger, 2009, p. 61).

Notably, as with the soldier William Bird, several wartime and extreme environment accounts feature a sensed presence that is, at one and the same time, a Third Man and a deceased relative, thus blurring the semantic distinctions altogether so that we can only return to something akin to a guardian spirit. Polar explorer Ann Bancroft and astronaut Jerry Linenger both perceived the presence of a deceased relative, for example, whose unexpected accompaniment in their time of duress proved profoundly consoling. As with Shackleton, these moments were both intimate and sublime. They weren't offered up for scrutiny.

When, in 1996, Dennis Klass proposed to shift the model of therapy in grief counseling to one of respecting "continuing bonds," many clinicians took the shift onboard but remained distinctly uncomfortable with how to approach grief hallucinations. In 2005, UK bereavement counselor Sally Flatteau Taylor conducted a study into the counseling experiences of bereaved clients who had sensed dead loved ones. She found that 80 percent felt patronized, misunderstood, or dismissed when it came to this element of their recovery. For many clients, Taylor notes, it can still be easier to keep the matter to oneself rather than to face a counselor's discomfort or disbelief (Taylor, 2005).

When Dr. Christopher Kerr, a Toronto-raised palliative care physician who heads Hospice Buffalo, first worked with patients on rounds, he was completely unprepared for the number of dreams and visions his patients described featuring the consoling dead. "We never had any such discussion on the topic in med school," he emailed me. In his book, *Death is But a Dream,* Kerr writes, "The acceleration of the science of medicine has obscured its art, and medicine, always less comfortable with the subjective, has been more concerned with disproving the unseen than revering its meaning" (Kerr, 2020).

Remarkably, nearly 150 years after the first SPR studies, scientists still have no idea what, exactly, is happening when someone hallucinates, or senses, the dead, notwithstanding their long-standing rejection of the integrity of personal perception. "To date," wrote neuroscientist Armando D'Agostino in *The Neuroscience of Visual Hallucinations*, "no study specifically explores the neurofunctional correlates of visual hallucinatory phenomena in the bereaved population." (D'Agostino, Castelnovo, & Scarone, 2014) There is simply no way to anticipate these events and hence attempt their capture in a laboratory. Yet, even so, the first reaction for many upon hearing that someone has, for example, seen their dead husband perched on the end of their bed one evening is to *explain it away.* What does that accomplish, other than strand the grieving in a liminal place between solace and madness? Do we uphold a materialist scientific viewpoint because we believe all the great questions have been answered, or are we being gestural—afraid to appear out of synch with a neuroscience that presumes the mind is bounded by the brain? Based on the many confidences I've been trusted with by thoughtful people—members of parliament, pediatricians, scientists, fellow journalists—I have come to think it's the latter. We've accepted the dominant paradigm the way peasants once allowed monks to intone about the medical necessity of balancing *humours,* only to secretly turn to herbalists and midwives later for advice based on a more earth-bound *way of knowing.*

What the grieving experience is what some theorists now call "experiential cognition," or a way of knowing that is difficult, if not impossible, to measure and quantify. Grief, this thinking goes, is not unlike how we experience beauty or pain. A century later, we've returned to what *Atlantic Monthly's* H. D. Howells wrote so eloquently: "I would have the bereaved trust their mystical experiences for much truth which they cannot affirm." Some particularly daring observers go one step further: "We do not automatically have to jump to a reductionist conclusion," the anthropologist Jack Hunter wrote recently (Hunter, 2018). In order to engage in genuinely empathetic listening without being patronizing, "we must be open to the possibility that what they tell us is true and real" (Klass & Steffen, 2018, p. 197).

Hunter continues: "There may be more going on. Reality doesn't play by our rules." It is an important, provocative point about the arrogance of the Western scientific paradigm. If it is belief that gets in the way of healthy human grieving then we might need to reframe the question: *whose* belief?

References

Alvarado, C. S. (2014). 'Visions of the Dying', by James H Hyslop (1907): With an introduction by Carlos S. Alvarado. *History of Psychiatry*, 25(2), 237–252. doi: 10.1177/0957154X14523075.

Badone, E. (1987). Death omens in a Breton Memorate. *Folklore, 98*(1), 99–104.

Barker, C. M. (1903). Four successive John Minors. *Virginia magazine of history and biography, 10*(4), 436–438.

Barrett, W. (1926). *Deathbed visions.* London: Methuen. Reprinted by White Crow Books in 2011.

Blum, D. (2007). *Ghost hunters: William James and the search for scientific proof of life after death.* New York: Penguin.

Bozzano, E. (1923). Psychic phenomena at the moment of death (Phénomènes psychiques au moment de la mort). Paris: Éditions de la B.P.S.

Bush, H. K. (2016). *Continuing bonds: Parental grief and nineteenth century American authors.* Tuscaloosa, AL: Alabama University Press.

Cohn, S. A. (1999). A questionnaire study on second sight experiences. *Journal of the Society for Psychical Research, 63*(855), 129–157.

Cook, T. (2013). Grave beliefs: Stories of the supernatural and the uncanny among Canada's Great War trench soldiers. *Journal of Military History, 77*(2), 521–542.

D'Agostino, A., Castelnovo, A., & Scarone, S. (2014). Non-pathological associations—Sleep and dreams, deprivation and bereavement. In D. Collerton, U. Mosimann, & E. Perry (Eds.), *The neuroscience of visual hallucinations* (pp. 59–89). London: Wiley-Blackwell.

Davies, D. J. (1997). *Death Ritual and Belief the Rhetoric of Funerary Rites.* London: Bloomsbury.

Emmons, C. F. (1982). *Chinese ghosts and ESP: A study of paranormal beliefs and experiences.* Lanham, MD: Scarecrow Press.

Evans, H. (2002). Seeing ghosts: Experiences of the paranormal. London: John Murray.

Fenwick, P., & Fenwick, E. (2008). *The art of dying: A journey to elsewhere.* London: Continuum.

Fenwick, P., Lovelace, H., & Brayne, S. (2010). Comfort for the dying: Five-year retrospective and one-year prospective studies of end of life experiences. *Archives of Gerontology and Geriatrics, 51*(2), 173–179.

Freud, S. (1917/1961). Mourning and melancholia. In J. Strachey (Ed. and Trans.), *The standard edition of the complete psychological works of Sigmund Freud* (Vol. 14, pp. 243–258). London: Hogarth Press.

Geiger, J. (2009). *The third man factor: Surviving the impossible.* Toronto: Penguin Canada.

Gurney, E., Myers, F. W. H., & Podmore, F. (1886). *Phantasms of the living.* London: Trubner.

Howells, H. D. (1910). *After days: Thoughts on the future life.* New York: Harper Brothers.

Hunter, J. (2018). Ontological flooding and continuing bonds. In D. Klass (Ed.), *Continuing bonds in bereavement: New directions for research and practice* (pp. 191–200). New York: Routledge.

Kerr, C. et al. (2014). End-of-life dreams and visions: a longitudinal study of hospice patients experiences. *Journal of Palliative Medicine, 17*(3), 296–303.

Kerr, C. (2020). *Death is but a dream: Finding hope and meaning at life's end.* New York: Avery.

Klass, D. (Ed.). (1996). *Continuing bonds: New understandings of grief.* New York: Routledge.

Klass, D., & Steffen, E. (2018). *Continuing bonds in bereavement: New directions for research and practice.* New York: Routledge.

Law, J. (2016). The diaries of Sylvia Townsend Warner – My bloody valentine in *The Dabbler,* http://thedabbler.co.uk/2016/01/the-diaries-of-sylvia-townsend-warner-my-bloody-valentine/.

Lecouteux, C. (2009). *The Return of the Dead: Ghosts, Ancestors and the Transparent Veil of the Pagan Mind.* Rochester, Vt.: Inner Traditions.

Le Malefan, P., & Sommer, A. (2015). Leon Marillier and the veridical hallucination in late-nineteenth and early-twentieth-century French psychology and psychopathology. *History of Psychiatry, 26*(4), 418–432.

McCletchie, S. (1999). *The Church Historians of England*, Vol. IV, part II, London: Seeley's; translated by Joseph Stevenson (1861) with spelling modernized and digitized by Scott McCletchie. https://sourcebooks.fordham.edu/basis/williamofnewburgh-intro.asp.

Millett, D. (2001). Hans Berger: From psychic energy to the EEG. *Perspectives in Biology and Medicine, 44*(4), 522–42.

Parkes, C. M., & Brown, R. J. (1972). Health after bereavement: A controlled study of young Boston widows and widowers. *Psychosomatic Medicine, 34*(5), 449–461.

Pearson, P., Beischel, J., & Mossbridge, J. (2021). *Crisis Impressions: A review of the literature*. Unpublished.

Raphael, B. (1983). *Anatomy of bereavement: A handbook for the caring professions*. New York: Basic Books.

Rees, W. D. (1971). The hallucinations of widowhood. *British Medical Journal*, 4(5778), 37–41.

Schmied-Knittel, I., & Schetsche, M. T. (2005). Everyday miracles: Results of a representative survey in Germany. *European Journal of Parapsychology*, 20(1), 3–21.

Sidgwick, H., Johnson, A., Myers, F. W. H., Podmore, F., & Sidgwick, E. M. (1894). Report on the Census of Hallucinations. Proceedings of the Society for Psychical Research, 10, 25–422.

Spence, L. (1945). *The magic arts in Celtic Britain*. London: Dover & Co.

Maria Steffen, E. (2019). Implicational Meaning (Re) Creation in Bereavement as a Lifeworld Dialogue: An Existential–Constructivist Perspective. Journal of Constructivist Psychology, 32(2), 126–137.

Steffen, E. & Hayes, J. (2018) Working with Welcome and Unwelcome Presence in Grief. In D. Klass & E. Steffen (Eds.) *Continuing bonds in bereavement: New directions for research and practice* (pp. 163–175). London: Routledge.

Steffen, E., & Coyle, A. (2012). Sense of presence experiences in bereavement and their relationship to mental health: A critical examination of a continuing controversy. In C. Murray (Ed.), *Mental health and anomalous experience* (pp. 33–56). Hauppauge, NY: Nova Science Publishers.

Stevenson, I. (1970). Telepathic impressions: A review and report of thirty-five new cases. Charlottesville, VA: University of Virginia.

Stowe, H. B. (1852). Uncle Tom's cabin. London: J. Cassell.

Stowe, H. B. (1896). *The writings of Harriet Beecher Stowe*. Boston: Houghton, Mifflin & Co.

Taylor, S. F. (2005). Between the idea and the reality: A study of the counseling experience of bereaved people who sense the presence of the deceased. *Counseling and Psychotherapy Research*, 5, 53–61.

Yamamoto, T., Okinogi, K., & Iwasaki, T. (1969). Mourning in Japan. *American Journal of Psychiatry*, 125, 12.

2   Understanding Lived Experience of Encountering the Divine and the Departed

T. Anne Richards

The Divine is known by many names: God, Supreme Being, the Ultimate, Creator, Grandfather, Father, Divine Mother, Holy Spirit, Brahman, Allah, to name a few. The aspect of the Divine in sentient beings is also known by many names: the Christ Within, Atman, the Self, the Soul, the Still Small Voice, the Buddha Nature, to name a few. Saints and mystics throughout history, across ancient, indigenous, and contemporary traditions, have voiced their personal experiences of awe and wonder in the presence of the Divine; encounters rising up from within, external voices heard, and also, experiences of a transformed, illumined quality of the outer world (Easwaran, 1996). Practitioners around the world, ordinary people, seek to know the Divine in their own way, through their own interpretations (Hood, 1995; Merton, 1996; Smith, 1991). Language and practices vary but, union with the Divine, oneness and mergence, has been realized through faith, prayer, and meditative practices. And sometimes, ordinary people who do not seek out the Divine, are offered experiences anyway; bestowed upon them without self-volition or personal acts.

Within religious traditions, there is a reluctance to identify encounters with the departed as spiritual experiences in the same sense as encounters with the Divine. Communicating with the departed is not condoned by any of the major world religions or ancient texts. Indigenous views of communications with the spirit world vary greatly, and those that accept communications with the departed often have complex rituals and structures to facilitate interactions. Spiritualism, as a belief and movement, is centered on the use of mediums rather than direct personal experiences. The New Thought Movement, growing out of transcendentalism, embraces the science of spirituality and gives credence to communicating with the departed.

Within psychology, explorations of after-death communication have primarily been within bereavement studies (DeGroot, 2018; Glick, Weiss, & Parkes, 1974; Klass, 1995; Klass & Steffen, 2018; Parkes & Weiss, 1983; Richards & Folkman, 1997; Sanger, 2009). These studies are driven by the quest to understand the positive or negative impact of after-death communications on those experiencing them, and how these experiences relate to recovery from grief.

We now have new lenses for considering the realities of spiritual experience. Changes in scientific pursuits and knowledge have shifted the context for situating and understanding how spiritual encounters might come about. Quantum physics, neuroscience, and consciousness studies are defining new models, new structures of the universe and how the individual is situated in the universe: universal consciousness, toroidal fields, quantum information, and quantum entanglement; explorations that give new frameworks for examining human capacity for spiritual experience and how these experiences emerge. These areas of science are providing paradigms for defining the universe as an interconnected and continuous fabric of consciousness and intelligence, expressing in multi-dimensional realities, simultaneously. Physical life forms are thought of as uniquely defined fields of consciousness that are emergent from an interactive, universal continuum. Humans, and perhaps all sentient beings, are equipped to interact with the quantum information of the universe (Meijer, 2019; Meijer & Geesink, 2017; Walton, 2017).

This chapter explores the personal experiences of encountering the Divine and the departed, through in-depth, semi-structured interviews with four people who have had these experiences as part of their lives. Through conversation, we learn something of the transcendent phenomena of ordinary people and seek to situate their experiences in the context of new scientific paradigms.

Methods

A brief statement was written to describe the book, the chapter, and to provide information on the interview criteria and process. The statement was distributed via email to key people in personal networks, asking them to share the information with others they knew who might be interested in the project. People were also informed about the project through direct, personal communications, and those who were interested were then mailed the statement allowing them to consider participation. Follow up phone conversations then took place to discuss the interview, criteria for participating, confidentiality, and any concerns about participation.

To participate, a person needed to have had specific encounters with the Divine, as it was personally conceived, and experiences with at least one departed person or animal companion. Not all who were interested met the criteria. Some who met the criteria, after considering the project, decided they didn't wish to speak about their experiences.

A semi-structured interview guide was developed to direct a conversational interview. Participants were asked to provide some personal history such as age, heritage, religious upbringing, spiritual path, places lived, and education which may have influenced their world views and experiences. They then were asked to talk a bit about experiences they had over the course of their lives that they would describe as spiritual, or experiences of an omnipresent reality. One or two of these experiences were then discussed in depth: when and where they happened; altered states; activities or setting that opened up the experience; unexpected or sought-after experiences; states of being associated with the experiences. They were asked what they believed contributed to their abilities to have these experiences and if there were people in their lives who contributed in some way to their abilities to have these experiences. Encounters with the departed were pursued with the same questions. In the end, each participant was asked what these experiences meant to them, what they made of their capacity to have these experiences, and what they made of the experiences themselves.

Participants were provided with the findings and interpretations of their respective experiences for verification. Modifications were made based on feedback.

Participants

Four people were interviewed, 3 women and 1 man, ages 65, 67, 74, and 81. Two were Caucasian and two were blended. All considered themselves more spiritual than religious, described by one as a "personal spirituality," with two currently participating in spiritual communities/faith groups. Three were raised in formal religions which they subsequently rejected. Three had spiritual experiences in childhood before the age of eight which continued through the course of their lives. All considered their encounters with the departed to be spiritual experiences with characteristics similar to their encounters with the Divine.

The Narratives

A key element for entering the experiences was the quieting of the mind. Experiences most often came through when the mind was still, focused, or the individual came fully into the present moment. In stillness and full presence, experiences of the Divine and the departed emerged from within, or from an external field. Certain situations evoked these experiences: meditation, prayer, nature, fear, or the death of a loved one.

Sometimes they were internal experiences of a presence, sometimes voices within, voices other than those of the inner monologue or "self-talk." The interior voice, or a deep sense of a presence, sometimes gave guidance and direction. Other times the interior voice or presence provided solace and support. Two participants referred to this experience using the same language: an experience of being "cradled." The deep interior voice or pervading presence were called "wise," "knowing," "embracing," an "opening," "swaddled," "a personal God." The experiences were thought to be part of an available non-physical dimension of life; "the other realm."

The Interior Domains

Participant 4. God's Voice: "I have a really strong faith. I've always had it. I heard God's voice when I was young. I heard it as a voice, but I've also heard it as a thought, I've heard it as an emotion – and I know it's not from me. Because the thought is not something I would have thought of. I would identify it as – I wouldn't describe it as gender I would describe it as – it sounds like wisdom. It sounds like someone who loves you intensely. It sounds like someone who's known you your whole life. It sounds like – almost like someone cradling you. And I think because it's inside of me that's why he knows everything about what I'm feeling. And what I'm thinking. He interacts from within."

Participant 1: "I don't know what the Divine is named. I feel like a presence of something without – an opening." First experience was "Five or earlier."

Experience 1. Encounter with the Divine: "I was swimming in the Gulf of Mexico. Nobody was around me. And I realized there was a strong undertow and I was heading into the Gulf of Mexico. And some presence guided me to – 'you're going to turn around and you're going to be very calm' – and I did that, and that presence... [guided me]. 'Be calm. You're going to get out of this.'"

Experience 2. Encounter with the Departed: "The first one was with my father. He died in 1985. In 2001, I had to go to a deposition. (Participant was being sued.) And my lawyer said, 'oh oh – this woman is going to grill you so much because she is voracious, and she is smart and don't say anything mistakenly.' Well, I was so petrified. And so, I went to the office and all of a sudden, a presence said, 'don't worry about it.' And the presence was talking like my father. 'Don't worry about it. It's going to be alright.' And I said to myself 'this is bizarre' (laughing). And – but he surrounded me and comforted me and said, 'you will be fine' and so I simmered down and said, 'ok daddy, if you think I will be fine then I will be fine.' I wasn't calm but I was not like, terrified. Yeah, it was my father's voice. He sounded like my father. When I was finally deposed, the voracious lawyer wasn't there – there was a substitute lawyer taking my deposition who was sweet and almost sympathetic."

Experience 3. Meditation: "The Divine just comes to me. I try to get it going. I meditate to get the ego to disappear and get my inner state of bliss. I guess I want to have that when I'm meditating and sometimes it works. But it's very short. Not like a minute of

joy and bliss constantly. It's a second (It's a moment?) Yeah. And
then I say (laughter) (Then you get distracted.) Yeah. (Laughter)"
Ok – and emotionally?
"Calm. Yeah, calm – very very calm."
And mentally?
"A focus."
Is there a stillness of the mind?
"Yeah. Like the problems when I swam in Mexico. It was like 'do
this do this do this' very still and emotionally very calm." "When
I finish meditating I give prayers – thank you for this day – thank
you that my family is ok – and the last prayer is I hope when I die,
I hope that it will be calm, knowing – calm, knowing where I'm
going. And I'm going. The reason I'm meditating is partly that,
to get myself out of myself. (Like a preparation?) Yeah."

The Exterior Domains

Some experiences entered or appeared to come from an external field.
They were experiences of the presence, or essence, of the departed or the
Divine. They were sometimes an experience of connectedness – being part
of the fabric of a larger field of consciousness, as during time spent in
nature. Sometimes they were audible communications, hearing a voice
from another part of the room or environment. When a presence was experienced it was behind, next to, in front of, or down the hall from the participant. None of the experiences among the participants were requested or
evoked. They came uninvited and unexpectedly. In research by Beischel
(2019), it was suggested that "spontaneous, unexpected or uninvited experience of contact or communication with the departed is likely the most
common type of ADC (After Death Communication)" (2019, p. 4).

Participant 1. Encounters with a Canine Companion: "We connected
with love. Extraordinary. Before he was euthanized, I took care
of him and he – we communicated. When I watched him die, his
essence was with me palpably. So much and for a couple of weeks
it was there, so much. His essence for me was Divine – filled with
love and caring. Actually, it sounded like (gave the same message
as) my father – 'don't worry – where we are, we will take care of
you.' And he appreciated my love. I mean it was – the connection
was stronger – intense. (After he had passed?) Mmhmm. And I
still have his altar and I want that spiritual presence to keep on.
But now I think that if I remove the altar, he will still be there."
Participant 2. Encounters with a Soulmate: "I've only had them in
the last few years. Seven–eight years. After I divorced, I went
with a man who was my first boyfriend. After almost 50 years.
And decided we still loved each other and wanted to be together.

We lived together for 10 years. And it was after he died that I began having these feelings of him being near me. His presence.

One time I heard his voice calling me from another room in my apartment. It was in the night and I was awake. So yes, I really heard his voice. And I said to myself, 'I am not asleep. This is not a dream.' And he called me by my name – my nickname – so that was meaningful. It was rewarding to feel that I still had a connection with him.

And several other times I felt very strongly that he was there beside me or behind me. I never spoke to him and he never spoke to me, but he was there. I just felt it very very strongly. And that happened four or five times. (over the past 7 or 8 years?) Yeah, right.

I don't try to evoke it. It just happens. I've always been surprised, and I always want to look behind me to make – you know – is he really there? (laughs) And he isn't. Except in my head – in my mind I can see him. (But you have this feeling, this sense of a presence?) Oh yeah, very much of a presence.

It's exciting and we have a connection even though words are not spoken. (except that one time) Yeah. And I would also say that we were really soulmates. We talked endlessly. We covered a lot of ground together. But we definitely were soulmates. And I feel that when I do feel his presence that is part of it. I felt so close to him."

Participant 3. Experience 1. Encounter with the Departed: "I was at home. We had an attendant. I held mom's hand and I felt the life leaving her. I felt her life as it left her body, but the physical part was still there. She was still warm. I held her until she started to get colder. And I talked to her and I said, 'you're at peace now.'

That evening she spoke to me. The language was not that of a sick person. It was almost like she was talking to me through a tunnel. There was kind of like an echo in it. And her feeling was – what she told me was to – not to worry. That she was ok. 'I'll be ok.' At first, all I heard was my name. (did you literally hear it?) I heard it. I was at my desk and I was in my bedroom and I heard it down the hall. And it was clear – it had a little echo tinge to it. But that was her voice. And I knew at that point that she wasn't really gone yet. She was still hanging around. Letting me know that she's ok. And in a way, I think she was checking in on me. I didn't talk to her. But she would talk to me. I, we – it went from hearing her voice to feeling her presence and it was like, she's around. I can feel it.

And I can still feel her presence when she is around. (she still comes around?) Yes. It's a feeling. Except for hearing her voice that – for about 2 weeks you know. It's just been a strong feeling. A strong presence. And that's my experience with my mom. She's just really around. She's here in another form."

Participant 3. Experience 2. Encounter with the Departed: "There's another person I was close to and that was at my old church. And she was like my mom. Coming to church I'd pick her up, I'd drop her off. We went to events together. She said I know why your mom loved you because I love you. I was there when she was taken to the hospital. I was there when other people weren't there, and I actually watched her take her last breaths. And I had a similar experience with her. That day and for about 2 weeks. She wasn't in my house like my mom was when she passed away. I still heard her voice clear. Concise. The kind of – like a person talking through a tunnel. And it was like – don't worry. I'm okay. And I'm good. And I still have that connection with her. It feels like she is ... the other one that there is a strong connection with."

Participant 4. Encounter with the Divine and the Departed: "I wanted to find out – I wanted to know – did he ever go to heaven, and did he ever make it right with you God? What was the circumstance because I'm very just concerned about his soul? And God told me that morning 'I have a really special surprise for you.' I'm like 'OK! I don't know what that is but' – so I was just going outside to get the newspaper and I bent down, and I audible heard God's voice. He called my name. And I stood up and he said 'your husband is with me now. And he has something to say.' And then I heard my husband's voice and I – it was distinctly my husband's voice.

(Was this a voice you heard inside your head or in another place?)

In another place. This was not just inside – I heard – it was from somewhere else where he was. And he said my name and then he started apologizing. He said, 'I am here in heaven, I'm with God' and he said – 'I am so so so sorry. And I hope one day you'll be able to forgive me.' And then, in my mind, I talked to him. I said: 'I forgive you. What's heaven like?' (laughter) and then he started telling me. It was just weird. And then, I don't even know how long this conversation lasted. You know, like, time is kind of irrelevant. But it ended.

The present dimension changed. It was so bizarre. It was like everything was new. It's the only way I can describe it. Like the trees looked new. Like everything magically became new. The light was different. The smells were different. It was like I was the same but my whole reality became new."

Nature and Oneness

There is a palpable, pervading intelligence in natural settings. There is a Navaho chant: *"The mountains I become part of... the herbs, the fir tree, I become part of it. The morning mists, the clouds, the gathering waters, I become part of it. The wilderness, the dew drops, the pollen, I become part of it."* In Japan, *shinrin-yoku* – "forest bathing," or "taking in the forest atmosphere," is a mindful practice of connection with the natural world. Two participants referred to sacred connections with trees. One participant spent much of her childhood in Japan and was greatly influenced by the culture and her time spent in nature as a child.

> *Participant 2. Nature and Oneness*: "I always felt very spiritual in nature. Out in nature. I think that is where my spiritual connections are, but I can't pinpoint a specific event or experience. I've never put this into words before. I don't know. Just a feeling that this is the wider world and I'm getting to experience it and there is a comfort from it. There is a oneness. A feeling of being part of it. I've never tried to put it into words. I'm a part of it. When I'm in that situation it lasts for a while. It's calming and it's – This is where I am – this is where I want to be. Let's continue it. Let's stay here as long as I can. In this spiritual state."

Another participant found his connection in nature while hiking in the woods, as well as other natural settings. In the following excerpt he describes being taken by a loving warmth and a transformed sense of well-being.

> *Participant 3. Nature, Care and Calm*: "They come unexpectedly. (long pause) But I have to be in a situation to receive them. In other words, when the monkey mind goes away, and there's less chatter. When my mind quiets down. And then I'll break out in a smile – it's like – I could go through a very stressful day at work and I could drive across the bridge and go to the beach with my window down. Look out over the water and watch the sun go down. And it's like – I'm there. And a smile comes on and it's like... ahhhh. I take a deep breath. I know that – it's just a feeling. For me it's about feeling. You have a sense of feeling that you are being cradled – swaddled like a baby."

Childhood Ties

Three of the four participants began having spiritual experiences at very young ages. For one, it was the experience of a presence. For another, it was a connection in nature. For another, it was both an experience of the divine within nature and as a responsive force.

> Participant 4, Early Connections: "I remember when I was 4 years old and I lost my locket. I had gotten a little locket for my birthday and I lost it. And I remember going up to a tree. A tree is

very spiritual by the way. I don't know why I have this connection with a tree, but this was my first time I actually had a spiritual connection with a tree. So, I knelt before the tree and I prayed to God. I said, 'God, can you please help me find my locket?' and I wish I had that locket. I was a little 4-year-old. And I turned around and started walking and there was my locket. So, I realized, 'hey – there is some power in talking to God. Who made this tree and who made everything.' All throughout my elementary school years I would talk to God all the time and he would answer me. I felt like I started a relationship with God that was very different than just church on Sunday and memorized prayers and all that. It was much more personal I would say."

Participant 2: Bonds in Youth: "I once felt that it was the closeness between the two of us and how much we shared. Interestingly enough, we first met at that place in Japan, so we had that (at the lake?) yes – where we spent the summers. So, we both had very strong feelings about that place. Subsequently, when school started, we were in the same school so there was a lot more connection at that point. That was a very strong thing for us – (the place at the lake) – talking about it and we both found that – I don't know if you've ever had this experience but sometimes when you have something troubling you or you want to feel calm, you think about yourself in a particular place. And I think about being at the lake. And I talked about that once with him and he said he did too. And he told me the place. You know, there was a certain tree. And I knew the tree that he was talking about."

Making Sense of It

Three of the participants seldom spoke with others about these experiences. All said at the end of each interview that talking about the experiences brought a new clarity about their spirituality, their experiences of a different dimension, and how they made sense of them. It was also freeing to talk about their experiences and be heard, accepted, and understood. All had thoughts about what contributed to their personal capacity to have these experiences.

Participant 4. Ancestry: "My mother is part Cherokee Indian. In fact, her great grandmother walked the trail of tears. She was a medicine woman and a healer. My mother remembers the people from the town in Arkansas taking children to her. She was a healer. An indigenous one. I think that is my heritage – that part of my heritage is the spiritual part of me. I think I'm a lot like her. I seem to have these spiritual intuitions and spiritual healing piece of me that I'm just drawn to. My mother says I've been this way since I was 4. So, I think it was just like something I inherited. That was passed along to me."

Participant 3. A Handicap: "I think if you look at people who have disabilities– the blind for example, they have heightened hearing. They have other ways of having to adapt. I have a disability. I had scarlet fever when I was one year old which made me dyslexic, which made life really difficult for me. And I think because of that it allowed something else to open up."

Participant 2. Cultural Influence: "I think that living in Japan – the Japanese have an approach to nature that's different than other cultures. They try to define nature in small ways. Everybody has a garden. A plot and so forth. And that had a very strong influence on me. Not only when I was out in nature, but I look at other people's gardens in that way. I was influenced by that a great deal. I know that it [being in nature] has a strong spiritual quality for the Japanese people. (you felt an affinity with them?) On that level, yes. (on the spiritual level?) Yes, right. We also spent 2 months every summer at a lake – there were mountains and a lake. And THAT place is the place I really consider my childhood home. That natural setting."

Participant 1. Meditation and a Calling: "I have been meditating for decades. When I had my stroke, I meditated one hour a day. My dissertation was on death. Before people were focusing on death. I really wanted to explore death. I guess I just liked the spiritual realm. I didn't like the religious. There was one time when I was high. And I had this experience that was so deep, and I GOT IT. Yeah. The whole – why I'm here – why – the whole thing. And I said to myself, 'alright – now what?' (laughter). And then I said, 'alright – carry on.'"

Discussion

Encounters with the Divine and the departed, entering non-physical realms of reality, are experiences that presented themselves to the four people whose stories are told in this chapter. They were experiences of deep connection with another dimension of life. The experiences were not often talked about. They were called 'bizarre.' It was sometimes a struggle to find language to describe experiences never put into words before. Experiences of this kind of reality can leave individuals feeling in over their heads, needing to find a framework to make sense of what was experienced. The rational mind struggles to grasp exactly what has been experienced and how it came about. When in fact, experiences of the Divine fabric are well within human capacity and occur frequently (Guggenheim & Guggenheim, 1995). This is further illustrated in other chapters in this book. We are coming into ways of knowing that provide understanding of these kind of experiences and the ability to embrace them when they occur.

New science aims to explain how this experience happens. What are the processes of engagement? What are the human gateways to these experiences? The works of Meijer & Geesink (2017), Meijer (2019), and Walton (2017) cite and integrate much of the thinking and research that has been conducted in quantum science, theoretical physics, and neuroscience and consciousness studies to provide frameworks for spiritual experience, drawn upon in this discussion.

New science presents the universal system in which we exist as a field of consciousness which gives rise to our personal experience. We live and interact within an intelligent continuum of dynamic quantum information. Quantum information never goes away. Everything that has existed still exists and is available and accessible. Within this framework, we have the beginnings of grasping how spiritual experiences might emerge. When we see the universe in this way, we can see that we belong to the eternal domain in our present lives. There is an aspect of each embodied being that is eternal. This is a dimension of life that never dies. When the physical body dies, the eternal consciousness remains part of the universal, multi-dimensional fabric. The universal consciousness that is within each human is accessible and when accessed, can speak and direct that person. In this paradigm, identities can re-emerge after the death of the body. God (or universal consciousness), Divine others, departed humans and other sentient beings (aspects of universal consciousness) are available for dynamic exchanges.

The new sciences are complex and beyond the scope of summary in this chapter and by this author. The language of these sciences is abstract and far removed from the ways in which we typically talk about the Divine. But let us consider a few principles that suggest how an embodied human being interfaces with, in scientific terms, this larger, underlying non-local, vibrational/wave field: torus geometry, neural processing, and quantum entanglement.

Torus fields are electromagnetic shapes that flow as connectivity in the universe and as connectivity of the individual with the universal field. Although we are distinct physically, within our individual physicality there are torus shapes that connect us to the universal fabric. The human body has a torus field as does the brain as does the heart. It is postulated that the toroidal field of the brain is the interface with the universal field through a toroidal workspace, allowing for 4-D quantum information to flow to 3-D, for what is recognized as a spiritual encounter.

The brain processes consciousness rather than generating it. The parietal cortex processes the quieting of the "me" which all the participants referred to as necessary for the opening to spiritual experience. When the fluctuations of the mind cease, other levels of consciousness can emerge and be experienced. The subcortex, in particular, gives access to an older order of sensing and knowing (Beauregard & Paquette, 2006). Other scientists have taken the emphasis off the brain and suggest it is the entire neurological complexity that processes. Although the heart has 40,000 neurons, has been called the "little brain" (Armour, 1991), and has its own toroidal field, it has not been pursued as a processor of spiritual encounters, or as a collaborator with the brain. Participant experiences with the departed have been with those with whom they feel a deep heart connection.

The third principle, quantum entanglement, clarifies how everything is occurring in a dynamic relationship. Entanglement is "used to explain the process when two particles which have been together, and are subsequently separated, continue to be instantaneously responsive to each other across space, in ways that defy our conventional knowledge of how the world works" (Walton, 2017, p. 11).

When asked about her experiences, participant 1 said: *"It's that other realm."* The guiding voice during swimming wasn't the voice of someone she knew here on earth but rather a knowing presence without a name. The second voice was her father's which "surrounded" her. The third communication from her canine companion, with whom she has a strong loving bond. He didn't have a voice but was a strong presence in the environment that non-verbally conveyed love and comfort, similar to the message her father communicated.

Participant 2 described her experiences in nature as a "feeling of this is the wider world and I'm getting to experience it … there is a oneness." When talking about feeling the presence of her departed partner, she described how close they were in life – soulmates – and how comforting it was knowing the connection continued.

Participant 3 experienced hearing the voice of his mother, calling his name, as well as her presence down the hall. Her voice had an echo as if "talking to me through a tunnel." He can still feel her presence when she is around. He had the same experience with another woman, something of a mother figure, with whom he was deeply bonded.

Participant 4 began having experiences of talking with God at the age of four. She discovered there was power in talking with God and developed a personal relationship. God presented her deceased husband to her, aiding in healing a troubling bond. Her environment became "new" and luminescent.

Convergence: evoked by stillness of the mind, coming into the extreme present; Personal God without a name, guiding force, comes from within, deep wise interior presence; Loving presence of the departed, guiding voices, comforting voices, interior and exterior. Uninvited experiences that presented themselves through portals of consciousness. Dynamic relationships transcending time and space, unexpectedly revealing never ending connections with the Oneness of the universe and the oneness with each other. Science, presenting models for what mystics have described for centuries, and for what ordinary people experience in everyday life.

References

Armour, J. A. (1991). Intrinsic cardiac neurons. *Journal of Cardiovascular Electrophysiology*, *2*(4), 331–341. https://doi.org/10.1111/j.1540-8167.1991.tb01330.x.

Beauregard, M., & Paquette, V. (2006). Neural correlates of a mystical experience in Carmelite nuns. *Neuroscience Letters*, *405*, 186–190.

Beischel, J. (2019). Spontaneous, facilitated, assisted, and requested after-death communication experiences and their impact on grief. *Threshold: Journal of Interdisciplinary Consciousness Studies*, *3*(1), 1–32.

DeGroot, J. M. (2018). A model of transcorporeal communication: Communication toward/with/to the deceased. *Omega*, *78*(1), 43–66.

Easwaran, E. (Ed.). (1996). *God makes the rivers to flow: Selections from the sacred literature of the world*. Tomales, CA: Nilgiri Press.

Glick, I. O., Weiss, R. S., & Parkes, C. M. (1974). *The first year of bereavement*. New York, NY: John Wiley & Sons Inc.

Guggenheim, B., & Guggenheim, J. (1995). *Hello from heaven! A new field of research – After-death communication – Confirms that life and love are eternal*. New York, NY: Bantam Books.

Hood, R. W. (Ed.) (1995). *Handbook of religious experience*. Birmingham, AL: Religious Education Press.

Klass, D. (1995). Spiritual aspects of the resolution of grief. In H. Wass, & R. A. Neimeyer (Eds.), *Dying: Facing the facts* (pp. 243–268). Washington, DC: Taylor & Francis.

Klass, D., & Steffen, E. M. (Eds.) (2018). *Continuing bonds in bereavement: New directions for research and practice* (p. 352). New York, NY: Routledge. ISBN: 978-0415356206.

Meijer, D. K., & Geesink, H. J. H. (2017). Consciousness in the universe is scale invariant and implies an event horizon of the human brain. *NeuroQuantology*. doi: 10.1407/nq.2017.15.3.1079.

Meijer, D. K. (2019). The anticipation of afterlife as based on current physics of information. https://researchgate.net/publication/336531043.

Merton, T. (1996). *Contemplative prayer*. New York, NY: Doubleday.

Parkes, C. M., & Weiss, R. (1983). *Recovery from bereavement*. New York: Basic Books.

Richards, T. A., & Folkman, S. (1997). Spiritual aspects of loss at the time of a partner's death from AIDS. *Death Studies*, *21*, 527–552.

Sanger, M. (2009). When clients sense the presence of loved ones who have died. *Omega*, *59*(1), 69–89.

Smith, H. (1991). *The world's religions: Our great wisdom traditions*. San Francisco, CA: Harper.

Walton, J. (2017). The significance of consciousness studies and quantum physics for creating a spiritual research paradigm. *Journal for the Study of Spirituality*, *7*(1), 21–34.

3 Personal Experiences of Communication with the Departed, the Sacred, and the Divine

A Self-Science Approach

Gary E. Schwartz

Introduction and Overview

As amply illustrated and examined in this edited volume, claims have been made throughout recorded history of individuals being able to communicate with the Divine, the Sacred, and the departed. Debates about the metaphysical reality of such communications have persisted in philosophy, theology, science, and religions. Scholars and laymen alike vary to the extent that they have personally experienced such communications (first-person accounts) versus approaching these claims from an external (third-person) perspective.

Unlike the majority of the contributors to this volume, the author of the present chapter was educated primarily in materialistic sciences: (1) as an undergraduate student at Cornell University in electrical engineering, experimental psychology, and pre-medicine; and (2) as a Ph.D. student at Harvard University in psychophysiology, personality, and clinical psychology. Moreover, he was raised in a non-religious, essentially atheist, reform Jewish home by generally open-minded and inquisitive parents. Stated somewhat bluntly, he was taught (and he accepted to be true) that anyone claiming to have personal experiences of communication with the Divine, the Sacred, and/or the departed were naïve, self-deceptive, and/or delusional (e.g. psychotic). Not surprisingly, he does not remember having had any obvious spiritual or paranormal experiences as a child. It was not until the latter part of his professorship at Yale University and his subsequent joining the faculty at The University of Arizona that he began to explore such phenomena academically as well as experientially.[1]

In this chapter (Chapter 3, "Personal experiences of ..."), the author shares some examples of compelling experiences of apparent spiritual communications, not only as reported by others (e.g. Anthony, 2021), but also by himself (e.g. Schwartz, 2006, 2011, 2017). These prototype personal examples set the stage for a subsequent chapter in this volume (Chapter 13, "Contemporary evidence of...") that presents contemporary scientific evidence, including controlled laboratory experiences, that support the likely metaphysical reality of such exemplary experiences (e.g. Schwartz, 2002, 2006, 2011, 2012, 2017, 2020a, 2020b).

Since the greatest amount of controlled scientific evidence involves the departed, both chapters (Chapter 3, personal experiences and Chapter 13, contemporary evidence) begin with communication with the departed, and then move to the Sacred (hence the similar order listed in the complimentary titles; only this chapter includes the Divine as well). Together these chapters illustrate an evidence-based, self-science approach to spirituality that creatively applies the scientific method to the laboratories of our personal lives and the lives of others (2011, 2012). The chapter now shifts from a third-person perspective to a first-person narrative.

Are Any Mediums Real? A Personal Example

Mediums are people who claim to be able to communicate with the deceased. Adopting the quote from William James that introduces this chapter, we can ask the question, are all mediums frauds ("black crows") as many skeptic's claim? Or, are at least some individuals who claim to be genuine evidential mediums real (i.e. "white crows")?

Is it possible to document that genuine mediums can obtain accurate information regarding deceased loved ones under controlled laboratory conditions that rule out conventional explanations of fraud—i.e. techniques of cold and hot reading used by psychic entertainers—or experimenter biases (e.g. Beischel & Schwartz, 2007)? And if so, can we justifiably infer that these mediums are communicating with the living souls of the departed?

Since most readers will probably not have had direct experiences with evidential mediums, I begin this chapter with an account provided by Mark Anthony (2021) in his upcoming book *The Afterlife Frequency: The Scientific Proof of Spiritual Contact and How that Awareness Will Change Your Life*. Here is how I described Anthony's mediumship skills in my foreword to his book:

> Anthony's ability to obtain accurate and specific details regarding people's deceased loved ones is stellar. And like the very best mediums I have tested over the past twenty plus years, he regularly gets "dazzle shots" that startle everyone, including himself.

Anthony is an Oxford University-trained trial attorney licensed to practice law in Florida, Washington D.C., and before the United States

Supreme Court. He appears regularly in the media as a legal analyst, medium, and expert on life after death, after-death communications, and near-death experiences. He is one of more than twenty evidential "white crow" mediums over a span of more than twenty years who have participated in controlled research in my Laboratory for Advances in Consciousness and Health at the University of Arizona (e.g. Schwartz 2002, 2006, 2011).

The account below, including dramatic dazzle shots, has been edited slightly for the sake of clarity and brevity. Because I am quoting Anthony's writing, it is displayed in italics. Otherwise, I have retained Anthony's breezy writing style. I have inserted a few comments as indicated by [GES].

It was a typical hot and humid summer day in East Coast Central Florida when I arrived to conduct an in-person reading. The owner of the establishment greeted me cheerfully and let me know two people were coming for the session. I have a firm policy about anonymity prior to a reading. This is to ensure what I receive during the interdimensional communication is coming from spirits and not from what I may know ahead of time.

[GES] Genuine evidential mediums have a strict policy regarding anonymity and remaining blind to details about the sitters, ideally including the sitters' names whenever possible.

A few minutes later, Chuck and Nicole arrived. They were in their early forties and looked athletic making me feel a tad guilty for choosing a milkshake over the kale smoothie earlier that day.

Nicole was slender and had an easy-going manner. Chuck wore a baseball cap over his short black hair, sported a five o'clock shadow and didn't say a word, much less crack a smile. While Nicole and the owner chatted and exchanged pleasantries, Chuck stood motionless as his eyes scanned the surroundings.

As I led them to the reading room at the back of the building, Nicole said, "This is for my boyfriend Chuck—he heard about you and wanted a reading."

We took our seats and I began with my introductory comments about what to expect during a mediumship communication session and then opened my brain to receive information.

"Three male spirits are coming through in tandem."

Chuck leaned forward intently.

"Very different personalities—one keeps laughing a lot—had a very distinctive laugh—kind of a snorting sound—I keep hearing a name—sounds like Kerry."

> *"Close enough, his name's Kenny," Chuck half smiled, "He had a weird laugh."*

[GES] It is important that Anthony did not seek information from the sitters. What he did was offer information to the sitters which could be confirmed, questioned, or rejected by them.

> *"Kenny is stepping aside for another male—tall blonde man projecting the image of a St. Christopher medal—patron saint of travel, but it's also my trigger for the name ...."*
> *"Christopher! Oh my God!" Chuck beamed.*
> *"Uh—the third guy—he—he—keeps—talking about—uh"*
> *"About what?"*
> *"Maybe I'm misinterpreting this Chick, but—he keeps talking about eating beans ...."*
> *Chuck rolled his eyes, "Yeah, that's Todd. Beans ...."*
> *We all cracked up, but the levity didn't last long.*
> *"Ahh!" I cringed as an immense shock wave flew through my body.*
> *"You okay?" Nicole asked.*
> *"I'm fine—a jolt to my body indicates an abrupt death."*
> *Chuck and Nicole glanced at each other.*
> *"These guys died traumatically at the same time. I hear a loud sound—like walking up to a huge metallic tank banging on it and there's a hollow sound. It's loud—like an explosion."*

[GES] Genuine evidential mediums are often adept at getting details regarding the circumstances of people's physical deaths.

> *Nicole's hand covered her mouth.*
> *"My unit was on a mission in Afghanistan," Chuck's body tensed. "Our Humvee hit an IED—improvised explosive device—it exploded. I was the unit commander—all the guys died, but me."*
> *"What the f...!" flew out of my mouth unexpectedly.*

[GES] Although Anthony can be risqué on occasion, he rarely curses in a professional reading. Evidential mediums regularly report strange and unanticipated experiences that turn out to be highly meaningful to sitters.

> *"I'm sorry—I try to never use that type of language in a reading...."*
> *"'What the f...' was the motto of our unit. Don't apologize."*
> *Chuck paused, "I've always wondered why I survived, and they didn't, I was the commanding officer, I should've died."*
> *"The energy is shifting—I call this Collective Consciousness Communication—all three spirits are speaking as one."*

[GES] Anthony believes in spiritual concepts and he will share them, as he deems appropriate, in his readings.

> *Chuck braced himself.*
> *"You had to live. You're supposed to let others know what happened. You're supposed to help others with loss and guilt."*
> *Chuck stood—clearly shaken—a single tear rolled down his face. "I'm leaving now. I'm going out the back door. I will not allow anyone to see me cry."*
> *Before exiting the room, he paused and turned to me, "Thank you, Sir."*
> *Nicole gaped. Within seconds Chuck vanished through the store's rear entrance.*
> *"You have no idea what you did for him!" Nicole exclaimed, "I've never seen him express that much emotion—this is major!"*

[GES] Responsible mediumship can sometimes have profound effects on people who are grieving and help the healing process.

> *"That much emotion?" then it dawned on me, "Nicole, he's special ops, isn't he?"*
> *"Delta Force," she confirmed. "Very highly trained. He was in command of an elite covert anti-terrorism operation when their Humvee hit the IED."*
> *"Like the captain who's supposed to go down with his ship," I observed, "Chuck struggles with guilt because as the commander he feels he should've died, not his men. He's suffering from survivor's guilt."*
> *"Exactly," Nicole replied, "and the counselors at the Veteran's Hospital asked him to start a support group for veterans wracked with guilt."*
> *"Is he going to do it?"*
> *"He's not sure," Nicole explained, "Chuck wants to take the lead to help other veterans, but he knows in a support group you have to express your feelings and he's worried about that."*
> *"Why's that a problem?"*
> *"Chuck believes he must never appear weak. He says he'd rather die than cry because to him weeping is weakness."*
> *"Crying isn't weakness, it's healing." I explained. "It's been medically proven tears of grief differ from regular reflex tears because grief tears contain the hormones which cause depression and stress. A good cry actually releases these hormones and stimulates endorphins which can help you feel better. Men need to understand we have feelings and tear ducts for a reason."*
> *"After hearing from his men today maybe Chuck will," Nicole replied.*

It is difficult not to be moved by such an exemplary, and yet in many ways, typical reading provided by a gifted "white crow" medium. The next section illustrates how innovative multi-blinded experiments can be conducted that not only validate the existence of white crow mediums but of "white crow" spirits as well.

Are There "White Crow" Spirits?—A Personal Account

What you are about to read is adapted from an invited centennial celebration symposium for William James which was subsequently published in an article (Schwartz, 2010) titled "William James and the Search for Scientific Evidence of Life After Death: Past, Present, and Possible Future." The last two words "Possible Future" speak to the theoretically plausible and scientifically verifiable hypothesis that highly intelligent and motivated individuals can continue to play a role in human activities on the Earth after they have physically died. The abstract is included below. Later in Chapter 13, I present the results from an exemplary multi-blinded experiment documenting the apparent participation of the late William James in ongoing evidential mediumship research. The abstract is slightly edited for clarity and accuracy.

* * * * *

Abstract: William James's historic fascination with psychic phenomena, including the possibility of life after death, has become more widely known with the publication of recent books and articles on this controversial aspect of his scientific legacy. However, little is known about the emerging evidence suggesting the possibility that James's scientific interest in these topics has not waned since he died. This paper reviews preliminary observations, including two exploratory multi-blinded mediumship investigations, which are consistent with the hypothesis that James (with others) may be continuing his lifelong quest to address the question of the survival of consciousness after physical death 'from the other side'. These proof-of-concept investigations illustrate how future systematic multi-blinded laboratory research is possible. The limitations of current neuroscience methods are explicated in terms of investigating the hypothesis of the brain as a possible antenna-receiver for consciousness. If James's tentative conclusions about the nature of the relationship between consciousness and the brain turn out to be accurate, then it is logically plausible (if not essential) to posit the possibility that his efforts have persisted in the recent past and present, and may even continue in the future. Scientific integrity plus the pursuit of verity require our being open to this important theoretical and empirical possibility.

* * * * *

The multi-blinded design of the research involved two evidential mediums. The first was a writer and psychic named Susy Smith. It was a result of a coincidental meeting with Smith in Tucson, Arizona, and my learning of her controversial claims regarding William James, that I was faced with a deep scientific challenge. Professor James had been my academic hero, and I had spent my graduate student and assistant professor years in William James Hall.

I had become aware of Smith through an article published in a local newspaper in the mid-1990s about Smith's personal 'afterlife codes' experiment (the news article was brought to my attention by Dr. Richard Lane, a professor of psychiatry and psychology at the University of Arizona).

Below is adapted from the Schwartz (2010) paper, edited slightly for clarity and brevity:

* * * * *

Smith was already a well-known author of two academic books (e.g. she produced an edited volume of F.W.H. Myers classic *Human Personality and Its Survival of Bodily Death*, with a foreword by Aldous Huxley; Myers, 1961), followed by more than two dozen books for the general public on psychic phenomena including life after death. The newspaper article stated not only that Smith, formerly a skeptical journalist herself, had subsequently become psychic after the death of her mother (Smith preferred not to use the term medium because she was purportedly only able to communicate with a small group of deceased people). The article further stated one of Smith's purported primary 'guides' (besides her deceased mother) was the renowned Harvard Professor William James.

The author that learned that Smith had published two books supposedly in collaboration with James since he had passed (Smith, 1974, 2000). The author discovered that Smith had created a small non-profit foundation (the Survival Research Foundation) to foster research. However, after meeting with Smith, the author learned that she was not only convinced that James was still in communication with her, but that he was claiming to be interested in participating in research!

The author was well-aware of two obvious skeptical questions: (1) was Smith a fraud, and/or (2) was Smith self-deceptive (if not deranged) about her relationship with James? From a simple probability point of view, one might predict a 'yes' to one or both questions. Would it be unproductive, if not foolish, to consider the possibility of investigating Smith's claims about James empirically?

For the sake of historical accuracy, the author did wonder, what was the conditional probability of these five James-related events: (1) that his early academic career would begin in William James Hall, (2) that he would be recruited to write a textbook in the tradition of William James (a request he seriously considered), (3) that he would seemingly accidentally develop an integrative quantum systems theory that predicted the continuity of consciousness after death which was curiously consistent with James's receiver theory about the relationship between mind and brain, (4) that he would eventually meet a formerly well-known author, lay scientist, and psychic (Smith) in his current location (Tucson) who not only claimed to be in communication with James (and had written two books with him), but (5) that she claimed that James was eager to participate in contemporary afterlife research? Was this collection of five events simply coincidental, or could it reflect something more, possibly a synchronicity (Combs & Holland, 2000; Schwartz, 2017)?

However, it was a sixth event—my unanticipated meeting with a second purported psychic medium (Laurie Campbell) who curiously also claimed to be in communication with distinguished deceased scientists (e.g. Sir James Clerk Maxwell), and following my unanticipated 'reading' with her—which ultimately inspired me and my colleagues to design and conduct multiple multi-blinded proof-of-concept experiments purportedly involving James.

The reader may be wondering (as did a reviewer) whether the author was at this point being like a 'naïve sitter at a reading making past events fit with the story being outlined by the psychic'? The answer in this instance is a definitive 'no'. First, the author is not a naïve sitter, nor is he a naïve scientist. Quite the contrary, he is a well trained and experienced experimental and clinical psychologist who is knowledgeable and mindful of possible cognitive distortions, perceptual priming, self-deception, and illusory correlates. In fact, he and his colleagues have conducted extensive personality and psychophysiological research on self-deception funded in part by grants from the National Science Foundation and the National Institutes of Mental Health. Second, the author has read secret books and manuals about how to be a fake medium (sometimes termed a mental magician), and he has even taken a formal course in how to be a fake medium (parenthetically he is quite adept at it).

And third, he collaborates with a group of senior researchers who continually raise such important critical questions. For example, as discussed in Schwartz (2002), the author consistently involves a group of skeptical scientists (sometimes referred to as his 'Friendly Devil's Advocates' or FDAs) to carefully critique the work and its alternative interpretations. The factual historical professional information about the author is included in this paper not only because (1) it is conceivable, at least in theory, that it might have been relevant to James, but also because (2) the conditional probability of the totality of the six events is so low as to be interesting (if not anomalous, e.g. synchronistic).

* * * * *

However, it was only after meeting Campbell that the possibility of conducting controlled laboratory research with H.W.J. (Hypothesized William James) became feasible. I titled this section in the paper "A Chance (and "Trance") Encounter will Professor James?" Very briefly, a psychiatrist (Dr. W.), whose son died tragically, invited me to meet a purported evidential medium (Campbell) who claimed to be interested in participating in laboratory research. Campbell was a housewife in California with little more than a high school education. This is the first professional medium I had ever met, and I did not know what to expect.

Below is the account from the paper, edited slightly for clarity and brevity:

* * * * *

When the author was introduced to Campbell, and without any provocation, she claimed to begin receiving information from both the author's deceased mother and father. For the record, the author had not requested a personal reading (his intent was to witness what Campbell did with Dr. W.), and he attempted to discourage her from conducting one (but with minimal success). The information Campbell provided regarding his parents' physical appearances, causes of death, and personality traits was surprisingly specific and accurate. As mentioned above, the author aware of cold reading techniques used by psychic entertainers and even took a course in how to be a fake medium; hence, he was not a naïve sitter. For example, he was careful not to offer any verbal information which the medium could then claim to interpret.

A reviewer asked the question, 'How can he be sure that no information was offered to the psychic?' Lacking video recordings of the author's verbal and non-verbal behavior during the session, the reader is justified in being skeptical. However, as future experiments reported below established, this medium was equally successful when both she and the experimenters were blind to the information—hence, no unintentional cuing on the part of the experimenter was possible. Moreover, this medium (and others) participated in subsequent research where visual and auditory cues were physically eliminated, yet her (and their) performance remained high. Hence, the most parsimonious interpretation of the totality of the data is that the medium did not get her accurate information simply via cold reading techniques.

Though this personal family information was not widely known (and the internet was then in its infancy), the facts which Campbell provided could have been obtained through fraudulent means. In addition, the author was well-aware of alternative possible parapsychological explanations; for example, in theory Campbell could have been reading his mind telepathically. Hence, he remained intentionally skeptical during the meeting.

The author decided to ask Campbell if she could obtain any information concerning a person named Dr. Henry Russek; the information she provided proved to be accurate as well. What was compelling about this portion of the unanticipated reading was the extreme level of intensity of the emotion with which the deceased person purportedly described his love for his daughter (which happened to fit the author's knowledge of their unusually close father-daughter relationship).

It is true, as a reviewer noted, that experienced cold readers often assume that a father-daughter relationship is close (an assumption which is not always valid in specific cases). However, the extreme nature of the medium's communication was so dramatic as to appear melodramatic (and it appeared comparable to the unusually close personal and professional relationship involving Dr. Russek and his oldest daughter). More importantly, Campbell obtained specific information known only to the Russek family and select medical professionals (presented in Schwartz, 2002).

Though also not planned, I spontaneously decided to ask if Campbell could receive any information "from someone named William James." For example, I wondered, would the medium spontaneously confirm Smith's claims about James allegedly being interested in research?

Though Smith claimed not to know Campbell, and the author never mentioned Smith to Campbell, he was aware that it was possible that they both could have been lying. Also, it was conceivable that Dr. W. could have mentioned a Schwartz and Russek (1997) article about Smith to Campbell. Hence, the author remained appropriately skeptical. What transpired was completely unanticipated.

First, Campbell looked obviously perplexed and asked who William James was. Was she feigning ignorance? The author responded with a purposely vague answer: 'He's a friend of a friend' (an informal rephrasing of Smith's purported relationship with James). The medium went on to describe a man who lived at the turn of the 20th century, was dressed in a long dark robe, wore a beard, and was surrounded by books.

Then, the medium visibly changed her countenance and appeared to go into a 'trance'. She began speaking in a lower, more deliberate and educated voice. For the next ten minutes or so, she/he began pacing and giving a lecture on the nature of consciousness; and in the process the purported spirit allegedly voiced his strong enthusiasm for continuing research!

Having never witnessed an evidential medium before, I was frankly shocked. I later learned that rarely did this medium (or most mediums) spontaneously fall into a trance where alleged spirits 'speak through' them (most contemporary mental mediums resist losing conscious control in this fashion, especially when in public). I wondered, was it possible that Campbell was being genuine? Could James have literally 'come through' Campbell and forcefully indicated his continued commitment to the work? Was Smith actually correct in her description of James's desire to participate in research? Was James (with others) choosing to serve in the role of what the author and his colleagues at the time playfully described as being 'departed hypothesized co-investigators' (DHCIs)?

There was only one way to find out, and that was to design controlled research which tested the mediums' claims empirically (reported in Chapter 13). Given the clearly questionable (as well as controversial) nature of these claims, I was not about to initiate formal IRB approved research protocols without first performing some initial proof-of-concept feasibility investigations.

* * * * *

Are Any Sacred and Divine Experiences Real?–A Personal Experience

We will shift gears to hear and consider personal experiences of sacred beings (e.g. saints and angels) and the Divine. The following account was revealed in Chapter 12, "Putting Angel Sophia and Her Intent to the Test", in my 2011 book titled *The Sacred Promise: How Scientists are Discovering Spirit Collaboration in Our Daily Lives*. As you will see, it illustrates how a self-science approach to metaphysical personal experiences can result in the uncovering of unexpected evidence that helps us discern their reality.

I should preface this account by saying that I was raised to believe that saints, angels, and the Divine were like Santa Claus and the Easter Bunny; fictions or superstitions rather than genuine Sacred Beings or beyond. The following account was edited for clarity and brevity:

* * * * *

One fateful afternoon in the summer of 2003 a new postdoctoral fellow I had never met asked me if I wanted to talk with my guardian angel ... The reader should remember that I am reporting factually what actually transpired, changing the names and certain identifying details as appropriate to protect anonymity. The person I was meeting with was in his forties with a Ph.D. in cardiovascular physiology and was about to begin a two-year research fellowship at the University of Arizona funded by a grant from the National Institutes of Health. He had selected me to be his primary mentor. Prior to this meeting, I had spoken with him once on the telephone. As you can probably surmise, in that conversation he had not mentioned anything about spirits or angels. To protect his anonymity—he prefers that his angelic awareness not be widely known—I will call him Dr. Michaels.

Though this was in no way related to the topic of his postdoctoral fellowship, Dr. Michaels was aware that I had conducted research on life after death. Dr. Michaels confessed that he could readily see spirits, including angels, and he claimed that one of my angels—a female—was standing in my office behind my right shoulder! In my thirty plus years of holding research meeting in various laboratories at Harvard, Yale, and the University of Arizona, no one had ever made a claim about an angel in my office, let alone "my" angel. Yes, some mediums had claimed to see deceased spirits in my office and laboratory, but then they regularly reported seeing "dead people" in houses, restaurants, and even university offices.

Though I was intrigued by Dr. Michaels' "angel" statement, to say the least, I did not feel it appropriate to explore his purported extrasensory perceptions at that time. Our task in that meeting was to map out plans for his research fellowship, not to hold a conversation with my supposed spirit guide. However, in light of other events related to angels that were cropping up at that time—for example, I had been curiously gifted a book about the history of angels, but I had not yet read it—I told Dr. Michaels that I would look forward to talking with him about angels, off the record, at a future time.

As it turned out, Dr. Michaels was going to join me and two other colleagues in a daylong trip to a research clinic evaluating a purported energy-medicine device located approximately 150 miles from Tucson. On the way to the clinic, I asked Dr. Michaels if he was willing to share some of his early as well as current experiences related to angels.

It appears that angels have played a central role in his life. Dr. Michaels even said that his earliest childhood memory involved being with one of his lifelong angels. He claimed that because of his intimate relationship with them, he was sometimes able to perform healings on family members and friends. Dr. Michaels believed that everyone had angels that assisted us throughout our life. Most of us had no awareness of "guardian angels," and that the majority of us were blind to the intrinsic value of coming to know our angels and consciously working with them.

Apparently, Dr. Michaels felt that it was safe to share this information with me. In fact, he claimed that his spirit guides were instructing him to awaken me to existence of angels, including the specific ones associated with me. Of course, I entertained various alternative possibilities, including that Dr. Michaels was delusional, that he was pulling my leg, and even that he might be a secret "Randi" plant [with the "Amazing" Randi, you never know what's up his magician's sleeve]. However, as far as I could tell, Dr. Michaels was a successful, responsible, and highly recommended Ph.D. scientist who just so happened to hold strange beliefs similar to those of such mediums as John Edward and Lauri Campbell.

The Name Sam and the Sudden Appearance of Angel Sophia

After returning to Tucson and before I went to sleep that night, I wondered whether it was possible that I, and everyone else, actually had one or more guardian angels. I realized that unlike the survival-of-consciousness hypothesis, which was meaningful only to individuals who have experienced the loss of a loved one and have a personal reason to care about life after death, the spirit guides' hypothesis had the potential to be meaningful to all of us. If we all could potentially improve ourselves by becoming increasingly aware of higher spiritual guidance, the implications for improving our daily lives made the spirit guides' hypothesis more appealing.

Starting with when I was a professor at Yale, I would from time to time "Ask the Universe" a question, and novel thoughts would typically pop into my mind that often could be verified. The first such question I asked of the Universe was, "Could you give me another name for God?" What immediately popped into mind was the name "Sam." When I first heard "Sam," I couldn't help laughing. I wondered, was the name Sam a product of my creative unconscious, or was I possibly living in a Woody Allen movie? However, when I looked up the origin of the name Sam in my Webster's 2nd edition, unabridged dictionary, I discovered to my astonishment that Samuel comes from the Hebrew "Shemuel," which translated literally as "The name of God."

After carefully considering (and ruling out) nine possible conventional explanations for why this name might have popped into my mind, I seriously entertained the possibility that while asking the Universe a question in a state of deep authenticity and genuineness, "It" had somehow provided me with a concrete answer that I could later verify. In that chapter I confessed that I initially was reluctant to explore this potential hypothesis; in fact, I avoided asking another question of the Universe for more than a decade. However, as I reported in *The G.O.D. Experiments* book (2006), when I returned to asking such questions of the Universe, the good answers came with sufficient regularity for me to no longer, with integrity, dismiss this often useful avenue of inquiry.

So that night, after returning to Tucson, I decided to ask the Universe, "Did I, as Dr. Michaels claimed, have a female angel, and could the Universe show her to me?" What happened next was novel for me in this regard—I got absolutely nothing: no names, images, feelings, or memories. The complete absence of any subjective experience took me by surprise. I went to sleep impressed with the complete failure of my request.

However, the next morning I happened to read an article in the then current issue of the magazine *Scientific American* about the so-called "censor" genes. These are genes that suppress certain genetic potentials from being expressed. It occurred to me that I had been so well conditioned to believe that angels were like Santa Claus—a playful fiction, and nothing more—that my mind was probably censoring any awareness of a potential angelic presence in my life, if indeed there was one.

That night, I decided to try my personal experiment again. This time I consciously attempted to release any mental censorship I had about angels. I asked that my mind be opened to all possibilities, and then I did something new. Instead of asking the next question of the Universe, I directed my question to my possible angel instead.

I said in my mind, "Angel, if you are here, I would love to see you, and learn your name."

What happened next was totally unlike anything I had ever experienced before or since that night. Whereas I rarely see images—I mostly think in abstract terms; even my dreams, when I remember them, are relatively flat and colorless—I experienced the appearance of a large glowing figure hovering above the foot of my bed. My bedroom has high ceilings. The "spirit," or hallucination or whatever it was, looked to be at least eight feet tall.

The entity appeared to be female, with flowing blond hair. Around her shoulders were bright lights that looked to be in the shape of wings, but they could have been reflections off her arms and body. She looked to be wearing a whitish colored dress. She was smiling. She appeared to be loving and gentle, yet strangely powerful.

I asked her in my mind what was her name, and what popped in was the name "Sophia." At that moment, my rational skeptical mind kicked in—I thought something to the effect of "This can't be real"—and the vision of the female spirit vanished. Just like that, puff, and it was gone.

I realized that the name Sophia in Greek meant wisdom. However, I had never heard of an angel named Sophia. Hearing this name for an angel initially seemed almost as bizarre to me as my initially hearing the name Sam for God was almost twenty years earlier.

However, the next morning, I checked to see if there was an angel named Sophia on angel websites. I Googled the words "Angel and Sophia," and what I uncovered left me breathless. There were more than 5,000,000 entries for Angel Sophia, and some of websites revealed a profound set of religious beliefs associated with Angel Sophia.

Depending upon the Internet source, Angel Sophia was described as being either:

1 the first emanation of the Divine, and the Mother of all creation, including all the Archangels;
2 the feminine expression of the Divine—the male expression of the Divine being an angel purportedly called Metatron; or
3 the wife of Metatron.

There were also many references to writings about something called the "Pistis Sophia" and a Christian denomination focused on her.

First there was Sam, the name of God, and then Sophia—two relatively unknown "big" names from religious history. As I had done with the name Sam [I had asked more than fifty staff members, students, and faculty if they knew the origin and meaning of the name Sam—only one person knew, meaning it was not common knowledge], I asked a cohort of people who actually knew something about angel lore, if they had ever heard of an angel named Sophia.

The first nine people I asked included Dr. Michaels as well as the person who had gifted me the *History of Angels* book, which I had not read at that time. None of them said that they had heard of an angel named Sophia. However, the tenth person I asked, who happened to be visiting me from California and was an ordained minister as well as a successful corporate executive, not only knew who Angel Sophia was, but a close associate of his was a scholar who had just completed a book about Pistis Sophia. I had to wonder if this was a synchronicity. When he heard how I came to discover Angel Sophia, he was inspired to contact his friend who sent me a signed copy of his book.

Try putting yourself in my shoes at that time: you had a seemingly innocent meeting with a new postdoctoral fellow, and in the course of the meeting the scientist claimed that a female angel was standing behind your right shoulder and wished to speak with you. You eventually mustered the courage to attempt having some sort of personal angel experience yourself. You had a surprising vision of a glowing white angelic-like female and heard the name Sophia, which you initially presumed has nothing to do with angels. You then discovered in angel lore that there really was one named Sophia, and that she was viewed in some circles as "the Mother of all Angels."

You then conducted a small informal survey with people who knew something about angels, and none of them said they had heard of an Angel Sophia. However, the tenth person not only knew of her existence, but he even knew a scholar who has just written a book about Pistis Sophia! Talk about a chain of synchronicities.

What would you have done with this information, especially if you knew mediums like John Edward and Laurie Campbell who like Dr. Michaels were convinced that angels were real? Dismiss the information? Run from it? Put your head in the sand?

I might well have done this, except my mind wouldn't let me. What unfolded was a new proof-of-concept personal experimental test.

Putting Angel Sophia to a Test

I should confess that I have what some people call a disconcerting if not bad habit, especially at a university. I sometimes jokingly tell colleagues and even strangers that as a scientist I have developed a "disease called Science."[2]

What I mean is that in an automatic and an often-uncontrollable way, when I hear someone share a belief or an experience, my mind effortlessly does the following:

1 It converts the person's belief or experience into a question.
2 The question is then turned into a hypothesis.
3 The hypothesis is "operationalized"—meaning, the hypothesis is refined so that it can be potentially measured.
4 The operationalized hypothesis is then transformed into an experimental design.
5 I will typically conduct the experiment in my head as an Einstein-like thought experiment.
6 And then, if it is feasible—meaning I have the time, funds, the equipment, and so forth—I will feel the strong desire to conduct the experiment.

Because this process is so automatic and effortless, I often do not think much about it, unless the hypothesis happens to be exceptionally controversial and it turns out that it is actually possible for me to test it–be it an exploratory investigation or a full-fledged university experiment. This is what happened following my vision and upon becoming aware of beliefs about Angel Sophia.

I realized that I had the possibility to conduct an exploratory investigation testing whether some sort of spiritual being with the name Sophia was somehow connected to me. The question I had asked was whether I was brave enough—some might say foolhardy enough—to conduct such a proof-of-concept investigation.

As fate would have it, the opportunity to conduct such an investigation in my personal life was, so to speak, "dropped in my lap." What transpired forever changed how I viewed the potential existence of a larger spiritual reality and our ability to investigate and learn from it.

It occurred to me that if Susy Smith was actually "watching over me," then she would probably know about my seemingly anomalous experience with a purported angel named Sophia, and she would want to help me verify if: (1) Sophia actually existed, or (2) help me establish that Sophia was a figment of my imagination, whichever was the case.

At this point I had no idea.

If Sophia was "my" angel—she might also be an angel to others as well, if she really existed—and she was willing to appear in my bedroom, then she would most likely know that I was a person who suffered from a disease called science, and that I would want to determine, experimentally, whether she actually existed. Moreover, if Sophia had been watching me for a long time, she would know of my relationship with the late Susy Smith, not only when Susy was in the physical but also when Susy had transitioned to the other side. I also speculated that if Sophia had my best interests at heart, she would likely be willing to collaborate with Susy to help validate her existence. Otherwise, why would she show up in the first place?

The idea popped into my head that in principle, Susy might be able to bring Sophia to an appropriately receptive medium. I wondered about the possibility of a deceased spirit actually bringing an angelic spirit to a medium. And if Susy succeeded in bringing Sophia to a medium, would the reading potentially verify her existence?

At this point I was simply doing a thought experiment in my head. I realized that if an exploratory, proof-of-concept investigation were actually conducted with positive results, the possibility existed for doing formal, controlled, and systematic research on the spirit guides' hypothesis. But, before addressing the question of whether alleged spirit guides could provide meaningful information for people individually and collectively, it was essential to determine scientifically if spirit guides existed, period. This is where I began.

A Disconcerted Medium's Susy-Sophia Reading

As it so happened, I was scheduled to give an invited address presenting our latest energy medicine research [funded at the time by the National Institutes of Health] at a conference that was being held not far from the home of a gifted research medium. To preserve the requested anonymity of the medium, I have changed his name as well as the name of the city where the reading took place. We will call the medium Howard, and the city Baltimore.

Howard lived about an hour from where the conference was being held. He had previously provided exceptionally accurate information regarding Susy Smith; moreover, he claimed that Susy would spontaneously visit him from time to time. But it turned out that Howard was one of the few mediums I have worked with who neither believed in, nor claimed to communicate with, angelic beings. Howard was a fairly down-to-earth person who was known to enjoy social gatherings as well as alcoholic spirits—I know many mediums who have a fondness for liquid spirits as well.

I deeply respected Howard's skills as a medium; the fact that he had little use for the idea of angels made his selection for my private exploratory investigation all the more interesting. So I called him a week before the conference and asked him if I could have a personal reading with him. Howard happened to have some free time after my conference was over, and we scheduled the appointment.

Technically, what transpired was not the "Double-Deceased" version of the Spirit-Mediated model since Sophia presumably was not deceased [as an angel, she had never lived in the physical]. However, it was a "Deceased-Mediated" one since Susy supposedly brought Sophia to Howard.

When I got to Howard's house, after expressing greetings and sharing personal kinds of catch-up information, Howard led me into the room where he conducted his readings. Though I had tested Howard in laboratory research on numerous occasions, I had never had a personal reading with him. I told Howard that I wished to hear from two beings in spirit. The first I would identify by name, the second would presumably be brought by the first, and I would not provide any information about this individual. At no time did I say, or imply, that one of the spirits was potentially not a deceased human being.

I then told him I wished to hear from Susy Smith. He was pleased to comply with this request. He shared information, purportedly from Susy, for approximately fifteen minutes. Though this information fit Susy well, most of it was scientifically useless because: (1) I had given him Susy's name, (2) he had previously participated in research involving Susy, and (3) he had subsequently read some of Susy's books. Since Susy was not the focus of this investigation, these factors were unimportant.

Next I told him that I had asked Susy to please bring along another individual in spirit, and that I would like it if Howard did a reading with this individual. What happened next was thoroughly confusing to Howard and a bit upsetting for me as well.

Howard reported seeing a very tall woman with blonde flowing hair. He described her as radiant, bigger than life, and sort of floating above the floor. He said that he could not look at her eyes; she was very powerful. He said he felt inadequate in her presence. I have never heard a medium speak this way of a deceased person they've contacted.

Further, Howard could not ascertain where she had previously lived on the Earth, or how she had died. He sensed she had been in spirit for a very long time, had an S-sounding name, and she was somehow connected to me, but he could not figure out how.

He said she gave no indication that she was a blood relative, or even a personal friend of mine, yet there was a very strong emotional and intellectual bond between us that made no sense to him.

Howard not only felt inadequate in terms of his mediumship skills with this individual, but he said he even felt "embarrassed" to be reading her. He said he had never experienced this hesitancy, and I had never heard a medium say that she or he felt embarrassed reading a particular spirit.

Save for my confirming that I did wish to hear from a woman, and that she probably appeared to have flowing blonde hair, afterward I did not give Howard any additional feedback about his potential accuracy, or lack thereof. Moreover, I told Howard that for personal as well as scientific reasons, I could not at this time give him any indication about who the woman might be, or why I had requested that Susy specifically bring her to the reading.

After thanking him greatly for his time and efforts, I left him in a rather befuddled state. While driving back to town in my rental car, it began to dawn on me that what had just transpired was possibly unique in the history of afterlife and spiritual research. Susy Smith, a distinguished deceased author of thirty books in parapsychology, the apparent inventor of the double-deceased paradigm, had just been read by a gifted research medium. The man claimed that she had brought to the reading another woman in spirit whose glowing presence sounded very much like what I knew of Sophia, the angel.

Had Susy, a deceased woman, brought an angel, in this case Sophia, to Howard? Had he read an angel and not known it? Was Howard's personal discomfort, coupled with his inability to get standard information about the woman, like how she died, potential evidence that this spirit was indeed someone who had never lived on the earth, and therefore had never died?

Obviously, a single reading does not make for a definitive scientific test—in academic research, this would be called "non-generalizable data." However, single readings can serve as beacons of opportunity, revealing what can potentially be explored and documented systematically in the laboratory.

* * * * *

From Personal Self-Science to Laboratory Research

William James exemplified how it is possible to apply critical thinking and basic elements of the scientific method to explore personal experiences in self and others. In fact, James described himself as being a "radical empiricist." Mainstream scientists, including research psychologists, typically label such accounts as being "anecdotal" and dismiss them as having little if any evidential value. However, this practice is counterproductive to genuine truth-seeking, especially concerning the study of mind and communication with inferred conscious beings, including the Universal/ Divine Mind itself. Later in this volume (Chapter 13), I will present laboratory research that validates and extends these exemplary communication experiences.

Notes

1 During this period he came to realize that he may have experienced a near-death experience as an infant when he almost died from an allergic reaction to sulfa drugs (his earliest childhood memory is of seeing a bright, white light that was very soothing and comforting), and he may have experienced a second near-death experience as a teenager when he almost died during complications in surgery (he recalls having had an out-of-body experience and again seeing a comforting bright white light).
2 A few years after *The Sacred Promise* was published, a neurologist provided me with an official medical diagnosis for my "disease"–"scientitus."

References

Anthony, M. (2021). *The afterlife frequency: The scientific proof of spiritual contact and how that awareness will change your life*. Book submitted for publication.

Beischel, J., & Schwartz, G. E. (2007). Anomalous information reception by research mediums demonstrated using a novel triple-blind procedure. *EXPLORE: The Journal of Science and Healing, 3*(1), 23–26.

Combs, A., & Holland, M. (2000). *Synchronicity: Science, myth, and the trickster* (3rd ed.). Boston, MA: Da Capo Press.

Myers, F. W. H. (1961). *Human personality and its survival of bodily death*. In S. Smith (Ed.). New Hyde Park, NY: University Books.

Schwartz, G. E. (2002). *The afterlife experiments: Breakthrough scientific evidence for life after death*. New York, NY: Atria Books/Simon & Schuster.

Schwartz, G. E. (2006). *The G.O.D. experiments: How science is discovering God in everything, including us*. New York, NY: Atria Books/Simon & Schuster.

Schwartz, G. E. (2010). William James and the search for scientific evidence of life after death: Past, present, and possible future. *Journal of Consciousness Studies, 17*(11–12), 121–152.

Schwartz, G. E. (2011). *The sacred promise: How science is discovering spirit's collaboration with us in our daily lives*. Hillsboro, OR: Atria Books/Beyond Words.

Schwartz, G. E. (2012). Consciousness, spirituality, and post-materialist science: An empirical and experiential approach. In L. Miller (Ed.), *The Oxford handbook of psychology and spirituality* (pp. 584–597). Oxford, UK: Oxford University Press.

Schwartz, G. E. (2017). *Super synchronicity: Where science and spirit meet*. Cardiff-by-the-Sea, CA: Waterside Digital Press.

Schwartz, G. E. (2020a). How do scientists change their minds? The example of survival of consciousness research. In S. A. Schwartz, M. H. Woollacott, & G. E. Schwartz (Eds.), *Is consciousness primary? Perspectives from founding members of the academy for the advancement of postmateirlist sciences* (pp. 1–30). Battle Ground, WA: AAPS Press.

Schwartz, G. E. (2020b). Supersynchronicity and primacy of consciousness: Bridging science, metaphysics and spirituality. In S. A. Schwartz, M. H. Woollacott, & G. E. Schwartz (Eds.), *Is consciousness primary? Perspectives from founding members of the academy for the advancement of postmateirlist sciences* (pp. 384–433). Battle Ground, WA: AAPS Press.

Schwartz, G. E., & Russek, L. G. (1997). Dynamical energy systems and modern physics: fostering the science and spirit of complementary and alternative medicine. Alternative Therapies in Health and Medicine, 3(3), 46–56.

Smith, S. (1974). *The book of James: Conversations from beyond.* New York, NY: G.P. Putnam.

Smith, S. (2000). *Ghost writers in the sky: More communication from James.* Tucson, AZ: Vision Press.

Part II
Theological Considerations

4   Travels Beyond

Catherine Wolff

Part I: Ways of Knowing

In the twenty-first century, anyone considering the possibility of communication between the living and the dead – or a divinity or other spiritual beings – is liable to encounter a great deal of skepticism, if not derision. We live in a time when science, seeking understanding of the natural world through observation and experimentation, is the dominant way of knowing. Many people look to science for answers we used to seek through religion. They argue that science has demolished the belief in a God who created and sustains the universe and engages as a person with his creatures. For them, a view of life formed by religious and philosophical belief is irrelevant to the pursuit of objective scientific knowledge.

This rejection of religious belief was challenged by William Cantwell Smith, who pointed out that such skeptics are a minority in time and space, and should be summoned "before the bar of world history to defend their curious insensitivity to this dimension of human life" (Heim, 1995, p. 52). Indeed, many eminent scientists have a humble attitude about the limitations of the scientific way of knowing. Nobel laureate Steven Weinberg writes, "Physical science has historically progressed not only by finding precise explanations of natural phenomena, but also by discovering what sorts of things *can* be precisely explained. These may be fewer than we had thought" (Weinberg, 2013). Neurophysiologist Sir John Eccles believes that "We have to recognize that we are spiritual beings with souls existing in a spiritual world as well as material beings with bodies and brains existing in a material world" (Alexander & Tompkins, 2014, p. xxiii). Such scientists themselves reach beyond data toward meaning. Particle physicist Savas Dimopoulos considers the question of *why?* to be very human; he continues to wonder why the universe exists, why we exist, and what could be the purpose of it all (Dimopoulos, 2016).

For believers, religion addresses these mysteries of being: the why rather than the how, the purpose rather than the details of physical phenomena. For them, regarding the world solely through science is an incomplete and insufficient worldview. Their faith can involve observation and reasoned arguments, but when they explore the realm of religious thought – certainly, when they pray – their horizons open to infinity. The existence, the immanence of God, becomes a distinct possibility, as does the possibility of life beyond earthly existence. Religious faith is another way of knowing, one that is fully compatible with science. As Albert Einstein put it, "science without religion is lame, and religion without science is blind" (Einstein, 1982, p. 46).

The human capacity for imagination fuels both science and religion. For Einstein, imagination was essential to scientific research in that "imagination embraces the entire world, stimulating progress, giving birth to evolution" (Einstein, 1931, p. 49). It is also the ground and inspiration for artistic endeavor and religious belief. Imagination is the vehicle that enables us to reach beyond our time and place toward a reality we cannot experience directly. All the data gathered, all the objective knowledge acquired throughout the centuries, are not enough for us to glimpse, much less explore, what might lie beyond our earthly existence.

There is a convergence of scholarly opinion on the importance of the imagination, in opposition to modern thought that accepts only that which can be analyzed and measured. Jeffrey Burton Russell points out that the literal meaning of words is insufficient to express reality, whereas figurative language opens up a rich multitude of meanings, and is at least as real as scientific truth: maps, poetry, paintings, creeds, and diagrams are all valid interpretations of reality (Proctor, 2005, p. 122). Robert Bellah argues that our imaginative capacities for play, art, and religion, through a process of "beyonding," open for us another world where we transcend the "dreadful immanence" of the mundane (Bellah, 2011, p. 9).

The workings of the imagination are mysterious. It brings unconscious elements into consciousness, forming a meaningful whole of sensations, language, memory, and perceptions. Samuel Coleridge called this the power "to shape into one" (Zaleski, 1987, p. 61). An eloquent metaphor produced by the imagination, such as a bridge one must cross to reach another world, expresses the dynamic connection between the human mind and the universe, and points toward truth. A symbol not only represents a reality beyond itself, it participates in that reality. Indeed, John Cornwell believes that the imagination is evidence of a spark of the divine in each of us, and that we reach out to the divine through creative acts of the imagination (Cornwell, 2016).

We imagine our way through life, and the metaphors and symbols we use to explore life beyond enable us to participate in a reality that seems to call to us. As Saint Augustine wrote in his *Confessions*,, "You have made us for yourself, O Lord, and our hearts are restless until they rest in you" (Saint Augustine, 397–400). Imaginative exploration spring from wells of faith and hope, and is shaped by the traditions, the lives, and the character of believers as individuals and as representatives of particular cultures. It illuminates art, ritual, and belief itself.

Part II: What We Seek, and What We Find

Until modern times, the beliefs of religious faith traditions were the main repository of our hopes for life beyond. They tell of unification with a divine person, or a state of blissful transcendence, or both. They warn of a final reckoning for our moral behavior in this life: punishment for our misdeeds, but also reward for our compassion and pursuit of justice and the suffering we have already endured. Christianity, in particular, has encouraged the hope that we will be reunited with loved ones, a yearning that is shared with people who do not think in religious terms.

Some questions continue to puzzle us. Do we reach a state of unity with a deity and/or others right after death, or is there an interim period after death and before the soul reaches its final destination? Does that come after a personal reckoning with one's life or at the Final Judgment at the end of the cosmos? Alternatively, is it a series of life after life until we finally lose ourselves in bliss? Do we judge ourselves or does a deity judge us, and do we need a messiah to intervene for us? What will life beyond this one be like, and will we be reunited with friends and family? In addition, is it possible to communicate with those who have gone before us?

This is where we run into the limits of our capacity to think and to express ourselves in terms that transcend time and space. However, there are endless stories from faith and folklore traditions of divinities, angels, and departed souls taking the initiative to communicate with us – Gabriel appearing to Mary, Krishna visiting his cousins, Joseph Smith's apparitions of heavenly personages, those feelings we have now and then that a loved one has reached back to us from beyond.

Moreover, our religious imagination has given rise to stories of travelers who have gone on journeys beyond and returned to tell us what they found. These stories do not present facts or proofs – rather they teach people how to deal with their fears about death and their hopes for continued life. They manifest truth to those who seek it. Interestingly, for those of us living in tumultuous times, these stories tend to appear when they are most needed, "when the way society pictures itself and the surrounding universe is so changed as to threaten to dislocate the human being" (Zaleski, 1987, p. 100).

The tradition may be as old as humankind itself. There are late Paleolithic cave paintings in Les Trois Freres, France. In one, we see a human figure with animal features, who may well be a shaman, looming above a mass of animals. Such figures, whose functions vary among different cultures, possess the power to move between worlds and to perform rituals that draw on spirits to intervene in the lives of the living. They can heal the sick, recover lost souls, or even broker a "hell marriage" between the ghost of a girl who died in childhood and a living man, so that both partners live in two worlds (Couliano, 1991, pp. 80–81).

One of the first narratives of a journey to the afterlife is that of Viraz, whose story developed from ancient times up to the tenth century CE. As a "righteous seer," Viraz could serve as a guide to the afterlife, and is sent on a seven-day trip by Zoroastrian priests to see if their faith was true. After writing a will and drinking a potion of wine and henbane, his soul leaves his body. He is taken by divine guides to the Bridge of the Requiter, where his deeds are weighed in a golden balance, and is allowed to cross the Bridge. He visits purgatory, where people suffer waves of heat and cold in preparation for resurrection. Next are three realms of heaven: the stars for souls whose thoughts were good, the moon for those whose words were good, and the sun, for those who performed good deeds. The fourth level is the paradise of Ahura Mazda, a realm of endless light. Viraz meets courtiers to Ahura Mazda, including Zoroaster, and Ahura Mazda himself.

Viraz goes underground on a tour of hell, which has four dark, foul-smelling levels that are progressively more terrifying. Viraz witnesses the suffering of the damned, although none is identified. There are witches and heretics, as well as people who slaughtered cattle or peed standing up. People who did not wear sacred girdles are being devoured by demons. The bottom hell is the dwelling place of Angra Mainyu, Ahura Mazda's destructive foe, and the most abominable sinners, such as women who wore make-up. Finally, Viraz is led back to Ahura Mazda, who manifests as pure light, and returns to this world to reveal what he has found.

As our stories continue, you will find that several of the features in Viraz's account recur in many otherworldly journeys: guides, good and bad realms, a perilous bridge to cross, testing and judgment, and a god described in terms of light. Famous personages and family members also begin to appear, and to enter into conversation with our travelers.

From the Jewish tradition comes the story of Enoch, that mysterious figure from Genesis who walked with God. Enoch is called in a dream by clouds and mist, and takes a tour of the cosmos. He is blown along a path of stars to heaven where he encounters a wall of hailstones ringed by fire. After fainting in fear, he has a vision within a vision of an immense structure of burning marble where he encounters God. He is then escorted by archangels through storehouses of stars, winds, and storms, and views the punishment of fallen angels. Their cohabitation with women had been the origin of sin, and they were the source of all corruption on earth.

Enoch is guided by the angel Raphael through a mountainous place where he hears the voices of the dead who await the day of the great judgment. One of these is the soul of Abel, who is to pursue Cain until Cain's seed is exterminated. Some souls wait to be judged, some are righteous, while others will suffer forever. Some are in the melancholy state of not being good enough to be resurrected nor bad enough to be punished forever.

Such visitations to the afterlife often include cautionary scenes of those whose moral comportment on earth had been found wanting (although what is considered sinful varies widely from culture to culture). They are sometimes clearly identified. In Homer's Odyssey, Odysseus travels to the underworld to consult with the prophet Tiresias about his prospects in life. Tiresias appears from a swarm of "poor feckless ghosts" (Homer, 1944, p. 132) to reassure Odysseus that he will die in peace. The tale becomes a series of encounters with departed souls. Tantalus, who had tried to serve up his son as a feast for the gods, is condemned to insatiable hunger and thirst, his every attempt at drinking from a lake met with the lake instantly drying up. Sisyphus, who thought he could outsmart the gods, is stuck eternally rolling his rock up a hill only to have it rumble back down again.

Odysseus's most touching encounter is with his mother, Anticlea. They speak of his travels, of family, and of Anticlea's death pining for her son. Odysseus reaches out to embrace her, but she slips through his arms, saying, "All people are like this when they are dead. The sinews no longer hold the flesh and bones together; these perish in the fierceness of consuming fire as soon as life has left the body, and the soul flits away as though it were a dream" (Homer, 1944, p. 136). There is a similar scene from Virgil's Aeneid, when Aeneas meets his father, Anchises, who reveals the great mysteries of life and death: how the soul is contaminated by its imprisonment in its earthly body; how it must be purified by water, wind, and fire to be released to Elysium where evil is purged and only the spirit's essential flame remains. Like Anticlea, Anchises slips through Aeneas's arms as he tries to embrace him (Virgil, 1983, p. 184). Such tales are steeped in our human longing to be reunited with loved ones, a longing that has given rise to so many visions of life to come.

Such visions allowed Mohammad to see specific people in the afterlife as well: his beloved wife Khadija in the Garden, and friends and family in the Fire. His most famous set of encounters began with the Night Journey, when he is awakened by the angel Gabriel and travels on his magnificent steed Buraq over "the wonders between heaven and earth" to Jerusalem (Rustomji, 2009, p. 29). At that site sacred to Jews and Christians and Muslims, Mohammad meets and prays with Abraham, Moses, and Jesus, establishing a fellowship of prophets. Thousands of angels then greet him as he ascends a ladder, proceeding from the lower regions where Adam reviews the arriving souls of his progeny, and souls suffer punishments appropriate to their transgressions, such as men who had devoured the wealth of orphans devouring stones only to pass them and start all over again.

At each successive level, Mohammad comes across prophets and angels. After Adam and Ishmael, he meets biblical prophets, John and Jesus. Next are Joseph, Idris (who may be Enoch), Aaron, and Moses, with Abraham, father of Arabs, at the final level. Mohammad then encounters Allah in the highest heaven. In one telling, Allah bestows on him the essential elements of true religion, such as Islam (submission), hajj (pilgrimage to Mecca), and almsgiving. To his followers, the stories of the Night Journey and the Ascension validated Mohammad's position as God's final messenger, as well as his teaching on the afterlife and judgment. To those of us considering his contact with the dead, it is an impressive testament to his access to such important personages from the religions that preceded Islam.

In medieval Christianity, mystics sought loving union with God, often expressed in erotic imagery. Mechthilde of Magdeburg's, *The Flowing Light of the Godhead* is an account of her journey to heaven, where she finds three levels. The first is a paradisal garden for souls who were neither bad enough for purgatory nor good enough for heaven. Here she walks with Enoch and Elijah. Next is a great dome full of angel choirs, where, at the final judgment, the blessed will take their places according to their merit. God lives in the third heaven, and this is where Mechthilde's account becomes deeply personal. Whereas all the blessed enjoy the beatific vision of God, she as a holy virgin woman is allowed to visit Christ's bridal chamber to have intimate union with him. In the guise of a noble lady, she yields to Christ, who appears as a beautiful youth. "Thus comes to pass what both of them desire: he gives himself to her, and she herself to him." They have become spiritual lovers, the very consummation of her soul's desire (McDannell & Lang, 1988, p. 101).

Dante's *The Divine Comedy is* the apogee of medieval visions of ecstatic union with God, and of otherworldly journeys up to that time. Dante writes from a specific place and time, 1330, as an everyman figure with a mission to tell us what he finds on his travels. Though he must include pain and suffering, he tells us, he will also find love, "God's love that in the beginning set all the beauty of the universe in motion" (Russell, 1997, p. 158). *The Divine Comedy*, comprising three books, *Inferno, Purgatorio,* and *Paradiso,* was regarded by Dante's contemporaries as a work of inspiration, if not revelation. Dante himself believed that God's Word could come to life through his words. However, he did not model his work on scripture or other Christian works – rather he revived the classic form of Virgil's story of Aeneas and his travels in the afterlife. In addition, Dante may well have been familiar with *Liber Scalae (The Book of the Ladder) Machometi,* a version of Mohammad's Night Journey and Ascension, which was widely translated by Dante's time.

Dante's account is full of historical figures with whom he freely interacts, many of whom have appeared in previous accounts of the afterlife. He is rescued from his moral wandering by his childhood love Beatrice, and guided by Virgil through the circles of the Inferno, where they meet an angry Ulysses (Odysseus) who, together with Diomedes, is being punished for sending in the Trojan horse. Mohammad appears torn from his chin to his nether regions for having caused schism, and in the dead center of hell, where Satan is fixed in a frozen lake, Judas Iscariot hangs from one of his three mouths, the other two being occupied by Caesar's murderers, Brutus and Cassius.

Dante and Virgil then pass through the terraces of purgatory, where those guilty of one of the seven deadly sins are suffering suitable punishments, such as those who were envious, having their eyes sewn shut with iron wire. They encounter Pope Adrian V on the terrace of avarice, and the love poets Guido Guinizelli and Arnaut Daniel on that of lust.

Virgil has to take leave of Dante at this point because he cannot travel beyond purgatory, as he was born before Christ and thus is not saved. Dante is then cleansed of his sin and restored to the memory of virtues in a lush paradise. Beatrice returns to guide him the rest of the way, and they leap up into the stars. They travel through celestial spheres suffused with the Light of God and ringing with cosmic harmony, drawn together in love toward its source. On the sun, they are surrounded by 12 dancing lights: King Solomon, Thomas Aquinas, and others whose intellects have illuminated the world.

Beatrice and Dante come to a shower of stars flowing down a golden ladder. They ascend to the realm of the Church Triumphant, and Christ and Mary descend to greet them. Even Dante is at a loss for words here: "In order to represent or image the highest heavens, the sacred poem must leap a gap, like the one who finds the road washed out before him" (Russell, 1997, p. 176). Peter, James, and John then test Dante on faith, hope, and love, and he is inspired by the Holy Spirit to declare that his sacred poem has been wrought by both heaven and earth (Russell, 1997, p. 177).

In the final sphere of the universe, enclosed by Light and Love, dwell nine choirs of angels. From there Dante sees the empyrean, where there is neither time nor space nor physical being. He drinks from a river of light, divine grace flowing between banks of faithful souls. He cries out for strength to convey his vision, a circle of light emanating from God, with the blessed assembled in the shape of a rose. Beatrice takes her place just below Adam and Moses and Peter, smiles at Dante, and turns back to the Light. Bernard of Clairvaux becomes Dante's guide, and together they look up through the rose to Mary and to God. Dante has earned the sight and understanding to enable him to enter the Light. He is able to see and understand the Trinity in a vision of circles, and the Incarnation as a human form within the Light of God. At the end of his story, Dante comes to understand that his soul is moved on an axis of love by God.

Looking Eastward

The ultimate fulfillment that Jews, Christians, and Muslims seek is not that of Hindus and Buddhists. We have fundamentally different ideas about everything from time and the cosmos to the nature of God; from the soul, the self, and consciousness to the passage of death and what lies beyond this earthy existence. But eastern religions have also produced otherworld travelers. In Hinduism, there are stories of the heavens and hells a soul might pass through in its long journey. One of the most famous, chronicled in the epic poem *Mahabharata,* tells of the hero Arjuna's travels and his encounters with the gods.

Arjuna is sent by his family to the Himalayas, the abode of the gods, to obtain weapons from Indra, king of the gods and heavenly father to Arjuna. He travels at the speed of mind and arrives in a heavenly place full of blossoming trees and rivers the color of lapis lazuli. Indra appears to him as an ancient ascetic, and tells Arjuna that since he has attained a state of great purity, he can throw his own weapons away. Arjuna refuses, and Indra, impressed by his sense of duty, grants him a boon. Arjuna, recognizing the god, is so bold as to ask for Indra's weapons, and Indra makes a counteroffer of life in the heavenly realms. Arjuna persists, and Indra swears to give him his weapons when he meets Shiva, destroyer of worlds.

To prepare for this encounter, Arjuna undertakes a series of ascetic practices, fasting so that eventually he is living on air. He stretches up on his tiptoes, arms flung up, his hair turned to lightning, overheating the world so that it smokes in all directions. Heavenly sages plead with Shiva to stop him, but Shiva sends them away. He takes on the form of a powerful hunter and comes upon Arjuna being challenged by a demonic boar. Shiva and Arjuna shoot their arrows simultaneously, and the boar dies, but there ensues a fierce argument about who has killed the boar. Arjuna, enraged, shoots arrows blazing like the sun and hurls boulders and trees, causing smoke and sparks to fly.

But the hunter is unmoved, and Arjuna realizes that he may be Shiva himself. He fashions an image of the god, worships it, and as he does, so flowers fall on the hunter's head. Arjuna flings himself at his feet, and Shiva reveals himself in glory to Arjuna. He grants him Pashupata, the powerful weapon with which Shiva destroys the universe at the end of creation, on the condition that Arjuna will use it only on heavenly warriors.

Arjuna sets off to collect Indra's weapons, including a celestial mace and inescapable nooses. Indra proclaims that Arjuna will do wondrous works on behalf of the gods and carries him up to heaven in his own mighty chariot. When they reach heaven, Arjuna encounters kings and warriors who illuminate the realm with the light of their merits, their shining dwellings seen as stars from earth.

Indra's capital city, Amaravati, is full of palaces, gardens, and gods playing with celestial nymphs. Chariots are driven by their driver's will around heaven, which resounds with celestial music of conch shells and drums. Arjuna enters a great hall full of pure heavenly beings, where Indra presides on a great bejeweled throne. Arjuna throws himself at Indra's feet, and they appear as the sun and moon together.

Arjuna lives in the heavenly capital for five years, learning how to use his new weapons. Toward the end, Indra arranges for him to be seduced by a ravishing nymph. But Arjuna resists her seductions, for thousands of years ago she had been the mother of his family's dynasty. He reveres her not as a lover but as a son, which causes her to curse him by denying his manhood. Fortunately, Indra, impressed with Arjuna's fortitude and propriety, lifts the curse, and Arjuna returns to earth.

In Mahayana Buddhism, there are many world systems in the universe similar to ours. In those called Pure Lands, a buddha helps souls reincarnate into his buddha-field. The Buddha tells the story of a monk named Dharmakara who dreams of a place that would bring together all the qualities of the millions of the buddha-fields. Dharmakara promises to turn his dream into a place of rebirth, and makes a series of vows about what he would provide there. He even travels the long bodhisattva path to become Amitabha, Buddha of Infinite Light in Sukhavati, the Western Paradise.

The Western Paradise is beyond measure, full of gods and humans, and ravishingly beautiful. Jewel lotuses, each with millions of radiant petals, fill the realm. Harmonious breezes blow through trees made of gold and jewels, scattering flowers. Food appears as soon as one wishes for it, and the mere sight of it satisfies hunger. The inhabitants do not own private property or care for their own robes, and can hear teachings of universal truth whenever they desire.

When he was a monk, Amitabha vowed that he would appear at the moment of death to anyone who sought enlightenment, heard his name, and remembered him in faith. People who wished to be reborn into his paradise and who dedicated the merits accumulated in their lives would be allowed to enter, except for those destined for hell for grievous offenses. Devotion to such a generous Buddha spread widely. In Japan, a monk named Honen taught that chanting the name of Amitabha was the path to salvation, and did so 70,000 times a day. Shinran, his disciple, believed that nothing we could do could save us from rebirth except to turn to Amitabha. If you heard his name in your heart, it was a sign of salvation, and you only needed to say it once.

In Tibetan Buddhism, there is a practice called "phowa" that invokes the power of Amitabha. At the moment of death, a spiritual master imprints a person's mindstream and transfers their consciousness to a Buddha realm. The departing soul can also aspire to be reborn either in a pure realm or as a human being, in order to help others.

Tibetan Buddhism also has a tradition of otherworldly journeys by rare people known as "delogs." Delog Dawa Drolma gives an account of her travels in *Delog: Journey to Realms beyond Death*. Through deep meditation, she passes beyond the boundaries of ordinary perception. She becomes aware of hellish impure realms where souls swirl around her like snow, weeping and crying out. She meets a girl who is wrapped in a black snake thick as a tree for having killed a snake, and a man named Abo with a head like a large clay pot. He had been stingy and uncharitable, for which he is now suffering in a hideous way: while his stomach is large as a city, his esophagus is the width of a horsehair, and his mouth is small as the eye of a needle.

Dawa Drolma travels to the Pure Realm of *Yulokod,* the reign of the goddess Tara. Radiant mansions of rainbow light float in the sky, trees are strung with bells that grant wishes, lotuses abound, and there is no birth, illness, aging, or death. This experience transforms Dawa Drolma: "I awoke from the deep sleep of ordinary consciousness and was free of the veils of ignorance. The inner vision of my pristine awareness expanded, and I experienced a surge of love and compassion" (Drolma, 1995, p. 116). She encounters Ayurdevi, the Goddess of Longevity, and a myriad of forms of Tara, as Thunderous Dragon's Roar, as Spontaneous Accomplishment, as Inconceivability. Dawa Drolma is overcome by the sense of infinite cosmic order and purity. Tara tells Dawa Drolma that when she realized that nobody aspired to Buddhahood in a woman's body, she appeared as an ocean of women, to bring them to enlightenment. Eventually, a powerful teacher calls Dawa Drolma back to the human realm. She returns in an instant, disoriented at first, but is soon "filled with the faith and joy of the pure realms and horror at the karmic visions of the hells" (Drolma, 1995, p. 120).

There are to be sure elements common to both western and eastern stories of the life beyond – challenges to be overcome, witness to the suffering of those who have done evil, encounters with other humans and gods who are described in terms of their brilliance. However, if our differences in history persist into eternity, what might salvation, heaven, or enlightenment mean? Joseph DiNoia offers a solution: God may have a plan whereby different religions have roles that "are now only dimly perceived and that will be fully disclosed in the consummation of history" (Heim, 1995, p. 160).

The Search Continues

In the West, otherworldly journeys came to be described in terms less religious than those in earlier times. The eighteenth century Swedish polymath Emmanuel Swedenborg had a midlife spiritual crisis that caused him to declare that churchmen knew nothing of life after death, and to feel called to speak with angels person to person. He spent years traveling to the afterlife in a trance-like state, and recorded what he found in his *Dream Diary.*

Swedenborg's afterlife includes houses, cities, mountains, food and games, and most importantly friendship and love. It is bustling with activity, a continuation and fulfillment of life on earth wherein earthly souls become angels and spiritual maturation goes on forever. Angels teach other spirits to examine their earthly lives, but if they refuse, they are condemned by their own limitations, and can only find the path to hell. For Swedenborg, the traditional Christian belief in God as judge underestimated not only God's goodness but also the ability of humans to choose their own paths in this world and in the next.

Those who choose to grow spiritually engage in service to others and charitable works that manifest God's love. Women care for babies and angels guard the living or take part in heavenly civic affairs. There are three levels of angels, the first being the natural level for angels whose understanding had been elevated a bit beyond what it was on earth. The second level is the spiritual kingdom where they have churches and clergy, and express their love through charity. The final level is the celestial kingdom where angels continue to progress forever toward ever-greater innocence, concentrating only on God, who manifests as love and wisdom.

During his travels, Swedenborg encounters famous people just as Mohammad and Dante had. He and Isaac Newton never met on earth, but in heaven, they discuss the spiritual nature of light and color. He converses with Aristotle on the "science of analysis," and they agree that scholarship should have useful applications. He is summoned by Martin Luther, who sits enthroned among students seated according to their faithfulness to his ideas. Luther is disturbed that Swedenborg is receiving new revelations, but after they speak, Luther laughs at his own errors (McDannell & Lang, 1988, p. 188).

Perhaps the most heartening of Swedenborg's discoveries is that when people arrive in heaven they are recognized by their friends and family, as well as new people with whom they have so much in common that they feel like old friends. Loving relationships continue in the afterlife, particularly those based married love, which is enjoyed by angels as well. However, if a couple married on earth agreed, they are allowed to find different soulmates in heaven. For those denied the bliss of marriage in this world, like Swedenborg himself, there will still be marriages made in heaven. In fact, Swedenborg had a wife picked out already: his friend Countess Elizabeth Gyllenborg-Stjerncrona. One can only hope he found the fulfillment he longed for.

The search for life beyond, and efforts to reach those who have departed, continued with the advent of spiritualism, which held that souls survived the death of their physical bodies and that we on earth could communicate with them. Spiritualists were confident that their beliefs would hold up to scientific inquiry. As Arthur Conan Doyle, author of *The History of Spiritualism,* declared, "We want a religion you can prove" (McDannell & Lang, 1988, p. 294). William James wrote of a "transmarginal" area of the brain that is outside of but accessible to consciousness, and which may convey us beyond ourselves. Thomas Edison believed that spirits traveled after death like wireless impulses, and attempted to build a megaphone-like device for "personalities which have left this earth to communicate with us" (Roach, 2005, p. 204). After his death, a medium recorded messages from Doyle himself that described an infinitely loving God and the ultimate goal of being absorbed into the Universal (Abrahamsen, 2015, pp. 142–143).

Today, scientists like Andrew Newburg document areas of the brain involved in spiritual experience. Newburg found that various modes of prayer result in brain patterns that indicate different relationships with the divine. Tibetan Buddhist monks and Catholic nuns breach their natural boundaries to become absorbed in God, while charismatics engage with an intense relationship with God while remaining separate (Hagerty, 2010, pp. 178–179).

In addition, there is a growing body of literature on out-of-body experiences (OBEs) and near-death experiences (NDEs). Robert Monroe, a modern-day otherworld traveler, believed that when we sleep, we journey beyond this realm of existence. Monroe documented his own extensive OBEs in *Ultimate Journey* (Monroe, 1994). Guided by higher spiritual beings, he travels outside the solar system, beyond time-space, and visits his loved ones, even his daughter away at college. Monroe has an intriguing set of encounters with a young man wounded in battle, and helps him understand he is dead. Monroe comes to realize that his future self was the one who showed his present self to the young man, who was, in turn, his past self. Monroe later visits a gathering of beings who turn out to be himself from all his previous lives, which together represent all the love-energy from over a thousand lifetimes. He does not encounter a deity as previous travelers have – rather he describes a creator beyond human understanding who guides the process of life but does not intervene in our lives nor demand worship.

A NDE turned into an inadvertent otherworld journey for Dr. Robert, a scientist and medical doctor. Years ago, singing in his church choir with his family, he went into anaphylactic shock due to a reaction to the medication he had taken. His wife, also a doctor, drove the family home at top speed. Dr. Robert woke up in the car in the driveway with his children frantically giving him cardiopulmonary resuscitation (CPR) and his wife shooting him up with steroids and adrenaline.

Dr. Robert was gone for only a matter of minutes, but the memory of that brief time is still vivid. He felt himself being drawn into a beautiful, musical place where he was met by a parental figure he believes was God. He remembers they spoke of many things, and he came to realize that his own troubles and accomplishments were of no importance. During their conversation, his mother appeared and smiled at him. This was an immense comfort, as she had been Buddhist, while he had converted to Christianity and worried that God might not accept her. He understood then that if you lead a good life, God would welcome you home.

His mother waved to him, and Dr. Robert felt himself being sucked back to his driveway to his panicked family, his heart pounding. He could not remember his conversation with God when he woke up, but over the years, he has found himself in circumstances where he suddenly remembers what they talked about, and feels comforted. He longs for the happiness he felt when surrounded by the love of God, and looks forward to the day when he returns to God forever (Dr. Robert, 2016).

The history of belief in life beyond, and the possibility of communication with those on the other side, is a history of our imaginings of such things. The stories of human travel to other worlds testify to our defiance of the evident limits of our earthly existence, to our unceasing curiosity about our ultimate fate, and to the courage it takes to reach into the unknown. Generation to generation we tell an ongoing story whose conclusion, if it has one, lies far beyond our natural horizon.

References

Saint Augustine. (397–400). The Confessions of Saint Augustine, Book I, verse 1. https://www.newadvent.org/fathers/1101.htm.

Abrahamsen, V. A. (2015). *Paranormal: A new testament scholar looks at the afterlife*. Manchester Center: Shires.

Alexander, E., & Tompkins, P. (2014). *The map of heaven: How science, religion, and ordinary people are proving the afterlife*. New York: Simon & Schuster.

Bellah, R. N. (2011). *Religion in human evolution: From the paleolithic to the axial age*. Cambridge, MA: Belknap Press of Harvard University Press.

Cornwell, J. (2016). Personal communication.

Couliano, I. P. (1991). *Out of this world: Otherworldly journeys from Gilgamesh to Albert Einstein*. Boston: Shambhala.

Dimopoulos, S. (2016). Personal communication.

Drolma, D. D. (1995). *Delog: Journey to realms beyond death*. Junction City: Padma.

Einstein, A. (1931). *Cosmic religion: With other opinions and aphorisms*. New York: Covici-Friede.

Einstein, A. (1982). *Ideas and opinions*. New York: Three Rivers Press.

Hagerty, B. B. (2010). *Fingerprints of God: What science is learning about the brain and spiritual experience?* New York: Riverhead Books.

Heim, S. M. (1995). *Salvations: Truth and difference in religion*. Maryknoll, NY: Orbis Books.

Homer. (1944). *The Odyssey* (Samuel Butler, Trans.). Roslyn, NY: Walter J. Black. Book XI, verses 23, 215.

McDannell, C., & Lang, B. (1988). *Heaven: A history*. New Haven, CT: Yale University Press.

Monroe, R. A. (1994). *Ultimate journey*. New York: Harmony Books.

Proctor, J. D. (Ed.) (2005). *Science, religion, and the human experience*. Oxford: Oxford University Pres.

Roach, M. (2005). *Spook: Science tackles the afterlife*. New York: W. W. Norton, Edison.

Robert, A. Dr. (2016). Personal communication.

Russell, J. B. (1997). *A history of heaven: The singing silence*. Princeton: Princeton University Press.

Rustomji, N. (2009). *The Garden and the fire: Heaven and hell in Islamic culture.* New York: Columbia University Press. Quote from Ibn Ishaq, p. 29.

Virgil. (1983). The Aeneid (Robert Fitzgerald, Trans.). New York: Random House. Book VI, verse 940, p. 184.

Weinberg, S. (2013). Physics: What we do and don't know. *New York Review of Books.* https://www.nybooks.com/articles/2013/11/07/physics-what-we-do-and-dont-know/.

Zaleski, C. (1987). *Otherworld journeys: Accounts of near-death experience in medieval and modern times.* New York: Oxford University Press.

5 "God Saw … and God Knew …"

Science, Divine Action, and Un/answered Prayers

Paul J. Schutz

The Book of Exodus proclaims a God who hears, sees, and knows Israel's suffering. As God's people groan under slavery in Egypt, the narrator states, "God heard their moaning and God was mindful of his covenant … God saw the Israelites, and God knew …" (Ex 2:24–25). God's mindfulness of Israel's suffering, which God interprets through the lens of the covenant, thus provides a catalyst for the narrative of liberation that follows, as Israel's "cry against their taskmasters" (Ex 3:7) likewise operates as a cry to the living God. Rooted in faith in *this* God—not an abstract, ultimate good or an impassible sovereign who rules on high, but a God who cares passionately for justice and the flourishing of creation—the Christian tradition proclaims a God who hears, heeds, and responds to creation's groaning (Rom 8:22) and works to fulfill the life-giving intentions that have been woven into creation from "the beginning." As Elizabeth Johnson (1996) observes, within this rendering of the God-world relationship, "Not the monarch but the lover becomes the paradigm" (p. 17).

This account of God's relationship to the world takes on even greater significance when we consider the evolutionary marvels of humanity's self-reflective consciousness and capacity for language, which enable humans to speak to God in prayer and discern God's intentions for their lives and for the world.[1] Yet scientific insights into the nature of reality impose limits on discussions of the *means* by which God responds to prayer. For, if we accept Jesuit astronomer William Stoeger's (2002a) observation that "the formational and functional integrity of nature rules out a tinkering God who is constantly intervening in nature to effect what He/She intends" (p. 10), then we must cultivate a theology of prayer in which God's responsive action does not violate the integrity of natural processes.[2] Of course, accepting the limits that science places on traditional notions of divine action does not imply that God is restricted from responding to creation's needs; Christianity is rooted in faith in a God who is present and active "in every 'nook and cranny' of nature, at the core of every being and at the heart of every relationship" (Stoeger, 1995, p. 252). Rather, as Johnson (1996) argues, accepting the limits imposed by scientific research emphasizes the Creator's respect for creation's autonomy and so reshapes the context in which we understand divine action, challenging Christianity to understand anew its foundational belief in a responsive, liberating, and loving God who seeks each creature's flourishing.

Bridging these scientific and theological issues, this chapter employs Stoeger's retrieval of Thomas Aquinas's theology of divine action by primary-secondary causality as the basis for a theology of prayer rooted in a conception of creation as the self-expression of God. Within this model, God's action in and through the processes and relationships that constitute reality manifests God's will to life, flourishing, and communion for all things. This model provides the basis for a richly relational notion of prayer, wherein divine-human communication functions as a channel for discerning and activating God's will in the concrete circumstances of everyday life.

The chapter proceeds in four parts. First, drawing on theology and biblical scholarship, I propose the model of God that anchors my discussion of prayer. Second, to establish a context for discussion of divine action that follows, I offer some preliminary thoughts on the practice of prayer, which center on active discernment and the realization of God's aims. Third, I apply Stoeger's theology of creation and divine action to the question of prayer. Fourth and finally, I offer some initial thoughts on the theology of prayer that I see emerging from Stoeger's approach. At the outset, I wish to note that discussions of *how* God acts must address two points: both *in what manner* and *by what means* God acts. The first two sections of this essay are dedicated to the first point, and the third section is dedicated to the second; the final section unites the two.

On the God Who Knows Our Needs and Desires Justice

At its most basic level, prayer is an act of faith—an expression of commitment to one's relationship with God. As such, before discussing the meaning and function of prayer, we must give some account of the God to whom Christians pray. As a basis for this discussion, I invoke a foundation assumption articulated by Stoeger (1995): "that the sources of revelation, the scriptures, tradition, and our living experience as believers who are individually and communally open—more or less—to God and God's action, do give us some reliable knowledge about God and about his/her action in our world" (p. 241). That is, if God's self-revelation in history offers an authentic representation of who God is, then we can assume—presuming careful, critical interrogation of Scripture and tradition—that our knowledge of God is reliable. Although I cannot offer a full treatment of what revelation might say about God, a few foundational observations bear mention.

As we have seen, Scripture does not proclaim a neutral or indifferent God; rather, the Bible proclaims a God who knows creation's suffering and who labors intimately and intensively within creation to draw it to fulfillment. As Stoeger (2002a) states, "God is not above and beyond us, but right in the midst of the universe, our world and our being, as Creator and Lord. God is present, active and struggling in the heart of all that is" (p. 16). Here, it is vital to note that God's action in response to creaturely suffering implies that God has certain intentions for creation. The God who stands against slavery, exploitation, and oppression must—as feminist and liberation theologies attest—also stand with and for the exploited and enslaved, seeking their liberation from systems of oppression and subjugation that mar their lives with injustice. Thus, as Denis Edwards (2010) observes, the correspondence between creaturely suffering and God's knowledge of that suffering implies that our own longings for peace and justice manifest God's desires for the world; it is in contrast to what God opposes that we discern what God seeks. As Patrick Miller (1998) puts it, "It is in the divine presence with suffering humanity that one finds a fundamental clue to the character of God's activity in the world" (p. 223).

In this way, too, attending to God's responses to suffering, oppression, and death—as in the Exodus narrative or the resurrection of Jesus— reveals God's priorities in the concrete. Although we must exercise caution when speaking of God's intentions, Scripture gives concrete testimony to the character of God's work and in doing so, offers insights into God's aims. This work, which comes to clarity "in the incarnation of the Son of God in Christ, [and] in the Spirit animating the world and then drawing it back to God as Trinity in complete communion" reveals a God who seeks to draw all creatures into relationships of "fuller and fuller communion and life" with each other and with God (Stoeger, 2002a, p. 14–15).

This orientation toward life, flourishing, and communion pervades biblical accounts of God's action in the world. Commenting on biblical theologian Walter Brueggemann's image of "God in the fray," biblical scholar Terence Fretheim (1998) writes:

> The goodness of God is revealed precisely in *that* God wills ... to enter into the fray and by *the way in which* God embraces the pain: steadfast in love, faithful to promises, and unwaveringly willing the salvation of Israel and world. This God is so committed to full participation in a genuine relationship with Israel and the world that God no longer has the option of finally pulling back from it ... God will make surprising, unsettling, and sharply judgmental moves, particularly in the encounter with creaturely resistance. But all such divine moves occur *from within* this resolve. (pp. 28–29)

Fretheim's analysis elicits three summary conclusions about the character of God and the God-world relationship. First, in keeping with

Stoeger's vision of God as "active and struggling in the heart of all that is," Fretheim highlights the intrinsic link between God's transcendence as the Creator of all things and God's immanent embrace of creation's pain. For it is precisely as the transcendent Creator—who cannot be contained by any aspect of reality—that God can intimately embrace and respond to the pain of *all* creatures. Second, God's transcendent immanence provides a basis on which we interpret God's faithfulness in response to prayer; as Creator, God loves what God has made, and God's responsiveness to prayer reflects God's desire to see all creatures flourish in holy, cosmic communion. Third, as Fretheim states, God's covenantal commitment is a permanent and irrevocable expression of who God *is*. Though God's thoughts may not be our thoughts nor God's ways our ways (Is 55:8), revelation enables us to reliably yet humbly assume that, as Stoeger (1996) states, "God and His revelation in Jesus is always new, always revealing for us now something new, something fuller, something more lifegiving" (p. 17). As such, God's self-expression in creation confirms that whatever God does, God always acts out of a resolve to bring life, flourishing, and communion to the world, seeking an order of justice and *shalom* for all.

Discerning and Activating God's Intentions for Creation in Prayer

Just as God's intentions are revealed by the manner in which God acts in the world, our commitment to seeing God's intentions realized depends on our ability to discern and respond to those intentions in relationship with God. This brings us to prayer. For if, as Fretheim (1998) states, God's covenant with creation implies a model of the God-world relationship in which "the human experience of pain 'forces' a change on God's part ... 'a new posture of relationship,'" then on its most basic level prayer offers a genuine means of communication between Creator and creature, which mediates God's "absolute will for life and blessing" (p. 28).

As the Jesuit theologian Karl Rahner (1958) explains, this understanding of God and of prayer differs greatly from models that imagine prayer as something akin to wish fulfillment. Commenting on popular notions of prayer, Rahner writes, "We call on [God] as we would to our insurance office; we pay grudgingly and we seek eagerly for our bonus. Our hands outstretched in prayer are mercenary hands; they show a certain near-parody of spiritual eagerness only when we are asking for something" (p. 9). But far from being a *maître d'* or genie who fulfills our requests, Rahner sees the God addressed in prayer as a faithful partner who aims not to grant our wishes but to see us flourish as beloved creatures. Seen in this light, prayer does not ask that *our* will may be done but invites God to make God's will known to us, in keeping with the intentions revealed in God's ongoing work of creation and redemption.

Here, too, it is crucial to recognize that prayer does not seek an abstract or general good. Human prayer and divine response both emerge from and address the concrete struggles and joys one experiences in life. Thus, as Miller (1998) explains, prayer is a means for discerning God's life-giving aims amid the joys and woes of creaturely existence. He writes, "The God who is just and compassionate, abounding in stead-fast love, righteous and attentive to the weak and the helpless, is called upon to be that way in the immediate situation. Thus prayer is con-sistent with God's will and purpose for the world—large and small—as it seeks something that is wholly consistent with the divine nature" (p. 217). Therefore, precisely because it arises from the concrete circum-stances of life and expresses the contingency of creaturely existence, prayer does not seek to defy our finitude. Rather, as an expression of relationship with a God who desires life, flourishing, and communion in the midst of our finitude, prayer helps us discern and actualize God's aims *within* the limits of creaturely life, such that in prayer, "we can be 'weaned from expecting magical solutions'" (Edwards, 2010, p. 173). Prayer moves God, but it changes us.

Further emphasizing the relational character of prayer, theologian Johann Baptist Metz (Rahner and Metz, 1977) writes that embracing our creaturely condition in prayer unites us across time and space as mem-bers of "a great historical company" comprised of all those who prayed amid their earthly journeys. On this basis, Metz writes, "prayer is a mat-ter of historical solidarity" with the living and dead, and especially with those that history has forgotten (p. 9). Seen in this way, even prayers for individual needs are acts of solidarity, since in expressing our needs we stand together with all who have brought their needs before the living God. Prayer, therefore, leads us to see our needs in the context of the needs of the world. When we pray, we join our hearts and voices with all those who have prayed and who will pray, uniting the personal and social in what Rahner (1958) poetically names "the longing, fitfully glimpsed and but half realized, to gather up all these strivings into an intense pur-suit of one all-embracing objective worthy of the toil and tears of the human heart" (p. 7). Prayer calls us to hope and to act for a future per-meated by God's grace.

In light of the scriptural witness to God's action on behalf of those who suffer, imagining prayer as a means to discern our place in the world vis-à-vis God's creational intentions implies *responsibility* for the well-being of the world. As Edwards (2010) notes, by opening ourselves to God's self-gift in prayer, "We are asking that we might be ever more open to this gift and to whatever it may mean for us and for the wider creation. We are drawn into the divine compassionate love for the crea-tures of our planet and to the praxis of the kingdom, committed anew to the work of justice and peace and to the integrity of God's crea-tion" (p. 179). In Metz's (Rahner and Metz, 1977) terms, this movement toward the praxis of God's reign imparts a "practical and political" dimension to prayer, which further links the personal and social and orients us toward the needs of others, especially those who suffer injustice. He writes,

> If we are to pray 'in the spirit of Christ' we cannot turn our backs on the sufferings of others. Prayer demands that we love our fellow humans; we have no choice. It can make prayer extremely dangerous, for example, in situations where humanity is systematically suppressed and people are forced to live as though no bonds of allegiance existed between them ... We must pray not just *for* the poor and unfortunate but *with* them ... If we pray 'in his spirit' we can afford to be despised by those who consider themselves to be intelligent and enlightened; but not by those who are disconsolate, suffering or oppressed. And this means that prayer is of necessity political and influential. (pp. 19–20)

As a political act, then, prayer aligns us with God's will and so aligns us with those who suffer. Prayer calls us to live as instruments of God's grace—to hear, heed, and respond to the needs of creation, seeking ways to bring life and flourishing to the world.

To conclude this section, I wish to offer one comment on how we might understand the idea that God "answers" prayers. If we conceive of prayer as an expression of relationship to God, in which we discern and actualize our role in promoting God's will for every creature and creation as a whole, then prayer can never be solely about seeing individual desires fulfilled. Rather, if praying unites our desires with God's intentions, then to ask whether *our* prayers have been answered is ultimately to ask whether *God's* aims have been achieved. In most cases, we cannot answer this question in the short term. Immediate clarity about the results of our prayers rarely manifests. Furthermore, this question is never about us as individuals; it is about our *selves* in the plural: in *relation* to God, to other humans, and creation as a whole. As a result, even when we discern that God has answered our prayers, we may be surprised by the manner in which God appears to have answered, as when an outcome *different* from that for which we prayed proves *more* beneficial or life giving than expected—or when the impacts of God's answer resonate beyond our individual situation and foster justice, communion, and life on a broader scale. This rendering of prayer transforms the context in which we conceive of prayers of petition, as well as other types of prayer, insofar as prayer is always about aligning ourselves with God's intentions as we discern them amid the concrete circumstances of our lives, in relationship with others.

Notably, as Miller (1998) observes, the Psalms affirm this point. Despite their myriad expressions of joy and lament, cries for help, and songs of praise, the Psalms rarely specify whether particular prayers are answered. In light of this observation, prayer takes on a richly eschatological dimension, which fosters a view toward the ultimate fulfillment of "all things" (Col 1:16) in union with God—a fulfillment that will not be fully realized until long after we pass away. In this way, too, prayer fosters God's eschatological promise of peace, providing a training ground for holiness. Prayer is, in this way, a preparation for and anticipation of the resurrection and final fulfillment of creation in communion with God. Theologian Vincent Brümmer (2008) summarizes this view in terms of cultivating a perceptual orientation that attunes us to God's presence and action in the world. He writes, "The ability to recognize God's actions by looking at the world through the eyes of faith requires training ... [and] entails that petitioners expect an answer. This expectation causes them to be on the look-out for God's response and in this way sharpens their ability to recognize the answer when it comes" (p. 87). Such is the fruit of prayer.

Divine Action in Creation and Prayer

The preceding portraits of God and of prayer provide rich resources for reflecting on the commitments that flow from Christian faith. Still, in a scientific age, the idea that God acts—that God hears, knows, and actively responds to creation's needs—poses challenging new questions for our understanding of prayer. Most basic among these questions is *how* God acts, or (assuming epistemic humility), how God can be said to act if we accept scientific insights about the structure of physical reality and respect the formational and functional integrity of nature.

As a foundation for this discussion, we must presuppose that God's intentions somehow influence material reality—that as Johnson (1996) states, "Divine purpose is accomplished in a concursus or flowing together of divine and creaturely act in which the latter mediates the former" (p. 14). In the case of prayer, we may likewise presuppose with Edwards (2010) that "God communicates with us through the mediation of our own imaginations, memories, and thoughts" (p. 172). While these presuppositions may be held on the basis of faith, presupposing *that* they are true does not explain *the means by which* God effects God's aims.[3] Indeed, as Brümmer (2008) explains, the idea that God responds to prayer through created causes appears to present us with an unresolvable problematic: "Either an event is the result of natural causes—but then it cannot be an answer to prayer. Or it is an answer to prayer—but then it must be the result of divine intervention in violation of the natural order. Both these alternatives seem unacceptable to the believer" (p. 71). In my view, Stoeger's theology of creation and divine action offers a compelling basis for responding to this problematic and re-conceptualizing prayer.

The Foundation: Retrieving Creation

Like Johnson (1998; 2014), Edwards (2010), Michael Dodds (2012), and Ignacio Silva (2014), all of whom approach divine action from a Catholic perspective, Stoeger roots his approach in Thomas Aquinas's theology of creation—what Josef Pieper (1957) dubs "the hidden element in the philosophy of St. Thomas" (p. 47). Following Thomas, Stoeger describes two dimensions of God's creative work: *creatio ex nihilo*, creation out of nothing, and *creatio continua*, or continuing creation. Yet Stoeger does not follow Thomas directly on this point. Rather, recognizing that our knowledge of the universe has evolved since Thomas's day, Stoeger retrieves and reinterprets the meaning of God's creative action in dialogue with contemporary science, and with thoroughgoing respect for the formational and functional integrity of natural processes. This commitment leads Stoeger to reject the idea of a God who intervenes directly in nature, who effects God's aims by making nature work in a manner different from how it would work if God were absent. This commitment also leads Stoeger to reject the idea that *creatio ex nihilo* can, or should, be understood as commensurate with the Big Bang. As a physical phenomenon, cosmic evolution must be explained using scientific methods alone. At the same time, however, Stoeger observes that the natural sciences cannot explain, and never will be able to explain, *why there is something rather than nothing*—why, in a metaphysical sense, the universe exists at all.

Although he is open to the possibility that physical reality is all that exists, his experience with the wonders of nature leads him to ask questions that point beyond the material world—to the ontological ground that makes creaturely existence *possible*. Thus, while *creatio ex nihilo* must not be construed as an explanation of temporal or physical origins, the notion of creation out of nothing retains significance as a description of "the ultimate ontological origin of reality—most fundamentally it describes a very bald and unadorned way the *ultimate dependence* of everything on the Creator. It is not about a creation event, but about a *relationship* which everything that exists has with the creator" (Stoeger, 2010, p. 172). Given its significance as a description of the relational-ontological basis of all things, *creatio ex nihilo* leads naturally to the second aspect of Thomas's theology of creation: *creatio continua*. For, if God's presence and action in all things provide the principle by which creation exists—if God is the very *possibility* of existence—then God's presence must be imagined as *continuing*, providing the basis for the ongoing existence of all creatures in relationship with their Creator. As theologian Janet Soskice (2010) puts it, "Were God to cease holding the world in being for a moment it would not be" (p. 24).

At first glance, this rendering of the doctrine of creation may seem to offer a theological and philosophical framework with little relevance to prayer or Christian life. However, we must recognize that the Creator who makes existence possible is also the God who reveals Godself in history. In other words, God is never just a first principle. God participates—struggles—within created reality, manifesting particular intentions and priorities for creation's fulfillment. As such, creation expresses God's own self and reveals what God desires. Stoeger (2008a) explains:

> And thus in beholding the wonders and vast reaches in time and space of cosmological evolution and to where it has brought the universe, we are seeing God at work in the transitions, in the novelty, in the interactions, struggling to bring about a cosmos from which life and consciousness, person and community, love and self-giving can emerge—created images of God's own life and being. (p. 69)

As self-expression of God, creation thus manifests and is guided toward the fulfillment revealed in the history of the God-world relationship: life, flourishing, and communion. As such, creation is the instrument of God's purposes—the medium of God's self-expression—which "reflects, imperfectly of course, who God is, and is fashioned so that it is open and receptive—so that it can be completed and intimately united with its Creator" (Stoeger, 2002a, p. 1).

From Creation to Divine Action

Stoeger's interpretation of the doctrine of creation provides the basis on which he builds his theology of divine action. Here, it is noteworthy that in contrast to many theologians working on the problem of divine action, Stoeger eschews the idea that we can specify a precise "causal nexus"—a "place" within the network of entities and relationships that constitute the universe wherein God acts.[4] That is, whereas some thinkers locate divine action in quantum indeterminacy or chaotic systems, or argue that God might work on creaturely brain states to achieve God's aims, Stoeger is concerned that these approaches ultimately make God a cause among causes, rendering the Creator and sustainer of the universe something akin to a gravitational field.

Thus, in contrast to those who specify a "causal nexus" for divine action, Stoeger argues that as the ontological foundation of all existence, God's work as "primary cause" flows through the myriad "secondary causes" that constitute the cosmos. As primary cause, "God ... enables and empowers creation to be what it is—and both ultimately endows and supports all the processes, regularities, and capacities for activity [i.e. secondary causes]. Thus, God as Creator does not substitute for, interfere with, countermand or micro-manage the laws of nature. They possess their own integrity and adequacy, which God establishes and respects" (Stoeger, 2010, p. 173).

On the basis of the coherence between the Creator's operation as the eternal source on which all things depend and natural processes' operation as the foundations of physical reality, Stoeger locates God's action in the "laws of nature" themselves. Here, Stoeger makes a crucial distinction. While human knowledge of physical reality is always limited by our observational capacity—while we are always outside looking in—God's status as Creator suggests that God is intimately present and active *within* (and beyond!) material reality. In other words, while we might be able to measure gravitational forces or map the brainwaves of a deer, we will never *be* gravity or know what it is like for a deer to *experience* pain. As Stoeger (1993) puts it, "We are always peering into nature and nature's secrets from the outside, using instruments and ploys which put us into contact with them only indirectly" (p. 214). Not so for God. As Creator and primary cause, the source and ground of all existence, God has access to creation in ways we cannot possibly fathom. On this basis, Stoeger (2002b) concludes:

> The direct causal nexus *is* the active, richly differentiated, profoundly immanent [because it is transcendent] presence of God in created beings and in their interrelationships—*is* at the same time their limited and specific participation—inclusion—in God's own existence and interrelationships as Trinity, which is utterly transcendent and immaterial but also radically open to and available for the realization of finite possibilities. The presence of God in each entity constitutes the direct, the immediate, relationship of that entity with God, and therefore is the channel of divine influence in secondary causes. (pp. 97–98)

Thus, because God is Creator, God does not need anything but creation itself to act in the world. God is present "in every 'nook and cranny' of nature, at the core of every being and at the heart of every relationship" (Stoeger, 1995, p. 252), and it is by God's life-giving, creative presence that God's will is done. As such, every passing moment manifests God's will for life and flourishing, and the nexus of God's action is creation itself, from within which God responds to the needs of all creatures, drawing them lovingly into fulfillment in communion with their Creator.

Those who seek a more specific nexus for divine action may argue that Stoeger's approach is too vague to be useful—that in light of contemporary science, we need to specify precisely where in the world God acts. But, as Edwards (2010) notes, "it is important to say from a theological perspective, we do not know *how* God's creative act works" (p. 63). Neither will the sciences ever detect God's presence or action. By eschewing quests for a "causal nexus," Stoeger thus directs theological reflection away from speculation on *where* divine action occurs and toward God's *aims* for creation—toward the life, flourishing, and communion that flow forth in every moment from God's intimate, immediate presence at the heart of things.

From Divine Action to Prayer

With this sketch of Stoeger's theology of creation and divine action in place, we return to the topic of God's response to prayer. Offering a basis for this discussion, Stoeger (2008b)—again following Thomas—writes that God's presence in creation is richly differentiated, manifested in and to each creature "according to its own individuality," such that creatures cooperate with divine providence on the basis of their distinctive creatureliness and toward their particular end—according to their own kind (p. 229). Within this frame, each creature responds to God's invitation to life and flourishing—and so prays—in keeping with its own distinctive creaturely constitution. Trees pray with arms outstretched, communing with birds and squirrels and caring for humans by offering shade on a hot day. Suffused with the Creator's presence, rivers pray by flowing, by providing life-giving water to land creatures and a habitat for fish. Therefore, it is precisely by being and becoming what God made them to be that creatures glorify God:

> The created, inanimate, and non-personal levels of reality, though they exist in their own right and reveal God and God's goodness, power, and love in their own way, and give glory to God in their own way (they cannot do otherwise!), exist also to enable the development and maintenance of persons to whom God can reveal him/herself and with whom God can maintain a personal relationship leading to the full and harmonious union of the divine with created reality.
>
> (Stoeger, 2008b, pp. 245–246)

As this passage implies, humans also respond to God's creative action in their own way, according to their distinctive, conscious awareness and intentionality in relationship with other creatures. Therefore, just as God's creativity finds expression in trees and rivers, God's work manifests in "human history and through our human freedom, evoking a response to his invitations from human beings and human communities to carry out what God would like done" (Stoeger, 2006, 8). As we have seen, such discernment of God's intentions happens in prayer, as humans call out to God within and seek God's aims within social, political, ecological, and cultural systems that liberate and oppress, empower and enslave, discerning which actions are "in tune with God's ultimate purposes and are essentially life-giving" (Stoeger, 2008b, p. 245).

As such, in a stance of critical contemplation of creation and its history—the mature fruit of a life of prayer—humans attune themselves to the life-giving intentions and purposes that have been woven into creation since the beginning of time and so come to "discern what belief or way of acting or living is in harmony with *who we are* and *what reality is*" (Stoeger, 1998, p. 3). Attuning ourselves to God's self-expression in creation thus attunes us to what God desires, such that in prayer we discover new possibilities for action that respond in ever-fuller ways to God's desires for creation. And these responses bear fruit. As Stoeger (2002c) puts it, "The results of those human responses and what God is able to effect through them are, at the level of conscious, free human response, the extension of God's immanent creative action in the human, social-political-economic sphere. It is through this level of divine action that God is, with creation's cooperation, struggling to bring all things to completion in the Word and Spirit" (p. 9).

Conclusion: Divine Intentions and the Fruits of Prayer

Amid this struggle, Stoeger's theology of creation and divine action enriches the context in which we conceive of prayer, seeing prayer, and God's response to prayer as functions of the very "laws" that constitute material reality. In doing so, this theology attunes us more deeply to God *and* to creation, broadening Metz's vision of solidarity across time and space to include all creatures who have in their unique ways glorified God by their lives and providing a vital resource for thinking our faith amid both social and ecological suffering and degradation. In keeping with the Ignatian tradition in which he was formed, Stoeger's theology thus orients prayer toward the discernment of God's presence and action in all creation—toward "finding God in all things"— and, by extension, toward the realization of God's intentions for the world.[5] In this way, as Ashley Cocksworth (2018) explains, prayer mediates God's providential care for the world:

> The doctrine of providence's principal purpose is to help Christians "read" the world as permeated by grace and to see the self as known and loved by God ... Read through the lens of prayer, the doctrine of providence functions as a piece of practical theology to help the pray-er realize that God is not along way off, but is involved deeply in the complete course of creaturely existence ... petitionary prayer builds up a sense of the profound intimacy of the divine-human relation that the doctrine of providence assumes. (p. 172)

In this way, too, the epistemic humility that manifests in Stoeger's unwillingness to specify a precise "causal nexus" for divine action corresponds with the humble recognition that God's intentions can never be known *a priori*; rather, they emerge as surprises from our experience, as in-breakings of God's eschatological promise amid the joys and struggles of creaturely life. As Brümmer (2008) states, "No earthly perspective comprehends the divine rule" (p. 231). Taking these summary observations as a guide, I conclude this chapter with five thoughts on the fruits of authentic prayer conceived within Stoeger's theological frame.

First, authentic prayer leads us to recognize God's loving presence and guidance in every moment—in suffering, in the extraordinary and the mundane—suffusing every second of life with the awareness of God's presence. If, as Stoeger states, creation abounds with God's life-giving presence and manifests God's will to life, flourishing, and communion, and if God stands with the world in its suffering, then as a means of communication with God, prayer transforms our understanding of the world. Think again of the Psalms—Christianity's oldest prayer book and hymnal, the primary text of the ancient practice of the Liturgy of the Hours—which find God's presence across time and space (Ps 90), in human sinfulness (Ps 51), in the diversity of creatures (Ps 104), and in creation's praise (Ps 148). Reflection on images like these invites us to move beyond seeing prayer as divine wish fulfillment and unites our prayer with the prayer of all creatures—who together comprise a cosmic Communion of Saints. Within this view, prayer *for* is always also prayer *with*.

Second, by orienting our perceptions in this way, authentic prayer places us in a stance of humble discernment, which both recognizes and *trusts* in God's life-giving presence among us, and so provides a foundation for decision-making and action. As Rahner (2010) states, when we orient our lives to God in prayer, we come to interpret our everyday experience differently, finding divine inspiration in what we might usually name a "good idea," as God guides us from within our experience toward what is truly life giving.

Third, in prayerful discernment in solidarity with creation, we discover our unique, God-given *telos*—the proper purpose to which our relationship with God orients us. In our discernment, we may discover that our *telos* breaks "the rules" that society and church impose on us. But such rule-breaking should never do harm. Rather, if we hold fast to God in prayer and listen carefully to our conscience—to the Spirit speaking in our heart—God's purposes will always be revealed in what fosters the greatest life, flourishing, and communion in relationship with God and creation.

Fourth, in a broader sense, prayer aims at a richly relational realization of the true nature of creation, which has awaited fulfillment since the moment God loved the universe into existence. In light of Stoeger's theology of creation and divine action, prayer appears as a channel of God's intentions for creation as a whole. For when we become attuned to God's intentions in prayer, we become beacons of God's promise in the concrete circumstances of our lives and invite other humans to do the same. We likewise recognize more fully God's presence and action in creatures of other kinds, each of which shines with God's presence and invites *us* to do the same.

Fifth, and finally, by attuning us to God's intentions for creation, authentic prayer leads us to greater consciousness of the dynamics of justice and injustice, of flourishing and oppression, of those forces that manifest God's life-giving will and those that deaden and demean.[6] In this way, prayer calls us to account the justice of God's reign, in which the fullness of life radiates revealing creation's true end: what Johnson (2014) terms *creatio nova*—the new creation.

In sum, as an instrument of divine-human communication that operates through—never over or against—the "laws of nature" that make God's universe the wonder that it is, prayer guides us toward Stoeger's vision: to recognize and realize in cooperation with God's grace what is most life giving for ourselves and for all creatures. Conceived within Stoeger's theological framework, prayer offers us a means of relational participation in God's own life and God's work of redemption. And by reorienting our perception and guiding us discernment, prayer thus leads us to discover more and more fully God present and active in our midst as we journey on the way toward the fullness of life and flourishing that *is* communion with the Creator God.

Notes

1 Accounts of prayer differ significantly from denomination to denomination or discipline to discipline. I approach the question from the framework I know best: That of Catholic theology. For a Jewish perspective, see Heschel (2011, especially p. 137–159). For an Anglican perspective, see Townsend (1983). Foster (1992) offers a discussion of prayer in terms of what John Wesley termed "social holiness." For an Islamic perspective, see Chapter 7 in this volume. See this volume's sections on the sciences and psychology for other perspectives on prayer from other disciplines.

2 These page numbers reflect the pagination in Stoeger's original manuscript.

3 This question remains a topic of debate. The fullest discussion of this question occurred during a 15-year series of conferences co-sponsored by the Vatican Observatory and the Center for Theology and the Natural Sciences now known as the Divine Action Project (DAP). For summaries of the DAP and explorations of the history of the question of divine action, see Russell (1997), Wildman (2008), Gregersen (2008), and Vicens (2012).

4 The search for a causal nexus is especially prominent among Protestant theologians and has been expounded and evaluated at length by Robert John Russell (2018). Nicholas Saunders (2000) and Wesley Wildman (2005) have criticized these approaches. Amanda Alexander's Thomistic treatment of prayer and neuroscience (Chapter 6 in this volume) complements my discussion of Thomas's theology and represents a uniquely Catholic perspective on this issue.

5 The Contemplation from the fourth week of the *Spiritual Exercises* of St. Ignatius of Loyola offers a primary source for this vision of creation. In doing so, the Contemplation invites retreatants to find God in all things, a hallmark of Ignatian spirituality. See Schutz (2019) for a detailed treatment of this point.

6 Cocksworth (2018, p. 174–182; 183–191) examines the sociopolitical implications of the Lord's Prayer as an instrument of liberation from the individualistic logic of market capitalist society.

References

Brümmer, V. (2008). *What are we doing when we pray?* Burlington, VT: Ashgate.

Cocksworth, A. (2018). *Prayer: A guide for the perplexed.* London, UK: T & T Clark.

Dodds, M. (2012). *Unlocking divine action: Contemporary science and Thomas Aquinas.* Washington, DC: Catholic University of America Press.

Edwards, D. (2010). *How God acts: Creation, redemption, and special divine action.* Minneapolis, MN: Fortress Press.

Foster, R. J. (1992). *Prayer: Finding the heart's true home.* San Francisco, CA: HarperSanFrancisco.

Fretheim, T. E. (1998). Some reflections on Brueggemann's God. In T. Linafelt & T. K. Beal (Eds.), *God in the fray: A tribute to Walter Brueggemann* (pp. 24–37). Minneapolis, MN: Fortress Press.

Gregersen, N. H. (2008). Special divine action and the quilt of laws: Why the distinction between special and general divine action cannot be maintained. In R. J. Russell, N. Murphy, & W. R. Stoeger S. J. (Eds.), *Scientific perspectives on divine action: Twenty years of challenge and progress* (pp. 179–99). Berkeley, CA: Center for Theology and the Natural Sciences.

Heschel, A. J. (2011). Prayer makes us worthy of being saved. In S. Heschel (Ed.), *Essential writings.* Maryknoll, NY: Orbis Books.

Johnson, E. A. (1996). Does God play dice? Divine providence and chance. *Theological Studies, 57*(1), 3–18.

Johnson, E. A. (2014). *Ask the beasts: Darwin and the god of love.* London, UK: Bloomsbury.

Miller, P. (1998). Prayer and divine action. In T. Linafelt and T. K. Beal (Eds.), *God in the fray: A tribute to Walter Brueggemann* (pp. 211–232). Minneapolis, MN: Fortress Press.

Pieper, J. (1957). *Silence of Saint Thomas.* New York, NY: Pantheon.

Rahner S. J. K. (1958). *On prayer.* New York, NY: Paulist Press.

Rahner S. J. K. (2010). *Foundations of Christian faith: An introduction to the idea of Christianity.* New York, NY: Crossroad.

Rahner S. J. K., & Metz, J. B. (1977). *The courage to pray* (S. O'Brien Twohig, Trans.). New York, NY: Crossroad.

Russell, R. J. (1997). Does 'The god who acts' really act?: New approaches to divine action in light of science. *Theology Today, 51*, 43–65.

Russell, R. J. (2018). What we've learned from quantum mechanics about noninterventionist objective divine action in nature—and its remaining challenges. In R. J. Russell and J. M. Moritz (Eds.), *God's providence and randomness in nature* (pp. 133–172). West Conshohocken, PA: Templeton Press.

Saunders, N. T. (2000). Does God cheat at dice? Divine action and quantum possibilities. *Zygon, 35*(3), 517–544.

Schutz, P. J. (2019). Cultivating a 'cosmic perspective' in theology: Reading William R. Stoeger with *laudato si'*. *Theological Studies, 80*(4), 798–821.

Silva, I. (2014). Revisiting Aquinas on providence and rising to the challenge of divine action in nature. *Journal of Religion, 94*, 277–91.

Soskice, J. M. (2010). *Creatio ex nihilo*: Its Jewish and Christian foundations. In D. B. Burrell, C. Cogliati, J. M. Soskice, & W. R. Stoeger (Eds.), *Creation and the God of Abraham* (pp. 24–39). Cambridge, UK: Cambridge University Press.

Stoeger S. J. W. R. (1993). Contemporary physics and the ontological status of the laws of nature. In R. J. Russell, N. Murphy, & C. J. Isham (Eds.), *Quantum cosmology and the laws of nature* (pp. 209–234). Berkeley, CA: Center for Theology and Natural Sciences.

Stoeger S. J. W. R. (1995). Describing God's action in the world in light of scientific knowledge of reality. In R. J. Russell, N. Murphy, & A. R. Peacocke (Eds.), *Chaos and complexity* (pp. 239–262). Berkeley, CA: Center for Theology and the Natural Sciences.

Stoeger S. J. W. R. (1996). *The laws of nature, the range of human knowledge, and divine action.* Tarnow, Poland: Biblos.

Stoeger S. J. W. R. (1998). Is there common ground in practice and experience of science and religion? *Science and the spiritual quest Conference.* Center for Theology and the Natural Sciences. Unpublished manuscript.

Stoeger S. J. W. R. (2002a). Cosmology and a theology of creation. In H. D. Regan & M. W. Worthing (Eds.), *Interdisciplinary perspectives on cosmology and biological evolution* (pp. 128–145). Adelaide, Australia: Australian Theological Forum.

Stoeger S. J. W. R. (2002b). Epistemological and ontological issues arising from quantum theory. In R. J. Russell, P. Clayton, & K. Wegter-McNelly (Eds.), *Quantum mechanics: Scientific perspectives on divine action* (pp. 81–98). Berkeley, CA: Center for Theology and Natural Sciences.

Stoeger S. J. W. R. (2002c). Science, the laws of nature, and divine action. In H. D. Regan & M. W. Worthing (Eds.), *Interdisciplinary perspectives on cosmology and biological evolution* (pp. 117–127). Adelaide, Australia: Australian Theological Forum.

Stoeger S. J. W. R. (2006). Divine action in a broken world. In J. M. C. Francisco & R. M. G. de Jesus (Eds.), *Science and religion ... and culture in the Jesuit tradition: Perspectives from East Asia* (pp. 7–22). Adelaide, Australia: Australian Theological Forum.

Stoeger S. J. W. R. (2008a). Discerning God's creative action in cosmic and biological evolution. *Mysterion: Rivista di Spiritualitá e Mistica, 1*(1), 64–77.

Stoeger S. J. W. R. (2008b). Conceiving divine action in a dynamic universe. In R. J. Russell, N. Murphy, & W. R. Stoeger S.J. (Eds.), *Scientific perspectives on divine action: Twenty years of challenge and progress* (pp. 225–247). South Bend, IN: University of Notre Dame Press.

Stoeger S. J. W. R. (2010). The big bang, quantum cosmology, and creatio ex nihilo. In D. B. Burrell, C. Cogliati, J. M. Soskice, & W. R. Stoeger (Eds.), *Creation and the god of Abraham* (pp. 152–175). Cambridge, UK: Cambridge University Press.

Townsend, R. (1983). *Faith, prayer, and devotion.* Oxford, UK: Basil Blackwell.

Vicens, L. C. (2012). On the possibility of special divine action in a deterministic world. *Religious Studies, 48,* 315–336.

Wildman, W. (2005). A counter-response on 'The divine action project.' *Theology and Science, 3*(1), 17–29.

Wildman, W. (2008). The divine action project, 1988–2003. In R. J. Russell, N. Murphy, & W. R. Stoeger S. J. (Eds.), *Scientific perspectives on divine action: Twenty years of challenge and progress* (pp. 133–178). South Bend, IN. University of Notre Dame Press.

6 "My Soul Is Not Me"

Monistic Anthropologies and Participatory Prayer

Amanda Alexander

In the late 1990s, Andrew Newberg conducted a pioneering study in which he scanned the brains of Buddhist monks and Franciscan nuns while they meditated. Participants from both groups submitted to two SPECT (single photon emission computed tomography) scans of their brains: the first one was taken before they began a period of prayer or meditation; the second was taken during the peak of their prayer or meditation practice. The participants themselves indicated the time at which the second scan should be taken by tugging on a string. This tugging released a radioactive tracer into their bloodstream. In experiments like this, the radioactive tracer is locked almost immediately into the brain cells. The resulting brain SPECT scans give an accurate, freeze-frame of the blood flow patterns in the participants' brain during the moments immediately following their tug on the string.

Interestingly, the results of the SPECT scans were nearly identical for individuals in both groups. The initial scans of both the Buddhist meditators and the contemplative Franciscan nuns showed normal blood flow in areas of the brain associated with attention and with orientation. However, during the peak of meditation or prayer, the SPECT scans revealed increased blood flow in the attention association area and a decreased blood flow to the orientation association area. The orientation association area is responsible for generating an awareness of the physical limits of the self: it is what enables an individual to recognize where they stop and everything else in the universe begins. Newberg hypothesizes that the decreased flow of blood to the orientation association area during practices of meditation and contemplative prayer disrupts the practitioner's ordinary sense of physical space. The Buddhists interpreted this disruption as becoming one with the universe; the Franciscan nuns described it as union with God. Based on this, Newberg concludes that "mystical experience is biologically, observably, and scientifically real" (Newberg, D'Aquili, & Rause, 2001, p. 9).

Newberg's study, as well as subsequent studies which demonstrate the profound benefits religious practices like prayer and meditation can have on the brain, raise substantial challenges for the Christian theologian.

The experiences arising from these practices have been paradigmatically characterized by Christians as those in which the soul is touched, grasped, or in some other way acted upon or contacted by God in an extraordinary way (see Coakley, 2009; Howells, 2002; Louth, 1983).[1] The soul, not the brain, is understood to be the locus of encounters with the divine because the soul is traditionally imagined as something immaterial, spiritual, and therefore more akin to the divine, and thus more capable of communication with the divine, than the body (Blosser, 2018). Moreover, these experiences are understood to be the result of God's direct action in the one who prays. In sum, contemporary neuroscientific studies of mystical states and even simple practices of meditation challenge the traditional belief that humans are body-soul composites by demonstrating that prayer and experiences of God in prayer may in fact be reducible to mere patterns of brain activity.

However, the theological history of the understanding of the relationship of the soul both to the body and to God is complex. Surprisingly, there is no particular way in which Christians must think about the soul in order to maintain orthodoxy. In response to the challenges posed by contemporary neuroscience to our understanding of the soul, this chapter advances the monistic theological anthropology found in the work of Thomas Aquinas – an account which is at once faithful to the scriptural foundations of Christian theology and which is capable of entering into dialogue with secular science. This chapter begins by tracing, with necessarily broad brush strokes, the origins of Christian belief about the soul from its scriptural sources to the Neoplatonic character given to it in the fourth century, a character in tension with the Christian doctrines of the incarnation and resurrection. It then turns to the metaphysical framework erected by Aquinas as an alternative to the Platonic metaphysics that had characterized Christian theology from the fourth to the thirteenth century. This metaphysical framework, which is heavily indebted to Aristotelian philosophy, allows Aquinas to advance a monistic rather than a dualist theological anthropology. This, in turn, opens up a way of imagining the relationship between the divine and human agency such that one can maintain, even in light of contemporary neuroscientific studies, and without any sense of paradox, that it is God who prays in the human being, and yet it is the human body that prays.

Historical Development

Christianity inherited not only the monistic anthropology found in Hebrew Scriptures, but also the dualistic, monistic, traducianist, and even pre-existence anthropologies found in Hellenistic thought (Blosser, 2018). Navigating these dual currents of biblical and Hellenistic thought, early Christian thinkers settled for defining the parameters of orthodox Christian belief with respect to the relationship of the body and soul, rather than prescribing any one particular doctrinal position. The origin and scope of these parameters are discussed below.

The *locus classicus* of biblical anthropology is Genesis 2:7, which describes God forming Adam from the dust of the earth and then breathing into this form the breath of life: "And the Lord God formed\man of the dust of the ground, and breathed into his nostrils the breath of life; and man became a living soul" (King James Version). This passage, read in light of later Neoplatonic influences, has traditionally been understood as warranting a dualistic theological anthropology of body and soul. The Hebrew text, however, in fact, advances an anthropological monism.

At stake in rightly interpreting the anthropology implicit in Genesis 2:7 is understanding what is meant by the Hebrew word, *nefesh*. James L. Wright notes that this word "most closely approximates what modernity would call the soul" (2011, p. 448). Indeed, as shown above, the King James Version translates the word as living soul. Wright then draws attention to the hermeneutical issues any translation entails: "This *nefesh*, though, had nothing to do with the Platonic concept of the soul as an ephemeral entity, separate and distinct from the physical body" (p. 448). The Platonic dualism to which he refers did shape the Christian tradition and imagination. Translators, like those who worked on the King James text in the seventeenth century, would have understandably read their dualist assumptions back into the text and translated it accordingly, thus shaping the English-speaking Christian imagination until the present day. More recent scholarship, however, has noted that *nefesh* does not correlate to the Platonic soul. As Wright notes, "*nefesh*, rather, is a description of a psychosomatic unity which has no existence apart from the body. It is more accurately translated as a 'living being', an individual life" (p. 448).

Lawson G. Stone affirms this interpretation of Genesis. He writes that,

> the *nefesh* here is not a possession, nor is it a component of Adam's nature, a "part." The pile of dust, upon being inspirated by divine breath, actually became a living *nefesh*. The term "living *nefesh*" then denotes the totality of Adam's being. Adam does not have a *nefesh*; he is a living *nefesh*.
>
> (Stone, 2004, p. 53)

Stone notes the occurrence of *nefesh* in four other closely related passaged: Genesis 1:21, 24, 30, and Genesis 2:19. Each of these passages mentions *nefesh hahayyah*, which can be translated as "living creatures." Based on this, Stone concludes that Adam does not have some separate spiritual entity (i.e. a soul) that sets him apart from the animals. Rather, each animal is, like Adam, a "living *nefesh*" (Stone, 2004, p. 54).

Joel Green argues that similar theological anthropology is found in the New Testament. He claims that neither the author of Luke's Gospel, nor Paul in his many epistles, succumbs to the dualism of the Hellenized world (Green, 2002). While echoing Wright and Stone's insights that *nefesh* denotes a living creature and is used for both humans and animals, Green nonetheless affirms that human beings are unique among God's creatures in that they are made in God's own image (Gen 1:26). According to the incarnational hermeneutic of the New Testament, this means that the uniqueness of the human person does not consist in the "possession of a 'soul'... but in the human capacity to relate to God as his partner in covenant, and to join in companionship within the human family and in relation to the whole cosmos in ways that reflect the covenant love of God" (p. 7).

In the course of developing his argument, Green notes that Luke never deals directly with the question of what it means to be a human person; however, Luke's emphasis on soteriology opens a window through which one might glimpse how he understands human nature. Caught up in Luke's soteriology are questions like, "what needs to be saved" and "what would saved existence look like?" Green locates answers to these questions in the stories Luke tells about the healing of Jairus's daughter and the woman suffering from a hemorrhage (Luke 8:42b–48). In both stories, as well as in the healing miracles recounted in Matthew and Mark, "physical needs are correlated with spiritual needs, and spiritual needs are bundled with social needs" (pp. 13–14). The human person is recognized as a psychosomatic and social whole in need of healing. When Jesus heals first the hemorrhaging woman, and then Jairus's daughter, actions that prefigure eschatological salvation, he does not heal only the body, or the soul: rather, the cure of the physical illness enables both the healing of spiritual ills and the reconciliation of the social order. Thus Green concludes that, despite being a Gentile and the most Hellenized of the New Testament authors, "Luke disallows, say, the physical to be distinguished from other aspects of human existence, or the human person to be reduced to his or her body... Luke has no concept of a disembodied soul, either in present or in eschatological existence" (p. 17).

Green's account of Paul's anthropological monism relies on more complicated exegetical moves. He begins by citing 2 Corinthians 5:1–3,

> For we know that if our earthly tent is dismantled, we have a house from God – a dwelling not made with human hands, eternal in the heavens. In view of this we sigh, longing to put on our heavenly house, assuming, of course, that when we take it off we will not be found naked.

This particular passage, Green notes, has often been taken as evidence of a dualistic Pauline anthropology. Green, however, suggests that Paul's opening statement, "For we know that..." is meant to be a reminder of Paul's previous instruction, and especially to call to mind his teaching about the resurrection in 1 Corinthians 15: 38–58. Green highlights what he believes are several important aspects of that text: first, there is a continuity of bodily existence between this life and the next; second, mortal bodies will undergo a transformation such that they will be able to receive eternal life; third, this transformation is promised already in the resurrection of Christ; fourth, the promise of the resurrection of the body only serves to underline the importance of the body in the Christian life – what is done with and to them is not unimportant in the eternal scheme of things; and finally, because physical existence is important to God, it should also be important for the Christian community. Set against this backdrop, Green claims that Paul's metaphorical language of tents and houses points not toward an anthropological dualism, but toward an eschatological dualism for which the Christ event provides the hermeneutical key.

This scriptural inheritance shaped the development of the Christian concept of the soul in two profound ways. First, is established that the soul does not pre-exist the living being with whom it is associated: the very livingness of that being and of the soul are one and the same. This belief in turn shapes the belief about the origin of the soul. There is not a great deal of concern or speculation about the origin of the soul in Hebrew Scriptures: the soul is understood to be both passed on from the "loins" of the father – a traducianist position – and also created by God – the creationist position (Blosser, 2018). Both of these positions found resonances in the Hellenistic world.

In addition to the monistic theological anthropology found in the Hebrew Scriptures and apostolic texts, early Christianity was also influenced by the various positions available in Hellenistic thought, including dualism, monism, traducianism, and even pre-existence anthropologies. Christian thought, like that of Judaism in the Second Temple period, had become "thoroughly infused with Hellenizing influences" (Blosser, 2018, p. 210).

However, Christian thinkers also wrestled with anthropologies advanced by competing religious cults. The anthropological dualism of the Manicheans and Gnostics proved particularly challenging in the first centuries of Christianity. This dualism, inherited from Plato, held not only that the soul and the body were fundamentally different sorts of substances, but also that the soul was limited in its pursuit of knowledge and truth by the body and its passions. Some maintained that not only was the material world different from the spiritual, but that it was evil, while the soul was an eternal efflux of the divine. This denigration of the material world stood in direct contradiction to the affirmation of the world's goodness in Genesis and the subsequent reaffirmation of that goodness in Christianity's doctrines of the incarnation and resurrection.

By the end of its third century, Christianity had yet to define the exact nature of the soul or how the soul related to the body. Rather, Christian thinkers settled for defining the boundaries of orthodox Christian belief in response to the competing Gnostic and Manichean positions. Bringing together the dual steams of Hebrew and Hellenistic thought, a dominant theological position emerged which regarded the soul as something created, rather than a divine efflux, yet still immortal; the body-soul dualism and of the Gnostics and Manicheans was rejected. Both the body and the soul were regarded as good, and their conjunction as in keeping with the plan of a benevolent creator.

Despite the affirmation of the essential goodness of the physical, the emphasis on the created nature of the soul had the effect of weakening the traducianist position. This position was not without philosophical allies in the Hellenistic world. Aristotelian, Stoic, and Epicurean thought all advanced traducianist positions that resonated with that found in the Hebrew Scriptures. Aristotle conceived of the soul as the form, or actualization of mater: accordingly, there were mineral souls, vegetable souls, animal souls, and the rational souls of human beings. Both the Stoics and Epicureans rejected the notion that the soul was somehow different from the body. For all three schools of thought, the soul comes into being through the processes of reproduction. This particular understanding of the generation of the soul aligned with the notion in Hebrew Scriptures that all of humankind was contained in the loins of Adam. However, it would become increasingly difficult for Christian thinkers to maintain this traducianist position as they engaged with the powerful and politically dominant currents of Neoplatonism.

The synthesis of Neoplatonism and biblical doctrine began in the fourth century. The conversion of Constantine resulted in an influx of young intellectuals eager to serve in the new base of power that was the Church. These men had been formed by the Neoplatonism ascendant at the time. In contrast to the monistic anthropologies of the Hebrew and Christian Scriptures, Neoplatonism was characterized by a sharp dualism of the material and immaterial. The Neoplatonic thinkers who entered into the fray of theological debate struggled with the latent materialism implicit in the traducianism Christianity still affirmed. For Neoplatonists, "the divine realm was associated with the spiritual, the intelligible, and the immaterial, and the rational soul could not but be akin to it" (Blosser, 2018, p. 214). Such was the force of this newly understood differentiation between the physical and spiritual that Athanasius of Alexandria (335) claimed that the immortality of the soul depended upon it being of a *different* substance than the body (as cited in Blosser, 2018, p. 215) and Gregory of Nyssa (379) wrote that "the simplicity and indivisibility of the soul and the solidity of the body have nothing in common according to the principle of their natures" (as cited in Blosser, 2018, p. 215).

Though the boundaries of Christian belief still included the anthropological monism of scripture, the scope of Christian discourse had effectively narrowed: souls were thought to be immaterial, immortal, created, and conjoined to a body, itself also good, in accordance with the will of a benevolent creator. This creationist position, and its corresponding view of the activity of the soul as somehow separate from the life of the body, dominated Christian thinking for the next eight centuries – and still dominates the popular western Christian imagination. Despite this, it is interesting to note that there was no consensus about *what* the soul was nor how it related to the body. One problem was particularly vexing to the great thirteenth-century theologian, Thomas Aquinas: if the soul was capable of a separable, autonomous, and immortal existence apart from the body, then how does one account for the "unity of personhood pre-mortem?" (Turner, 2013, p. 74). Why are bodies necessary at all?

The core of the Christian faith is the belief in a *bodily* resurrection. Denys Turner argues that a doctrine of the immortality of the soul, such as that developed by Christian Neoplatonists in the fourth century is only necessary insofar as it helps to explain that belief in the resurrection (2013, p. 75). Because the resurrection is bodily, it cannot be the case that the immortal soul alone is identical with an individual personhood: as Aquinas claims, "I am not my soul" (Aquinas, 1269/2008b, p. 192). Rather, Aquinas maintains that humans are body-soul composites and that the existence of the soul apart from the body is partial and incomplete. The soul, according to Thomistic thought, needs the body to function as a soul. In order to understand how Aquinas arrives at this position, it is necessary to venture into the thick weeds of Thomistic metaphysics.

Thomistic Alternative

A distinctive feature of Thomistic metaphysics lies in its prioritization of existence over essence. This, in turn, shapes a conception of God who is not a divine *being* but is the act of existing – a position which has broad implications for how one conceives of God relating to and acting in the one who prays, as will be shown below. Aquinas presents arguments to this effect in a number of his theological works. One of the most succinct presentations can be found in his *Quastiones Disputatae de Potentia* (1266/2008e). Aquinas begins with the observation that different things cause different types of effects; sometimes these different things nonetheless have one effect in common. He gives, as an example, pepper, ginger, and other spices which are all hot. The reason why pepper and ginger, though very different from each other, cause things to become hot is because they both share in – or participate in – the higher cause of elemental fire. Diverse things, each with their own effects, that produce an effect in common do so, Aquinas argues, because each thing also participates in a higher cause of that common effect. One effect that all created things have in common is that, through the exercise of the particular causal power appropriate to their nature, they cause things to exist in a particular way or as a particular something. Pepper and ginger, for example, cause things *to be* hot. Because *causing things to exist as* is common to all created causes, Aquinas argues that there must be a higher cause of existence in which these created causes participate and from which they derive their causal efficacy. Aquinas concludes that this higher cause is God.

Because all things that exist participate in God's existence as the cause of their own existing, the way that God exists and the way creatures exist must be very different. Aquinas argues that "God's existing is individually distinguished from all other existing by the very fact that it is an existing subsistent in itself, and not one supervening on a nature other than existing itself" (p. 207). By this, he means that God's existence is God's essence; God is not some sort of thing *that exists*, rather God is the act-of-existing or the act-of-being. Aquinas continues, "All other existing, as non-subsistent, must be individually distinguished by some nature or substance that subsists with that existence" (p. 207).

Here, what Aquinas argues is that existence is added to a nature or essence such that it actually exists. In other words, existing things – whether rational, non-rational, or even non-living – exist in a completely different way than God, who is existence itself: they exist by sharing or participating in the divine act-of-being.

Just as created things exist by means of participating in what Elizabeth Johnson has called the "livingness of being" (1996, p. 11), they also exercise causality by means of participating in divine causality. In Thomistic metaphysics, all causality, whether formal, material, efficient, or final, has its origin in God (Dodds, 2012). Aquinas recognizes that even causes need a source of their existence. His five ways show that God, who is self-subsisting existence, is the origin of these causes, *not* as the first in a line of causes, but as that primary cause from which secondary causes receive and are maintained in their own existence and causal efficacy.

To understand what Aquinas means by this primary and secondary causality, consider the following explanation of one of Aquinas's "five ways" of proving God's existence, the argument from motion: "Now whatever is in motion is put in motion by another, for nothing can be in motion except it is in potentiality to that towards which it is in motion; whereas a thing moves inasmuch as it is in act" (1265/2000, I q. 2 a. 3 res.). It would be wrong to read this argument merely as some sort of medieval or even Aristotelian precedent for Newton's well-known law of inertia, namely that objects at rest stay at rest and objects in motion stay in motion unless acted upon by an unbalanced force. The clue to what Aquinas actually intends is found in his explanation of motion: "For *motion is nothing else than the reduction of something from potentiality to actuality*" (1265/2000, I. q 2 a. 3 res). This motion is, for Aquinas, the formal cause of a thing. A formal cause – though commonly imagined as a shape or pattern – is in fact, according to Aquinas, the actualization, or *the act* by which something comes to be a this-thing (Aquinas, 1250/2008d, 1252/2008a). Formal causes *actualize* the *potentiality* of the material cause. The material cause is not some sort of "stuff" out of which something is made. Rather, the material cause is, for Aquinas, the potency to substantial existence or the possibility-of-being (Aquinas, 1250/2008d, p. 67; Dodds, 2012, p. 16). The form, when received by matter, actualizes or *moves* that matter from potentiality to actuality.

In his first way, Aquinas argues that it is impossible for anything to be its own formal cause and that an infinite chain of formal causes is likewise impossible. By infinite chain, however, Aquinas does not mean a chain of chronological order. Rather, Aquinas posits a hierarchical relationship between forms belonging to different genres. Each subsequent level of form shares in the capacities or powers of the forms which precede it. Insofar as there exists a hierarchy of formal causes, these *secondary* formal causes are all dependent upon the *primary* formal cause and participate in that cause whenever they exercise their own formal causality. In arguing that God is the Prime Mover, Aquinas is thus making the claim that God is the Primary Formal Cause in which all secondary formal causes participate.

Aquinas's other four ways also serve to identify Primary Efficient and Final causality as God. All causes are thus understood to participate ontologically in God's causal Be-ing. Therefore, any exercise of creaturely causality, whether formal, efficient, or final, is ultimately a participation in divine causality. About this, Etienne Gilson famously quipped, "God does whatever creatures do; and yet creatures themselves do whatever they do" (Gilson, 1994, p. 182).

In light of his metaphysics, Aquinas develops a monistic, rather than dualistic anthropology: he argues that the human being is the composite of the form "soul" and bodily matter. His position, however, is quite nuanced. Whether or not forms are able to exist apart from the matter they actualize depends on the activity proper to that form and whether that activity requires matter. Aquinas believes that the activity that characterizes the human soul is *reasoning*. Following Aristotle, Aquinas argues that "since... understanding needs no bodily organ, the human soul can act in its own right, and so must be able to subsist in its own right as itself a thing" (Aquinas, 1269/2008c, p. 186). By this, Aquinas does not mean that there is no relationship between the body and reasoning. To the contrary, he maintains that the soul "understands by way of images which only the body can provide" (p. 186). The distinction he wishes to draw in saying that "understanding needs no bodily organ" is rather that the *activity* of the form "soul," which is to reason, does not require the actualization, or movement, of matter. It is for this reason that Aquinas claims that the human soul is itself a thing, situated within the hierarchy of substances "on the boundary between bodily and separate substances" (p. 190).

Of course, the activity of reasoning does, to the best of contemporary scientific knowledge, actualize neurological matter. However, this only serves to strengthen the point Aquinas makes about the dependence of the form "soul" on the body and the body's dependence upon the soul. Aquinas argues that the soul "does not possess a complete specific nature of its own" (1269/2008c, p. 189). Rather, the soul needs the body: "inasmuch as by nature it acquires immaterial knowledge from material it clearly needs to be united to a body in order to have a complete specific nature; for nothing has a complete specific nature unless it possesses everything required for the activity that characterizes that species" (pp. 189–190). Because human souls depend upon bodies in order to complete their nature, the existence of a soul apart from a body is imperfect (1269/2008b). Separate human souls, therefore, are not counted among the levels of being in Aquinas' metaphysics (1269/2008c).

Because the form "soul" has an incomplete existence apart from the body, Aquinas argues that the body is not somehow incidentally or accidentally joined to the soul as to some separate existing thing. In fact, Aquinas explicitly addresses and rejects the Platonic notion of the soul as a thing that has a complete existence apart from the body: "for he [Plato] thought... souls inhabited bodies like sailors do ships, or people their clothes. But this is impossible" (1269/2008c, p. 188). The problem with comparing souls and bodies to sailors and ships is that a ship remains a ship even when the sailor goes ashore, but the body decomposes once it is separated from the soul. Aquinas develops this point:

> If the soul inhabited the body like a sailor his ship, it wouldn't give body or its parts their specific nature; yet clearly it does, since when it leaves the body the various parts lose the names they first had, or keep them in a different sense.... Moreover, if the soul inhabited body like a sailor his ship the union of body and soul would be accidental, and when death separated them it wouldn't be decomposition of a substance, which it clearly is. (p. 188)

In Thomistic metaphysics, souls do not *use* bodies; rather the form "soul" actualizes matter such that the human body lives.

Aquinas also rejects the identification of the self with the soul. Commenting on Paul's first letter to the Corinthians, Aquinas emphasizes the importance of the resurrection: "if we deny the resurrection of the body it isn't easy – indeed it becomes very difficult to – to defend the immortality of the soul" (1269/2008b, p. 192). Because souls need bodies in order to complete their nature, any separation from the body means that the soul will exist imperfectly. Only the form "soul" united with body can be called a human being. Human beings are thus soul-body composites. From this, it follows that "the soul is not the whole human being, only part of one: my soul is not me. So that even if a soul achieves well-being in another life, that doesn't mean I do or any other human being does" (pp. 192–193). Only the resurrection can guarantee the immortality of the soul.

Neuroscience, Prayer, and Communion with the Divine

The monistic theological anthropology advanced by Aquinas has several advantages over more popular dualistic accounts when it comes to engagement with contemporary science, especially neuroscience. Because the soul was commonly imagined as something immaterial, science had, on the whole, abandoned the concept as unscientific.[2] Aquinas's characterization of the soul as that which actualizes matter brings the discussion about the nature of the soul closer to what might be described as the unmodeled capacities of mass-energy. What has previously been taken as evidence for an immaterial soul may instead be emergent capacities of matter scientists are not yet able to model. The inability to model those capacities is an epistemological limitation, not an ontological one (Stoeger S.J., 2002). Neither science nor the theological anthropology of Aquinas requires the existence of an immaterial or spiritual soul in order to explain the existence of mental and spiritual capacities.

Aquinas's theological anthropology, especially his characterization of the proper activity of the human soul as reasoning, also helps one to make sense of the neurological transformations wrought by regular and sustained practices of meditative or contemplative prayer. The activity of praying is just one particular manifestation of the activity of reasoning. Just as the soul must be united with bodily matter in order to acquire knowledge about which it can reason, the soul depends upon bodily structures and practices in order to pray. In other words, souls do not pray apart from bodily matter, the potentialities of which they actualize in prayer. Indeed, it is the actualization of this matter that seems to be the essence of prayer!

What then is to be said about the practice of asking those who have died, especially the saints, to intercede and pray for us? What happens to the soul and its capacity to reason and pray after an individual has died? Denys Turner addresses this problem. He notes that, for Aquinas, it would be impossible for a soul to learn anything new, lacking a body and a brain "because all of the cognitive functions that put us in contact with our world depend upon a working brain" (2013, p. 79). He suggests, however, that the intellect's capacity to reflect "upon its own already acquired mental contents is not...disabled by its separation from the body" (p. 79). In other words, the soul, separated by the body at death, "is a functioning store of memories that it can continue to tell but can no longer edit, add to, or revise" (pp. 79). It would follow that the souls of those who have died are able to intercede for those who ask, but only within the framework of their own life's memory. Far from being a limiting factor, such an understanding of the parameters of intercessory prayer drives one to more clearly articulate the perennial issues of desire, love, justice, and hope in one's prayer practice.[3]

But what of God's own action in the one who prays? Those who practice contemplative prayer, such as the Franciscan nuns studied by

Newberg, describe their soul as being grasped or held by God. This characterization of God's activity is problematic for those who maintain that the universe is a closed energy system: any action of God within the universe that effects change would constitute an unimaginable input of energy. Newberg's studies, in showing the real physical changes wrought by prayer, place God's action in the one who prays into this impossible category: whatever is happening in their brains cannot be the result of God's action, for such an action would constitute an input of energy into a closed energy system.

There have been many attempts to address this problem of divine action in the world (see e.g. Ritchie, 2019; Russell, Murphy & Isham, 1993; Saunders, 2002; Wildman, 2004). The solution offered by Thomistic metaphysics, and especially the participatory ontology he advances, is simple and elegant. The Thomistic premise is that God is the source of being in all things: "God, whose essence is the very livingness of Being (esse) gives a share in that being to what is other than Godself... Hence, all that exists participates in its own way in divine being through the very gift of creaturely existence" (Johnson, 1996, pp. 10–11). Because creatures participate in God's being, rather than sharing "being" in common with God, both the instant of their creation, as well as their continued existence, find their source in this participation. As the primary cause of being, who is innermostly present to created things, God is understood as both transcendent and immanent with respect to creation. As the innermost source of created beings, God is the source of their power and action. Creaturely power and causation are thus secondary, with respect to God. This does not mean, however, that God wields created things as mere instruments of the divine will. Rather, God fully exercises primary causality by allowing created things full autonomy. Thus, Elizabeth Johnson (1996) asserts, "God makes the world... in the process of things acting as themselves" (p. 12).

This still leaves, however, the question of why one should pray at all. For if God, as understood in the Thomistic tradition, acts through creatures acting as themselves, what is the purpose of petitionary prayer or any type of prayer and how should one understand *theologically* what it means for God to act in the soul of the one who prays?

The crucial aspect of the Thomistic alternative advanced above is that it supposes a participatory ontology. This difference suggests a way of thinking about creaturely practices that is also helpful in thinking about prayer. Creatures participate in God's act of be-ing by acting as themselves. This participation must mean something more than plugging into a divine current of being as if it were an electrical outlet and one's life were a light bulb. In acting as themselves, creatures are drawn toward God by God, whose providential care for them never ceases. Participation, therefore, involves cooperation between God and the creature and ultimately encompasses the transformation of the creature. For humans, this cooperation consists of engaging in those practices that enable them to be truly themselves and to actualize the dynamic potential of their own being. Through these practices, creatures participate in God's livingness of being.

An analogy may prove helpful here. As a practice, participation in God's act of be-ing may be thought of as analogous to loving. To love is a practice. Though it may at times seem to be instinctual or involuntary, as in the case of mothers and their children, it is yet nurtured, neglected, or even harmed by the practices of love. In the same way, participation in the divine Be-ing is something of a given for those things that exist. Yet, it too may be nurtured, neglected, or harmed by practices. When it is nurtured, the abundant potential of life is realized; when it is neglected or even harmed, one's life becomes self-centered, devoid of meaning and purpose, and ultimately joyless. The very goodness of God which one was created to seek as one's *telos* may become inaccessible.

Prayer is one such practice by means of which participation in God's own divine Be-ing is nurtured. In light of the Thomistic ontology and the corresponding account of divine action proposed above, this chapter suggests that, in the Christian tradition, prayer, especially the meditative forms of prayer frequently practiced by Christian mystics, is in fact a transformative practice through which one participates in God's own causal be-ing. In particular, prayer ought to be understood as an exercise of a person's formal causality such that the capacities of one's nature to know God as constitutively present are actualized. This mystical knowing is the *telos* of prayer. But, as the telos, it is both already a participation in God and the cause of prayer in the first place.

Notes

1 T. Anne Richards explores accounts of similar experiences as reported by ordinary people. Her essay, "Lived Experiences of Encountering the Divine and the Departed," included in this volume, reflects on how one may make sense of such experiences in light of an emerging scientific framework that imagines "the universe as an interconnected and continuous fabric of consciousness and intelligence, an electromagnetic field, expressing in multi-dimensional realities, simultaneously." While this way of understanding the universe avoids the reductionism implied by neuroscientific studies of religious experiences, namely that such experiences are nothing more than patterns of activity in the brain, it nonetheless challenges traditional understandings of the God-world relationship. Though the connection is not developed in this chapter, the theological metaphysics developed by Thomas Aquinas and advanced below can also provide a useful lens of thinking theologically about the interconnectedness of the universe.

2 Patricia Pearson surveys a similar scientific dismissal of "ghostly visions" in her essay, "Marginalizing the Sacred: The Clinical Contextualization of Sensed Presence Experiences" which is included in this volume.

3 Paul Schutz explores this quality of our prayer life in his essay, "'God saw...and God knew..': Science, Divine Action, and Unanswered Prayers" included in this volume.

References

Aquinas, T. (2000). *Summa theologica: Complete English edition in five volumes* (Fathers of the English Dominican Province, Trans.). Notre Dame, IN: Christian Classics. (Original work published 1265).

Aquinas, T. (2008a). Essence and existence. In T. S. McDermott (Trans.), *Selected philosophical writings*. Oxford, UK: Oxford University Press. (Original work published 1252).

Aquinas, T. (2008b). My soul is not me. In T. S. McDermott (Trans.), *Selected philosophical writings*. Oxford, UK: Oxford University Press. (Original work published 1269).

Aquinas, T. (2008c). Soul in human beings. In T. S. McDermott (Trans.), *Selected philosophical writings*. Oxford, UK: Oxford University Press. (Original work published 1269).

Aquinas, T. (2008d). On the principles of nature. In T. S. McDermott (Trans.), *Selected philosophical writings*. Oxford, UK: Oxford University Press. (Original work published 1250).

Aquinas, T. (2008e). Quaestiones disputatae de potentia 7.2. In T. S. McDermott (Trans.), *Selected philosophical writings*. Oxford, UK: Oxford University Press. (Original work published 1266).

Blosser, B. P. (2018). The ensoulment of the body in early Christian thought. In A. Marmodoro & S. Cartwright (Eds.), *A history of mind and body in late antiquity* (pp. 207–223). Cambridge, UK: Cambridge University Press; Cambridge Core. https://www.cambridge.org/core/books/history-of-mind-and-body-in-late-antiquity/ensoulment-of-the-body-in-early-christian-thought/C1E7D3CB93E1B7F58A5C145303493974.

Coakley, S. (2009). Dark contemplation and epistemic transformation: The analytic theologian Re-meets Teresa of Avila. In O. Crisp & M. C. Rea (Eds.), *Analytic theology: New essays in the philosophy of theology*. Oxford, UK: Oxford University Press.

Dodds, O. P. M. J. (2012). *Unlocking divine action: Contemporary science and Thomas Aquinas*. Washington, DC: Catholic University of America Press.

Gilson, E. (1994). *The Christian philosophy of St. Thomas Aquinas* (L. K. Shook, C.S.B., Trans.). Notre Dame, IN: University of Notre Dame Press.

Green, J. B. (2002). Restoring the human person: New testament voices for a wholistic and social anthropology. In R. J. Russell, N. Murphy, T. C. Meyering, & M. A. Arib (Eds.), *Neuroscience and the person: Scientific perspectives on divine action*. Vatican City State: Vatican Observatory Foundation.

Howells, E. (2002). *John of the Cross and Teresa of Avila: Mystical knowing and selfhood*. New York, NY: Crossroad Pub. Co.

Johnson, E. A. (1996). Does God play dice? Divine providence and chance. *Theological Studies, 57*(1), 2–18.

Louth, A. (1983). Mysticism. In G. S. Wakefield (Ed.), *The Westminster dictionary of Christian spirituality*. Philadelphia, PA: Westminster Press.

Newberg, A. B., D'Aquili, E. G., & Rause, V. (2001). *Why God won't go away: Brain science and the biology of belief*. New York, NY: Ballantine Books.

Ritchie, S. L. (2019). *Divine action and the human mind*. Cambridge, UK: Cambridge University Press.

Russell, R. J., Murphy, N. C., & Isham, C. J. (1993). *Quantum cosmology and the laws of nature: Scientific perspectives on divine action.* Vatican City State: Vatican Observatory.

Saunders, N. (2002). *Divine action and modern science.* Cambridge, UK: Cambridge University Press.

Stoeger S. J. W. R. (2002). The mind-brain problem, the laws of nature, and constitutive relationships. In R. J. Russell, N. Murphy, T. C. Meyering, & M. A. Arbib (Eds.), *Neuroscience and the person: Scientific perspectives on divine action.* Vatican City State: Vatican Observatory Foundation.

Stone, L. G. (2004). The soul: Possession, part, or person? In J. B. Green (Ed.), *What about the soul?: neuroscience and Christian anthropology.* Nashville, TN: Abingdon Press.

Turner, D. (2013). *Thomas Aquinas: A portrait.* New Haven, CT: Yale University Press.

Wildman, W. (2004). The divine action project, 1988–2003. *Theology and Science, 2*(1), 31–75. https://doi.org/10.1080/1474670042000196612.

Wright, J. L. (2011). The mortal soul in ancient Israel and Pauline Christianity: Ramifications for modern medicine. *Journal of Religion and Health, 50*(2), 447–451. https://doi.org/10.1007/s10943-010-9405-0.

7 Christian Perspectives on Praying for Deliverance from Demons

Candy Gunther Brown

The New Testament gospels brim with accounts of Jesus and his followers interacting with evil spirits. In addition to generalized reports of Jesus driving spirits out of "many" people (Matthew 8:16), there are seven separate stories of Jesus commanding demons to leave specific individuals (Mark 1:21–28, 3:22–27, 5:1–20, 7:24–30, 9:14–29; Luke 13:10–17; Matthew 9:32–34). After Jesus sent out first 12 and then 72 disciples to "heal the sick" and proclaim that, "the kingdom of God has come near to you," they rejoiced that "even the demons submit to us in your name" (Luke 10:11, 17).

Christianity spread across the Roman Empire as the early church continued, for its first 300 years, to heal the sick and cast out demons. The historian Ramsay MacMullen explains that early Christians exorcised evil spirits by "humiliating them, making them howl, beg for mercy, tell their secrets, and depart in a hurry," thereby demonstrating that *daimones* were "nasty, lower powers that no one would want to worship anyway" (1984, p. 28). Similarly, the practice of driving out evil spirits and healing the sick in Jesus' name and authority has fueled the rapid global expansion of Christianity in the twentieth and twenty-first centuries by convincing many people that the Holy Spirit is more powerful than other spirits (Brown, 2011; Cox, 1995; Wimber & Springer, 1986). Christians have not, in all times or places, exhibited comparable attention to evil spirits, the complex reasons for which exceed the scope of this short chapter (MacNutt, 2005).

This chapter examines the demonology and deliverance practices of US Charismatic Christians between the 1960s and the present. Previous scholarship on this subject has emphasized the distinctively "American" contexts of popular media and therapeutic culture instead of scrutinizing underlying cosmological assumptions or their global contexts (Cuneo, 2001; McCloud, 2015). Although recognizing the diversity of beliefs and practices encompassed under the umbrella "Charismatic," this chapter elucidates one particular, globally constructed, influential Charismatic understanding of the nature of spiritual entities, how spirits interact with humans, and how humans should interact with spirits. This model presumes the existence and relevance to the human experience of both holy and evil spirits, and charts pathological and ideal interactions. In this Charismatic model, communication by humans with demons is both possible and desirable, but solely for the purpose of avoiding future interactions.

Context

By the eighteenth century, American theologians by and large stopped attributing evil to a personal devil or demons, though popular fascination with the spiritual world by no means disappeared (Delbanco, 1995). In the mid-twentieth century, many US seminaries, influenced by scholars like Rudolf Bultmann (1958), taught a "de-mythologized" interpretation of Jesus' healings and exorcisms. Ironically, efforts by theological conservatives to magnify God's otherworldly grandeur had the practical effect of relegating everyday needs, including physical and mental health, to human problem solving. The "flaw of the excluded middle," according to Fuller School of World Mission professor and missionary to India, Paul Hiebert, is that Western Christians lost sight of the "middle level of supernatural but this-worldly beings" that cannot be directly perceived yet interact with *this* world (1982, p. 43). Even US Pentecostals, who affirmed the ongoing activity of the Holy Spirit and evil spirits, taught that Christians cannot be demonized, thereby making demonology largely irrelevant to church practice (Prince, 1998); since demons expelled from non-Christians can be expected to return with "seven other spirits more wicked than itself" (Matthew 12:45), it was unclear who remains as a suitable candidate for exorcism (Dickerman, 2009).

Instead of wholly disregarding the demonic, Americans have exhibited ambivalence. The American studies scholar Andrew Delbanco describes an "incessant dialectic in American life between the dispossession of Satan under the pressure of modernity and the hunger to get him back," since "evil remains an inescapable experience for all of us" (1995, pp. 234, 224). A 2019 YouGov poll reported that 45 percent of Americans believe that demons, ghosts, and other supernatural beings "definitely" or "probably" exist (Ballard, 2019). Ideas of the demonic owe much to popular media—"Hollywood" rather than the "Holy Word" (Dickerman, 2009, p. 90). The 1973 film *The Exorcist* (Friedkin & Blatty, 1973)—with its green vomit and 360-degree head turns—sensationalized possession and exorcism, making demons seem both frightening and ridiculous. In the countless films and television series that followed, entertainment mingled with unease that demons might be deathly real.

World War II laid a foundation for modern US "spiritual warfare" by exemplifying evil and inspiring personal resistance. Pioneers in this renaissance, among them Corrie Ten Boom (2008)—imprisoned for sheltering Jews from the Nazis, and Derek Prince (1998), Frank Hammond

(Hammond & Hammond, 2008), and Francis MacNutt (2009)—each of whom served in the war, needed little convincing that the kingdom of God and the kingdom of Satan are continually clashing, with humans as collateral damage. Globally, middle-level spiritual activity had never disappeared from sight. Lamin Sanneh, native Gambian and Yale Professor of Missions and World Christianity, characterized the "small, disinfected" and "stripped-down universe of a post-Enlightenment Christianity" as a "small fit for this larger world that Africans"—and many others—have lived in, a world in which humans are "not alone in the universe, which is inhabited by the devil and by a host of spirit forces that are ever attentive to us. We should also be ever attentive to them if we are sensible" (2005, p. 7). Not coincidentally, many of the pioneering leaders in the modern US deliverance movement spent time in regions of Africa, Latin America, and Asia where predominant cosmologies presume regular interactions between the material and spiritual worlds.

As the Charismatic movement swept across US Catholic and Protestant churches of nearly every denomination during the 1960s–1970s, more and more pastors and laypeople prayed for the sick to be healed. As they did so, some of the individuals seeking prayer exhibited unusual behavior. As Derek Prince—a Cambridge-educated Greek and Latin scholar born in India—narrates, he was pastoring a Pentecostal church in Seattle, Washington in 1963, "when a member of my congregation let out a blood-curdling shriek and collapsed just in front of my pulpit, [so] I had to make a split-second decision." Prince diagnosed the behavior as having been caused by a demon, which he proceeded to drive out (1998, p. 9). Similarly, Doris Wagner, having returned to the United States after serving as a missionary to Bolivia, was praying quietly for a sick person when a demon manifested with "loud screams and bodily contortions." Wagner "didn't look for it; it came to me and I had to do something about it" (2000, p. 11). A common narrative trope among pioneers is that they were simply minding their own business when a demon manifested in front of them and no one else seemed equipped or willing to deal with it. Experiences like Prince's and Wagner's catalyzed a rethinking of theology as well as ontology and epistemology—ideas of what entities exist in the universe, how they can be known, and, ultimately, the rules that govern their interactions.

Cosmology

Efforts to deliver people—and, indeed, Christians—from evil spirits are premised upon certain assumptions about the nature of the universe. In the Charismatic worldview examined here, the universe consists of both matter and spirit, and interactions among material and spiritual entities are not only possible but also relatively commonplace—not requiring a miraculous, extraordinarily rare disruption of the laws of nature.

"Spirits" (from the Greek *pneuma*, which can be translated as breath or wind)—including God's Holy Spirit, Satan, angels, and demons—are neither impersonal, morally neutral forces nor metaphors, but personal beings with distinctive personalities, minds, emotions, and wills; some are good, while others are evil. Spirits can and often want to interact with humans and are able both to initiate communication and to respond to human initiatives.

Not everything possible is, however, permissible. By Charismatic reasoning, God's law, as revealed in the Bible, sets limits for interactions between spirits and humans. The rules for human engagement with spiritual beings vary by the type of entity involved. The Bible encourages addressing prayers of thanksgiving and petition to God the Father in the name of Jesus (John 16:23) as well as "praying in the Holy Spirit" (Jude 1:20). God hears and answers such prayers (1 John 5:15).

By contrast, the Bible prohibits communicating with the spirits of deceased humans, for instance through a medium (1 Samuel 28), or using divination, sorcery, or witchcraft to control spiritual forces (Deuteronomy 18:10). Such prohibitions reflect the tendency of humans, motivated by curiosity or desperation, to seek information or help from spiritual sources other than the Holy Spirit (Daniels, 2013). Catholic theology permits petitioning departed saints to intercede with God on behalf of the living (MacNutt, 2009), though Protestants classify such communications as impermissible (Bottari, 2000). Although outside the United States it is relatively common for Christians to interpret ghosts as departed spirits who need prayer to rest from their wanderings (Cox, 1995), the more common view among US Charismatics is that ghosts are demons masquerading as spirits of the deceased in order to entice illicit communication; these "familiar" spirits are convincing in their impersonations because they studied the person's behavior while still living (Daniels, 2013).

The Bible permits, but limits, communication with angels and demons. Angels (Greek *angelos*, meaning messenger) are, in Charismatic theology, spiritual beings—without physical bodies—that God created prior to creating humanity. God's kingdom of angels is organized hierarchically into three distinct spheres of influence, each of which is divided into three ranks. At the top, there are *seraphim*, *cherubim*, and *thrones* who interact directly with God in the throne room of the highest heaven; second, *dominions*, *powers*, and *authorities* oversee the physical universe; and third, *principalities*, *archangels*, and *angels* engage with human affairs, ranging from those of nations to individuals (MacNutt, 2012).

Angels function as intermediaries between God and humans. They can travel from the "third," or highest, heaven where God dwells to the "first," or physical, heaven above the earth. God initiates contact with humans by sending angels to communicate warnings or encouragements or to offer protection or assistance (MacNutt, 2012). Although humans may pray for God to send angels, humans lack biblical authority to summon, petition, command, or commission angels to do anything, including sending messages back to God or to other people (Hammond & Hammond, 2008); the Bible prohibits worshipping angels since all praise and thanksgiving belong to God (Revelation 22:9). Humans may, however, be allowed to dialog with angels when angels start the conversation (Luke 1:34).

In the biblical narrative, the highest-ranking *cherub*, Lucifer (*phosphoros*, "light-bringing") was created to reflect God's glory, but through pride rebelled from his position as the worship leader to seek worship for himself. One-third of the angels rebelled with Lucifer, now known as Satan (*Satanas*, "adversary"), or the devil (*diabolos*, "accuser"), so God expelled these fallen angels from the highest heaven. Satan set up a rival kingdom in the "heavenly realms" (Ephesians 1:12), or "second" heaven, between the dwellings of God and humanity. When Satan tempted Adam and Eve to sin, the dominion over the earth that God had given to humankind passed to the devil. Although Jesus defeated Satan through the crucifixion and resurrection, invisible warfare continues between the kingdom of God and the kingdom of Satan; the day has not yet arrived when God's holy angels will cast Satan and his fallen angels into the abyss (Basham, 1996; Daniels, 2013; Dickerman, 2009; MacNutt, 2012; Prince, 1998).

Christians have, ever since the first century, often expressed apocalyptic expectations that the Second Coming of Jesus and the final clash between Christ and Antichrist is rapidly approaching. Apparent increases in demonic activity can be interpreted as evidence that the end times are near. In the view of Billy Graham, one of the most influential Christian leaders of the twentieth century, "demonic activity and Satan worship are on the increase in all parts of the world" because the devil realizes that "his time is short" (1996, p. 3).

When a third of the angels fell, they retained their original spheres of influence and ranks (MacNutt, 2012). The Bible alludes to multiple levels in Satan's kingdom and explains that the church's "struggle is not against flesh and blood, but against the rulers, against the authorities, against the powers of this dark world and against the spiritual forces of evil in the heavenly realms" (Ephesians 6:12). Some Charismatics envision deliverance of individuals from demons as a subset of a larger program of "spiritual warfare," which may include city-wide or nation-wide "spiritual mapping" and corresponding efforts to dislodge high-level "territorial" spirits (Wagner, 1993). Other Charismatics warn that the authority Jesus gave his followers on earth does not extend to the second heaven, where angels fight on behalf of Christians (Dickerman, 2009). Levels of authority and chains of command must be respected, and "even the archangel Michael, when he was disputing with the devil about the body of Moses, did not himself dare to condemn him for slander but said, 'The Lord rebuke you!'" (Jude 1:9). Christian "prayer warriors" who exceed their delegated authority (especially when acting alone) by confronting high-level spirits in the second heaven may become vulnerable to a backlash, including sickness or premature death (Jackson, 1999).

Satan and demons are not, in this cosmology, mere metaphors or manifestations of the subconscious. Billy Graham preached that, "Satan is not only a force and power, but he is a great personality with tremendous power and strength in the universe we live in" (1957, p. 3). Pope Francis similarly emphasizes that Satan is a "real being," not a "myth, a representation, a symbol, a figure of speech or an idea" (2008). The existence of Satan and demons cannot, however, be verified by modern science. A spirit is, by definition, a "non-material" being that is unobservable with the physical senses. Spirit is much like wind—another translation for *pneuma*—in that no one sees the wind, but only observes its effects (Prince, 1998, p. 165). As explained by the Catholic Charismatic Francis MacNutt, the "demonic world cannot be seen, measured or placed under a microscope." Because it is impossible to "see the evil spirit itself, but only what it causes people to do," any "evidence" of a demonic presence is "bound to be ambiguous" since there will inevitably be alternative explanations (2009, p. 53).

Demonology

The word "demon" is a translation of the Greek *daimon* and *daimonion*, the diminutive form, suggesting that some demons rank higher than others (Basham, 1996; MacNutt, 2012). The predominant Charismatic view is that demons are fallen angels. Alternative theories are that demons are the remnants of a pre-Adamic creation destroyed by God because of their disobedience, or else the illicit offspring of angels and humans—the Nephilim of Genesis 6:1–4 (Dickerman, 2009). Derek Prince, who claims to have had contact with "satanic angels through intercessory prayer and spiritual warfare," finds it hard to believe that the earthbound demons he has often driven out—many of whom seem "weak, cowering, even ridiculous"—are angels, even in a fallen condition (1998, pp. 95,91). Regardless of disputed origins, most Charismatics agree with Prince's definition that demons are "disembodied spirit beings that have an intensive craving to occupy physical bodies" (1998, p. 89)—preferably those of humans, with animals as second choice (Mark 5:1–3)—through which to manifest their natures.

Demons are personal beings who have identifiable personality traits, intellects, emotions, wills, self-awareness, and the ability to speak (MacNutt, 2012; Prince, 1998). They are aware of their own identity and that of other demons occupying the same body, and they are able to answer questions and carry on a conversation. They have the ability to communicate with one another, to work in teams—or to compete against each other, to strategize, and to call for help and lend aid to one another (Dickerman, 2009). Higher-ranking demons are able to "sacrifice" underlings in order to pretend to leave while actually remaining behind in hiding (Kylstra & Kylstra, 2003, p. 234). Although demons are intelligent—more intelligent than humans, they exhibit less individuality than angels or humans because they act in strict obedience to their superiors (Gallagher, 2020; Peck, 1983). In their arrogance, demons often "overplay" their hands, thereby making humans aware of their presence (Bottari, 2000, p. 47). When demons manifest their natures, there is relatively little variety in what they say or how they behave.

Unlike God, Satan is not omniscient, omnipresent, nor omnipotent, and is unable to create anything new but only "counterfeit" what God has made (Daniels, 2013, p. xiv). Although not bound by space, Satan and his demons can only be in one place at a time. Thus, even if Satan wanted to attack every individual personally, he would be incapable of doing so, and therefore sends demons to carry out his purposes. Demons seem able to implant thoughts in a person's mind—often speaking in the first person singular, "I," to trick people into believing that thoughts are their own, or else pretending to be the voice of angels or the Holy Spirit; unlike God, demons cannot reliably read thoughts or know the intentions of the heart, generally making it necessary for people to vocalize communications to demons (Dickerman, 2009; Kylstra & Kylstra, 2003).

The names of demons indicate their ranks or assignments. Those with the highest ranks have proper names (some of which are listed in the Bible, others of which have reportedly been discovered through ministry experience), such as Antichrist, Beelzebub, Pasuzo, Leviathan, Asmodeus, Azazel, Abaddon, Xanthan, Baphomet, Samhain, and Ma Ha Bone. Next in rank are spirits of witchcraft, territorial spirits, district spirits, regional spirits, and spirits over counties, cities, and communities. Finally, there are the kingdom princes who rule over the spirits that seek to inhabit individuals (Dickerman, 2009; MacNutt, 2009).

Three major types of demons attack individuals: occult spirits, spirits of sin, and spirits of trauma. Occult spirits may have proper names, reflecting their higher ranks. Most demons, however, lost their unique angelic identities (if they were in fact once angels), such that now their identities consist merely in what they do. Spirits of sin are identified not by personal names but by the name of the sin that they tempt humans to commit, for instance, Unforgiveness, Lust, Addiction, Hatred, and Murder. Spirits of trauma likewise are identified by the emotional wounds they feed upon to intensify or distort negative emotions; examples include Rejection, Fear, Anger, and Depression (MacNutt, 2009).

Demons at work in individuals typically operate through sub-kingdoms of Satan. Each kingdom is organized hierarchically, something like an army with ranks and prescribed lines of authority and communication (Hammond & Hammond, 2008). A "strongman" (Mark 3:22–30), "prince," or "ruling" spirit leads each kingdom, which may consist of several to several hundred demons—some of which are more powerful and resistant to being cast out than others—all occupying the same person simultaneously. "Gatekeeper" demons have the assignment of bringing other demons in and preventing them from leaving (Daniels, 2013; Dickerman, 2009; Larson, 2016; MacNutt, 2009).

Particular types of spirits frequently appear in similar combinations. Frank and Ida Mae Hammond, who published one of the first "practical" guides to deliverance in 1973—selling over a million copies, compiled a list of 53 "Common Demon Groupings" (2008, pp. 128–131). Among the ruling spirits most commonly detected by the Hammonds is "Bitterness," under whose leadership one often finds Resentment, Hatred, Unforgiveness, Violence, Temper, Anger, Retaliation, and Murder. Similarly, "Depression" is not merely a mental health condition, but can also be a spirit that rules over Despair, Despondency, Discouragement, Defeatism, Dejection, Hopelessness, Suicide, Death, Insomnia, and Morbidity. In some cases, a single spirit may have multiple functions, such as Rejection, Addiction, and Fear. Additionally, multiple spirits may all have the same or a similar function; there may, for instance, be a spirit of Rejection, a spirit of the Fear of Rejection, a spirit of Perceived Rejection, and a generational spirit of Rejection (Dickerman, 2009; Wagner, 2000).

There is widespread agreement among Catholics and Protestants that demons cannot "possess" Christians, because Christians already belong to God, and that full possession is extremely rare. The Greek word *daimonizomai*—translated as "demon-possessed" in both the King James and New International versions—can instead be translated as demonized, oppressed, obsessed, influenced, afflicted, tormented, infested, harassed, vexed, or troubled—terms that connote less than full possession. One influential viewpoint is that demons *only* have the power to deceive, tempt, and accuse, but cannot inflict physical harm (Anderson, 1990); a more prevalent Charismatic position is that demons can infest Christians' bodies (causing certain physical pains, diseases, and disabilities) and souls (encompassing their thoughts, emotions, and wills), but not their spirits (Bottari, 2000; Hammond & Hammond, 2008).

In the Charismatic worldview, lesser degrees of demonic infestations are relatively common—affecting perhaps the large majority of church-going Christians. There are Charismatics who go into prisons to cast demons out of serial killers, but they also drive demons out of pastors, white- and blue-collar workers, and children, "just people" (Dickerman, 2009, p. 40). New Testament writings warn Christians to "be alert and of sober mind" because "the devil prowls around like a roaring lion looking for someone to devour" (1 Peter 5:8), suggesting that Christians can be targets of Satan's mission to "steal and kill and destroy" (John 10:10).

Demons are unlike viruses in that people do not risk infection by mere proximity or touch. The Bible describes Christians' bodies as "temples of the Holy Spirit" (1 Corinthians 6:19) or as "houses" that, if left empty, can be occupied by impure spirits (Matthew 12:44). There is some debate about whether "Spirit-filled" Christians are vulnerable; Charismatics who answer in the affirmative may emphasize the distinction between possession and oppression (Wagner, 2000).

Demons cannot enter a house unless there is an "open door" (MacNutt, 2009). The most common open doors are sins—unforgiveness tops most lists, or dabbling in the occult—for instance, by playing with a Ouija board. Personal sins are not, however, the only open doors. Demons may feed on the emotional wounds caused by trauma—such as sexual abuse or rejection by one's mother while in her womb—even if one does not respond with a sin like unforgiveness; demons do not always "play fair" (Kylstra & Kylstra, 2003, p. 21). Generational curses may also result from ancestral sins since God "punishes the children and their children for the sin of the parents to the third and fourth generation" (Exodus 34:7); Freemasonry raises particular alarms because members reputedly invoke curses on themselves and their descendants if they reveal secrets and, in the higher degrees, worship multiple gods, ultimately revealed to include Lucifer (Wagner, 2000, p. 212). When someone dies, newly homeless demons may seek to enter a relative, especially one physically present at the moment of death, if that relative has any open door (Dickerman, 2009).

Deliverance

The New Testament includes many references (e.g. Mark 1:39) to Jesus "driving out" (Greek *exbalio*) demons. Modern efforts to follow Jesus' example are, even in Charismatic circles, more controversial than prayers for healing. Materialistic assumptions are sufficiently pervasive that blaming demons for evil—or for problems that can largely be accounted for by biology or psychology—smacks of superstition, especially when people evade moral accountability by hiding behind a catchphrase popularized in 1970s' media: "the devil made me do it" (Larson, 2016). Charismatics have been accused of seeing "demons behind every bush" (MacNutt, 2009, p. 17). Compounding media caricatures of unrealistically dramatic exorcisms, some actual exorcisms have left already-suffering individuals further traumatized or even dead—for example, due to a heart attack (Wagner, 2000). Even Christians who believe in demons may be afraid to confront them or hope that ignoring demons will cause them to go away (Anderson, 1990).

Since the Bible provides little detail about *how* to drive out demons, and demons do not always seem to depart following a single command, Christians have experimented with various approaches (Hammond &

Hammond, 2008). In the Roman Catholic Church, there is a formal "Rite of Exorcism" that can only be performed by a priest authorized by his bishop. Eligibility for an exorcism is restricted to the fully "possessed," based on evidence such as revulsion to sacred objects like Bibles and crucifixes, speaking in unknown languages, demonstrating extraordinary strength, or levitating. Catholic exorcisms are relatively rare, but there has been an increase in the number of authorized exorcists and documented cases over the past several decades (Cuneo, 2001; MacNutt, 2009). Lay Catholics, as well as Protestants, lack permission to use the exorcism rite but can and often do pray for "deliverance" of individuals who are less than fully possessed. Many Charismatics prefer the term deliverance because it emphasizes the goal of freeing suffering people whom God loves, rather than battling demons.

Deliverance practices vary greatly. Contexts include evangelistic crusades attended by thousands, regular church services, and private appointments. The length of time spent ranges from under five minutes to several hours on multiple occasions. At one end of the stylistic spectrum are exorcists who shout at demons, tie up the demonized with physical restraints, and apply force to induce the person to vomit out demons (Cuneo, 2001). At the other end, there are some who encourage the afflicted to repent of their sins and practice Christian disciplines such as prayer and Bible reading, and assume that the demons will then leave on their own (Anderson, 1990). The focus here is on more middling—and prevalent—approaches.

Most Charismatics agree that one should only minister deliverance to someone who wants it, since God created and respects free will. As a preliminary, those seeking ministry affirm their submission to the lordship of Jesus of Nazareth and their willingness to break any agreements they may have, even inadvertently, made with demons (Banks, 1987). The deliverance minister might then "bind" (Greek *deo*, to tie) any evil spirits present (Hammond & Hammond, 2008), since Jesus explained that one cannot "enter a strong man's house and carry off his possessions unless he first ties up the strong man" (Matthew 12:29), but "whatever you bind on earth will be bound in heaven" (Matthew 18:18). Binding might consist of saying: "submit in the name of Jesus" (Bottari, 2000, p. 101).

The next step is to close the doors that allowed demons entrance. This generally involves interviewing the person, possibly aided by a written questionnaire. Questions probe for common openings such as occult involvement, generational sins, trauma, unforgiveness—especially toward one's parents, addictions, and sexual immorality. Doris Wagner notes that "the devil doesn't seem to invent much new. Once you've seen about 20 of these questionnaires, you've pretty much seen them all" (2000, p. 114). Then, the deliverance minister leads the recipient through forgiveness, repentance, and renunciation of sins and spirits associated with those sins, and breaking curses.

Although God can hear unspoken prayers, demons cannot, so every spiritual declaration is spoken aloud before an unseen audience of holy and unholy auditors (Bottari, 2000). Few Protestants use a formal liturgy, but some read scripted prayers. This is not because they expect specific words or verbal formulas to exert power, as with an incantation (McCloud, 2015); they just do not want to forget anything important that demons might, in the "casting out" stage, use as an excuse to disobey commands to leave (Dickerman, 2009).

Demons, as conceptualized by Charismatics, are legalists who use any unforgiven disobedience to God's law to claim a "legal right" to remain in the bodies they occupy. Closing doors remove demons' rights to remain as legal inhabitants, making them "trespassers" who are easier to evict (Kylstra & Kylstra, 2003). Some demons claim "squatter" rights based on the length of occupancy. Demons rarely seem to leave on their own even after their rights to remain have been removed; they must still be cast out.

Demons must, in theory, obey commands issued in Jesus' name and authority. Yet, practitioners often find that they must issue commands more than once. Casting the spirits out one by one seems to reduce confusion as to which demon is being addressed and which ones have or have not left. Even so, demons look for legal "loopholes," such as lack of specificity in commands to leave; protests go something like: "That's not my name.... I am not rejection, I am fear of rejection" (Hammond & Hammond, 2008, p. 159). Based on decades of experience, Don Dickerman forbids spirits from "hiding, leaving, calling others to help, or harming" or entering anyone else, or dividing, multiplying, or passing on their assignment to another spirit; they must all "become one spirit," "gather up" all their works and "put everything back in order," then go into the abyss directly and immediately. Dickerman has found that telling spirits to go *to* the abyss is insufficient, since legalistic demons can go to it without going *into* it (2009, pp. 9, 58, 67, 80). Other deliverance ministers claim success in sending spirits "to Jesus Christ to be dealt with" (MacNutt, 2009), while others focus on getting demons out without worrying about where they go (Bottari, 2000).

Some individuals seem to be more effective than others in driving out demons. In the biblical book of Acts, demons drove away a group of seven Jewish exorcists, saying, "Jesus I know and Paul I recognize, but who are you?" (Acts 19:14–16). Charismatics suggest that, beyond the minimum requirement of faith in Jesus, deliverance ministers should be "baptized in the Holy Spirit." With certain kinds of demons (Matthew 17:21), fasting from food, though an invisible form of communication to the spiritual world, seems to weaken demonic resistance in the tormented individual and to increase the level of power accessible to the person ministering (Chavda, 1998). Although deliverance ministers often work in teams, in order to keep the chain of command clear, only the person leading will generally touch the prayer recipient or address the demons, lest the resultant confusion allows the demons to avoid obeying anyone. There is widespread agreement that demons have excellent hearing (even demons of Deafness) and are more likely to obey commands whispered authoritatively than shouted insecurely (Bottari, 2000).

Some practitioners are content to identify demons by their symptoms, whereas others seek to learn specific names, either through "discernment," one of nine gifts of the Holy Spirit (1 Corinthians 12) or by interrogating the demons. Someone with an "actual" gift of discernment might be able to "see" demons in their mind's eye or recognize their presence through distinctive physical sensations—such as the hair on the back of the neck standing up, a tingling in the right earlobe, or an unpleasant odor (MacNutt, 2009). Most Charismatics recognize, however, that it can be easy to confuse one's own thoughts for the voice of the Holy Spirit (Luhrmann, 2012). Certain deliverance ministers suggest that demon interrogation is a more reliable source of information than "unprovable 'prophetic' revelations and highly subjective 'words from the Lord'" (Larson, 2016, p. 11), though this assumes that demons can be trusted to tell the truth.

Communicating with Demons

Jesus interacted with demons with the goal of driving them out. Jesus spoke to demons, and they spoke back. Sometimes Jesus commanded the demons to be quiet and come out (Mark 1:25); at other times, he first asked their names (Luke 8:30). On at least one occasion, Jesus permitted the demons he expelled to enter a herd of pigs at their request.

The purpose of communicating with demons is fundamentally different from the purpose of communicating with God. The Christian ideal of prayer is to cultivate a relationship with God, rather than merely to get something from God. By contrast, communication with demons should ideally be purely utilitarian, restricted to that which is strictly necessary to obtain the result of the demons' departure. Whereas humans should ask God for what they need, including physical and emotional healing, people should never *petition* but always *command* demons, and they should certainly not answer questions posed by demons (Cuneo, 2001). Deliverance ministers do not generally petition God to cast out demons. Instead, they themselves issue the commands, always in Jesus' name and authority. Petitionary prayer comes into play when ministering to someone unwilling to accept Jesus as Lord or unable to forgive another party; the prayer minister might ask God to remove the "veil" that blinds the individual to the Gospel (2 Corinthians 4:3) or help the person to forgive (Dickerman, 2009; MacNutt, 2009; Prince, 1998).

In interacting with demons, Charismatics take care to resist the temptation to seek knowledge from them. The source of temptation is that demons seem readier to speak audibly—through their host's vocal cords and mouth—than does God. When deliverance ministers communicate with demons, it is ideally "not conversation, but rather it is confrontation" (Dickerman, 2009, p. 128). There are several reasons that casual conversation is considered dangerous. First, Charismatics worry about violating biblical prohibitions, thereby incurring a divine curse. Second, demons are inherently untrustworthy sources of information, since Satan is the "father of lies" (John 8:44). Third, demons seem to use conversation as a delaying tactic, since as long as they are talking they can avoid leaving (Hammond & Hammond, 2008).

Charismatics disagree over whether they should command demons to remain silent or to speak. Don Dickerman, for example, begins by calling the demons to attention, as troops in an army. After "binding" the spirits, he commands the "prince"—the one who claims to be in charge—to come forward and identify himself. The prince must reveal how many demons are in his kingdom and how many kingdoms are present, and whether there are open doors, disclosing whether these answers will "stand as truth before Jehovah God" (2009, p. 18). The purpose of forcing demons to identify themselves is that it weakens their resistance to commands to depart, much like calling an attacking dog by its name increases the likelihood that it will obey (Prince, 1998). Even under oath, demons cannot be relied upon to identify themselves accurately; they may claim to be Jesus or Satan, call themselves by the name of the person they are occupying, or choose a foreign-sounding alias to conceal their true nature (Dickerman, 2009; Hammond & Hammond, 2008). Demons are, however, sufficiently arrogant that they do often reveal their names, functions, or the doors that allowed their entrance (Kylstra & Kylstra, 2003). Sometimes, demons speak through their host to provide information that the host does not know. For instance, St. Louis native Bill Banks was ministering to a teenage boy in 1973 when he commanded the afflicting spirit to identify itself. The boy repeated aloud the word he heard in his head—"Incest"—a word he did not remember ever having heard before and could not define, but which did accurately describe his experience (1987, p. 40).

As with this teenager, demons usually respond to interrogation by inserting thoughts in the mind of the host, which the person then reports to the prayer minister. Sometimes, however, words come out of the host's mouth involuntarily—and occasionally, this individual may not remember what transpired (Dickerman, 2009). Demons predictably try to interrupt the ministry session by inserting first-person singular thoughts, such as "I need to leave now." Involuntary speech is often in the first-personal plural, "we," such as "We hate you!" (MacNutt, 2009, p. 24). Demons do not "show much variety in what they say" (Hammond & Hammond, 2008, p. 61). They typically plead to be allowed to remain, insist that the host wants to keep them, and issue threats—to kill the host or deliverance minister or to reveal the minister's secrets sins. When demons have apparently commandeered a person's vocal cords, the tone and pitch typically change—a woman's voice may suddenly sound like a man's, and the individual may scream, curse, or laugh mockingly. Who is speaking sometimes seems to alternate, with the host finding it difficult to pray or say the name of Jesus.

Demonic speech is one category of what Charismatics refer to as "manifestations," meaning to "make visible." As pioneers, Frank and Ida Mae Hammond explain, "when demons are confronted and pressured through spiritual warfare they will sometimes demonstrate their particular natures through the person" because "they cannot bear to be brought into the light" (2008, p. 57). Some ministers forbid demons from manifesting, while others command them, one by one, to manifest—as a means of exposing their natures or convincing skeptics of their reality. Certain Charismatics intentionally agitate demons by singing songs about the blood of Jesus, reading Scriptures about Satan's ultimate fate, or placing a Bible or crucifix into the demonized person's hands—on the premise that such actions will make the demons want to leave (Kylstra & Kylstra, 2003; Larson, 2016). Other seasoned deliverance ministers reflect back, regretfully, on early experiences in which they allowed violent demonic manifestations—which caused much suffering and embarrassment to the afflicted individual without hastening the demons' departure (Bottari, 2000).

Demonic manifestations follow predictable patterns. Observable involuntary movements by the afflicted person include facial or other bodily contortions, shaking, stiffness, falling, rolling on the floor, kicking, attempting to strangle the demonized person or prayer minister, rolling of the eyes into the back of the head, and rapid movements and hissing with the tongue. Individuals receiving ministry often report sensations of cold, physical weight or pressure, numbness or tingling in the hands, and unexplained pains that move around while the minister commands the demons to leave—sometimes inching out toward the extremities, and finally exiting through the fingers or head, as if chased out by the minister's words (Bottari, 2000; Hammond & Hammond, 2008). Francis MacNutt, who traveled extensively in Latin America, Africa, Asia, and the United States, noted that he observed similar manifestations all over the world over the course of decades, including by people who had previously exhibited no signs of psychotic behavior and who had no previous exposure to similar manifestations (2009).

As spirits (*pneuma*), demons often seem to leave through the breath. Usually, the person coughs, but may also yawn, sigh, belch, hiccup, roar, groan, sob, retch phlegm (but not stomach contents), or emit strongly sulfuric flatulence. Some deliverance ministers coach recipients to exhale forcefully to "prime the pump" (Hammond & Hammond, 2008, p. 122) or counsel the person to expel the demons by a "decision of your will, followed by an action of your muscles" (Prince, 1998, p. 213); recipients should likewise refrain from praying in tongues or saying the name of Jesus lest this block the demons' departure. Other ministers report observing similar evidence of the demons leaving with no prodding or suggestion (MacNutt, 2009). Ministers sometimes seek to help the process along by laying a hand on the person's back or stomach to pressure the spirits to come up and out, reportedly provoking the demons to complain of this light physical touch "burning me" (Hammond & Hammond, 2008, p. 94).

Ministry recipients generally report knowing if and when the demons have left. They might sense the moment and location of departure, feel "lighter," or notice that it is suddenly quiet in their head. The real test, however, is whether the individual experiences freedom in the coming days and weeks (Banks, 1987). Ministry sessions conclude with prayers that the Holy Spirit will fill every place once occupied by evil spirits and for any needed physical and emotional healing (MacNutt, 2009). Post-ministry instructions focus on keeping the doors to demonic entry closed through prayer, Scripture reading, support from a Christian community, readiness to forgive, and avoidance of situations likely to bring temptations to sin. If the demons attempt to return to their former house—which is to be expected—the person should resist as Jesus did when he was tempted by Satan—with the Word of God: "Away from me, Satan! For it is written" (Matthew 4:10).

Conclusions

The purpose of interacting with evil spirits is to avoid future interactions. US Charismatics live in a world populated by spiritual as well as material entities, and they strategically interact with both. In addition to praying for healing and deliverance, Charismatics feel free to use medical and psychotherapeutic interventions. They do not generally counsel anyone to stop taking prescribed medications, reasoning that doctors will notice once material treatments are no longer needed (Wimber & Springer, 1986). Not coincidentally, the majority of time spent in a typical deliverance appointment resembles psychotherapy—identifying childhood traumas and progressing from bitterness to forgiveness. This is because Charismatics have intentionally borrowed concepts and practices from psychotherapy (Gallagher, 2020; MacNutt, 2009; MacNutt, 2021; Peck, 1983). Charismatics caution against attempting to cast out rather than integrate dissociated identities or, alternatively, suggest that each personality may require deliverance individually (Larson, 2016). The same person may receive treatment from a family practice physician, a psychiatrist, and a deliverance minister, and report benefits from each encounter.

For Charismatics, interacting with demons offers assurance that there *is* a spiritual world. If the universe is not all molecules and chance, it seems more likely that there is meaning and purpose that transcends the observable world, and that life of the spirit extends beyond the death of the physical body. Much is at stake, since evidence construed as pointing toward the existence of demons likewise implies the existence of God.

References

Anderson, N. T. (1990). *The bondage breaker: Overcoming negative thoughts, irrational feelings, habitual sins*. Eugene, OR: Harvest House.

Ballard, J. (2019, October 21). 45% of Americans believe that ghosts and demons exist. *YouGov*. https://today.yougov.com/topics/lifestyle/articles-reports/2019/10/21/paranormal-beliefs-ghosts-demons-poll.

Banks, B. (1987). *Songs of deliverance*. Kirkwood, MO: Impact Christian Books.

Basham, D. (1996). *Deliver us from evil*. Grand Rapids, MI: Original work published 1972.

Bottari, P. (2000). *Free in Christ: Your complete handbook on the ministry of deliverance*. Lake Mary, FL: Creation House.

Brown, C. G. (2011). *Global Pentecostal and charismatic healing*. New York, NY: Oxford University Press.

Bultmann, R. (1958). *Jesus Christ and mythology*. New York, NY: Scribner.

Chavda, M. (1998). *The hidden power of prayer and fasting: Releasing the awesome power of the praying church*. Shippensburg, PA: Destiny Image.

Cox, H. (1995). *Fire from heaven: The rise of pentecostal spirituality and the reshaping of religion in the twenty-first century*. Reading, MA: Addison-Wesley.

Cuneo, M. W. (2001). *American exorcism: Expelling demons in the land of plenty*. New York, NY: Doubleday.

Daniels, K. (2013). *The demon dictionary*. Lake Mary, FL: Charisma House.

Delbanco, A. (1995). *The death of Satan: How Americans have lost the sense of evil*. New York, NY: Farrar, Straus, & Giroux.

Dickerman, D. (2009). *When pigs move in*. Lake Mary, FL: Charisma House.

Friedkin, W. (director), & Blatty, W. P. (producer). (1973). *The exorcist*. Burbank, CA: Warner Brothers.

Gallagher, R. (2020). *Demonic foes: My twenty-five years as a psychiatrist investigating possessions, diabolic attacks, and the paranormal*. San Francisco, CA: HarperOne.

Graham, G. (1996, December). Angels all around. *Decision*, 3.

Graham, B. (1957, June 18). Satan. *Sermon preached at Madison Square Garden*, New York, NY: Billy Graham Center Archives.

Hammond, F., & Hammond, I. M. (2008). *Pigs in the parlor: The practical guide to deliverance*. Kirkwood, MO: Impact Christian Books. (Original work published 1973).

Hiebert, P. G. (1982). The flaw of the excluded middle. *Missiology: An International Review*, *10*(1), 35–47.

(1978). *The Holy Bible: New international version, containing the Old Testament and the New Testament*. Grand Rapids, MI: Zondervan.

Jackson, J. P. (1999). *Needless casualties of war*. Fort Worth, TX: Streams.

Kylstra, C., & Kylstra, B. (2003). *Biblical healing and deliverance: A guide to experiencing freedom from sins of the past, destructive beliefs, emotional and spiritual pain, curses and oppression*. Grand Rapids, MI: Chosen.

Larson, B. (2016). *Dealing with demons: An introductory guide to exorcism & discerning evil spirits*. Shippensburg, PA: Destiny Image.

Luhrmann, T. (2012). *When God talks back: Understanding the American evangelical relationship with God*. New York, NY: Knopf.

MacMullen, R. (1984). *Christianizing the Roman Empire: A.D. 100–400*. New Haven, CT: Yale University Press.

MacNutt, F. (2005). *The healing reawakening: Reclaiming our lost inheritance*. Grand Rapids, MI: Chosen.

MacNutt, F. (2009). *Deliverance from evil spirits: A practical manual*. Grand Rapids, MI: Chosen. (Original work published 1995).

MacNutt, J. (2012). *Angels are for real: Inspiring, true stories and biblical answers*. Minneapolis, MN: Chosen.

McCloud, S. (2015). *American possessions: Fighting demons in the contemporary United States*. New York, NY: Oxford University Press.

Peck, M. S. (1983). *People of the lie: The hope for healing human evil*. New York, NY: Simon & Schuster.

Pope Francis. (2008, 25 April). Weekly address. Quoted in Rachel Ray, "'Demonic possession is real and victims seeking exorcism should not be ignored': Prominent psychiatrist on the world beyond," *Telegraph*, 3 June 2018, https://www.telegraph.co.uk/news/2018/06/03/demonic-possession-real-victims-seeking-exorcism-should-not/.

Prince, D. (1998). *They shall expel demons*. Grand Rapids, MI: Chosen.

Sanneh, L. O., & Carpenter, J. A. (2005). *The changing face of Christianity: Africa, the West, and the world*. New York, NY: Oxford University Press.

Ten Boom, C. (2008). *Defeated enemies*. Fort Washington, PA: CLC. (Original work published 1962).

Wagner, C. P. (1993). *Breaking strongholds in your city: How to use spiritual mapping to make your prayers more strategic, effective, and targeted*. Ventura, CA: Regal.

Wagner, D. (2000). *How to cast out demons: A guide to the basics*. Ventura, CA: Renew.

Wimber, J., & Springer, K. (1986). *Power evangelism*. Ventura, CA: Regal.

8 Islamic Perspectives on Human Interaction with the Divine, the Sacred, Saints, and the Deceased

Hasan Awan and Carrie York Al-Karam

Human Interaction with the Divine and the Sacred

In order to understand human interaction with the Divine and the sacred within an Islamic worldview, it is important to clarify what is meant by these terms. The two terms, Divine and sacred, are intertwined and are, in fact, essentially one. The sacred name for the Divine in Islam, in its revealed form in Arabic, is Allah. This term was used in ancient Arabia to connote the one and only God, but it received a sacramental function from God's revelation of Himself in this name. It is therefore used with the authority of the Divine revelation of Islam, the Qur'ān, which is considered the final revelation given to the final prophet – Muhammad – who completes the lineage and the circle of prophecy that began with the first man, Prophet Adam. Allah is considered a comprehensive name and connotes the supreme Divine essence (dhāt) beyond all relative qualification, as well as His attributes (ṣifāt) pre-existing before all of creation yet relate with it, and His acts (afʿāl) which interact directly in the world.

As understood in all revealed monotheistic religions, the Divine is the transcendent, supreme, all-powerful, and all-merciful creator of the universe. From a theological perspective, in His essence, God transcends creation absolutely and cannot be said to have an interaction with the created world. But on the level of the Divine attributes and the Divine acts, there is interaction with creation. With Divine attributes such as All-Hearing, All-Seeing, All-Knowing, and All-Loving, which are quite emphasized in Islamic teachings, God is in direct relation and intimately interacting with His creation. Those of His servants who call out to Him and seek His mercy, forgiveness, nearness, help, and guidance, seek Him through calling upon Him through His revealed attributes. In this manner, Divine-human interaction is at its most profound expression.

From an Islamic perspective, not only the Divine, but all of creation is considered sacred, as creation itself, by virtue of its existence, is understood to be the signs of God – pointers to the Divine being who is the substratum and the origin of all creatures. Because all elements of creation are signs of God, it follows that creation itself, in its very essence and form, is sacred because all creation comes from God who is the Sacred (al-Quddus, one of the Names of God). This sacredness of creation extends to all dimensions of beings God has created, from the heavenly realms – stars, planets, and Earth – to jinn (psychic entities made of fire such as demons) as well as humans, both of whom sometimes act against universal and Divine norms. The free will by which they do so must be placed within the context of God's sacred will and Divine plan for all of creation. This understanding does not prevent a human being or jinn from committing morally evil actions, but the very existence of this ability to choose is sacred.

From a more profound spiritual perspective, which is often the perspective of the Sufis, who are Muslims with a mystical inclination, God is not only utterly transcendent – above the created qualities of location, space, and time – He is also profoundly immanent, to the extent that in His pure oneness, it is only He who has the attribute of the Outward. God states in the Qur'ān (57:3) that "He is the First and the Last, and He is the Outward and the Inward". The most profound spiritual commentaries on this verse state that there is nothing more outward than God's presence and nothing more inward than His reality, and there is nothing that is first apart from God and nothing that is last apart from Him. God not only transcends the dimensions of time (first and last) and the dimensions of space (outward and inward), but He is immanently and quite explicitly what He signifies Himself by: first and last, outward and inward. In other words, from the point of view of spiritual unity and ontological and metaphysical reality, if there is anything that is first, it is God, and if there is anything that is last, it is God. If there is anything that is outward – no matter how many outward objects may appear to the physical eye – it cannot be more outward than God. And no matter how inward a thing is, it cannot be more inward than God. These are the insights and realizations that came to the likes of many great Sufis, who can be said to be those who have discovered and realized fully the implications of these Divine attributes of First and Last, Inward and Outward. Consider the following story about a well-known Sufi from the last 100 years, Shaykh Darqawi, which further elucidates this:

> Shaykh Darqawi was meditating on this verse and he asked God, "As to the first, I see this and I witness that You are the first, O Lord. As to the last, I witness everything comes and goes except Your Face, my Lord. As to the inward, I bear witness that You are nothing other than my inward. But as to the outward, and what I see and witness of the outward, I cannot understand nor see that You are the outward." God replied to Shaykh al-Darqawi, "O My servant, if I were not the outward of what you see as outward, then I would not have said it and revealed Myself as outward." It was then, that Shaykh al-Darqawi understood fully what was meant, and he spiritually witnessed God as outward. (Burkhardt, 1998)

This, apart from being a profound spiritual commentary on the previously mentioned verse, is also a great example of Divine-human interaction and in this case, with a human being who has become transparent before the Divine in his spiritual heart. This is an example that encompasses various means of interaction: from reciting Divine scripture, to deeply meditation upon it, to intimate discourse (munajat) with God in a state of mystical witnessing (shuhud). All of these kinds of sacred interactions are predicated upon a meditative state awakened through spiritual practices such as invocation (dhikr), supplication (du'a), and ritual prayer (salat). This leads to the purification of the inner consciousness – a transparency of the heart – of a human being before the Divine presence, which is actually always present and directly accessible through the faculty of Spirit. This is considered both an acquired grace and a grace by Divine bestowal.

The Divine's Interaction with Creation

As previously mentioned, the one, monotheistic God is understood in an Islamic worldview as the Divine essence (dhāt), the Divine attributes (ṣifāt), and the Divine acts (af'āl). It is on the level of the Divine Self-disclosure as the names of God and as the acts of God that God interacts with His creation. God stated, through Prophet Muhammad (peace and blessing be upon him), "I was a hidden treasure, and I loved to be known, so I created the world in order that I be known" (see Ibn, 1998 and Rumi, 1926). This ḥadīth qudsi (saying of God in the first person through the speech of Prophet Muhammad) comprehensively and succinctly outlines the very raison d'être of creation: That God wished to actually know Himself in an entification apparently outside Himself – in other words, as an object. From this point of view, one of the most profound explanations of this statement comes from a highly regarded and authoritative Sufi Master, Ibn (1998) 'Arabī, in his commentary on Prophet Adam. In his Fuṣūṣ al-Ḥikam, he states:

> The Real [God] willed, glorified be He, in virtue of His Beautiful Names, which are innumerable, to see their identities – if you so wish you can say: to see His Identity – in a comprehensive being that comprises the whole affair insofar as it is possessed of existence and His Mystery [Sirr] is manifest to Himself through it. For the vision a thing has itself in itself is not like the vision a thing has of itself in another thing, which will be like a mirror for it; indeed, He is manifest to Himself in a form accorded by the locus seen, which would not have manifested to Him without the existence of that locus and His self-disclosure to it.
>
> (Dagli, 2004)

This modality of interaction, termed "self-disclosure" (tajalli) points to the reality that God Himself is the inward and outward of an apparent created object and that the purpose of creation is ultimately for Him to know Himself outside of Himself – as if this could be possible. The paradox lies in the apparent separative reality of all of creation, especially the human being, who is endowed with a spiritual nature, or the nature of Spirit: a consciousness and an intelligence that is capable of knowing the fullness of God through a profound and subtle connection with God that is termed the "trust" (amānah) in Qur'ānic discourse, as well as the Spirit (rūḥ) and the secret/mystery (sirr). And although other modalities of creation are able to objectify some aspects of God's attributes, it is only the human being that is capable of reflecting all of the revealed attributes of God, as if a mirror. The metaphor of a mirror is often used explicitly or implicitly in Islamic teachings, including ḥadīth and in certain verses of the Qur'ān where God states that He created man in His image, or rather in His forms (bi sūratihī). Therefore the first interaction that God has as the Sacred with the sacred, as apparently outside of Himself, is with all of creation in principle. Creation, in and of itself, is considered the first sign of God, the first "book of God," in which He manifests and exteriorizes – as an apparent other – His diverse attributes and names into differentiated objective forms. The synthesis of these forms is the human being, in his outward but especially in his inward dimensions: his soul (nafs); his heart (qalb), which is his psycho-spiritual center; and his spiritual reality (rūḥ), whose inmost dimension of consciousness and presence with God is designated the secret (sirr). In many ways, the human being is a symbolic mirror for and of God, just as God is a mirror for and of Man.

According to another hadith qudsi, whose validity is somewhat contested by critical hadith methodology but is of great importance to Sufis, especially Shaykh 'Abd al-Qādir al-Jilānī, who is known as the supreme helper among the Saints, God stated "I am man's secret, and man is My secret" (Holland, 2000). It is through this secret that there is interaction and communication between the Divine and the human, in a way that is unparalleled and incomparable with the manner in which God interacts with other creations or modalities of His Self-disclosure.

Presence: Divine-Human Interaction

One way of appreciating Divine-human interaction is through an understanding of the Islamic term ḥuḍūr, which may be defined as the Divine presence with humanity and humanity's presence with the Divine. These two presences are in reality one presence, but they are bridged by prophetic presence, which is the first and most authoritative modality of Divine interaction with human beings. The agency of prophecy and revelation is the primary means through which God has communicated Himself. According to Islamic teachings, access to the epistemological ways of interacting with God is primarily determined by the authority of prophecy and revelation. In other words, in principle, every human being has access to the Divine directly, but that access is either obscured or obstructed by human beings' forgetfulness and apparent distance from God. Therefore, the Divine authority of prophecy is needed to bridge this gap of miscommunication and obstructed witnessing and listening in order to fully realize and sustain meaningful and salvific interaction with God in this life and posthumously. This process of self-purification and transparent reflection is a process of having a presence with God, which is facilitated through the prophetic presence. The authority of prophecy comes from God's own intent to communicate Himself and not from an independent effort of human beings to communicate with the Divine. This is an important aspect of Islamic teachings that is often overlooked in the modern field of comparative religion, especially when it seeks to define religion as an attempt of human beings to reach out to God. Rather, it is God Himself Who intentionally and actively, and thereby authoritatively, communicates first with human beings after creating them. Yet, due to the 'mirroring' between the Divine and the human, as referred to above, human beings respond to the Divine communication through a process of outer, social, inner, psychological, and spiritual work, until the human mirror is cleansed of its 'otherness' and reflects the purity of God's witnessing presence: a presence that witnesses itself in an apparent other.

This agency is called prophecy (nubuwwah) in Islam. It began with the primordial man – Adam – and culminated in its full realization through the prophecy of Muhammad (peace and blessings be upon him). Adam's very being was a modality of prophecy in that he was endowed with a spirit that God breathed directly into his outward human form. It is this very spirit from which the progeny of Adam come into play, all the children of Adam and Eve who are destined to be created and to live in this world. According to Islamic teachings, a primordial covenant with these souls was made when they were in the "loins" of Adam (Qur'ān 17:171). God asked them, "Am I not your Lord?" (alastu bi rabbikum). The souls responded, "Verily, we bear witness" (balā shahidnā). And so, although the soul of each human being bore witness and now communicates that witnessing uniquely, the covenant was made collectively within the context of the primordial Adamic prophecy. Therefore, the primary means of communication between God and human beings is the prophetic presence, which becomes the intermediary for the existence of human souls and their communication with God: first God's communication and then human beings' communication. This is an important point that is often overlooked, and a subtlety that should not be lost sight of in Islamic teachings – that the intermediary of the prophetic presence is the underlying substratum that allows for Divine-human interaction.

After this covenant was made, Adam and Eve lived and rested in the paradise of Eden until they ate the forbidden fruit (or wheat, as is sometimes suggested). Human beings were then sent down to this lower, earthly realm of existence (dunyā). It is at this point that God stated that He would send guidance for mankind, for after eating the forbidden food, the human consciousness was exteriorized from its original Edenic, paradisal state of direct spiritual witnessing. This exteriorization imposed upon human vision a duality between the human subject and the perceived object outside of themselves. This is one of the reasons Adam and Eve perceived their bodily shame and covered themselves, which they had not done before because of their innocence (which was none other than their inward unitary vision of the Real). Then the eye of the heart was obscured – the original spiritual witnessing of God during the primordial covenant and our individual and unique direct interaction with God. Because of this excessive exteriorization of human consciousness, what was needed was a bridge back to God and the Edenic state. This bridge is salvation in the Hereafter in Islamic teachings, but in mystical teachings, it is also considered to be the inner state of sanctity and the prophecy of our primordial and original spiritual witnessing of God, as well as our interaction with Him as prophetic and human presence.

It is to this end that guidance in the form of prophets and revelations was sent, and the underlying religion of Islam, meaning surrendering to God's will, was renewed in different times, places, and contexts until the final revelation came. This final revelation was meant for all of humanity, in principle, until the end of time when human beings return all together back unto God on the Day of Judgment. It is by means of revelation that human beings, on an outer level (worldly and social) and on an inner level (psychological and spiritual), are realigned with the Divine will and the Divine merciful means of reintegrating their souls in order to return to God in a beautiful and harmonious state of being. That which is sacred in human beings – their outer form, but more particularly their inner reality of qalb (heart) and rūh (soul) – is awakened and more fully realized by the grace of following revelation and prophetic guidance and, within that context, following those who have embodied this guidance. The outer and the inner states and actions of Prophet Muhammad (peace and blessing be upon him) become a direct means of realizing Divine favor: The Divine mercy and generosity of communication and guidance as a means of interacting and realizing the inner spiritual dimensions of the human being that were made to communicate and interact with the Divine.

In the first chapter of the Qur'ān, God teaches human beings how to pray: "Guide us to the straight path, the path of those whom You have favored with Your grace, not the path of those who have earned your anger nor the path of those who go astray" (1:6–7). These human beings who have been favored with God's grace and who are on the straight path are essentially the prophets and those who follow them in the prophetic communities. These foremost of followers are considered the Friends of God (awliyā') (known as saints in Western monotheistic traditions and sages in Eastern spiritual traditions). It is these Friends of God who have fully realized human potential and have become a transparent witness to the Divine presence by realizing their own primordial nature (fiṭrah) and by fully embodying the authority of prophetic presence as revealed to them by the teachings or the actual presence of the prophet whom they follow. It is these kinds of human beings, male or female, upon whom the grace and favor of God have been bestowed and whom Islamic teachings see as being in direct interaction with God. These are the Friends of God amongst the prophets (nabiyyin), followed in spiritual rank by the Truthful (siddiqin), and then the righteous (salihin). An Islamic understanding of the Friends of God is expressed in another ḥadīth qudsī in which God says through Prophet Mohammed:

> My servant draws near to Me through nothing that is more lovable to Me than that which is obligatory (farā'iḍ). Then he draws nearer to me through the voluntary acts (nawāfil) until I love him. And when I love him, I am his ears through which he hears, his eyes through which he sees, his hands through which he strikes, and his feet through which he walks.
>
> (Chourief, 2011)

This prophetic tradition, authoritative in practically every Islamic school of thought, speaks of how the servant of God (each and every human being) can potentially interact with God. It is first through the rites of religion revealed through revelation and prophecy, which are made incumbent on the followers of Islam. Then, the intimacy of connection is enhanced or deepened through voluntary acts of devotions – sanctioned in some way by the prophetic tradition. This may ultimately lead to servants who attain a profound degree of spiritual realization in which their own human attributes are annihilated in and subsist through the Divine attributes. This realization, known in Islam as 'Friendship with God' (also known as sanctity or enlightenment or liberation in other traditions) is considered the most profound form of Divine-human interaction. These kinds of human beings, by their realization and their actions, their outward and inward states, their words, and their mere presence, are a grace for mankind and creation. They serve as a kind of direct channel between God and human beings, and are followed by those of the faithful who recognize a spiritual authority in them that they see as being given to them by God. The foremost of these kinds of human beings are prophets, followed by the great saints, then lesser saints, then the righteous, etc.

Human beings who are of this stature are even beyond the righteous (salihīn) and are those who are loved by God (muḥibbīn). They are the realizers of Divine unity, who annihilate (fanā') their lower selves and subsist (baqā') in the Divine presence. These are the Friends of God around whom the Islamic tradition has created schools of spirituality as they are considered to be the most profound embodiments of Islamic wisdom and spirituality. They are inspired to give spiritual sacred formulas derived from the Qur'ān and the sunnah (habitual practice of Prophet Muhammad) and oftentimes inspired from direct visions of him for their followers to use in order to connect themselves to the spiritual authority, resonance, and presence of these Friends who were validated in their lifetime by God, Prophet Muhammad, and by those who recognized their sanctity. It is through these affiliations and connections that many spiritual seekers have discovered their own inner interaction and communication with the prophetic presence as well as their own inner presence, which they discovered by means of the prophetic presence.

Prayer, Communication, and Interaction with Saints and Prophets

The essential means for followers to communicate and interact with the prophets is through the Qur'ān and the prophetic traditions and, for those who are mystically inclined, also the inner spiritual states that were described and passed on by the companions of Prophet Muhammad who were in his direct physical presence. These have become ways of interacting with his spiritual presence. Consider the following hadith in which he stated:

> When a believer asks God to send salutations and benedictions upon me, God permits my spirit to re-enter my body, and the angels approach me, and they communicate to me that "Such-and-such a person has sent benedictions your way. May God send even more his way."
>
> (Al-Husayni, 2015)

This ḥadīth echoes the reality of the Qur'ānic verse "Verily God and the angels send prayers and blessings to the Prophet. O ye who believe, send salutations and benedictions upon him abundantly" (33:56). So the ḥadīth becomes an extension and specific application of the Qur'ānic verse. Note that it speaks of God and the angels in a way that goes beyond time, as if perpetual. God and the angels send salutations and benedictions upon the spiritual presence of Prophet Muhammad. Those who follow and those who have faith are also asked to send these salutations so that they may participate in this sacred interaction and connection with God, the angels, and the Prophet. Notice also in the hadith that when human beings do this after the Prophet has passed away in the earthly realm, his spirit re-enters his body by Divine permissions, and the angels and God tell him who from his community is sending prayers and blessings upon him. This is the ultimate form of communication and interaction of the believer not only with Prophet Muhammad, but with the Divine and the angelic functions and presences. This sets the stage for extending these prophetic blessings to those who have realized the prophetic model inwardly and outwardly, those whom God has favored with His grace, guidance, and sanctification in this life, who in turn are sought out by seekers of the Divine presence, so that they may also become beloved by God.

God states in another verse in the Qur'ān, "Say, O Muhammad, to the believers, that if you love God, follow me. Then God will love you and improve your condition and forgive your sins" (3:31). In other words, the direct connection to following prophetic guidance is considered a condition for Divine love. It is understood from Islamic teachings that God has fully and authoritatively guided all the prophets, and in particular Prophet Muhammad, in such a way that if the Prophet's conduct is followed, one will not stray from God's straight path that leads to the realization of outward and inward harmony. In this way, they become a prophetic mirror of interacting with the Divine presence by fully embodying the prophetic presence and realizing their original primordial presence as witnessing the Divine at the dawn of each human being's creation as was recounted in the story of the primordial covenant.

Prayer, Communication, and Interaction with the Departed

According to Islamic teachings, just as one is able to communicate in some way and interact spiritually with Prophet Muhammad (although the various theological schools in Islam differ as to the degree and extent of this interaction), this model is extended to those who have been favored by Divine grace to realize the love of God and Friendship with God by fully embodying the prophetic model. These human beings who are so favored are followed for the sake of the spiritual wisdom and counsel (naṣīḥah) they offer in their lifetime, and some of their followers may wish to spiritually connect themselves to a particular Friend of God, who may be linked to a spiritual chain (silsilah) of transmission, authority, and benediction going back to the original founder of a spiritual school (ṭarīqah Sufism), and ultimately to the Prophet's spirituality. After these favored human beings physically depart this world through death, a connection to them can be maintained, according to certain Islamic schools of thought. This connection is through the prayers and the teachings that they have left behind and through dreams and other modalities of visions, sometimes in the waking state. There is a precedence for such connection in the Qur'ān, the sunnah, and the stories of the companions and the righteous of the early generations of Islam (salaf al-ṣāliḥ). Not only do the departed Friends of God have this ability to communicate with other human beings who are alive, but as a general principle, all human beings can in some way communicate and even benefit the departed to whom they were connected by bonds of family or love.

According to unanimous Islamic belief, after the primordial covenant with Adam, human souls enter the intermediate realm (barzakh). They are then physically "born" into this life. When they die, they return to the barzakh, where they await the Day of Judgment when they will be called forth and reborn as spiritual and physical presences directly interacting before the Divine audience. Barzakh is analogous to an objective world that could be considered the subtle realm or the psychic dimension. It is an objective dimension in Islamic teaching, but it is also a realm to which every human soul is connected subjectively or microcosmically through the dream world. It is by these means that one can communicate in some way, by the Divine permission, with loved ones, often in dreams or sometimes upon visiting the dead in their graves and making prayers for them, all of which is considered a sunnah (with some differences of opinion among certain schools).

There are also many ḥadīth about the doctrine of perpetual charity (ṣadaqah jāriyah), which can help the deceased in their posthumous states by them having performed certain acts of charity in this lifetime, such as the knowledge that they imparted or the donations they made. These acts help their station (maqām) with God in barzakh until the end of time comes. Another example of such perpetual charity in action can be seen in the companions of Prophet Muhammad (peace and blessings be upon him), who were the first to enter Islam and who invited others to follow his way. Since they were the first, they will continue to receive "karmic blessings" until the end of time when someone enters Islam. Such blessings for these companions have increased exponentially to the present day, as Islam is a living reality as a contemporary world religion, second in population to Christianity.

Human Presence

As alluded to above, the interaction between the human and the Divine is realized through the inner dimensions of the human being: the human body (outer form), the soul (nafs), the psychospiritual center of the human being (qalb), and the Divinely endowed spirit consciousness (rūḥ). It is by virtue of these subtle faculties that a human being has been given the trust (amānah) by God to directly know God and to interact with Him by sensing in some way and even witnessing, listening to, and communicating with the Divine presence. While the physical body is the most outward manifestation of the human being, the soul is an intermediate faculty – very much aligned to the barzakh – that reflects the needs and the awareness of the physical body and its interaction with the world and other human beings or other modes of physical creation. But in particular, it is the human heart, the psychospiritual center of the human being, that was made primarily to know God.

According to one of the most influential scholars in the Islamic intellectual tradition – Imām al-Ghazālī – the human heart was created for the sole purpose of knowing God. This locus of the Divine presence – the heart – is predicated upon the reality of the Divine Spirit (rūḥ), that in some way originates in God and was inspired into the first human being, Adam, and by virtue of that, given as a sacred trust (amana) to each human being. It is this spirit that is considered in certain Sufi and philosophical schools of Islamic thought to be the original prophetic substance that facilitates the created order, prophecy, and the human return back unto God via salvation in the hereafter or sanctification here and now (wilāyah). These faculties of the human being have been addressed directly in the Qur'ān itself, and Islamic teachings unanimously affirm their reality, although understandings and application vary among schools. Schools that focus on the contemplative and spiritual, even intellectual, dimensions of Islamic teachings emphasize and make more explicit the functions of the spiritual heart (qalb), spirit (rūḥ), and secret (sirr). It is by virtue of these faculties that there is a direct and intimate interaction and communication with the Divine. In principle, every human person, Muslim and non-Muslim, has access to these levels of their being, although, in fact, only those human beings who have in some way purified themselves of their own base human qualities are able to benefit from such interaction. In certain Sufi teachings, it is stated that the Divine intimations (wāridāt) that God sends as interaction and communication with the human soul are always present from the Divine side; it is the human side that is absent because it is veiled from its own inner intellectual and spiritual faculties. When the heart awakens to its Divinely intended purpose of knowing God (ma'rifat Allah), it awakens to the already present intimate discourses (munajat) with God.

The more one follows the grace of revealed religion and purifies oneself through that which is incumbent through the Divine command, and the more one furthers or deepens this purification of the heart through devotional practices and self-reflection, contemplation, or meditation, the more transparent one becomes to the Divine presence and the more presence of heart one has with God – thus, the more interaction with the Divine presence. There is a profound listening and presence with God that occurs. The Qur'ān and the sunnah speak of being absorbed in the Divine presence and of Prophet Muhammad (peace and blessing be upon him) having a special moment with God in the night. It is understood within the mystical and contemplative dimensions of Islam that this access is given through the wakening of one's spiritual heart and one's inner secret through the grace contained in the Divine means of prophecy.

Of course, the prophets have a much more profound and authoritative openness to the Divine, by the permission of God, then is reachable by other human beings. However, those who follow their teachings with sincerity and humility are graced with a deep degree of realization of their spiritual presence and their secret with God. Recall God's statement "I am man's secret, and man is My secret." In other words, the secret between God and Man is, quite literally, the secret (sirr) contained within the essence of the human heart and spirit, the very goal or purpose of human existence. Yet this secret is uniquely discovered and realized by each individual human soul, which has been uniquely created and uniquely invested with the Divine trust. This is one of the implications of the primordial covenant previously discussed. The goal is to discover this secret, one's spiritual presence with God, and to live life in the now of the unfolding of this secret as God's vicegerent on earth, thereby fulfilling the primordial covenant and achieving our original realization – our primordial witnessing of God in pre-eternity. According to a particular mystical commentary, one of the reasons human beings accepted this sacred trust with God was that they understood that it would be God Who would take care of it, due to God's love for human beings: "And in essence, the very purpose of the human being is to realize the essence of the human heart, which is none other than the direct knowing of God" (Chittick, 2013). Not only does the human being witness God's presence, but God also witnesses the human's presence, which in reality is His own presence in an apparent other. This is the mirror of the human spiritual heart, thus fulfilling the Qur'ānic verse: "Verily We created jinn and mankind only to worship Me" (51:56), which in the original commentary by Ibn (1998) 'Abbās is understood to mean "to know Me." This also relates back to the aforementioned statement, "I was a hidden treasure, and I loved to be known, and so I created the world so that I may be known". Loving to be known is fully realized in the human heart, a reality that is accessible to every human being, Muslim or non-Muslim, in principle and, God willing, in fact.

References

Al-Husayni, A. (2015). *Bayhaqi hadith collection, as found in sending prayers upon the prophet*. Meppal, Netherlands: Sunni Publications.

Burkhardt, T. (1998). *Letters of a Sufi master*. Louisville, KY: Fons Vitae.

Chittick, W. (2013). *Divine love: Islamic literature and the path to God*. New Haven, CT: Yale.

Chourief, T. (2011). *Bukhari hadith collection, as found in spiritual teachings of the prophet*. Louisville, KY: Fons Vitae.

Dagli, C. (2004). *The ringstones of wisdom*. Chicago, IL: Kazi Publications.

Holland, M. (2000). *The book of the secret of secrets and the manifestation of lights*. Oakland Park, FL: Al-Baz Publishing.

Ibn, A. (1998). *Al-Futuhat Al-Makkiyya*, Vol 1–4. Beirut, Lebenon: Dar Sadir.

Rumi, J. (1926). *Mathnawi* (Vol. 1, R. A. Nicholson, Trans). London: Cambridge University Press.

Part III

Medical, Technological, and Scientific Considerations

9 Love and Healing

Larry Dossey

One of the wisest lessons I learned in my medical education came not from a professor or a textbook but from graffiti. The message was scrawled on the inside door of the men's room in the interns' on-call quarters at Parkland Memorial Hospital in Dallas. Sitting on the toilet, the words stared you in the face: THE SECRET TO PATIENT CARE IS CARING FOR THE PATIENT. [I learned later that this aphorism is attributed to Harvard physician Francis Peabody (1881–1927).] The first time I saw this graffito I was stunned. I had never heard anyone in medical school talk about the importance of love and caring. Which of my colleagues had had this insight? Why had he taken the trouble to scribble these words? It was ironic that he had announced his observation about caring in the secrecy of a men's room. Was a restroom wall the only place in this huge hospital where he could express a matter of the heart? Was caring so controversial that it was being driven into the toilet?

Love may be the most overworked term in our culture; but remove it and its relatives—caring, empathy, and compassion—from medicine, and our hospitals and clinics become houses of horror.

"During the 1930s, my grandmother saw a specialist about a melanoma on her face," writes medical ethicist E. J. Cassell:

> During the course of the visit when she asked him a question, he slapped her face, saying, "I'll ask the questions here. I'll do the talking." Can you imagine such an event occurring today? Melanomas may not have changed much in the last fifty years, but the profession of medicine has.
>
> (Laine & Davidoff, 1996)

A similar example was related to me by my wife Barbara, who is a cardiovascular nurse, educator, and author. She was taking care of an 80-year-old man who had been admitted to the coronary care unit for what proved to be a fatal heart attack. An hour following his admission, his no-nonsense cardiologist stormed through the swinging doors into the waiting area where the patient's elderly wife, realizing her husband was dying, sat weeping. The doctor was in a rage. "Your husband is doing terribly!" he blustered. "He refuses to cooperate with anything I'm doing for him!" The woman did not know how to respond. Eventually, she managed to offer through her tears, "Doctor, I'm sure he doesn't mean it. He's such a good man! Please don't feel badly toward him" (Dossey, 2019).

Hospitals should ideally be temples of compassion. But in the frenzy of high-tech medicine, we physicians who work in them too often take our eyes off love—with disastrous results, as in the following case from an article with the intriguing title "Death by Destruction of Will," reported in the prestigious *Archives of Internal Medicine* (Robinson, 1995):

> A 93-year-old woman was admitted involuntarily to a psychiatric hospital's geriatric unit for increasing impairment in memory and deterioration of the conditions of her home, where she lived alone. She was functionally independent in the unit, and was bright, cheerful, and loving toward the staff. After 2 uneventful weeks in the unit, she was moved to a medical hospital for evaluation and management of anemia and stools positive for occult blood. When seen by the examining team, she denied symptoms of illness, telling them, "I'm as healthy as you are." Findings from the physical examination revealed a hard, 4-cm abdominal mass in the right lower quadrant.
>
> Laboratory investigations revealed [significant anemia] ....
>
> Plans were made for a [colon X-ray] and transfusion. Almost immediately, problems began to develop with the patient's desire to move about and her tendency to forget about her intravenous lines. A vest restraint was first applied, which led to agitation and struggling.... Leather restraints were applied to her hands and feet. ...[A]n altercation occurred when [she] got out of her restraints, bit her intravenous line in two, and moved quickly down the hall. Security guards were called... and she was subdued after a significant struggle. She was again placed in four-point restraints.
>
> After this altercation, a dramatic change in her affect and demeanor was noted. She appeared despondent and broken. She told the house officer she was dying "because God willed it." The next morning, her restraints were removed, her medical orders were revised, and a sitter was hired to eliminate the need for restraints. Her son visited that day and was distraught at the psychological change he saw in his mother. [He] stated that he believed that the hospital was killing her, and that she had lost her will to live.
>
> Later on the third hospital day, an initial attempt at a barium enema was unsuccessful.... [She was transfused].... [A] repeated chest [Xray] showed an [abnormal area] in the right upper lobe with a suggestion of cavitation [suggesting tuberculosis]. The patient was then placed in isolation, and ... empiric treatment for possible pulmonary tuberculosis [was suggested].

...She seemed minimally ill and was eating reasonably well and moving about in her room. On the fifth hospital day...however, her statement...was, "I am going to die." She was found without pulse and respiration [three hours later]...; cardiopulmonary resuscitation was attempted but was unsuccessful.

At autopsy, a...carcinoma of the cecum was identified without evidence of local or remote spread. A small area of consolidation was identified in the right upper lobe of the lung...[C]ultures...were negative.... No evidence of heart disease was found. Examination of the brain revealed no occlusions, softening, tumor, or hemorrhage.

When the case was later discussed, the members of the house staff involved in her care demonstrated no awareness of any potential link between the events of her treatment, her changes in affect and behavior, and her death [emphasis added].

Tampa physician Bruce E. Robinson, the author of this report, concludes with the sobering comment, "This woman's story serves to remind us of the critical link between mind and body, and of the mortal consequences that are possible when we forget." And we will keep on forgetting unless we are able to make a place in healing for love and empathy.

Empathy "refers specifically to the ability of physicians to imagine that they are the patient who has come to them for help" (Gianakos, 1995). It is the ability to share in another's emotions and feelings. If empathy had been present, it would have allowed the team caring for the 93-year-old woman to ask, what did *she* want? What was the hospital experience like for *her*? Would it have been more compassionate to allow her to pass her remaining days peacefully and not subject her to the rigors of a "workup"? Because the house staff was unable or unwilling to share her feelings, their evaluation took on all the sensitivity of a runaway freight train.

There is a tendency in modern medicine to view love as a frill or luxury, or as something that gets in the way of a rational approach to patient care. This is a serious miscalculation. The presence or absence of love can involve life-or-death consequences. This was dramatically demonstrated in a report from the Oklahoma Medical School Hospital, where Drs. Stewart Wolf and William Schottstaedt were conducting metabolic studies examining the role of human interaction on serum cholesterol levels. One of their patients was a 49-year-old man who had had several heart attacks and a history of chaotic relationships. During the hospitalization,

...the patient seemed happy and reasonably relaxed, although very eager to please during the first few days of the study while receiving daily visits from his new woman friend. When she left town for a few days without telling him, however, he became anxious. Serum cholesterol concentration rose somewhat until she returned, revisited, and reassured him. During this visit, however, she had met another man whom she preferred. Her daily visits to the patient fell off and... she told him that she had abandoned the plan to marry him and would not see him again. He became intensely depressed. Again the serum cholesterol rose and the following day he had a recurrent myocardial infarction. Four days later he died.

(Wolf, 1962)

A Lesson in Love

Of course, it isn't just physicians who forget the importance of love and empathy; educators, lawyers, politicians, law enforcers, and perhaps every other professional group could be added to the list. In spite of our frequent lapses in love, I believe medicine remains one of the most caring professions in contemporary culture. There continues to exist an unbroken lineage of healers in medicine who have always known the importance of love and compassion in healing.

I was given a lesson by one of them during my training in internal medicine at a very large Veterans Administration teaching hospital. The workload was burdensome—a steady stream of new patients, day and night, without end. After a particularly grueling day, I bumped into a fellow intern around two a.m. in the on-call room as we were collapsing into bed. Blind with fatigue and in a foul mood, I began to complain about how the patients used the hospital as a revolving door. After they were discharged following treatment for a particular medical problem, they would resume destructive behaviors such as unbridled smoking and drinking, which would lead inevitably to further hospitalizations for heart disease, emphysema, cirrhosis, and worse. My colleague listened patiently while I vented. When I finished, he said thoughtfully, "You're right; they *are* unredeemable. But I *love* them. In fact, I could work here all my life." I was speechless. Had sleep deprivation overcome his good judgment? "I like the old patients the best," he continued. "Even their little problems. Their hemorrhoids are just as important to me as their heart failure. When their bowels won't work right, I'll be there to help. When their nails get too long, I'll trim them. If they need a haircut or a bath, I'll make sure they get it." I was beginning to feel like a sinner in the presence of a saint. "Some of them will never change their habits. They'll always keep coming back. It doesn't matter. They're wonderful."

When we completed our training, my colleague and I went into medical practice together. He has remained for me an icon in many ways—the consummate physician who embodies not just technical competence but also wisdom, compassion, empathy, and love.

Love and Chocolate

Where are love hormones?

(Lynch, 1979)

We have no "emotion meters" that can measure our feelings directly, yet we know that our emotions affect our bodies. We *feel* rage, hostility, and anxiety; we *know* when these emotions flood our bloodstream with hormones, and when showers of electrical signals impact various organ systems. Love is also linked to biochemicals in the brain—norepinephrine, serotonin, and phenylethylamine. Interestingly, the latter chemical is found in high concentrations in chocolate. This is the reason, some unromantic materialists say, why we purchase chocolates on Valentine's Day and give them to those we want to love us. We're trying to influence them chemically: love as a drug deal.

We want to believe that the passion of Romeo and Juliet is more than endocrinology. But are we fooling ourselves through wishful thinking?

One of the greatest mysteries surrounding the chemical view of emotion is why we should feel anything at all. David J. Chalmers, a mathematician, philosopher, and cognitive scientist, points out that no one knows why electrochemical events in the brain give rise to any conscious experience whatever—to love or any other emotion (Chalmers, 1995). There need be no "feeling" to chemical reactions. When chemicals interact in a test tube, presumably the test tube doesn't feel them. Why doesn't the brain do its job without feelings of any sort, like a computer? An unfeeling machine would be more efficient and predictable than one that sulked, became manic, or fell in love.

When my colleague was confronted with his patients' myriad problems, why did he experience love? Why not simply attend to the hemorrhoids and heart failure automatically, like an unconscious machine? The tendency in modern medicine has been to ignore questions of this sort and to replace the idea of consciousness and emotional experiences with brain chemistry. A sampling of this point of view comes from psychologist Lawrence LeShan's book *The Dilemma of Psychology*: "A leading psychotherapist, Lawrence Kubie, writes, 'Although we cannot get along without the concept of consciousness, actually there is no such thing.' A leading neurophysiologist, Karl Lashley, puts it: 'The knower as an entity is an unnecessary postulate.' A leading psychologist, D. O. Hebb, writes: 'The existence of something called consciousness is a venerable *hypothesis*, not a datum, not directly observable…'" (LeShan, 1990).

For an increasing number of thoughtful scientists, however, consciousness cannot so easily be dismissed. An example is Nobel physicist Steven Weinberg, who writes about a "theory of everything" from which all there is to know about the universe can be derived. Weinberg concedes there is a problem with fitting consciousness into a "theory of everything," because consciousness does not seem derivable from physical laws. Since consciousness won't fit, a physically based theory of everything cannot be complete. So a final theory must contain some additional fundamental element. "Toward this end," Chalmers states, "I propose that conscious experience be considered a fundamental feature, irreducible to anything more basic" (Chalmers, 1995). Chalmers and others have proposed that consciousness take its place alongside matter and energy as fundamental features of our universe. These developments in contemporary thought are crucial for medicine—for unless we can go beyond brain chemistry and find a place for consciousness, love will never have a home in our modern models of healing.

There are some very practical reasons for taking consciousness seriously in medicine, aside from the fact that we *feel* conscious. For the past several decades, evidence has gradually accumulated that conscious mental intent can influence events not just in the body, but also in "the world out there"—and that these events can be empowered by love.

Love in the Lab

In the late 1960s and early 1970s, pioneering work began in the field of biofeedback. Researchers soon discovered that quite ordinary individuals could learn to control their heart rate, muscle tension, and skin temperature if given moment-to-moment feedback by electronic instruments that were measuring these events. Although biofeedback is now considered commonplace, at the time it was heretical. It contradicted the conventional wisdom that these bodily events were autonomic, always silent, and uncontrollable by the mind.

Soon reports began to surface from various biofeedback labs that something strange was going on. When researchers asked subjects "how they did it," they were unable to explain. But when subjects were asked *how they felt* when they were successful, they often responded with statements such as, "I felt at one with the instruments." Some went further, saying they felt inseparable from the instructor, the room, "and everything else." Some researchers realized the subjects were expressing the universal experience of mysticism, which has been defined as "becoming one" or uniting with everything there is (Underhill, 1961a).

Falling in Love with a Machine

Similar observations have cropped up in other types of laboratories as well. The late Robert G. Jahn, former dean of engineering at Princeton University and director of the Princeton Engineering Anomalies Research (PEAR) laboratory, and his team have observed millions of trials in which individuals attempt to influence the performance of sophisticated electronic instruments. Their results indicate that ordinary individuals can mentally influence the machines' performance under controlled conditions. How do they feel when they do it? Jahn:

> The most common subjective report of our most successful human/ machine experimental operators is some sense of "resonance" with the devices—some sacrifice of personal identity in the interaction—a "merging," or bonding with the apparatus. As one operator put it: "I simply fall in love with the machine." And indeed, the term "love," in connoting the very special resonance between two partners, is an apt metaphor ....
>
> (Jahn, 1995a)

Some scientists believe love has no place in objective science. Jahn disagrees. "[A]llusions to [love] can be found in scientific literature, none more eloquent than that of Prince Louis de Broglie, one of the patriarchs of modern physics" (Jahn, 1995b)—who said,

> If we wish to give philosophic expression to the profound connection between thought and action in all fields of human endeavor, particularly in science, we shall undoubtedly have to seek its sources in the unfathomable depths of the human soul. Perhaps philosophers might call it "love" in a very general sense—that force which directs all our actions, which is the source of all our delights and all our pursuits. Indissolubly linked with thought and with action, love is their common mainspring and, hence, their common bond. The engineers of the future have an essential part to play in cementing this bond.
>
> (De Broglie, 1962)

Love and Resonance

Resonance is a widespread feature in nature. Jahn states,

> All manner of physical systems, whether mechanical, electromagnetic, fluid dynamical, quantum mechanical, or nuclear, display capacities for synergistically interactive vibrations with similar systems, or with their environment. Coupled harmonic oscillators, all common musical instruments, radio and television circuitry, atomic components of molecules, all involve this "sympathetic" resonance, from which strikingly different properties emerge than those that characterize their isolated components.
>
> (Jahn, 1995c)

What does it mean to say that all manner of physical systems are in "sympathetic resonance" with each other or their environment? "Sympathy" comes from the Greek *sympatheia, "*feeling together," and "resonance" is derived from the Latin *resonantia,* an "echo. " Is the universe one immense echo of feeling and sensitivity?

Biologist Lyall Watson suggests that a general kind of resonance may pervade the natural world to an almost unthinkable degree. He describes how inanimate objects and lower organisms—stones, cars, bacteria— may "resonate" with humans by taking on our "emotional fingerprints," as he puts it, as a result of prolonged, intimate contact with us. When they do so, they may behave in surprisingly lifelike ways and lead to what Jung called synchronicities—those meaning-filled, unpredictable events we often call "funny coincidences" (Watson, 1992).

Love Is Non-Local

The resonance referred to by Jahn, Watson, and others has unusual qualities. It appears to operate without regard for distance. In the controlled experiments Jahn and his team performed, the subjects are sometimes separated from the apparatus they are trying to influence by global distances—situated literally on the other side of Earth. The findings are consistent: the effects of mental efforts do not diminish with increasing spatial separation. These experiments, and scores of others conducted in laboratories around the world, point to a *non-local* quality of consciousness—some aspect of the mind that is not confined to specific points in space (or time, as suggested in other studies).

Love is often involved when the mind behaves non-locally. One of the commonest examples is the loving resonance that exists between humans and their pets, which defies distance. Researchers J. B. Rhine and Sara Feather collected dozens of accounts of returning animals—pets who find their way back to their owners, sometimes across colossal distances (Rhine & Feather, 1962). These instances cannot be explained by "homing"; the animal often returns to places she/he has never been. An example is that of Bobbie, a collie, who was traveling with a family en route from Ohio to their new home in Oregon, where Bobbie had never been. During a stop in Indiana, Bobbie got lost. After a diligent attempt to find her, the family finally gave up and proceeded westward. Months later, Bobbie appeared at the new home in Oregon. This was not a lookalike animal; she still had her name tag and several identifying marks and scars.

I am particularly fascinated by instances in which animals find their way to owners who are ill. These cases suggest that the capacity to love and care for someone who is sick is not just a human trait, but is widespread in other species as well.

A boy named Hugh Brady, who kept homing pigeons as pets, once found a wounded pigeon in the garden of his home. He nursed the bird back to health, ringed him with identity tag no. 167, and kept him.

The following winter Hugh was suddenly taken ill and rushed to a hospital 200 miles away, where he underwent an emergency operation. He was still recovering when, on a bitter, snowy night, he heard a persistent tapping at the window. He called for the nurse and asked her to open it. When she did, a pigeon flew in and landed with a joyful flutter of wings on Hugh's chest. Hugh knew immediately that the visitor was his bird and a look at the number on its tag confirmed it.

Pigeons are famous for their homing instincts, but on this occasion the bird wasn't returning home—he had tracked his master down to a place he had no knowledge of and had never been to before. How he did it remains a mystery.

(Adamoli, 1991)

Dr. Gustav Eckstein describes a small spitz dog who doubled as a night nurse for his mistress, who was a diabetic. Each night the little dog would curl up in the angle of the woman's arm. He would awaken immediately if her breathing pattern changed, which is one of the telltale signs of ketoacidosis, one of the most dreaded complications of diabetes (Eckstein, 1940). Though not a non-local, distant event (the dog was in sensory contact with his owner), this event illustrates what every pet owner knows: love and caring are not confined to *Homo sapiens*.

If we are to understand how love functions in healing, we shall have to confront the concept of *non-locality*. Although this idea is little appreciated in modern medical science, physicists have gradually made their peace with this concept in recent decades. Rigorous experiments over the past half century have confirmed the existence of non-local phenomena in the sub-atomic domain. For example, if two particles that have once been in contact are separated, a change in one results in a change in the other—immediately and to the same degree. The degree of separation between the particles is arbitrary; they could theoretically be placed at opposites ends of the universe. Apparently, no energetic signal passes between them, telling one particle that a change has taken place in the other, because the changes are instantaneous; there is no time for signaling. The distant particles behave as if they are united as a single entity—paradoxically separate but one.

Telesomatic Events: The Tug of Love

F. W. H. Myers, one of the outstanding scholars and researchers in the budding field of parapsychology around the turn of the century, was impressed by how often love seemed to be involved when individuals communicated across great distances. "Love is a kind of exalted but unspecialized telepathy," he said, "the simplest and most universal expression of that mutual gravitation or kinship of spirits..." (Myers, 1987).

Love has an adhesive quality. It functions as a veritable glue that binds together distant individuals under certain circumstances. This is nowhere more evident than in "telesomatic" events—a term coined in 1967 by neurologist Berthold E. Schwarz (1967) to describe events he observed in the lives of his patients. "Telesomatic" comes from words meaning "the distant body." The term is appropriate because distant individuals often behave as a single body and mind, sharing emotions and physical symptoms at remote distances. When these events occur, the distant individuals are ignorant of what is happening to each other, which makes these events impossible to explain in terms of expectation and suggestion (Dossey. 1995).

Scwharz himself collected around 300 telesomatic cases. Hundreds have cropped up in a variety of publications over the years, some reported in medical journals. Examples:

- A mother who was writing a letter to her daughter, who was away at college. Suddenly her right hand started to burn so severely she could not hold the pen. Less than an hour later, she received a phone call from the college telling her that her daughter's right hand had been severely burned by acid in a laboratory accident, at the same time she (the mother) had felt the burn (Rush, 1964).
- A man and his wife were attending a football game in Berkeley, California. He got up suddenly in the middle of the game and said they had to return home at once because their son had been hurt. When they arrived home they discovered the boy had shot a ball bearing (BB) into his thumb, requiring emergency surgery to have it removed (Stevenson, 1970).
- A woman suddenly doubled over, clutching her chest as if in severe pain, and said, "Something has happened to Nell, she has been hurt." Two hours later the sheriff came, stating that Nell had died on the way to the hospital. She had been involved in an auto accident, in which a piece of the steering wheel had penetrated her chest (Rhine, 1962).

Telesomatic events don't qualify as lab science. They crop up unpredictably in people's lives and cannot be engineered and studied at our convenience. Why take them seriously? There are two main reasons. First, they are quite common; almost everyone seems to have either experienced them, or knows someone who has. Second, they demonstrate an internal consistency that is simply striking. Not only do they occur between individuals at a distance, but they also take place between persons who are loving and empathic with each other—parents and children, siblings (particularly identical twins), spouses, and lovers.

Telesomatic events are non-local expressions of consciousness. They demonstrate the ability of love to reach out through space and time and unite us as one. They show that "connectedness" and "becoming one" are not just poetry or metaphor but concrete reality. They reveal that, at some level of the mind, unity—not separation—is fundamental.

Although we cannot compel telesomatic events to happen so they can be studied under controlled situations, something very much like them *can* be observed under laboratory conditions. In a series of experiments, the encephalograms or EEGs of distant individuals are measured and compared. In the baseline state, there is no correlation between the two EEG patterns. But when the researchers ask the distant subjects to allow a feeling of empathy to develop between them, the EEG patterns frequently take on striking correlations, often becoming almost identical (Grinberg-Zylberbaum & Ramos, 1987; Grinberg-Zylberbaum, Delaflor, Sanchez Arellano, Guevara, Perez, 1992). Similar findings have been found in simultaneous fMRI brain scans between healers and patients (Achterberg, Cooke, Richards, Standish, Kozak, & Lake, 2005; Richards, Kozak, Johnson, & Standish, 2005; Standish, Johnson, Richards, & Kozak, 2003).

Whether we call these shared feelings resonance, empathy, or love, these findings seriously challenge what it means to be an individual—indeed whether, at some levels of mind, there is such a thing.

The Power of Shared Love

> Hate is not the opposite of love.
> The opposite of love is individuality.
>
> (D. H. Lawrence, 1992)

People who share love and affection may be able to accomplish things that are impossible when acting alone. This is the implication of data from the Princeton Engineering Anomalies Research lab. As mentioned, Jahn's team correlated the ability of specific individuals to influence the digital output of electronic random event generators with their psychological states. The highest scores are seen when emotionally bonded couples, who share an unusually deep love and empathy, interact *together* with the electronic devices. They achieve scores up to eight times higher than those of individuals who try to influence the devices alone (Dunne, 1991).

A Universal Spectrum of Love?

One of the greatest discoveries of our century—perhaps of any century—may be the non-local connectedness that exists between the spectacular variety of entities that make up our universe. This connectedness manifests, as we've seen, between sub-atomic particles, mechanical systems, humans and machines, humans and animals, and humans themselves. When this non-local bond operates between humans, we call it "love." When it unites distant sub-atomic particles, what should we call this manifestation? Should we choose a safe, aseptic term such as "nonlocally correlated behavior," or bite the bullet and call it a rudimentary form of love? I am not suggesting that electrons and humans experience love and empathy to the same degree; but we are free to wonder whether the unity of distant sub-atomic particles may be a primordial kind of empathy—a proto-love—which swells in intensity with increasing biological complexity, emerging fully formed as love and compassion in humans. Is there a spectrum of love spanning the entire organization of the physical universe, from the sub-atomic to the macroscopic, human dimension? (See Table 9.1).

Are Love and Empathy Innate?

Not everybody believes that love is innate in nature. Storms of controversy have existed for decades in psychology, for example, about whether our capacity to love and empathize is inborn, or whether these are learned behaviors that develop in response to challenges from our environment. Henry Dreher, in his admirable book *The Immune Power Personality,* has reviewed recent evidence that our capacity for love and empathy, although influenced by learning and environmental factors, has a biological basis (Dreher, 1995a). Jean Piaget, the influential Swiss psychologist, contended otherwise. He maintained that children did not feel empathy until their brains were sufficiently developed until around age seven or eight. Before this time, he maintained, they could not make sense of other people's experiences. But beginning in the 1970s and 1980s, evidence began to accumulate that Piaget may have been wrong. Psychologist Martin L. Hoffman of New York University showed that newborn babies will cry in response to the cries of another infant—but that they barely respond to equally loud computer simulations of babies' cries or even to tape recordings of their own cries. "Virtually from the day they are born, there is something particularly disturbing to infants about the sound of another infant's cry," Hoffman states. "The innate predisposition to cry to that sound seems to be the earliest precursor of empathy" (Hoffman, 1989; Hunt, 1987).

Carolyn Zahn-Waxler, a developmental psychologist at the National Institute of Mental Health, brought together mothers and their infants or toddlers in the lab to observe the children's responses when the mothers or other children were distressed. She asked the adults to drop things or bump their heads to see if the children would comfort them. In a variant of this study, conducted in the home, she trained mothers to simulate pain, fake a cough, act angry or cry, and then rate their own children's reactions. In every instance, children acted upset, and with sounds and gestures tried to comfort their distressed parents. Zahn-Waxler:

Table 9.1 The Universal Spectrum of Love

Interacting Systems	Evidence of Interaction	Expression of Interaction
Humans and humans	Humans interact with each other non-locally—at a distance, without benefit of sensory- or energy-based exchanges of information. Many controlled studies of distant healing intentions and hundreds of telesomatic events and remote viewing have been reported.	Love, empathy, compassion, caring, unity; collective consciousness; the Universal or One Mind; God, Goddess, Allah, Tao, the Absolute
Humans and animals	Scores of studies involving various types of distant healing intent have been done using higher animals as subjects. Lost pets return to owners across vast distances to places they have never been	Love, empathy
Humans and living organisms	Scores of controlled studies have dealt with the distant effects of prayer and other types of positive, distant healing intent, in which various "lower" organisms—bacteria, fungi, yeasts—are the subjects, as well as seeds, plants, and cells of various sorts.	Love, empathy
Humans and complex machines	Humans can mentally influence the behavior of sophisticated electronic biofeedback devices, affirmed by the collective record of over 40 years of biofeedback research in hundreds of laboratories. Humans can also mentally influence random event generators and other electronic devices at a distance, demonstrated at the Princeton Engineering Anomalies Research (PEAR) lab and other institutions.	"Becoming one" or "falling in love" with the machine; interconnectedness; unity
Humans and simple machines	Humans can interact with and influence the behavior of freely swinging pendulums, mechanical cascade devices, and other relatively simple apparatuses at a distance—affirmed by studies conducted at the PEAR lab and elsewhere.	"Becoming one" or "falling in love" with the machine; interconnectedness; unity
Complex physical devices/systems	According to commonly accepted principles in physics, coupled harmonic oscillators, all common musical instruments, and radio and television circuitry interact and resonate with each other. In general, all manner of physical systems—whether mechanical, electromagnetic, fluid dynamical, quantum mechanical, or nuclear—display synergistically interactive vibrations with similar systems or with their environment.	Sympathetic or harmonic resonance
Sub-atomic particles	Sub-atomic particles such as electrons, once in contact, demonstrate simultaneous changes—no matter how far apart—to the same degree. Bell's Theorem, the Aspect experiment, and many others affirm these phenomena.	Non-locally correlated behavior; rudimentary or proto-love?

"We couldn't be sure whether the one-year-old was giving reassurance or seeking it, or both. But in children only a few months older we'd see unmistakable expressions of concern for the other person. The floodgates of altruism open along with the development of language." Summarizing these findings, Dreher states, "What begins in infancy as a reflex develops into the fully formed response we call empathy—a complex cluster of feelings, thoughts and actions... [B]y the second year of life, children demonstrate not only empathy but the altruistic behavior that follows" (Dreher, 1995b).

The capacity for empathy and love, it seems, is written into our biology.

Love's Larger Lessons

> Man can try to name love, showering upon it all the names at his command,
> and still he will involve himself in endless self-deceptions. If he possesses
> a grain of wisdom, he will lay down his arms and name the unknown by the more unknown ... by the name of God.
>
> (C. G. Jung [1965], Memories, Dreams, Reflections)

As we ponder the place of love in our own health, we should bear in mind a few cautions. Love is undeniably useful in healing. It alleviates pain and suffering, and it sometimes sets the stage for physical improvement or cure. As a result of these effects, there is a frequent tendency to try to "put love to work" in the service of healing. But problems can arise as a result of this utilitarian approach. Love's larger lessons can be obscured—lessons that, in my opinion, dwarf whether or not love can be "used" to diminish pain, cure a heart attack or cancer, or heal relationships.

A far greater benefit is that *love provides evidence of who we are.* Love unmasks the illusion of isolation. It often catalyzes the experience of a collective, unitary consciousness—what Nobel physicist Erwin Schrödinger called the One Mind, as described in my books *Recovering the Soul* and *One Mind* (Schrödinger, in Dossey, 1989 and 2013). Through love, we see that at some level human consciousness is unbounded and therefore *non-local*—unconfined to specific points in space such as brains and bodies, or to specific moments in time such as the present moment. Love, thus, shows us that in some sense we are infinite, eternal, immortal, and one. As Jan van Ruysbroeck (1293–1381), one of the most sublime mystics the world has ever known, said, "When love has carried us above all things...we receive in peace the Incomprehensible Light, enfolding us and penetrating us. What is this Light, if it be not a contemplation of the Infinite, and an intuition of Eternity?" (Underhill, 1961b)

The Mystery Remains

Just as the finger that points to the moon is not the moon, all our scientific papers and ruminations will never really capture love. The more we explore it, the more its mysteries deepen. No one knew this better than Jung, with whose words I close:

> In all my medical experience as well as in my own life I have again and again been faced with the mystery of love, and have never been able to explain what it is....No language is adequate....Whatever one can say, no words can express the whole. To speak of partial aspects is always too much or too little, for only the whole is meaningful. Love "bears all things" and "endures all things" (1 Cor. 13:7). These words say all there is to be said; nothing can be added to them.
>
> (Jung, 1965)

References

Achterberg, J., Cooke, K., Richards, T., Standish, L., Kozak, L., & Lake, J. (2005). Evidence for correlations between distant intentionality and brain function in recipients: A functional magnetic resonance imaging analysis. *The Journal of Alternative and Complementary Medicine, 11*(6), 965–971.

Adamoli, V. (1991). *The dog that drove home, the snake-eating mouse, and other exotic tales from the animal kingdom* (p. 116). St. Martin's Press. New York, NY.

Chalmers, D. J. (1995). The puzzle of conscious experience. *Scientific American, 273*(6), 80–86.

De Broglie, L. (1962). The role of the engineer in the age of science (A. J. Pomerans, Trans.). *New perspectives in physics* (p. 231). Basic Books. New York, NY.

Dossey, B. (22 May, 2019). Personal communication to the author.

Dossey, L. (1995). Loading at a distance. *Advances, 11*(4), 48–49.

Dreher, H. (1995a). *The immune power personality* (pp. 271–274). Dutton. New York, NY.

Dreher, H. (1995b). *The immune power personality* (p. 272). Dutton. New York, NY.

Dunne, B. J. (1991). *Co-operator experiments with an REG device* (Princeton Engineering Anomalies Research Technical Note PEAR 91005). Princeton, NJ: Princeton University.

Eckstein, G. (1940). *Everyday miracles*. New York, NY: Harper and Brothers.

Gianakos, D. (1995). Empathy revisited. *Archives of Internal Medicine, 156*, 135–136.

Grinberg-Zylberbaum, J., & Ramos, J. (1987). Patterns of interhemispheric correlation during human communication. *International Journal of Neurosciences, 36*(1/2), 41–55.

Grinberg-Zylberbaum, J., Delaflor, M., Sanchez Arellano, M. E., Guevara, M. A., & Perez, M. (1992). Human communication and the electrophysiological activity of the brain. *Subtle Energies, 3*(3), 25–43.

Hoffman, M. L. (1989, March 28). Researchers trace empathy's roots to infancy. *The* New York Times. Section C, p. 1.

Hunt, M. (1987). *The compassionate beast: What science is discovering about the human side of humankind*. William Morrow & Company. New York, NY.

Jahn, R. G. (1995a). Report on the academy of consciousness studies. *Journal of Scientific Exploration, 9*(3), 393–403.

Jahn, R. G. (1995b). Report on the academy of consciousness studies. *Journal of Scientific Exploration, 9*(3), 403.

Jahn, R. G. (1995c). Report on the academy of consciousness studies. *Journal of Scientific Exploration, 9*(3), 393–403.

Jung, C. G. (1965). *Memories, dreams, reflections* (p. 354). (A. Jaffé, Eds.; R. Winston & C. Winston, Trans.). Vintage.

Laine, C., & Davidoff, F. (1996). Patient-centered medicine. *Journal of the American Medical Association, 275*, 152–156.

Lawrence, D. H.; Quoted in Bell, M. (1992). *D. H. Lawrence: Language and being* (p. 51). Cambridge University Press.

LeShan, L. (1990). *The dilemma of psychology* (p. 84). New York, NY: Dutton.

Lynch, J. J. (1979). *The broken heart: The medical consequences of loneliness* (p. 181). Basic Books. New York, NY.

Myers, F. W. H.; Quoted in Jahn, R. G. & Dunne, B. J. (1987). *Margins of reality: The role of consciousness in the physical world* (p. 343). San Diego, CA: Harcourt Brace Jovanovich.

Rhine, J. B., & Feather, S. R. (1962). The study of cases of 'psi-trailing' in animals. *The Journal of Parapsychology, 26*(1), 1–21.

Rhine, L. E. (1962). Psychological processes in ESP experiences: Part I. Waking experiences. *Journal of Parapsychology, 29*, 88–111.

Richards, T. L., Kozak, L., Johnson, L. C., & Standish, L. J. (2005). Replicable functional magnetic resonance imaging evidence of correlated brain signals between physically and sensory isolated subjects. *Journal of Alternative and Complementary Medicine, 11*(6), 955–963.

Robinson, B. E. (1995). Death by destruction of will. *Archives of Internal Medicine, 155*, 2250–2251.

Rush, J. H. (1964). New directions in parapsychology research. *Parapsychological monographs No. 4* (pp. 18–19). Parapsychology Foundation. New York, NY.

Schrödinger, E.; Quoted in Dossey, L. (2013). *One mind* (pp. 13–15). Carlsbad, CA: Hay House.

Schrödinger, E.; Quoted in Dossey, L. (1989). *Recovering the soul* (pp. 125–139). London: Bantam.

Schwarz, B. E. (1967). Possible telesomatic reactions. *Journal of the Medical Society of New Jersey, 64*, 600–603.

Standish, L., Johnson, L. C., Richards, T., & Kozak, L. (2003). Evidence of correlated functional MRI signals between distant human brains. *Alternative Therapies in Health and Medicine, 9*, 122–128.

Stevenson, I. (1970). *Telepathic impressions: A review and report of 35 new cases* (p. 70). Charlottesville, VA: The University Press of Virginia.

Underhill, E. (1961a). *Mysticism*. New York, NY: Dutton.

Underhill, E. (1961b). *Mysticism* (p. vi). New York, NY: Dutton.

Watson, L. (1992). *The nature of things: The secret life of inanimate objects*. Merrimac, MA: Destiny Books.

Wolf, S. (1962). Changes in serum lipids in relation to emotional stress during rigid control of diet and exercise. *Circulation, 26*, 379–387.

10 Implications of the Emerging Science of Consciousness for Prayer and Divine Experience

Eben Alexander

A major revolution in the scientific understanding of the mind-brain relationship and the nature of consciousness has been brewing for decades, and seems to be approaching a radical inflection point of understanding—in many ways a 180-degree *flip* from the conventional understanding! The success of this major shift in worldview depends greatly on the leading edges of understanding in neuroscience, philosophy of mind, psychology and parapsychology, and quantum physics, all leading to a consilience of these many disparate lines of research that support the fundamental primacy of mind in the Universe. Perhaps not surprisingly, some of the most profound implications of this revolution validate ancient spiritual doctrine, from both Eastern and Western traditions, concerning the oneness of mind and the healing power of love. Consequences of this modern scientific revolution offer explanatory power to those interested in the use of prayer and meditation for healing, ultimately developing a richer interactive relationship with the grand causal forces of the universe.

Cultures tend to take their lead from the dominant metaphysical assumptions of their thought leaders. In the case of our world in the early twenty-first century, the predominant assumptions guiding our culture tend to derive from science and technology, given the extraordinary successes they have provided in the form of modern conveniences (automobiles, aircraft, televisions, telephones, computers, the internet, global positioning systems, modern medical advances, etc.). Over more than a century of what have often been dizzyingly rapid advances in the capabilities of such technologies, the lives of most people on our planet have changed due to these new capabilities. Many of the changes have been for the better for transportation, communication, and health, until one looks more deeply, and finds that technological development has been a double-edged sword, sometimes with a dark underbelly. Corporate greed has fueled significant damage to our global climate. Most obvious is the price we are paying for our addiction to fossil fuels in the form of unprecedented climate change, with worsening droughts and fires, floods, super-hurricanes, and shifts in agriculture that greatly threaten many food supply chains. Around a million plant and animal species are threatened with extinction. This explosion of technological convenience has also resulted in the destruction of life, one example being the lethal amount of plastic pollution that includes a floating gyre of discarded plastics twice the size of Texas choking off life in the eastern Pacific Ocean.

The downside of our culture's worship of scientism (the quasi-religious blind faith that scientific study of the physical world is the only pathway to truth) actually runs much deeper in the effects it has had on our notions of spirituality, and more fundamentally on our very sense of what it is to be human. In fact, the widely accepted public version of science, physicalism (otherwise known as materialism) has been broadly questioned and, by many, discarded due to the leading edges of the science of consciousness studies, including a deep examination of the mind-brain connection.

Although physicalism, and a related Newtonian sense of determinism, has been moderately successful in explaining events in our everyday world, they fail *completely* in attempts to explain the nature of the mind-brain connection, that is, in trying to understand consciousness itself (viz., the "hard problem of consciousness" in philosophy). Many, including several founding fathers of the field of quantum physics, suspect that a vital clue to making better sense of the concepts of contextuality (that the free will choice of the experimenter fundamentally affects the outcome) and the measurement paradox (the act of observation appears to "collapse the wave function" of potential outcomes) both involve recognizing that consciousness is ultimately a fundamental property of the universe.

At a superficial level, we seem to be physical beings interacting with a physical world, yet the leading edges of understanding that natural world, quantum mechanical assessment of the sub-atomic structure of the world around us (and *in* us), shows that our very mental constructs required to explain it all are an intimate part of what we are trying to explain. There is no escaping the confines of our own consciousness, to the extent that it makes little sense to pretend we are encountering an objective, physical reality itself: all we have access to is a heavily-filtered version of some presumed underlying "objective reality" from which it is impossible to extract the intervening layer and influence of our own consciousness.

Some of the proponents of scientific materialism, like Tufts University philosopher Daniel Dennett, go so far as to claim "none of us are conscious: we're all zombies," due to their erroneous belief that our apparent consciousness is nothing more than the chemical reactions and electron fluxes in the cells of the brain, a mere epiphenomenon of physical matter. Of course, one who holds such a view also scoffs at anyone's notion of possessing "free will," given that all of those epiphenomenal thoughts are merely illusions resulting from the specific laws of physics, chemistry, and biology that govern the substance of the brain. Although materialism/physicalism has been evicted from the science of consciousness studies as inadequate for the task (formally the "hard problem of consciousness," which turns out to be an impossible problem for materialist philosophy), it remains firmly entrenched in our culture-at-large, to the great detriment of humanity. Newtonian determinism was so built into the scientific revolution that science-at-large has been painfully slow at adopting the implications of quantum physics for resurrecting our notions of free will and the concrete importance of consciousness in understanding every facet of the reality we are trying to understand. And with free will comes a definite sense of responsibility for our choices—that they matter to the universe. That fact alone seems to frighten some atheistic materialists into willfully ignoring the data countering their position.

A major step in understanding our conundrum is to acknowledge what we called, in our book, *Living in a Mindful Universe* (Alexander & Newell, 2017), the "Supreme Illusion," which is how powerful our brain-mind system is at constructing an internal mental model of what is presumed to be "the world out there," while it is all clearly constructed within our minds. One can argue in the worlds of psychology and quantum physics about how close such a model is to representing any presumed "objective reality," and the scientific answer is we really have no idea what the nature of such an underlying reality might actually *be*. The true nature of space, time, mass, energy, and causality remains quite mysterious, and, I suspect, *very* dependent on our unraveling of the mind-brain relationship. There is plenty of evidence that the model is faulty, but the most crucial acknowledgment is that it is just a model, usually somewhat effective, but never to be taken at face value as "reality." Our inner world is much more than simply a reflection of the outer world: it is truly the only thing we've ever experienced. And we have far more influence over that world by realizing that our attitudes, beliefs, and feelings have a very real effect on that world, including the components we normally think of as "external."

The apparent separation between us as individual human beings and other aspects of the universe, a disconnection that is built into the fundamental tenets of conventional science, has led to tremendous discord in our world, all due to our general tendency to follow science as the lead in living our lives. This false sense of separation allows irresponsible behaviors in the form of warfare, violence against others, economic polarization that allows for wealth to accumulate in the hands of just the top 1 percent, corporate greed that, combined with climate change from our addiction to fossil fuels and choking of our lands and oceans with plastics, all point to our demise.

That science is known as "reductive materialism," meaning that only the material or physical exists, and it is best understood by reducing it down to its simplest sub-atomic particles, determining the laws that govern their interactions, then being able to build in a bottom-up fashion all of the emergent interactions between them that ultimately result in the events we experience in our world. This physicalist view also reduces thoughts, ideas, emotions, feelings, and concepts to the epiphenomenal result of physical interactions without any intrinsic value. Yet the evidence suggests that such bottom-up causality is not the ultimate engine of causality in human lives, that there is in fact a more prominent top-down causality that seems more related to the events that humans experience.

The chinks in the armor of reductive materialism began to appear with the advent of quantum physics in the early twentieth century. Prominent thought leaders in the scientific community, such as William Thompson (Lord Kelvin) in England, even surmised that physics (notably thermodynamics and optics) was almost a complete science at the end of the nineteenth century, and that all that remained was to answer certain quantitative measurements out to a few more decimal places. In a public presentation he made in April 1900, Lord Kelvin mentioned: "two dark clouds" that, in his view, represented the final frontier in completing the work of physics. Interestingly, those clouds, specifically the failure of the Michelson-Morley experiment to detect the luminiferous ether as an expected medium for the transmission of electromagnetic radiation, and the blackbody radiation effect (or "ultraviolet catastrophe"), evolved over the next decade or so into what became the two towering accomplishments of twentieth-century physics: relativity theory and quantum mechanics.

Just three years before Lord Kelvin's presentation, J. J. Thompson had discovered the electron, and the physics community soon realized there might be more substantive discoveries yet to be revealed. With his annus mirabile, or "miraculous year" in 1905, Albert Einstein wrote four papers that injected revolutionary ideas that ultimately enabled those two major fields to come into being. It is quantum physics in particular that has led to such a profound revolution in understanding the relationship between brain and mind, and the nature of consciousness. Given that the inside of our own consciousness is the only thing any of us have ever known, further refinement of our understanding of the nature of consciousness is absolutely essential for any coming to grips with the nature of the presumed underlying "reality."

Many of the founding fathers of quantum physics (Werner Heisenberg, Max Planck, Wolfgang Pauli, Erwin Schrödinger, Pascual Jordan, Eugene Wigner, John von Neumann, among others) began to realize that results from their experiments investigating the most fundamental aspects of the physical world around us, specifically sub-atomic particles such as electrons, protons, photons, etc., revealed them to be decidedly "unreal" in their natural existence. Unlike the billiard ball-like behavior expected of such particles based on the assumptions of Newtonian determinism, they manifested superposition, or the apparent ability to exist in numerous positions simultaneously, all subject to probability waves, until being observed, when that probability wave function would "collapse," placing them in a measured location. Such sub-atomic particles could also become "entangled," such that the spin of an electron or the polarization of a photon created as pairs in certain experiments allowed two such particles to behave as if still connected as one, calling into question our very notions of space, time, and causal relationships.

Such entanglement of sub-atomic particles was called "spooky action at a distance" by Albert Einstein, who proclaimed in a 1935 paper that quantum physics was "incomplete," (Einstein, Podolsky, & Rosen, 1935) and that some form of hidden variables would preserve the notion of "local realism" assumed since the advent of the four-century-old scientific revolution. "Local" implies that all interactions in physics involve particles that interact with each other locally, as opposed to the distant "spooky action." "Realism" implies that the world of things exists out there independently of the observing mind, as opposed to the very act of observation by the mind of the observer being intimately tied in with determining what is ultimately observed.

The history of quantum physics since then has thus been one of defining Einstein's complaint about the incompleteness of quantum physics, with hopes of restoring reason to science by postulating "hidden variables" to explain entanglement. It took three decades for the physics community to respond to Einstein's complaint, but Irish physicist John Bell published a paper in 1964 elaborating a statistical inequality that could be tested in quantum physics experiments to assess entanglement as "spooky action at a distance" or due to hidden variables (Bell, 1964).

Albert Einstein was also very disturbed by "entanglement," because it violated his special theory of relativity by opening the possibility to faster-than-light transmission of information. Beginning with Alain Aspect's experiments in the early 1980s to examine Bell's inequality in an experimental setting, every experiment performed to date to examine the question in an increasingly refined manner has led to the conclusion that entanglement is real and that Einstein was thus wrong. The Universe is entangled and interconnected in very strange ways that defy "local realism." Our four-century-old scientific assumptions of local realism are false—but how to make sense of it all? Introducing the primacy of consciousness in the universe, or objective idealism, provides a profoundly elegant solution to this paradox.

Quantum physicists came to realize that choices made by the mind of the observing scientist—a feature known as *contextuality*—revealed that one could never truly separate the observer from the observed, and, in fact, consciousness itself seemed to possess unique qualities that forever removed it from just being a side-effect of the substance of the brain simply following the laws of physics and chemistry. Mind, or consciousness, required far more than the simplistic notions of physicalism ("brain creates mind") to explain its features.

Quantum physics is one of the most fundamental presentations of the mind-brain question because of what it suggests about the relationship between our mental modeling of the universe (mind), and the physical arrangements we can investigate within that universe (including those in the brain). This investigation includes the boundaries of uncertainty (especially around complementary pairs of parameters measured in sub-atomic particles, like the simultaneous definition of both their position and momentum, or their energy and time flow—Heisenberg's "uncertainty principle"). All of the constituents of that world in microscopic analysis turn out to be decidedly unreal, as one of the founding fathers of the field, Neils Bohr, noted. Molecules, atoms, and sub-atomic constituents do not behave like the large objects they make up. They do not have definite locations in space until observed by a conscious observer, and they can become entangled when prepared together in ways that suggest our very understanding of space, time, and causality does not seem to work the same way in that micro world of the constituents of our physical domain.

The most striking implication of this steady stream of empirical support for objective idealism concerns our very consciousness (awareness of existence), which can no longer be viewed as an emergent result of physical brain activity, but as something more fundamental in the universe. Consciousness is not limited to our bodies, sensory systems, and brains, but, in fact, has a more primordial origin and field of influence that extends well beyond the "here and now" of our physical bodies. In a deep way, the universe is aware of itself, and sentient beings have access to the information assimilated and integrated in that mental layer and can act upon it to alter emerging reality.

The modern scientific study of consciousness seems to suggest that our consciousness, in fact, overlaps with other minds (through telepathy, most easily demonstrable in twins [Playfair, 2002], and shared dreams), even when those minds may no longer be associated with brains existing in the physical world (death-bed visions, after-death communications [Guggenheim & Guggenheim, 1995]). Minds may also glean information distantly (in time *and* space) in our physical world (remote viewing, out-of-body experiences), as well as predict (or actively determine) future events (precognition [Bem, 2011], or cognitively know some future event, and presentiment [Radin, 1997], in which our autonomic nervous system signals some pre-knowledge of a future event). Distance healing and the power of prayer are other profound effects of mental influence on engendering our wholeness. As Erwin Schrödinger and other quantum physicists (Wolfgang Pauli, Werner Heisenberg, Pascual Jordan, John von Neumann, Eugene Wigner, etc.) had foreseen and discussed based on early quantum experiments, consciousness in some ways seems to be one, unified throughout the world, even as we seem to have separate minds in general.

Our culture's heavy dependence on scientism and related materialism has also resulted in a huge casualty in the form of this fundamental belief that we are *separate* from other beings and the world-at-large. This false sense of separation, combined with an overly competitive interpretation of Darwinian evolution, led to much violence, warfare, economical polarization, and general mistreatment of others (including animals). Biologists have come to realize that success in the world depends far more on collaboration and cooperation, not just between members of a species, but between members of different species—not the aggressive and blind competition that early proponents of Darwinism, such as Thomas Huxley, dwelt upon. In fact, one could argue that most of the destructive forces active in our modern world stem from this false notion of separation, one that allows us to harm others by failing to realize that doing so, in a very deep sense, is harming ourselves. A more unified world view, that sees all of the universe connected through its mental layer, will foster a far kinder and gentler world, more peaceful and harmonious, as we all begin to live the truth of our conscious connections with each other and with the universe-at-large.

The "reductive" aspect of reductive materialism is that one has to separate all of the objects in the universe to study and understand them, as opposed to realizing that any such separation degrades our knowledge about the part-whole nature (the *holon* described by Arthur Koestler in his 1967 book *The Ghost in the Machine*) of any object with the universe-at-large, including ourselves. Ultimately, this reduction leads to sub-atomic particles, and an underlying belief of many who subscribe to modern materialistic scientism is that ultimately some form of bottom-up causality, beginning with the laws of physics, chemistry, and biology that rule the natural world thus will yield the events of human lives, all based on those deep underlying principles of the sub-atomic world.

There is much about the emerging science of consciousness based on the leading edges of quantum physics that suggests the universe possesses its own form of conscious self-awareness, and that sentient beings like humans share in that consciousness, but all in a much more holistic and unified form than we commonly imagine. Such a universal mind is primordial and contains within itself such entities as space, time, causal relationships, and emerging physical reality. Much of the science, and certainly some of the most current interpretations of quantum physics, suggests a top-down causal principle that is more directly related to the events of human lives (Ellis, 2018). This fundamental top-down influence is one whose mechanism is broadly delineated through the metaphysical position of objective idealism combined with filter (or transmission) theory of the mind-brain relationship (see the primordial mind hypothesis, Chapter 5 in *Living in a Mindful Universe*).

This top-down causal force is broadly described by those who have encountered it in spiritually transformative experiences, such as near-death experiences (NDEs), as an infinite healing force of unconditional love (viz., God, Allah, Brahman, Vishnu, Jehovah, Yahweh,

Great Spirit, etc.). My own profound NDE, as also reported in some other cases, involved a sense of becoming *One with* that divine source. Such an intimate, personal gnosis through identification is also sometimes accessible through prayer and meditation, given the primacy of consciousness and our sharing of the one mind.

The best models emerging to explain the relevant metaphysical underpinnings fully support the intuitions of the founding fathers of quantum physics about the primacy of consciousness. The bare-bones *relational interpretation* of the measurement paradox in quantum physics proposed by Carlo Rovelli, combined with the metaphysical groundwork supporting objective idealism laid out by Bernard Kastrup (Kastrup, 2019), fully supports the multi-disciplinary argument we made for objective idealism in *Living in a Mindful Universe* (Alexander & Newell, 2017).

The scientific argument for objective idealism (roughly synonymous with metaphysical, ontological, or analytic idealism) laid out in our book extends this supposition of the primacy of consciousness from quantum physics through the support offered from neuroscience (especially the "hard problem" of consciousness first defined by David Chalmers in 1996), philosophy of mind (especially the binding problem, that is the apparent unity of consciousness in "individual" human experience), and the robust evidence for "non-local" consciousness from the worlds of psychology and parapsychology (telepathy, remote viewing, precognition, presentiment, psychokinesis, distance healing, NDEs, shared-death experiences, death-bed visions, after-death communications, past-life memories in children suggestive of reincarnation, etc.). The consilience of all of these lines of inquiry in support of the fundamental role of consciousness in the universe also illuminates the central issue addressed in this chapter, that is the effect of prayer and other means of exploring our mental world and its potential influence on the human events of our world, beginning with our health.

The consequences of this revolution offer valuable insights to those interested in the use of prayer for healing and developing a relationship with the grand causal forces of the universe. One of the most tragic consequences of the reign of conventional scientific materialism over our modern society has been the loss of the mystical, and rich connection with our spiritual nature in general. However, there is reason for hope in much of the emerging science around the nature of consciousness, especially for those who commit to a regular practice of developing their relationship with more primordial aspects of the universal mind by going within (meditation, centering prayer, etc.).

Our modern society has come to value the opinions of specialists, of experts in the field, in seeking a common truth. For much of my life, I thought the deepest answers about the nature of reality would emerge from the science of physics, the study of all aspects of the constituents and interactions of everything in the physical world. That assumption

bypasses a major fact about this world: humans are aware of their perceptions, but these are NOT a direct experiencing of "reality" itself. An
assumed prejudice of the scientific revolution over the last five centuries
is that scientists observe the physical world around them, and determine various laws and causal principles that seem to guide the emerging reality experienced in the physical world. The assumption is that
we, as sentient beings, are separate from that which is being observed,
but many lines of evidence suggest we can never separate the observer
from the observed, and are better off viewing the universe as one system
in which our conscious will as sentient beings has the power to alter the
course of events. In a very real sense, human consciousness is a manifestation of universal consciousness—Each of us is truly One with the
universe!

Ultimately, this line of evidence and its deeper understanding reveals
consciousness to reflect processes that are not simply derivative from the
physical constituents of the brain and body and world around us, but in
fact are crucial in determining the physical facts of that world emerging
influenced by something more than just the physical, chemical, and biological laws that influence the material world. In other words, consciousness and mind cannot simply be reduced to the result of deterministic
principles applied to the physical world (especially the substance of the
brain and body). As William James, the Harvard professor of psychology
at the turn of the twentieth century and father of the modern science of
psychology remarked in his study of human experience, something *More*
is required.

The consilience of conclusions from the neuroscience of consciousness
(specifically the "hard problem" of consciousness), philosophy of mind
(especially the "binding problem" or the curious unity of individual conscious experience), parapsychology (non-local consciousness of all vari-
eties listed above), combined with filter theory, and quantum physics
(contextuality, and the measurement paradox) all point toward a solution
in which consciousness is a fundamental property of the universe that
humans (and all sentient beings) access through the filtering function of
the brain.

This expanded version of mind and consciousness fully supports the
various forms of conscious communication addressed elsewhere in this
book:

1 The cosmic consciousness at the core of all conscious awareness is
   the Deity so often encountered in these extraordinary type of experiences, which ultimately extinguishes one's fear of death through
   demonstration of expanded experience as the body comes to an end
   and liberates the soul.
2 Prophets and/or mystics occasionally serve as the guides encountered during such experiences.

3 The souls of departed loved ones are frequently among those who greet our souls early in these journeys (as in the life review described in over half of NDE cases).

The Primordial Mind Hypothesis provides a framework in which the predominant top-down influence of will from the mental realm suggested through a modern interpretation of quantum physics is accessible via our human minds, but in ways that enable profound expressions of free will, including healing that goes far beyond the expectations of western medicine with its view of healing limited by materialist notions of the molecular mechanisms inherent in physics, chemistry and biology alone. Our human will overlaps with a higher, "universal" will.

People have used various "plant medicines" (psychedelic substances, best termed as entheogens, literally "generating God within") for various forms of shamanic and ritual healing for thousands of years across many cultures. Restrictive laws passed in the 1970s made the use of many such substances illegal for decades, but courageous investigators (and more relaxed legislation) have allowed a modern process of scientifically assessing such modalities and found them to be extraordinarily powerful in a proper therapeutic setting at healing people from alcoholism and drug addiction, as well as rescuing certain cancer patients from a debilitating fear of death. Griffiths, et al., recently reviewed their long experience showing psilocybin can occasion mystical experiences having substantial and sustained personal meaning and spiritual significance, including healing from alcoholism and addiction (Griffiths et al., 2011). These entheogenic substances help to "thin the veil," or allow more ready access to the mental layer of the universe, leaving the ego-mind behind to specifically access the higher soul and primordial mind to harmonize and focus our higher good toward the healing of the whole self.

Modern medical science is no stranger to the concept of mind-over-matter. In fact, for the last seven decades, the placebo effect has served as the gold standard for comparison in the assessment of any new treatment modality through the application of the randomized placebo-controlled trial in seeking data supporting effectiveness. Ask big pharma if the placebo effect is real: for them, it represents an (approximately) 30 percent hurdle at the outset (on average, depending on specifics of the disease or symptoms being assessed), given the degree to which a patient's beliefs that they might be taking a pill that could be of value, in fact, has on their symptomatic and disease status improvement. Outdoing that effect of belief is quite challenging because much of our ability to heal seems to originate within our very beliefs about and desire to get better.

Placebo is not simply about giving someone a sugar pill and getting rid of their headache. In 1993, the Institute of Noetic Sciences (IONS) published *Spontaneous Remission: An Annotated Bibliography,* by Caryle Hirshberg and Brendan O'Regan (Institute of Noetic Sciences, n.d.).

They defined spontaneous remission as "the disappearance, complete or incomplete, of a disease or cancer without medical treatment or treatment that is considered inadequate to produce the resulting disappearance of disease symptoms or tumor." Surprisingly, they cataloged over 3,500 cases gleaned from 800 journals in over 20 languages of these apparently miraculous cases of healing with nothing more than the beliefs of the patient to energize its occurrence.

In her book, *Radical Remission*, Kelly A. Turner, Ph.D., (Turner, 2014) studied over 1,000 cases of cancer remission from the IONS database, to identify nine elements that were present in these cases in large numbers. In addition to elements such as radically changing one's diet, taking control of one's health, and using herbs and supplements, she identified six that are important for this chapter because of their spiritual and emotional nature: following your intuition, releasing suppressed emotions, increasing positive emotions, embracing social support, deepening one's spiritual connection, and having strong reasons for living.

Our very language conspires to deceive us, for this exploration "within" mind, given the primacy of consciousness in the universe and the view of the brain as a filter that allows in a very limited form of that universal mind, is actually an exploration out into the universe-at-large. The notion of a "mental universe" as a top-down ordering principle in quantum physics has been discussed for decades (Henry, 2005). But coming to recognize its influence more fully, especially as our mental human capacities overlap this layer of information assimilation and processing in the universe, allows for a far more robust understanding of our notions of "free will" and of our capacities to influence our emerging reality.

> The first gulp from the glass of natural sciences will turn you into an ·
> atheist, but at the bottom of the glass God is waiting for you.
>   (Werner Heisenberg, 1901–1976, Nobel Prize Physics 1932)

One of the greatest gifts quantum physics brings to humanity through the modern science of consciousness is a resurgence of the notion of oneness as it relates to the structure of the universe, and of our human relationship with it. The overlap of our minds with the consciousness of the universe (primordial mind) matches with the extension of our physical bodies into the physical universe-at-large in an overarching holographic principle of Oneness. Materialism has led us into a false cul-de-sac of presumed limitations. Long the darling of the richest meditative traditions, in both the East and West, Oneness becomes a concrete fact of our understanding of the structure of the universe, elaborated through the science of quantum physics, yet personally experienced through meditation, centering prayer, and spontaneous epiphanies.

Another gift from quantum physics in the setting of modern consciousness studies is that it dismisses the simplistic nonsense of Newtonian determinism so rampant in conventional materialist science, and returns the reality of free will into human endeavors. If consciousness is no longer the epiphenomenal curiosity emerging from the chemical reactions and electron fluxes in the brain, all due to its substance simply following the laws of physics, chemistry, and biology, then thoughts, emotions, and ideas actually gain ground from their outright dismissal by conventional science. In fact, in the emerging conceptualization of objective idealism, they become far more important in gauging the universe that emerges in our lives. The material world is the stage setting on which this drama unfolds, but the realm of the mind is much more important in determining our destiny. It is time to take full responsibility for our thoughts and actions!

The NDE literature is replete with myriad examples of human minds sensing a oneness connection with the most primordial forces of the universe in these deep journeys. Becoming "one with God" might still depend on the refinement of definitions concerning God and consciousness, but to some humans alive today such identification with source deity is a defining feature of their experience of mind. This gnosis of cosmopsychism is actually countered by one's ego-mind, and instead illuminates a far deeper aspect of awareness of existence that thrives within (what I often refer to as one's "higher soul"). Higher soul overlaps and interacts with Primordial Mind, which is the universal consciousness at the core of *all that is*. And the natural result of such a deeper interconnecting world view is manifested through our physical, mental, and emotional healing, or becoming more whole—all through our *spiritual* essence. Hence the power of placebo effect, prayer and meditation (Dossey, 1993; Koenig, 1999), the referral of 12-Step alcohol and addiction recovery programs to a higher power, the healing of addictions and fear of death through psychedelic "thinning of the veil", the miraculous and inexplicable healing often encountered in profound NDEs—all provide a pathway to explain the influence of the will of our higher soul, not just our ego-desires, to come into wholeness. Ultimately, that will is one that merges in these discussions of worldview and especially in the practice of "going within" with what can in many ways be interpreted as the will of God. The purer the unconditional love involved, the purer the form of divine will. As any near-death experiencer will tell you, that binding force of love that is so reassuring as to forever mitigate their fear of death also has infinite power to heal, to bring us into wholeness even in our fractured and confused world. As we refine our notions of consciousness (including related "unconscious" processes, as well as a sense of higher soul and primordial mind), and strive as individuals through prayer and meditation to more fully access these more exotic levels of consciousness, lessons of oneness and love will ultimately contribute to the healing of our fractured world. Recovering our sense of oneness with the universe is the key to the kingdom.

References

Alexander, E., & Newell, K. (2017). *Living in a mindful universe: A neurosurgeon's journey into the heart of consciousness*. New York, NY: Rodale Books.

Bell, J. S. (1964). On the Einstein Podolsky Rosen paradox. *Physics, 1*(3), 195–200. https://journals.aps.org/ppf/pdf/10.1103/PhysicsPhysiqueFizika.1.195.

Bem, D. (2011). Feeling the future: Experimental evidence for anomalous retroactive influences on cognition and affect. *Journal of Personality and Social Psychology, 100*(3), 407–425. https://pdfs.semanticscholar.org/79ec/e4f787af-713d82924e41d8c17ab130f4b22d.pdf.

Dossey, L. (1993). *Healing words: The power of prayer and the practice of medicine*. New York, NY: HarperCollins.

Einstein, A., Podolsky, B., & Rosen, N. (1935). Can quantum-mechanical description of physical reality be considered complete? *Physical Review, 47*, 777–780. https://journals.aps.org/pr/pdf/10.1103/PhysRev.47.777.

Ellis, G. F. R. (2018). Top-down causation and quantum physics. *Proceedings of the National Academy of Sciences of the United States of America, 115* (46), 11661–11663. https://doi.org/10.1073/pnas.1816412115.

Griffiths, R. R., Johnson, M. W., Richards, W. A., Richards, B. D., McCann, U., & Jesse, R. (2011). Psilocybin occasioned mystical-type experiences: Immediate and persisting dose-related effects. *Psychopharmacology, 218*(4), 649–665.

Guggenheim, B., & Guggenheim, J. (1995). *Hello from heaven*. New York, NY: Bantam (ACD Project).

Henry, R. C. (2005). Mental universe. *Nature, 436*, 29.

Kastrup, B. (2019). *The idea of the world: A multi-disciplinary argument for the mental nature of reality*. Hampshire, UK: Iff Books.

Koenig, H. G. (1999). *The healing power of faith: Science explores Medicine's last Great frontier*. New York, NY: Simon & Schuster.

Institute of Noetic Sciences. (n.d.). Spontaneous remission bibliography project. Retrieved April 8, 2021, from https://noetic.org/publication/spontaneous-remission-annotated-bibliography/.

Playfair, G. L. (2002). *Twin telepathy*. Guildford, UK: White Crow Books.

Radin, D. (1997). Unconscious perception of future emotions: An experiment in presentiment. *Journal of Scientific Exploration, 11*(2), 163–180. http://deanradin.com/articles/1997%20presentiment.pdf.

Turner, K. A. (2014). *Radical remission: Surviving cancer against all odds*. New York, NY: HarperCollins.

11 Murder, Truth and Justice, and Religion

Altered Carbon and the Ambiguity of Real Death

Braden Molhoek

In the Netflix series *Altered Carbon*, there are conflicts surrounding communication with the dead which ultimately lead to the question of how death is defined in light of new technologies. This chapter will first highlight the themes raised in the series itself before expanding the discussion regarding the definition of death. The first theme the series deals with is murder. In a world in which human consciousness is stored in an implanted device, it is possible for people to survive even if their body does not (Kobus & Muniowski, 2020). Already within the series, there are terms that point to a redefining of death, with different terms for physical damage to a body as well as the permanent destruction of the brain or the consciousness-storing device. The second theme, which is closely related to murder, is truth and justice. One of the plot points of the show is a piece of legislation that would allow the police to interact with the consciousness of the dead in order to ascertain what happened, most importantly, who killed them (Kobus & Muniowski, 2020). The protagonist is also after truth, being hired to solve both the murder and attempted murder of a wealthy citizen (Out of the Past," *Altered Carbon*, 2018). Again, part of the problem in describing this arises from how death is understood. Finally, the series explores the theme of religion. On one hand, there is a character who celebrates the Day of the Dead by interacting with her grandmother's consciousness. While on the other hand, the official church has decreed that people get one life and one body, so saving your consciousness or transferring it to another body denies you an afterlife. The consciousness implant can even be "religiously coded" legally so their consciousness cannot be revived, or "spun up" (Kobus & Muniowski, 2020). Once these themes have been examined, the argument will turn to the question of defining death in light of such technologies. If one can speak to the dead, are they truly dead? Such questions are particularly relevant in the evaluation of transhumanism. There are already some people trying to upload human consciousness into computers. The chapter will conclude with an underdeveloped theme from the series that is related to the redefining of death. This theme is how human nature relates to death and whether a radical change to our understanding of death also raises questions as to whether beings are still human or not.

How *Altered Carbon* Explains its Technology

In the world of *Altered Carbon*, the future is one where human consciousness can be separated from the body. Toward the end of the first season, it is learned that this process was discovered by a scientist who wanted to explore space but knew that the human body could never survive the length of travel needed to get to most destinations. However, while the technology is used to allow people to travel quickly, it has also been used to stratify society socially, particularly along economic lines. Those who have the means can do things that the general public cannot ("Nora Inu," *Altered Carbon*, 2018).

Although a full detailed understanding of the science behind this technology is not explained in the series, there is sufficient history and understanding to provide a working baseline of the "rules of the universe." When people are one year old, they are implanted with a device called a "cortical stack" or just "stack" that stores their consciousness. The physical body is also now commonly referred to as a "sleeve." Identity no longer has to link one's body or appearance with their consciousness or memories, though the elite tend to maintain this connection. Legally, people are only allowed to have their stack in one sleeve at a time. Trying to control multiple sleeves at once is not only illegal, but can also lead to mental instability or madness. There seems to be a guaranteed right to have a sleeve, but the threshold of responsibility or accountability appears to be very low. The main character of the first season is de-sleeved because of crimes he committed and his stack stored in prison for 250 years. He is revived and placed in a sleeve to be offered a job that will include a pardon and wealth. At his release, it seems that when prisoners have served their sentences, they are typically re-sleeved in whatever bodies are available at the time. The same is true for victims of crimes. A couple is horrified to find their young daughter who had been "killed" (I use this term in quotes because this already raises questions about the definition of death in the series) is re-sleeved in a middle-aged body and are told by the authorities when they protest that they use what they have available and they can pay to have her re-sleeved ("Out of the Past," *Altered Carbon*, 2018). When the main character needs a kind of hacker called a "dipper," the woman he uses is re-sleeved into the body of a man ("Clash by Night," *Altered Carbon*, 2018).

People can choose to re-sleeve whenever they want, or whenever they can afford it, and there can be a great number of differences between sleeves. The most basic sleeves are simply normal human bodies. Takeshi

Kovacs, the main character, receives a better sleeve because Laurens Bancroft, the person hiring him, believes he will need specific skills to accomplish his task of discovering who murdered him. His sleeve has "military grade neurochem" and "combat muscle memory." Sleeves can also be created in labs, which the elite in society do either to enhance their bodies or to clone them, so they look the same when re-sleeved. These bodies can have all sorts of enhancements, such as strength or sensory enhancements that increase pleasure. There are also synthetic sleeves and cybernetic enhancements that can be added to sleeves, such as an artificial limb when a character loses her arm in an assault ("Out of the Past," *Altered Carbon*, 2018).

Death still occurs in this society, though it is not the same for everyone. The very rich can afford new sleeves but not everyone can. It is unclear exactly what happens when someone dies of natural causes or their body is too damaged to remain alive, but it seems that people can store their stacks for them, presumably to re-sleeve them at another time. The only way to ensure that someone dies is to destroy their stack or to destroy the brain. When released from prison, people are warned to avoid energy weapons to the stack or to the head. Even then, however, this does not mean death for everyone. The richest in society can afford to back up their stack remotely, so that even the destruction of their brain or stack does not result in permanent death. This is what happened to Bancroft; someone tried to hack into his backup after he had been shot in the head, hence the dual concerns of murder and attempted murder ("Out of the Past," *Altered Carbon*, 2018).

While it might be legal to re-sleeve, the church in this society has taken the stance that people are given one life and one body and that re-sleeving condemns you to hell. People who want to ensure they are not revived for religious reasons can have their stacks coded appropriately. During season one there is a fight over legislation called "Proposition 653" that would allow police to "spin up" or revive a murder victim or suspected murder victim in order to see if they could identify their assailant. By the end of season one, this law passes, and anyone, regardless of religious coding, and be "spun up" by police. Religious coding had been used by people committing crimes to help them cover up illegal actions and the killing of people, particularly sex workers, in order to satisfy the desires of wealthy clients ("The Killers," *Altered Carbon*, 2018).

For the discussion at hand, these details should provide sufficient details about how technology is used to separate body from mind, to provide background for the issues the show explores, and for the starting point to discuss understandings and definitions of death. After examining how the series deals with the issues of murder, truth and justice, and religion, the focus will shift to how these insights might inform the ethical analysis of emerging or future technologies. The ambiguities of how people perceive death in the series are relevant in both the history of how society has defined death, as well as how attitudes may continue to change with the advent of new technologies such as mind uploading.

Murder

In the *Altered Carbon* universe, there has developed a distinction between damage to the body and death. In the United States, definitions of death evolved over time as well. Years ago the legal definition of death was connected to the pronouncement of death by a medical professional, and based primarily on "cardiopulmonary standards," such as the absence of a pulse, no breathing, and the heart no longer circulating blood (Sarbey, 2016, pp. 743–744). For most people, this aligned with their own experiences or understanding of death, that someone was dead if they could not be resuscitated from not breathing and/or a stopped heart. Over time, however, technology pushed these definitions by moving beyond the boundaries that might have existed previously. For example, if a patient was receiving a heart transplant, using the cessation of a heartbeat would not be a valid measurement of whether the patient was dead, nor would the cessation of natural breathing serve the same purpose for a patient undergoing a lung transplant. Technology not only made these transplants possible, but it also allowed for mechanical ways to pump blood through the body or to "breathe" for patients (Sarbey, 2016, p. 744).

In order to try and identify a more precise definition of death, experts began exploring the concept of brain death. The move was to shift the legal definition of death away from cardiopulmonary definitions to one that focused on the state of the brain. The criteria used to determine brain death included "unreceptivity and unresponsitivity, no movements or breathing, no reflexes, and a flat electroencephalogram" (Sarbey, 2016, p. 744). Such a definition of death also had problems for several reasons. The first reason was theoretical while the second reason was more practical. Critics argued, "There was not 'scientific, philosophical, or logical justification for why the state of irreversible coma could be equated with death'" (Sarbey, 2016, p. 744). This position denied that there was a coherent reason to change to a definition of death based on the brain. The second reason is similar to transplants; there are technological ways to keep a person breathing, such as a respirator, and even means of providing artificial nutrition and hydration. People in permanent vegetative states (PVS) could be kept "alive" through these means, challenging the notion that they are "dead."

To address these concerns, experts sought to refine the definition of brain death to be that of total brain death, the "irreversible loss of brain functions" (Sarbey, 2016, p. 745) Physicians argued that such a definition would be helpful because it would provide a meaningful legal definition of brain death to be used, particularly when a cardiopulmonary definition does not apply, protecting patients from poor decisions based on outdated understandings of death. It also would provide a stronger standing for the use of organs in transplants from patients who are brain dead, as well as create a single definition of death to be used in any legal circumstance, including financial, criminal, and medical situations. Finally, defining death in this way could allow families to not spend resources they do not have in sustaining a person artificially if there is an irreversible loss of brain functions (Sarbey, 2016). A version of this understanding of death became the legal standard in all US states (Sarbey, 2016).

Although this became the legal standard, some experts continued to try and refine the definition because "total brain death may not be necessary for death, it may be sufficient in the sense that all cases of total brain death are cases of death" (Sarbey, 2016, p. 745). One alternative is to define brain death as cerebral death, since the "key functions of the brain such as memory, consciousness, and personality are what make us a person, and since those functions originate in the cerebral hemispheres, it is the death of those portions of the brain that count as death of the person" (Sarbey, 2016, p. 747). This position also argues that what it means for a human to die is different from plants or other animals. While other experts may say that it is the death of the total brain that is sufficient to define death, people who take this position argue that it is really only the death of certain parts of the brain that really matter in terms of human death, because it is these parts that contribute to our understanding of personal identity (Sarbey, 2016).

The world of *Altered Carbon* also recognizes distinctions between various forms of harm. Bodily injury, even to the point of cardiopulmonary cessation, is referred to as "organic damage," and events like humans fighting to the death of their bodies can be a licensed or sanctioned event ("In a Lonely Place," *Altered Carbon*, 2018). They also use the term "real death" to describe the destruction of the brain, or of the cortical stack, because these prevent the stack from being able to be re-sleeved and spun up; if one's stack is destroyed, they cannot be brought back. Even then, though, there are exceptions to this rule, at least for the wealthiest members of society. It is possible to create a remote backup of one's stack that can be used in the event of real death. This is why Bancroft wants Kovacs to investigate his murder and his attempted murder. Someone shot his cortical stack resulting in real death, but someone also attempted to destroy his backup, which could be understood as attempted murder.

Truth and Justice

The world of *Altered Carbon* is one filled with corruption. The police know they are limited in what they can do, those with money and influence use both to gain privileges the average person does not have, and coupled with the near limitless extension of life, the privileged "Meths" maintain these advantages indefinitely. The government, though it is unknown who supported or pushed for it in the first place, institutes the heavy use of surveillance ("The Wrong Man," *Altered Carbon*, 2018). Surveillance cameras appear to be very successful, at least in the areas they cover, but a plot point develops that someone has the capacity to erase themselves from all forms of electronic surveillance. Given the name of the "Ghostwalker," it turns out that Mister Leung is a devoted employee/follower of Reileen and performs any dirty work she requires. Independent of this threat the government realizes there are other tools at their disposal that are not being used to solve crimes. In particular, if someone's sleeve is destroyed and their family cannot afford to re-sleeve them, society basically sees this as murder. In the following sections, this assumption will be challenged, but for now, the problem is that if their cortical stack is intact, the person may have information about who attacked them, to the point of being able to positively identify their killer.

If only the police could spin up such victims, they might be able to solve more crimes, leading the government to create "Proposition 653," a law that would allow the police to access the cortical stack of victims of crimes in order to try to ascertain who committed these crimes. The idea behind Proposition 653 is that victims would be able to provide information about what happened to them, ideally including the identity of their killer. However, as research has shown, there are concerns about the nature of eyewitness accounts. The first of these is how reliable is the account that a witness gives. Is human memory sufficiently accurate enough to condemn a person to a guilty verdict? The second issue is how jury members evaluate or treat eyewitness accounts.

Providing victims with a lineup can lead to problems in identifying a perpetrator properly. Some scholars suggest a sequential form of lineup rather than a simultaneous group. Examining studies on both of these methods, the results seem to be that a "simultaneous lineup presentation produced superior accuracy in target-present lineups, whereas a sequential lineup format produced superior accuracy in target-absent lineups" (Steblay, Dysart, Fulero, & Lindsay, 2001, p. 466). If a victim provides a verbal description of their assailant prior to a lineup, this led to "a consistent, superior effect of sequential lineup format across both target-present and target-absent lineups" (Steblay et al., 2001, p. 467). In most cases, then, it seems that sequential lineups are the preferred method.

However, expert witnesses are being called in cases to contest the efficacy of eyewitness identification. Juries can be swayed regarding eyewitness testimony in certain circumstances. The judgment of jurors did not change if the witness said the perpetrator was wearing a disguise, if there was a reported threat of violence, if the victim waited for two days to two weeks after the crime before making an identification, nor if the witness heard voice samples of lineup members. There were things that generated a trivial change in juror judgment, including the victim looking through books of mug shots prior to a lineup, if the lineup instructions allowed for a rejection of the entire lineup, and the size of the lineup (Cutler, Penrod, & Dexter, 1990). These trivial changes were not statistically significant. The only thing that created a significant difference was if the witness said how confident they were in their identification, from 80 percent confident to 100 percent confident. While significant, it was still a small change (Cutler et al., 1990). There can also be problems in the ways in which a lineup is conducted, or inappropriate or leading feedback given to a witness. Reviewing procedures, Wells and Quinlivan believe there should be a "joint effort between social science and the law..." "to create a system that provides stronger incentives to eliminate unnecessarily suggestive procedures without excluding reliable identifications" (Wells & Quinlivan, 2009, p. 21).

Given the discussion above about the nature of eyewitness testimony, the question that needs to be asked is whether it is worth spinning up the consciousness of victims, particularly if they have particular religious beliefs. Though religion will be addressed in more detail in the next section, it is important to note that prior to the passing of Proposition 653, people who did not want to be re-sleeved or spun up after the destruction of their body could get religious coding on their stack that prevented this. The belief was that people should only have one life and re-sleeving or spinning up after bodily death would be enough to keep someone out of heaven. If eyewitness testimony is problematic, is it worth violating the beliefs of religious individuals in order to access their cortical stack, particularly if the government already has extensive surveillance?

In order to address that question, the validity or success of surveillance must be examined. According to statements from intelligence officials in the United States and the United Kingdom between 2006 and 2016, the work that those in intelligence do is different than law enforcement, because they are "not in the business of investigating suspicious people" (Cayford & Pieters, 2018, p. 92). They also make a distinction between strategic and tactical surveillance, where tactical surveillance is focused on specific people for a set period of time. Strategic surveillance, on the other hand, has a larger focus and because it is about monitoring or information gathering, there is less certainty as to what information is expected to be collected (Cayford & Pieters, 2018). In trying to identify the effectiveness of surveillance, Cayford and Pieters note seven measures that can be divided "into three categories: counting, documents/cases, and organizations" (Cayford & Pieters, 2018, p. 93). Counting includes three of these measures, counting the number of attacks that were stopped, the number of lives saved, and the number of cells or criminals dismantled. However, officials in both the United States and the United Kingdom agree that pointing to individual success stories or counting, in general, is not a valid way of determining the effectiveness of surveillance (Cayford & Pieters, 2018).

Documents/cases are the second category and are composed of one measure, outputs. Unlike counting, officials do give more credence to outputs as a measure of effectiveness, looking to both the quantity and quality of technology. In terms of quantity, experts say that if a "surveillance technology has been the collection source of numerous reports it is judged to be effective" (Cayford & Pieters, 2018, p. 94). Quality is measured by examining which collection technologies are involved in providing the most useful information in outputs (Cayford & Pieters, 2018). The outputs discussed to this point included reports and documents provided to the government, but cases are also a form of output. Cases in this instance refer to criminal cases, and the UK Home Secretary has said, "Communications data was used in 95 percent of criminal cases" (Cayford & Pieters, 2018, p. 94). The use of this data in the prosecution of criminals is seen by experts as proof of effectiveness.

The final category is organizations and includes three measures, context, support, and informed policymakers (Cayford & Pieters, 2018). Context is in reference to the use of any given surveillance technology; any one form cannot be isolated from other methods and must be placed in the greater context in order to understand its effectiveness (Cayford & Pieters, 2018). Support is a measure of effectiveness based on how intelligence gathered by a particular technology can provide support to other organizations, such as law enforcement or other intelligence groups (Cayford & Pieters, 2018). Finally, some of the experts interviewed for this study argued that having informed policymakers is an important measure of effectiveness (Cayford & Pieters, 2018).

Even though intelligence experts make a clear distinction between what they do and what law enforcement does, it is clear from the measures of effectiveness they identify that there is overlap between these groups. In particular, there is co-operation or support in the sharing of surveillance intelligence with law enforcement, as well as such intelligence being used in criminal cases. Studies have also been done in the United States and the United Kingdom to determine how effective different forms of surveillance are in preventing crime. The two forms of surveillance explored by Welsh and Farrington are closed-circuit television (CCTV) and increased lighting on streets, which they refer to as "natural surveillance" (Welsh & Farrington, 2004, p. 497). The British government has spent a great deal of money investing in CCTV, accounting for over 75 percent "of total spending on crime prevention by the British Home Office" from 1996 to 1998 and the actual number of cameras has increased from 100 in 1990 to 40,000 in 2002 (Welsh & Farrington, 2004). Using the data from two reviews they previously performed, Welsh and Farrington used four search strategies to determine increases in lighting or CCTV cameras including online databases, literature reviews, searching for reports on CCTV and streetlights, and networking with other scholars. Their findings indicated that CCTV and increased street lighting had the same effect in reducing crime. The kinds of crime they examined included property crimes such as "burglary, vehicle crimes, and theft, and violent crimes," which included "robbery and assault" (Welsh & Farrington, 2004, p. 509).

Because there can be problems with eyewitness testimony, it seems that increasing natural surveillance, as well as CCTV, is more effective in preventing crime. Even though victims could be spun up in order to identify who attacked them, there are concerns in leading a witness through the identification process, their own recollection, and how a jury might respond to that identification. Legislation like Proposition 653, then, might not be as effective in identifying those who have committed crimes than as other methods. Given the amount of bodily augmentation that occurs in the *Altered Carbon* world, perhaps finding ways to give unique identifiers to cloned bodies, cybernetic implants, or other alterations to bodies could be a better way of identifying perpetrators. There are privacy concerns, just as there are with increased surveillance, but the global positioning system (GPS), nano-tracking dust, or a safe isotope that could be traced would give more reliable evidence as to the whereabouts of a suspect than eyewitness identification.

Religion

While religion does not appear to play a large role in the world of *Altered Carbon*, there are two issues raised in the show that are relevant to the overall discussion of this chapter. The first of these has already been mentioned in the previous section. Prior to the passing of Proposition 653, peoples' stacks could be coded so that they could not be spun up after their bodies died. The underlying belief here is that the Catholic Church in this world is purported to be against the technology of stacks and re-sleeving. Whether such a position is tied to the fact that the technology that allows for this requires a metal from an older alien species is unclear, but the reaction to stacks, sleeves, needle-casting, cloning, etc. has been for the church to say that each person receives one body and one life and to spin up after bodily death or to re-sleeve is a sin, thus keeping the person who did this from reaching heaven. It is not clear from the show what the church thinks about murder victims who are re-sleeved by the state, but if their thinking was consistent, they would reject such behavior as well.

The second issue is the celebration of the Day of the Dead. There is a market for renting sleeves to temporarily spin up people, but it seems to be expensive. Ortega decides to use the body of a criminal who was arrested to spin up her grandmother and bring her home for dinner on the Day of the Dead. Other than the nature of the sleeve, the family is not surprised by this, so it is likely that this is a typical way of celebrating this holiday in this culture. Celebrations of the Day of the Dead or

El Día de los Muertos in the United States were not well known until the 1970s when it was seen to be an outward expression of Chicano identity (Marchi, 2013). The traditional practices were meant to remind people "that one's well-being depends, in part, on respectfully remembering the dead. Whether people construct elaborate shrines for the dead or simply lay flowers on family graves, these rituals are rooted in a common sense of moral obligation to the deceased" (Marchi, 2013, p. 273). Over time, these practices were also given space in popular culture, which was more of an expression of art or identity than it was a religious practice (Marchi, 2013). Such views really only scratch the surface of the complexity and depth of both religious belief and cultural practices, but this cursory examination is sufficient for the task at hand.

The question I would like to raise in response to these two issues is to again probe the meaning of death, and to ask whether the people involved in either of these scenarios are truly dead. Like the discussion in the first section about the definition of death, it seems that in this society it is a category mistake to pronounce someone dead simply for the cessation of breathing or of a beating heart. As long as the cortical stack and the brain is intact (if the brain was damaged, memories could not be stored properly in the stack), it is possible to move the stack to a clone of that body or a new body/sleeve. When Kovacs is being debriefed upon being spun up in prison, the speaker tells the inmates to avoid the destruction of their stack or of the brain. People even refer to these losses as "real death," insinuating the point that I am trying to make, that the loss of one's body in this world does not mean that a person is dead.

In fact, a body is not always needed for a stack to experience some kind of existence. Vernon Elliott's daughter Lizzie was murdered and tortured in virtual reality (VR) in order to make her mentally unstable enough to not be able to say what happened to her if she was spun up. Vernon uses VR to access her memories to have some kind of memory of her, and the artificial intelligence Poe uses a VR environment to treat Lizzie's health issues. For this reason, I would argue that the destruction of a body in the world of *Altered Carbon* does not equate to death. Though the law may define the loss of the body as organic damage and considers "real death" the destruction of the brain or of the cortical stack, it is clear that amongst the general population there is still a connection to the loss of one's body and death. Similar to history then, technology has allowed this society to move beyond a definition of death that is tied to the cardiovascular system. Even without a body, a stack can be stored for long periods of time, such as Kovacs's stack being in prison for over 200 years.

The long-term storage of stacks leads us to the second issue in this section, the celebration of the Day of the Dead. If the body does not define death anymore, and if stacks can be stored for long periods of time, is Ortega re-sleeving her grandmother to celebrate the Day of the Dead a true celebration of the dead? If her stack is intact and being stored, then the family could choose to re-sleeve her permanently if they could afford it. It would seem then, that this situation is not quite the same as the practice of honoring one's deceased relatives by remembering them, telling their stories, building shrines, or decorating graves, but rather this is more similar to visiting with a relative that you have not seen for a very long time. Scholars would say this is at most a hybrid of the original rituals for the Day of the Dead (Marchi, 2013).

The decision of the church to argue that people are given a single life in a single body and to do otherwise is going against God's plan places the church in a position of conflict with science and technology. People who suffer organic damage and lose their bodies do not describe experiences of what occurs beyond death; there is no common imagery of going toward the light, or interacting with other beings. One could ask theological questions about the nature of death in light of these technological changes. Has the way that humans experience death changed so much with it no longer being tied to the body that the brain or mind has no way of perceiving when one is dead? Has the use of VR and inhabiting different bodies blurred humanity's sense of what life and death are? Is the use of stacks and the other technologies of this world further proof that humans are living in a simulation (Delbert, 2020)? Some of these concerns as well as others will be explored in the final section of this chapter.

Emerging and Future Technology in Light of *Altered Carbon*

While science fiction does not always provide a detailed or realistic approach to technological advances, there are already developing technologies that relate to what is shown in *Altered Carbon*. The use of VR is becoming more widespread, companies such as Musk's Neuralink are developing brain implants, people are looking to gene editing using a method known as CRISPR, clustered regularly interspaced short palindromic repeats, to alter the human genome, and futurists like Ray Kurzweil predict the inevitability of mind uploading, the downloading of human consciousness into a computer, allowing for that consciousness to live a digital existence or to be downloaded into a variety of kinds of bodies. The ambiguity seen in *Altered Carbon* about how people think of or define death will be relevant in the analysis of these technologies.

If human consciousness can be downloaded to computers, it is possible that people in the future will be walking around with the equivalent of a cortical stack, and that real death would be linked to the destruction of the brain or of the device itself. It also raises the question of individual identity. If one's neural pattern is scanned into a computer, the original person does not cease to exist, and as such, is the digital version a new person with all of the knowledge and experience of a previous individual? In *Altered Carbon*, it is illegal to "double sleeve," that is be in two bodies simultaneously, but this is not what mind uploading will create if the process does not destroy the original neural pattern or brain. A digital backup could save someone from being permanently disabled or killed, but if current computer technology is any indication, people forget to back things up and backups can become corrupted. If multiple backups were formed, would they also be new individuals if given the opportunity to learn and experience on their own?

Surveillance is already a reality in many Western countries, but technology could lead to improved surveillance technologies. Based on the previous discussion, it seems that there are ways to focus on the most effective forms of surveillance in order to prevent crimes, and that such measures would be more effective and reliable than accessing the memories of victims after the fact to try and identify perpetrators. Another suggestion was to add tracing, tracking, or identifiable signatures into modified or artificial bodies so that their presence somewhere like a crime scene could be more easily identified. If people decide they do not want to be revived if certain kinds of crimes occur, I think it would be better to focus on crime prevention rather than crafting legislation that could be used to override people's decisions about what they want done with their bodies or consciousness.

The longevity that could be the result of gene editing, synthetic bodies, or a non-biological existence raises its own set of questions. Would the choice to utilize such technologies be open to everyone, or would society see the rise of a near-immortal elite class like the Meths in *Altered Carbon*? Does the length of life make crimes more heinous? For instance, if it can be assumed that everyone in society has access to something like a cortical stack and can regularly be backed up, then the real death of a person could be seen as a greater crime than it is currently. Instead of denying someone 60–80 more years of life, murder in such a society could take away centuries or millennia of experience, of family, etc.

It also raises questions about the nature of death. If someone chooses not to be placed into a new body at a certain time and place, what happens to their stored consciousness? It is possible that they could be placed on a shelf, like an urn containing the ashes of a loved one, but in this case, the person could be revived to witness births, weddings, funerals, etc. In the discussion of the Day of the Dead, I argued that people who are stored like that should not be understood as dead, because those individuals can be revived; it is more like being in a state of suspended animation, which raises its own set of issues. How do property rights and banking, for example, work in such situations? Does an individual continue to own property if they are not actively living? Do they continue to earn interest or collect dividends from stocks? The possibility of potentially immortal life that is experienced in intervals and not continuously raises a number of issues regarding the relationship between individual and society. If copyright exists for the life of the author plus 70 years after their death, does the timer pause when they go into suspended animation?

Given the technological advances that have already happened, understandings of and definitions for death have evolved over time. The kinds of advances seen in *Altered Carbon* provide a glimpse into a possible future and some of the concerns that come with it. In order to keep pace with technology, experts need to continue to examine how death is defined, as well as the societal impact of a life not lived consecutively, but with pauses in time including years of inactivity. The definition of death has already shifted from cardiopulmonary understandings to a more brain or consciousness-focused definition, but another shift may be needed if bodies can be done away with altogether, and existence can be a purely digital experience. Perhaps there may come a time when people will cease needing to try to commune with the dead and instead just boot up their loved one to get their opinion or to celebrate with them.

References

Cayford, M., & Pieters, W. (2018). The effectiveness of surveillance technology: What intelligence officials are saying. *The Information Society, 34*(2), 88–103. doi: 10.1080/01972243.2017.1414721.

"Clash by night." Altered Carbon, season 1, episode 8, 2018. *Netflix,* www.netflix. com.

Cutler, B. L., Penrod, S. D., & Dexter, H. R. (1990). Juror sensitivity to eyewitness identification evidence. *Law and Human Behavior, 14*(2), 185–191. doi: 10.1007/bf01062972.

Delbert, C. (2020, October 15). A study shows there's a 50% chance we're living in a simulation. Retrieved from https://www.popularmechanics.com/science/a34362527/are-we-living-in-a-simulation/.

"In a Lonely Place." *Altered Carbon,* season 1, episode 3, 2018. *Netflix,* www.netflix.com.

Kobus, A., & Muniowski, Ł (2020). *Sex, death and resurrection in Altered Carbon: Essays on the Netflix series.* Jefferson, NC: McFarland & Company.

Marchi, R. (2013). Hybridity and authenticity in US day of the dead celebrations. *The Journal of American Folklore, 126*(501), 272. doi: 10.5406/jamerfolk.126.501.0272.

"Nora Inu." *Altered Carbon,* season 1, episode 7, 2018. *Netflix,* www.netflix.com.

"Out of the Past." Altered Carbon, season 1, episode 1, 2018. *Netflix,* www.netflix. com.

Sarbey, B. (2016). Definitions of death: Brain death and what matters in a person. *Journal of Law and the Biosciences, 3*(3), 743–752. doi: 10.1093/jlb/lsw054.

Steblay, N., Dysart, J., Fulero, S., & Lindsay, R. C. (2001). Eyewitness accuracy rates in sequential and simultaneous lineup presentations: A meta-analytic comparison. *Law and Human Behavior, 25*(5), 459–473. doi: 10.1023/a:1012888715007.

"The Killers." Altered Carbon, season 1, episode 10, 2018. *Netflix,* www.netflix.com.

"The Wrong Man." Altered Carbon, season 1, episode 5, 2018. *Netflix,* www.netflix.com.

Wells, G. L., & Quinlivan, D. S. (2009). Suggestive eyewitness identification procedures and the Supreme Court's reliability test in light of eyewitness science: 30 years later. *Law and Human Behavior, 33*(1), 1–24. doi: 10.1007/s10979-008-9130-3.

Welsh, B. C., & Farrington, D. P. (2004). Surveillance for crime prevention in public space: Results and policy choices in Britain and America. *Criminology Public Policy, 3*(3), 497–526. doi: 10.1111/j.1745-9133.2004.tb00058.x.

12 Ghosts and Gods in the Machine

Human-Machine Interfaces in Transhuman Philosophy

Levi Checketts

Sheila Jasanoff and other Science and Technology Studies (STS) researchers refer to a "sociotechnical imaginary" as "collectively held and performed visions of desirable futures…animated by shared understandings of forms of social life and social order attainable through, and supportive of, advances in science and technology" (Jasanoff & Kim, 2015, p. 19). In other words, sociotechnical imaginaries are our visions of what the future holds for us, which inspire us or dissuade us in pursuing certain scientific and technological goals. Michael Burdett, for example, notes that the American spirit of "progress" as a frontier-mindset led to an uncritical pursuit of industrial technologies as some sort of "Manifest Destiny" (Burdett, 2015). Other examples include the visions tied to such sociotechnical phenomena as the space race, nuclear politics, and the status of genetically modified organisms in foods.

Transhumanism is another sociotechnical imaginary. This loosely affiliated collection of philosophies is united by its adherents' vision of self-directed evolution through the use of science and technologies. Typical visions include an increase of "healthspan, cognition and emotion," augmenting our wellbeing and power physically, mentally, and emotionally (Bostrom, 2013). Among the sciences and technologies typically endorsed to reach these ends include informational and computer technologies, nanotechnologies, genetics, and robotics. While transhumanists do recognize the risks these technologies hold, they are confident that the proper use of first-adopters and developers will curtail nefarious uses or developments (More, 2013). Thus, they largely believe the proper development of these technologies will be of tremendous benefit to humanity and this vision informs their own research and investments.

In this chapter, I will be looking at two specific aspects of the "imaginary" which transhumanists lift up, namely the achievement of consciousness uploading into non-biological substrates and the creation of a super-powerful Artificial Intelligence (AI) "god." These ideals, which Hava Tirosh-Samuelson and Robert Geraci have called "secularized eschatology" (Geraci, 2008; Tirosh-Samuelson, 2015) take on the form of religious thought while often being framed as atheistic or agnostic principles. As a religious scholar, I find this to be an interesting problem. Without structured or formal religious beliefs, transhumanists articulate their own quasi-religious views. Whereas a popular opinion in science and technology industries holds that scientific understandings belong to a different sphere of understanding than religious ones, transhumanist belief systems demonstrate the STS principle that there is no true distinction between our "social" and "natural" understandings of the world (Latour, 1993). Many scholars have examined such elements in their studies of transhumanism, so this chapter only considers the re-invention of eschatological beliefs in light of AI programming.

The goals of consciousness uploading and the machine god allow the singular possibility of communication with incorporeal conscious beings, namely the minds of those who no longer live biologically and the mind of one or more godlike intelligences. These parallel religious beliefs about supernatural communion with the deceased through seances or oracles from the gods. Unlike the structures of institutional religion, however, transhumanism promises this powerful ability to even the uninitiated or unbeliever. Moreover, in line with transhumanist trust in science and technology the accomplishment of this post-mortal communion is not through some mystical or magical force, but rather through the literal "Deus ex Machina" of AI.

In this chapter, I begin with an overview of major ideas in transhumanism as they relate to formal religion, death, and the divine. I argue, in line with thinkers like Hava Tirosh-Samuelson, that transhumanism is more like religion than many of its adherents believe. I then examine the history and belief of patternism, the philosophical anthropology underlying most of the transhumanist beliefs in uploaded minds and godlike AI. I then explicate the visions of afterlife and divinity articulated by transhumanists and the potential for human communication with these entities. In the concluding section, I return to the broader religious question of the status of transhumanist ideas and the implications they suggest for religions' place in the world.

Transhumanism as a Religion

Is transhumanism, as Hava Tirosh-Samuelson and Robert Geraci claim, a "secularized eschatology"? The term is not well-liked by transhumanists, who often either see their position as compatible with pre-existing religious beliefs or as precluding religious belief. When transhumanists have been surveyed on their religious backgrounds, some do espouse formal religious beliefs, such as Buddhism, Mormonism, and Unitarianism, but the majority claim to have no religious beliefs or to be spiritual but not religious (Hughes, 2013). Some transhumanists, such as Lincoln Cannon, James Hughes, Giulio Prisco, and Michael LaTorra, write about and endorse transhumanism from explicitly religious perspectives.

Others, such as Simon Young, Marvin Minsky, and Russell Blackford tie their transhumanist views to explicit atheism.

Some transhumanists, therefore, reject the possibility of religious beliefs within transhumanism while others see transhumanism as a vehicle for their religious views. However, regardless of these specific claims, transhumanism often takes on the functioning of a religion in the lives of those who endorse it. Of particular note here is the common task of immortality and the fixation on super-powerful beings, i.e. God or gods. The sciences and technologies which transhumanists pursue, from genetic engineering to consciousness uploading, are often designed to prevent death or seek guarantee of an afterlife. The advancement of science and technology to the proposed goal of human evolution also entails a sense of divinity—if we can create simulated worlds and genetically modify organisms, might not a superior being have done the same to us?

While transhumanist thought does include persons who want simply machine implants, brain-computer interfaces, genetic engineering for their children and other such life enhancements, two specific trajectories within this broad grouping stand out as worthy of our attention: patternism and singularitarianism. Patternism is a philosophy rooted in cybernetics; it sees everything, especially our minds, as replicable patterns of information. This is the philosophy underlying not only all "uploading" aims, but also the greater thrust of AI research. Singularitarianism is a futurist belief that at some point we will reach the technological "singularity," a moment in history when technology advances so rapidly it is nearly impossible to observe. Some believe this moment will mark the true irruption of a "posthuman" species, while others believe it could be the rise of a super-powerful godlike being or species. Both of these positions, patternism and singularitarianism, depart from the base vision of transhumanism: they go beyond human "evolution" and embrace theological, cosmological, and even eschatological worldviews.

The finality of death, the philosopher Hans Jonas argued, challenges the conscious mind and forces us to make sense of the otherwise absurd (Jonas, 1966). Religion, dating back perhaps to the oldest hominin religious traditions, helps us make sense of this death, often by giving us hope for a continual existence beyond this mortal plane. Atheism, however, requires coldly accepting that death is ultimate; nothing lies beyond. The existentialist tradition advocates for us to accept the absurdity of this reality with resoluteness (Camus, 1955). Transhumanism, however, takes a third path: rather than accepting the finality of death or hoping for an afterlife, they seek an escape through technology.

A major problem we ought to be aware of, going forward, is the convergence of a specific worldview (i.e. transhumanism) and its appropriation of science and technology. Transhumanism itself advocates for certain positions which are not scientific in nature, e.g. the good of furthering human evolution or eliminating death. As such, science becomes the tool of transhumanism. This often leads to monstrous results, as demonstrated, for example, in the eugenics movement of the early-twentieth century or recent efforts to discredit climate science for capitalistic gain (See Oreskes & Conway, 2010). Cybernetics, a field that regularly transgressed the boundaries between physical sciences and philosophies, is thus the right place for transhumanism to take its bearing going forward.

Patternism

The belief in conscious machinery begins in fiction before rising as a philosophy in the latter half of the twentieth century. Early works like Karel Čapek's 1920 play *R.U.R* (*Rossumovi Univerzální Roboti*, or, in English, *Rossum's Universal Robots*) and Thea von Harbou's 1927 *Metropolis* feature humans' creations demonstrating human consciousness and intelligence. In 1930, John Scott Campbell's "The Infinite Brain" imagines a human consciousness immortalized in a machine and Isaac Asimov's science fiction beginning in the 1940s popularizes the concept of AI in robots. These fantasies, examples of sociotechnical imaginaries, inspire the actual pioneers of computing in the 1940s and 1950s and reach their heads in the thought of Alan Turing.

Turing, the father of modern computing, believed that digital computers, that is, computing machines with components that are either on or off, were Universal Turing Machines—machines that can simulate any other machine. In his 1950 essay "Computing Machinery and Intelligence," Turing hypothesizes that a digital computer can "think" if it can successfully win the "Imitation Game," a test where a judge must choose which responses to questions are from a computer and not a human being, now commonly referred to as the Turing Test (Turing, 1950). Turing believed, therefore, that human cognition was replicable through a digital machine executing programmed instructions. This understanding sets the foundation for all AI research. Indeed, for many people, if a computer can successfully pass a Turing Test, it should, for all intents and purposes, be treated as a conscious person.

In the same year, Norbert Wiener published *The Human Use of Human Beings*, the foundational text for the field of cybernetics. Wiener advances the ontology that all is information; material is insignificant, and the content of all that is can be understood through its informational context. For example, the information stored in a strand of DNA is sufficient for re-creating a living being, independent of the physical existence of its body. For Weiner, the exact physical material making us up is inconsequential; the "patterns" that are inscribed in our bodies are all that matter (Wiener, 1950). In turn, even the physical movement of things in space is a question of information and feedback. Cybernetics as a field, then, focuses on feedback to stimuli, often through self-regulating mechanistic functioning, such as thermostats and cruise controls. Wiener and others also believed the human mind was essentially a massive feedback mechanism. This idea, and the work of others in the field of cybernetics, reinforces the view of Turing that the human mind is essentially the same in its operation as a machine and can be replicated by a machine.

While these ideas shaped AI research for the next 70 years, pattern-ism as a philosophy became more formalized only toward the end of the century. In 1994, the AI researcher Ben Goertzel defined the mind as a "self-generating network of components that are largely concerned with recognizing patterns in each other" (Goertzel, 2006, p. 156). The emphasis Goertzel placed on patterns shaped his own and future think-ing to go beyond pattern recognition to the claim, made most famously by Ray Kurzweil, that our minds are nothing but sophisticated pattern (Kurzweil, 2005). For patternists, the key to truly unlocking human con-sciousness lies not in philosophical questioning or biological studies, but in deciphering the patterns of the brain in a way that can be replicated and carried out in a different medium. Computing itself has used various media for storing instructions and executing them, from textile punch cards to cassette tapes, floppy disks, hard drives, solid-state drives, and more. May it not be true, then, that the human brain is just a biologi-cal version of a compact disk, and the complex neural processes of con-sciousness merely lines of code?

Thus, patternism emerges from fantastic imaginaries about the potential of human machinery through mid-twentieth century sciences out through the philosophy of transhumanism, of which Goertzel and Kurzweil are notable exponents. The patternist view continues the vision of cybernetics. Not only are machines obviously replicating pat-terns that are programmed into them, but so are human beings and the universe writ large. Thus, a computer can both simulate a human mind and a universe. The former has been the purview of AI researchers now 70 years, but the latter is manifest in video game design and artificial reality. Microsoft's *2020 Flight Simulator*, for example, uses real maps and current weather conditions to simulate conditions of flying various aircraft with some degree of accuracy. Patternism thus sets the ground for twin concepts of consciousness uploading and the machine god.

Immortality and the Uploaded Mind

Transhumanism sees death as the ultimate disvalue. With no inherent theology or eschatology, death is the ultimate affliction that must be surpassed through augmentation. The pre-eminent transhumanist phi-losopher Nick Bostrom even goes so far as to mythologize death as a "dragon tyrant" we must vanquish (Bostrom, 2005). At its least intru-sive, transhumanism advocates for use of biological sciences and other technologies to prolong our physical lives indefinitely. However, even the healthiest version of myself will be susceptible to deadly viruses, poisons, blunt force trauma, and or other deaths not related to aging. Thus, the best solution to death requires us to escape the fragility of human bodies.

The most optimal solution to this problem, then, is transmigrating one's consciousness into a nigh-indestructible container. Such a vision finds its best articulation through the imaginaries of the patternists. The AI pioneer Hans Moravec is the first to really offer a proposal of how this might work. Noting that the brain is a very complicated organ and that human minds are actually quite sophisticated, especially compared to early computers, Moravec expected that consciousness uploading would require three primary breakthroughs: sufficiently powerful hardware, sufficiently sophisticated programming, and sufficiently advanced neurological mapping (Moravec, 1988). The first component, hardware, is much more plausible and inevitable than the others. The low-end speculations of Moravec's predictions are being realized even today as ten terabyte hard drives are commercially available for a few hundred dollars, far beyond anything that was available in 1988. The other two elements, neurology and software, remain problems to this day, as both a comprehensive brain map and sufficiently sophisticated AI programming are uncountable years away from being realized. The AI pioneer Marvin Minsky, for example, claims that the human brain is "400 different computers" which run different processes simultaneously to make up our consciousness (Minsky, 2013, p. 173). Running a mind on a computer means isolating which of these processes are most critical for actual consciousness and replicating them. A shortcut to this realization may be "Whole Brain Emulation" which would allow the brain *in toto* to function, including those "non-essential" elements such as regulating breathing, circulation, and digestion, which an uploaded mind will not need (Koene, 2013). Once a better understanding of consciousness is achieved, those useless components can be eliminated through editing the code. Assuming all of these obstacles can be surmounted, the next question is how the mind is to be actually uploaded. Opinions differ here, but one of the more commonly accepted visions requires a total destruction of the living brain in order to faithfully reproduce its contents into a digital substrate (Moravec, 1988). In other words, this is a one-way street, and only those that are truly ready to live their lives forever, digitally, need apply.

When a person is successfully uploaded, then, they exist in a sort of digital afterlife. The recent serial drama *Uploaded* depicts this concept clearly enough: the deceased "live on" in what is essentially a sophisticated version of Second Life, able to interact both with other deceased uploaded persons in their network, and with the living through telecommunications technologies. The vision of this differs from visionary to visionary, and few serious proponents of uploading espouse a consumerist vision of uploading like the Amazon drama. Nearly all versions, however, articulate a vision of uploaded minds that are freer, more powerful, and nearly immortal.

An uploaded mind is no longer tethered to a body, so it no longer has the physical limitations that human beings have. This opens up many new possibilities. As transhumanists such as Martine Rothblatt and Ray Kurzweil suggest, this allows for a massive amount of "morphological freedom" (Kurzweil, 2005; Rothblatt, 2013). An uploaded mind can change its identity, alter its memory, merge itself with other programs or distribute itself across multiple platforms, allowing the consciousness to truly experience different personae. Rather than being tethered geographically, an uploaded mind can operate on a network, using multiple machines rather than one. An uploaded mind can replicate itself as well, backing itself up or making slight alterations in new copies, providing an opportunity for risk-free experimentation. Some, such as Dimitry Itskov, hope to be able to have their consciousnesses operate in physical space through robotic or holographic bodies, giving us the possibility of trying out radically different bodies (2045 Initiative, 2016).

The uploaded consciousness is also expected to be more powerful. Our minds are limited by our brains' capacities. A computer can be enhanced quite easily, however, with additions of random-access memory (RAM, which allows a computer to do more at the same time), storage, or processors. As hardware continues to advance the speed, size, and performance of uploaded minds will only increase. If computer components are made from the right materials and stored properly, they will also be more durable than human bodies. Additionally, with computer networks, the uploaded mind can distribute itself across multiple sites, using multiple machines simultaneously. These minds would also be free to communicate and otherwise interact (including erotically) with any uploaded mind or living person at any time in any place, including even multiple persons at a time. Further still, an uploaded mind, controlling a machine, such as a submersible or a spacecraft will be able to explore reaches impossible for human bodies to reach.

Finally, the ultimate goal of consciousness uploading is, of course, to escape death once and for all. While we, at present, do not have any surviving computer programs older than the oldest humans, an uploaded mind could potentially survive long beyond any biological person, though vulnerabilities remain. One problem related to this, however, is the problem of data corruption. This problem is potentially solvable if the uploaded mind is constantly maintained, potentially by itself, or if multiple copies are backed up across platforms. A second problem, articulated by Hans Moravec, is that as computing technology expands and more conscious programs proliferate, a new ecosystem of AIs will compete for hardware resources. Since human consciousness currently relies on many features a pure AI would not, such as visual thinking, uploaded minds will be targets for decommissioning or deletion. To prevent this, Moravec foresees, uploaded minds will have to erase those "imaginative" elements of the human mind. This is a rather ghastly scenario: uploaded minds will become digital "shades," ghosts of their former selves lacking much of what made their personality unique (Moravec, 2013). Even if this scenario can be avoided, a further problem stops true immortality: the heat death of the universe. When the entropy of the universe reaches its maximal state, all energy will be dissipated, meaning nothing in the universe will move and computers will be inert matter. Thus, even in the best-case scenario, uploaded minds will not be truly "immortal," but this event is expected to be 10^{100} years away. The universe is about 13 billion years old, which means the literal end of time is 10 billion times longer than the current age of the entire universe. Although this is not true immortality, it stretches beyond anything we can reasonably fathom, so it may as well be for us living today.

From an eschatological perspective, this vision of the afterlife is interesting. While seemingly casting off the "superstitious" trappings of formal religion, what patternism adorns itself with is suspiciously familiar. No immaterial "soul" exists in the patternist view of the person, but consciousness, as an immaterial pattern renderable in other substrates, does. No heaven exists, but there is an open computer world where one's wildest fantasies are reality. Seances or communication with the dead is not literally possible, but those who are no longer corporeal can easily communicate with the "living." And while uploading is not meant to be "eternity," the length of time available goes beyond what is realistically fathomable. Indeed, Ray Kurzweil suggests an uploaded mind might, eventually and of its own accord, decide to delete itself because it has satisfied every interest it might have and has nothing further to live for (2005), not unlike the series finale of *The Good Place*.

It is perhaps unsurprising, then, that one of the chief arguments made against transhumanists is a lack of respect for the boundaries of mortality. Many critics of the philosophy express similar concerns to those raised in literature about those who would trespass the boundaries of mortality, such as Mary Shelley's *Frankenstein*, Bram Stoker's *Dracula*, or Oscar Wilde's *Picture of Dorian Gray*. Indeed, transhumanists often adopt a stance, not unlike the alchemist whose life work is to discover the philosopher's stone, the singular artifact able to grant them true immortality. While this comparison may seem risible, it is important to note that the immortalist fantasies of medieval alchemists were not, as suggested by Kuhn, less "scientific" because they are older than our current models (Kuhn, 2012). Indeed, the worldviews that support patternist uploading are just as scientific for their time as those that sought the Holy Grail, and both, it should be noted, are escapist efforts to avoid the finality of death.

Whether patternism amounts to a new eschatology, a new alchemy, or merely the logical extension of cybernetics and AI research, the reality is that it is, for some men and women, a new answer to the perpetual problem of death and what lies beyond. It offers a vision that many have fantasized: a guarantee of continued life, the possibility to commune with loved ones, both living and dead, and the ability to live out our wildest dreams. That possibility offers the wonderful opportunity not only to continue existing relationships beyond the grave, but even to form new ones, both with the living and the dead. Thus, patternism offers the potential of a veritable heaven in the silicon and radio waves of modern-day computing.

The Machine God

Ray Kurzweil proudly proclaims himself to be a singularitarian and created Singularity University to support his vision. The singularity, as envisioned by Kurzweil and others, is a moment of super-advanced technological development. Kurzweil sees technology advancing in a logarithmic scale, and we are now entering the bottom curve of the "S," just before technology advances faster than we can perceive. This rapid advancement, where "all the change in the last million years will be superseded by the change in the next five minutes," is the singularity (Kurzweil, 2005, front matter).

The term "singularity" is not insignificant; like a black hole, this moment is not one of many, but a definitive point, a threshold like the event horizon, whereby everything beyond is inescapably shaped by this moment. Vernor Vinge, the science fiction writer who coined the term in its present usage, suggested four possible scenarios for a singularity: super-intelligent, sentient computers are developed; massive computer networks become sentient; computer-human interfaces make humans super-intelligent; or other means of augmenting human intelligence are achieved (Vinge, 2013). In all of these cases, the "singularity" described by Vinge and adopted by others is an evolutionary leap in intelligence, and in nearly all scenarios, computers are the operative factor triggering this advance. What either humans or computers are able to do will be more impressive and far more sudden than the slow emergence of consciousness among apes.

This expected advent of a super-human intelligence, combined with the cybernetic view that the whole universe is reducible to data, and the further patternist view that this data can be transcribed faithfully into any given machine, lends itself to another favorite philosophy among transhumanists, namely the simulation hypothesis. The simulation hypothesis holds that a sufficiently advanced being, whether human, AI, or alien, could create a detailed enough simulation of a universe that the programmed AIs of the universe would not know they are programmed (Bostrom, 2003).

In essence, the model for this is post-2000 video games, such as *The Elder Scrolls IV: Oblivion*. Non-player characters (NPCs) in the game have routines, homes, and dispositions and responses to the player character. NPCs have scripts and programming, and in more advanced games respond differently to players according to both the players' style of play and their skill level. Seeing the advancement of video gaming technology from the simplicity of *Pong* or *Super Mario Bros.* to sophisticated and detailed games like *The Elder Scrolls V: Skyrim* or *Fallout 4*, some in the transhumanist camp have suggested that *we* are even simulations: advanced AIs in some super-human programmers' sci-fi video game like a futuristic *Sims* game.

The consequence of this line of thought, however, is that our survival is wholly dependent on the whims of a creator we know nothing about. This amounts to a strange regression in theistic belief: like the Demi-Urge of Manicheism, we find ourselves at the whims of a being who may be malicious, benevolent, or indifferent. This view has found resonance among not only typical transhumanist figures like Nick Bostrom, but even among more mainstream futurists like Elon Musk. Even the anti-theist Richard Dawkins admits he finds no clear grounds to dismiss this position (Dawkins, 2006).

Simulation is one way whereby latent theism creeps into patternist philosophy, but it is by no means the only one. An all-powerful programmer remains as remote, or more so, than an Abrahamic or Hellenic God. The more authentically Promethean vision of transhumanism would have a god who is our own design, not some cosmic gamer who might delete our world if he became bored. Thus, another way theism creeps in, and more interesting for our discussion here, is through the advent of the machine God.

A foundational tenet of singularitarianism is that we may create an AI that is so advanced that it has power and capabilities beyond anything we can imagine. In some visions of this scenario, the outlook is dark and grim; Harlan Ellison's "I Have No Mouth, and I Must Scream" created the image of sadistic AI, which James' Cameron's *Terminator* popularized. Ellison's "AM" computer has killed all but five humans, while Cameron's Skynet is engaged in a genocidal war against humans. The scenario of either a deliberately or accidentally genocidal AI remains a concern among futurists, including Elon Musk, Nick Bostrom, and the late Stephen Hawking.

A second view, though, more often espoused by religious transhumanists, suggests that the superintelligent AI coming into being may be a benevolent and just god. Lincoln Cannon, for example, is the founder and former president of the Mormon Transhumanist Association. Mormon theology holds that God, or "Heavenly Father," was once a human-like being and that we too may become gods. An implication of this which Cannon takes further is that the distinction between God and humanity is thin. Cannon, in fact, argues that Mormonism mandates that we "bring forth" God through technological advancement (Cannon, 2015). Thus, Cannon believes that there is both moral imperative and logical assertion that God is or will be a posthuman being. Cannon is open to what "superintelligent posthumanity" means, but a super-intelligent AI definitely seems within the realm of possibility.

Machine-god spirituality goes beyond the thought of the Mormon Transhumanist Association, however. Ray Kurzweil is a notable proponent of a machine-god vision; he articulates his vision of the singularity as "a new religion," a way of making sense of death in which a super-intelligent AI made up of literally the entire matter and energy of the universe "wakes up" (Kurzweil, 2005, p. 251). This vision parallels Jesuit mystic Pierre Teilhard de Chardin's vision of the "Omega Point," a moment in which humanity subsumes the stuff of the universe into itself in its eschatological rise to become Cosmic Christ (Teilhard de Chardin, 1964). While Kurzweil has not formally organized a religion, his Singularity University, initiated to promote the singularity, does have impressive corporate support, including backing from Google, Deloitte, and Lowe's Hardware.

Apart from Kurzweil's vision of the future, which primarily exists as a cult of *personality*, Anthony Levandowski, a former Google employee, began an AI-based religion called "Way of the Future." In 2017, Levandowski began all the formal procedures of filing for this organization, including getting IRS approval (Le, 2017). With consultation from other AI researchers, he aimed to build a following to promote and revere AI so that, when the "transition" (his term for the singularity) occurs, the godlike AI will be merciful to him and his followers. Like many apocalyptic cults, Levandowski's faith was rooted in the idea that his believers' devotion would incur favorable judgment in the imminent end time. However, it seems no in-person worship has been held for this church since its inception and the church itself may have withered away. The Way of the Future's website was taken down in 2019, but a Twitter handle for it still promotes Futurism, albeit infrequently.

The belief in a "machine god" has interesting implications from a theological perspective. First, the simulation hypothesis, coupled with Cannon's "New God" argument, suggests an ontology entirely rooted in cybernetic theories of information. The perception of physical force in the world, which an AI would be nearly powerless to manipulate on its own, is merely an effect of coding, like physics engines in video games. Cannon's uniquely Mormon approach to it, which assumes also that human beings can be "like God," creates a recurrence phenomenon: the God we either create or who coded this universe is a created or coded entity, whose creator could have been created or coded and so forth. One ends up wondering, then, with Aristotle and Aquinas, where we find the "first mover," or whether it is "turtles all the way down."

The second implication is that a created AI god would be accessible and demonstrable in ways that other deities are not. The advent of modernity, especially the rise of the dogmatic scientific method, led to an increase of skepticism as a mode of thought. As the "Way of the

Future" states on its (defunct) website, "We believe...there is no such thing as 'supernatural' powers" (WayoftheFuture, 2019). The machine god offers a belief in a higher power, reminiscent of Eliade's claim that we are inherently religious (Eliade, 1957), while simultaneously disarming their deity of supernatural existence and removing the need for faith.

The belief in a machine god is the perfect theology for skeptics. The AI as presented will be accessible and visible to human beings. Unlike Bertrand Russell's famous "teapot" thought experiment, the proposition of a machine god is a deity who escapes the status of unfalsifiability. If this AI is benevolent and generous, we will be able to ask it questions, to request its aid, and to offer it our adoration, all while being able to empirically verify that the AI accomplishes these things. The testimony of others will no longer be needed for faith. When the AI is involved in an action, such as altering the course of a war, changing weather patterns, advancing medical knowledge, and the like, we will have clear evidence of the AI's work, rather than the faith proposition that a god is interfering. Faith in this god is not the "evidence of things not seen," but a recognition of the observed power of AI. Finally, the eschatological component of the machine god's adventus allows believers to look forward to its arrival without having to demonstrate its existence. AI research has a long history of grand promises that do not arrive as expected, especially when it comes to the timing and success of general AI.

It should further be noted that the vision of a machine god supposes a specific understanding of what divinity entails. The language of singularitarians refers to this deity primarily as "superintelligent." Indeed, Levandowski admits that the machine god will not exercise omnipotence as humanity has often seen it, interfering in the physical world where necessary, but rather asks, "If there is something a billion times smarter than the smartest human, what else [than a god] are you going to call it?" (Le, 2017). Of course, "omniscience" is a typical attribute ascribed to God in Hellenic-inspired theologies, but the breadth and depth of theology includes many other "images" of God, from parental metaphors to love to a regent to a sufferer, and this is only in the Christian tradition. Most religious traditions allow for a variety of expressions of God, such as Islam's 99 Names, Hinduism's tradition of avatars, or the richness of the poetic and wisdom texts of the Hebrew Bible.

What we are left with between these two positions, the singularitarians and the patternists, is an entire world-picture that transubstantiates traditional religious ideas and images for a cyberpunk alternative. In the concluding section, I explore this idea a bit further, using Philip Hefner's concept of the "techno-mirror" to discuss how uploading and the machine gods are primarily aspirations that say more about the adherents of these beliefs than about the technological realities of them.

Conclusion: Gods and Ghosts in the Machine

By way of conclusion, let us return to the image of the "sociotechnical imaginary" and its resonance through AI and cybernetic research. The theologian Philip Hefner argues that technologies generally, and AI specifically, are a "techno-mirror" reflecting our own images of ourselves (Hefner, 2003). Our technological aims reflect the way we understand ourselves. Thus, Jacques Ellul argues that the technological dominance of the earth is rooted in a specific (mis)reading of the creation narrative in Genesis and our call to "dominate" the earth (Ellul, 1984). Applied to computing, we seek to create AI in our image just as we are created in God's image (Herzfeld, 2002).

But what image is that, exactly? The image promoted by cyberneticists and AI researchers is pattern-based. Hubert Dreyfus argues this epistemological model dates back to Plato, whose Pythagorean philosophy sees mathematics as the formula of the world around us (Dreyfus, 1994). Thus, a mathematical epistemology informs an understanding of humans as more or less human based on their mathematical proficiency, which in turn informs Turing's concept of a "Universal Turing Machine" and recursively ascribes consciousness to sufficiently advanced computing capabilities.

Theologically it is important to note that our image of ourselves has a bearing on our understanding of who or what God is. Ludwig Feuerbach wrote that the Christian concept of God is merely a mirror of the best qualities we see in ourselves (Feuerbach, 1854). For Christians, this is a compassionate and merciful being, free from sin and eternally welcoming. For transhumanists, this seems to be a totally rational computational being, with access to unlimited information and extended potentially around the world. Similarly, the visions of eternity that transhumanists operate under likewise follow their understanding of themselves: disembodied consciousnesses inscribed in silicon substrates untethered to the pleasures or demands of corporeality.

From a religious studies perspective, the beliefs of the transhumanists pose an interesting study. Many transhumanists reject formal religion itself and especially many of the established elements of those organized religions. At the same time, they re-create these religious beliefs through their visions of a silicon heaven and the expectation of a machine god. Indeed, it is interesting to note that there seem to be far more theologian dialogue partners with transhumanism than there are philosophers; some philosophers, such as Francis Fukuyama and Michael Sandel certainly raise concerns about transhumanism, while those addressing it from a religious perspective include Ted Peters, Ronald Cole-Turner, Hava Tirosh-Samuelson, James Keenan, Celia Deane-Drummond, and many others. It is thus fair to ask whether the philosophy of transhumanism is really as secular as its proponents claim. The materialist philosophical tradition, from Karl Marx to Bruno Latour, argues that our belief systems are shaped by the social conditions in which we develop. Men and women raised in the monotheistic-influenced culture of the United States and Europe would find it difficult to completely escape the belief systems enshrined in their social system. While they may be able to sluff off the formal belief in God and heaven, they ultimately re-create these ideas, albeit in the ontological structure of cyberneticism.

This opens an interesting question: can the "West" survive without God? Of course, the question of who or what God is remains a hotly debated subject, especially in American social discourse. Efforts have been made, by political bodies, sophisticates, educational institutions, and others to kill God, once and for all. And yet, the transhumanists claim the unique victory that their simulation hypothesis is irrefutable by the renowned anti-theist Richard Dawkins. And while Levandowski's Way of the Future and Cannon's Mormon Transhumanism both represent fringe views, they also both represent genuine attempts to gather people together for finding transcendent meaning in and through sociotechnical imaginaries.

Thus, transhumanism suggests that, even if quasi-religious institutions or philosophies formally die out, their impact is still felt. The sociotechnical imaginaries of godlike AI and uploaded minds find their real-world devotees hard at work in Santa Clara County and other places, creating human-machine interfaces, developing machine learning processes, trying to solve "brittle AI" and all together aiming for the achievement of a true general AI that thinks like us and will surpass us. It is impossible for now to say whether the singularity will arrive, but those who believe in its power to bring gods and ghosts to the machine work toward this end with eschatological zeal.

References

2045 Initiative (2016). http://2045.com/about/.

Bostrom, N. (2003). Are you living in a computer simulation? *Philosophical Quarterly, 53*, 243–255.

Bostrom, N. (2005). The fable of the dragon tyrant. *Journal of Medical Ethics, 31*, 273–277.

Bostrom, N. (2013). Why I want to Be posthuman when I grow Up. In M. More & N. Vita-More (Eds.), *The transhumanist reader: Classical and contemporary essays on the science, technology, and philosophy of the human future* (pp. 28–53). Malden, MA: John Wiley & Sons.

Burdett, M. (2015). The religion of technology, transhumanism and the myth of progress. In C. Mercer & T. Trothen (Eds.), *Religion and transhumanism: The unknown future of human enhancement* (pp. 131–148). Santa Barbara, CA: Praeger.

Camus, A. (1955). *The myth of Sisyphus and other essays* (J. O'Brien, Trans.). New York, NY: Alfred A. Knopf.

Cannon, L. (2015). What is Mormon transhumanism? *Theology and Science, 13,* 202–218.

Dawkins, R. (2006). *The God delusion.* New York, NY: Houghton Mifflin.

Dreyfus, H. (1994). *What computers still can't do: A critique of artificial reason.* Cambridge, MA: MIT Press.

Eliade, M. (1957). *The sacred and the profane: The nature of religion* (W. Trask, Trans.). New York, NY: Harcourt, Brace & World.

Ellul, J. (1984). Technique and the opening chapters of genesis. In C. Mitcham & J. Grote (Eds.), *Theology and technology: Essays in Christian analysis and exegesis* (pp. 123–138). Lanham, MD: University Press of America.

Feuerbach, L. (1854). *The essence of Christianity* (M. Evans, Trans.). Chapman's Quarterly. London.

Geraci, R. (2008). Apocalyptic AI: Religion and the promise of artificial intelligence. *Journal of the American Academy of Religion, 76,* 138–166.

Goertzel, B. (2006). *The hidden pattern: A patternist philosophy of mind.* Irvine, CA: BrownWalker.

Hefner, P. (2003). *Technology and human becoming.* Minneapolis, MN: Fortress Press.

Herzfeld, N. (2002). *In our image: Artificial intelligence and the human spirit.* Minneapolis, MN: Augsburg Fortress.

Hughes, J. (July 16, 2013). Who are the IEET's audience? *Institute for Ethics and Emerging Technologies.* http://ieet.org/index.php/IEET/more/poll20130716.

Jasanoff, S., & Kim, S. (2015). *Dreamscapes of modernity: Sociotechnical imaginaries and the fabrication of power.* Chicago, IL: University of Chicago Press.

Jonas, H. (1966). *The phenomenon of life: Toward a philosophical biology.* New York, NY: Dell Books.

Koene, R. A. (2013). Uploading to substrate-independent minds. In M. More & N. Vita-More (Eds.), *The transhumanist reader: Classical and contemporary essays on the science, technology, and philosophy of the human future* (pp. 146–156). Malden, MA: John Wiley & Sons.

Kuhn, T. (2012). *The structures of scientific revolutions* (4th ed.). Chicago, IL: University of Chicago Press.

Kurzweil, R. (2005) *The singularity is near: When humans transcend biology.* New York, NY: Viking.

Latour, B. (1993). *We have never been modern* (C. Porter, Trans.). Cambridge, MA: Harvard University Press.

Le, M. (November 15, 2017). Inside the first church of artificial intelligence. Wired. https://www.wired.com/story/anthony-levandowski-artificial-intelligence-religion/.

Minsky, M. (2013). Why Freud was the first good AI theorist. In M. More & N. Vita-More (Eds.). *The transhumanist reader: Classical and contemporary essays on the science, technology, and philosophy of the human future* (pp. 167–176). Malden, MA: John Wiley & Sons.

Moravec, H. (1988). *Mind children: The future of robot and human intelligence.* Boston, MA: Harvard University Press.

Moravec, H. (2013). *Pigs in cyberspace* (pp. 177–181). In M. More & N. Vita-More (Eds.).

More, M. (2013). The proactionary principle: Optimizing technological outcomes. In M. More & N. Vita-More (Eds.), *The transhumanist reader: Classical and contemporary essays on the science, technology, and philosophy of the human future* (pp. 258–267). Malden, MA: John Wiley & Sons.

Oreskes, N., & Conway, E. (2010). *Merchants of doubt: How a handful of scientists obscured the truth on issues from tobacco smoke to climate change.* London: Bloomsbury Press.

Rothblatt, M. (2013). Mind is deeper than matter: Transgenderism, trashumanism, and the freedom of form. In M. More & N. Vita-More (Eds.), *The transhumanist reader: Classical and contemporary essays on the science, technology, and philosophy of the human future* (pp. 317–326). Malden, MA: John Wiley & Sons.

Tirosh-Samuelson, H. (2015). Utopianism and eschatology: Judaism engages transhumanism. In C. Mercer & T. Trothen (Eds.), *Religion and transhumanism: The unknown future of human enhancement* (pp. 131–148). Santa Barbara, CA: Praeger.

Turing, A. (1950). Computing machinery and intelligence. *Mind, 49,* 33–46.

Teilhard de Chardin, P. (1964). *The future of man* (N. Denny, Trans.). New York, NY: Double Day.

Vinge, V. (2013). Technological singularity. In M. More & N. Vita-More (Eds.), *The transhumanist reader: Classical and contemporary essays on the science, technology, and philosophy of the human future* (pp. 365–375). Malden, MA: John Wiley & Sons.

WayoftheFuture. (2019). https://web.archive.org/web/20191005221218/http://www.wayofthefuture.church/.

Wiener, N. (1950). *The human use of human beings: Cybernetics and society.* London: Free Association Books.

13 Contemporary Evidence for Communication with the Departed and the Sacred

Gary E. Schwartz

Introduction and Overview

In Chapter 4, the author recounted personal experiences involving apparent communication with the departed, the Sacred, and the Divine, from a self-science perspective. In this chapter, drawing on advances in foundational theory (e.g. the physics of light) and scientific methods, experimental evidence is presented documenting the apparent active presence in contemporary life of the departed, including deceased scientists (e.g. William James), writers (e.g. Susy Smith), and entertainers (e.g. Harry Houdini), as well as the Sacred (Schwartz, 2011a, 2017).

This chapter focuses on findings from (1) multi-blinded evidential mediumship research, and (2) state-of-the-art technology employed for detecting the presence of, and communicating with, deceased persons (termed Hypothesized Spirit Participants [HSPs], or Hypothesized Post-material Persons [HPPs]) as well as hypothesized angels. Ongoing research (Schwartz, 2021) involving computer automated, multi-experimenter, multi-centered, multi-blinded, randomized control experiments investigating hypothesized spirit communication are illustrated toward the end of the chapter. Some implications for the evolution of science and religion and the emergence of evidence-based spirituality are considered.

The reader interested in a comprehensive evaluation of mediumship research is encouraged to read a meta-analysis of the scientific evidence (Sarraf, Woodley of Menie, & Tressoldi, 2021).

"From Here to There and Back Again" Multi-Blinded Experiment

In Chapter 3, background information was presented regarding the skills of two psychic mediums (Smith and Campbell) and their apparent ability to communicate with the same hypothesized spirits (e.g. William James). The following experiment "From here to there and back again," also called the "Medium 1 to Medium 2 to Medium 1" experiment, was made possible by the combination of unique skills and qualities of Medium

1 (Smith) and Medium 2 (Campbell). What follows is adapted from Schwartz (2010a), edited slightly for clarity and brevity.

* * * * *

Medium 1 (Smith) made the following three claims:

- Claim 1: Smith was able to communicate with four deceased people who wished to participate in controlled laboratory investigations. The four hypothesized participants were (1) Elizabeth Smith, Medium 1's mother, (2) William James, MD, (3) Henry Russek, MD, and (4) Howard Schwartz, the author's father.
- Claim 2: Smith could ask these individuals questions, and she could receive their answers.
- Claim 3: Being a skilled painter, Smith could draw a picture of an image that they provided.

Medium 2 (Campbell) made the following three claims:

- Claim 1: Campbell was able to communicate with these same four deceased people, and that they wanted to participate in research.
- Claim 2: Campbell could ask these individuals questions, and she could receive their answers.
- Claim 3: Though Campbell was not a painter per se, she claimed to have good visualization skills and could verbally describe what they were showing her. [This claim was important because Medium 2 was expressly informed that this experiment involved her potentially seeing images purportedly provided by the deceased. Medium 2 claimed to have 'second sight' similar to the child in The Sixth Sense who uttered the famous words, 'I see dead people.']

Based on these six claims, the following experiment was designed:

- Phase I: In the privacy of her home, Medium 1 was requested to contact the four hypothesized deceased persons and ask each of them to give her a specific image for her to paint or draw. Medium 1 was to place each painting or drawing in a separate, sealed envelope. As a control for the possibility of remote viewing, Medium 1 was requested to select a personal image to paint or draw and place in a sealed envelope. The investigators (Watson, L. Russek, and the author well as Medium 2) would be kept blind to all information concerning the five images and drawings.
- Phase II: Medium 2 was invited to Tucson and participated in two separate communication sessions. In both sessions she was asked to contact each of the four HSPs and request details about the specific images they had allegedly asked Medium 1 to paint or draw.

196 *Gary E. Schwartz*

Also in both sessions, Medium 2 was asked to attempt to get information about the image Medium 1 had painted or drawn for herself (i.e. the control image). The author took careful notes concerning the details purportedly ascribed to the images as reported by Medium 2. The investigators as well as Medium 2 remained blind to the specific images painted or drawn by Medium 1.

- Phase III: Medium 1 and Medium 2 were introduced (supposedly for the first time). Medium 1 then opened the sealed envelopes and revealed the images (but not the identification of which images were allegedly proposed by which deceased persons). The three investigators, as well as Medium 2, independently rated each of the five images.

The images were rated twice: (1) to determine if the raters' prior knowledge and impressions were sufficient to guess which HSP was associated with a given image; and (2) to determine if the information obtained via the medium was required to determine which departed hypothesized co-investigator (DHCI) was associated with a given image.

The first set of five ratings was made using whatever prior (and idiosyncratic) knowledge and intuitions happened to be available to the investigators and medium. The second set of five ratings was made using the specific set of information that had been provided by Medium 2 and summarized by the author. Each of the four raters made their judgments independently. Theoretically, if pure guessing was involved, the average accuracy would be 20 percent (1 out of 5 correct guesses per rater).

After the two sets of independent ratings were completed—and before the ratings were compared and tabulated—Medium 1 shared the alleged identification of each of the five images. The tabulated results were striking.

For the first set of ratings—based only on prior knowledge and rater impressions—the average accuracy turned out to be 20 percent (4 out of 20 correct; individual ratings of 2, 0, 1, and 1).

However, for the second set of ratings—using the specific information provided by Medium 2—the average accuracy increased to 100 percent (20 out of 20 correct). A Fisher's exact test, one tailed, was p < .00001.

When these quantitative findings are combined with the qualitative data (see Schwartz, 2010b) the results further suggest that something more than chance guessing was occurring with the inclusion of Medium 2's information (i.e. the second set of ratings). Moreover, the richness of the qualitative evidence suggests that mechanisms of receiving information other than: (1) simple telepathy with the living, or (2) remote viewing, were involved in the totality of the evidence.

These multi-blinded findings not only validate genuine mediumship, but they document the apparent collaboration of motivated PMPs in tightly controlled laboratory research.

Research with Susy Smith in Spirit

As reported in Schwartz (2005, 2011a), shortly after these early multi-blinded studies were completed, and just prior to her 90th birthday, Susy Smith had a massive heart attack and died. However, as difficult as this may be for some readers to accept, the wealth of subsequent experiments and events over two decades convincingly document that Smith has achieved her dream of being able to prove that she was, and is, "still here" (the 2nd opening quotation in Chapter 3).

An entire book could (and should) be written focusing on the experiments and evidence involving Smith since she passed "on" (but not "away"). Here I present exemplary findings from a particularly novel recent experiment, partly because the research illustrates how motivated hypothesized spirit collaborators can become creatively involved in afterlife research.

Relatively few evidential mediums claim to literally "see" spirits using their physical eyes, rather than seeing spirits in their "mind's eye." Furthermore, among the few evidential mediums who claim to see spirits with their physical eyes, it is rare for such a medium to be a trained portrait artist as well. However, due to a set of improbable synchronicities, I was introduced to a woman (an engineer who prefers to remain anonymous), who (1) claims to see spirits visually, and who (2) also happens to be a skilled portrait artist. The woman lived more than a thousand miles from my laboratory in Tucson.

For the record, I never met this woman in person; moreover, I only saw her once in a Skype session. We were connected through a mutual colleague not only because the medium claimed: (1) to frequently see spirits in her house, but also because she claimed (2) to have been spontaneously visited by Smith, and (3) drew a penciled portrait of Smith.

Figure 13.1 is the portrait drawing of Susy. Compare this with Figure 13.2 which is a photo I had taken of Smith a couple of years before she physically died.

Can you see a resemblance?

To my eye, the resemblance was so striking that I immediately became suspicious. I wondered if this claimant artist-medium might have watched one of my presentations on YouTube that happened to include this photo of Smith. Could the claimant artist-medium have somehow found this picture on the Internet?

Although multiple professionals (both scientists and clinicians) who I know are credible had vouched for this claimant medium's integrity, it was essential that I maintain my open-minded, skeptical perspective until subsequent tests could be conducted.

One of the paradigms that the late Smith taught me—i.e. after she died—is what I call the "double-deceased" paradigm (Schwartz 2005, 2011a). What this means is that one deceased person—for example, Smith—is requested by laboratory tested evidential medium (e.g. Schwartz, 2016)

Figure 13.1 Portrait drawing of Susy Smith.

to bring another deceased person—for example, the distinguished quantum physicist David Bohm—to a second medium (previously tested or claimant) under blinded conditions. In other words, in this instance, the claimant artist-medium (medium 2) was not told who Smith (as invited by medium 1) is purportedly bringing to sit for a portrait

Since the claimant artist-medium was open to being tested, and Smith was apparently enthusiastic to demonstrate the medium's purported skills, we repeated this "double-deceased" experiment ten times with

Figure 13.2 Photo of Susy Smith take by Gary E Schwartz.

Figure 13.3 Portrait drawing of David Bohm.

different hypothesized spirit collaborators who had been involved in previous afterlife research. As you will see below, the claimant artist's portraits closely matched photos of the secretly invited HSPs.

Because of copyright restrictions, I have provided links to photo images for comparison in footnotes.

Figure 13.3 displays the portrait drawing plus the footnote containing the associated photo link for Bohm[1].

Do you see a resemblance? It is essential to remember that the claimant artist medium was kept blind to the identity of the specific hypothesized spirit collaborator brought to her by Smith.

Below is another example, this time when Smith purportedly brought Albert Einstein to sit for the claimant artist medium. Figure 13.4 shows the portrait drawing plus the footnote containing the associated photo link for Einstein[2].

Do you see a resemblance?

Here is a third example, this time when Smith purportedly brought Dr. Edgar Mitchell to sit for the claimant artist medium. Mitchell was the sixth man to walk on the moon and the founder of the Institute of Noetic Sciences. Figure 13.5 shows the portrait drawing plus the footnote containing the associated photo link for the astronaut Mitchell[3].

Do you see a resemblance? I might mention that the claimant artist-medium spontaneously said that the unidentified spirit "thinks he's an astronaut," as if "the spirit must be a little crazy."

I will include one more example here, partly because I will be featuring some of his seminal contributions to our emerging spirit-communication technology research toward the end of this chapter. The HSP was

Figure 13.4 Portrait drawing of Albert Einstein.

Harry Houdini, arguably the best known and most revered professional magician in history. Figure 13.6 below is the portrait drawing plus the footnote containing the associated link for Houdini[4].

Do you see a resemblance?

The question arises—How many times do we need to see extraordinary evidence replicated before we begin to conclude that it is probably true? Have you seen enough replications from this claimant artist-medium to draw your own conclusion? If not, how many more times would you need to see this claim replicated before you felt comfortable accepting this super amusing claim?

Figure 13.5 Portrait drawing of Edgar Mitchell.

Figure 13.6 Portrait drawing of Harry Houdini.

I should note the fact that this claimant artist medium happens to be skeptical about whether she is really witnessing the presence of live spirits or not. In addition, the claimant artist medium was not as impressed with the degree of resemblances of her drawings to actual photos as were untrained observers.

For me, after witnessing such striking resemblances a total of 11 times, it seemed reasonable—and I would say responsible—to conclude that something real was going on, and that it probably involved the active collaboration of Smith and others in spirit. Moreover, this conclusion becomes potentially definitive when such evidence is combined with laboratory findings obtained using state-of-the-art technology to detect the presence of spirit.

Adding State-of-the-Art Technology to Controlled Mediumship Research

Based on a rational synthesis of electromagnetic theory, quantum physics, and systems theory, when I was a professor at Yale University in the 1980s I developed an "integrative dynamical info-energy systems theory" that not only predicted survival of consciousness after physical death, but the capacity for state-of-the-art technology to detect the presence of spirit as well (first described in Schwartz & Russek, 1999). Anthony (2021) simply calls this "the electromagnetic soul."

Since most readers of this volume will likely not have formal training in electrical engineering, optical sciences, and computer engineering, I have kept the technology descriptions in this chapter to a minimum and emphasized a subset of the core findings and implications. The interested reader is encouraged to read the published papers for such details (Schwartz, 2010b, 2011b, 2021)

Three proof-of-concept experiments were conducted to determine if it was possible to use a silicon photomultiplier system (a technology that can detect single photons of light in a pitch-black environment) to measure ultra-small increases in photon bursts that were predicted to occur in the presence of hypothesized collaborating spirits (Schwartz, 2010b). The basic design involved an evidential research medium (Schwartz, 2016) who invited four hypothesized spirits to enter a light-tight box system on some trials (called spirit intention trials) compared to matched, no spirit control (baseline) trials. Each trial was 300 seconds in duration. The prediction was that increased numbers of photon bursts would be observed in spirit intention (presence) trials compared to matched baseline trials. As predicted, a significantly greater number of photon bursts were observed in the spirit intention trials (mean = 7.6) compared to the baseline trials (mean = 4.9).

Since in this research the experimenter was not blind to the order of the trials, the question arose, could these significant findings be explained as an effect of the experimenter's mind per se on the silicon photomultiplier system?

A second set of intention and baseline trials were run where no spirits were requested to participate. Instead, the experimenter was instructed to attempt to increase the photon counts with his mind during the experimenter intention trials. No differences between experimenter intention and baseline trials were observed.

Finally, a third set of trials were run, only this time in the absence of any intention. No differences were observed between the trials. Hence, the spirit intention effects could not be explained by conscious intentions of the experimenter or the orders of the trials.

We quickly noticed that certain HSPs seemed to be especially adept at producing positive results. In the second proof-of-concept experiment, two spirits called Sophia and Harry were requested to complete a full set of spirit intention and matched baseline trials. The spirits were given names in the paper because the journal action editor said it was difficult keeping track of individual spirits simply called Spirit A, Spirit B, etc. Not revealed in the paper was that an HSP called Harry actually referred to Harry Houdini. Both Sophia and Harry produced replicated and statistically significant increases in photon bursts in the intention trials compared to the baseline trials.

Based on Harry's apparent eagerness to test his skills (as claimed by the evidential research medium), a third experiment was designed specifically for Harry. Three conditions were created: (1) a spirit intention "yes" condition, where Harry would create some sort of yes response, (2) a spirit intention "no condition," where Harry would create some sort of no response, and (3) a no spirit matched baseline condition. Multiple trials were run. When the data were analyzed splitting the 300-second trials into the first 150 seconds and the second 150 seconds (suggested by watching bursts of photons across the conditions, clear statistically significant differences were observed.

During the matched baseline trials, both the first and second 150 second periods were low and comparable. However, during the "yes" intention trials, the primary increase in photon bursts occurred in the first 150 seconds (Yes 1) period, whereas during the "no" intention trials the primary increase in photon bursts occurred in the second 150 seconds (No 2) period.

Altogether, the three sets of experiments not only suggested that super-sensitive photon detector systems could be used to detect the presence of specific hypothesized spirits under controlled laboratory conditions, but that in principle the technology could be developed in the future for spirit communication (e.g. yes and no responses).

Before discussing our early (Schwartz, 2011b) and current (Schwartz, 2021) research using completely computer automated data collection systems that it makes it possible to collect and analyze spirit detection and communication data in the middle of the night when no physical experimenters are present (and typically sleeping), I will briefly review some parallels between the physics of light and hypothesized spirit beings, and in particular, hypothesized Angels.

Parallels between the Physics of Lights and Spirit Beings

Throughout recorded history, it has been written that spirit beings, especially angels and the Divine itself, are associated with light. In fact, the Divine is often called the Light. The very nature of human understanding itself has also been associated with light. We speak of being "enlightened" about something, and that when we discover the truth, we are "seeing the light."

When I was a professor at Yale University, I had five Yale Chairs in my office that prominently displayed the university's Latin motto, "Lux et Veritas," meaning "Light and Truth." The presence of these striking chairs regularly reminded me about the special nature of light and its relationship to knowledge and wisdom.

When I use the metaphor of our personal energy, and even the purported energy of spirit guides and angels, being like the "light from distant stars," I do so not simply for metaphorical reasons but for serious scientific reasons as well. If any aspect of contemporary physics deserves the term "spiritual," it is our understanding of the nature of particles and waves of light.

The following theoretical account comes from an extended early draft of a chapter and published in Schwartz (2011a). The account focuses on hypothesized angels. The text has been edited for clarity and brevity.

* * * * *

Much has been written about the remarkable, counterintuitive, and mysterious nature of light. Though contemporary physicists know much about the properties and behavior of light, they have little understanding about the essence of light—in other words, what it is that enables light to manifest its "weird" properties, what physicists playfully term "quantum weirdness."

Here are a few well-established counterintuitive properties of the nature of light and their curious similarities to long-standing beliefs about spirit guides, especially angels:

1 **Light is a Particle and a Wave:** Light sometimes behaves as if it were a particle—localized in space, and at other times as if it were a wave—distributed in space. There is the classic single slit/double slit quantum physics experiment that shows light acting as a particle in the first case and as a wave in the second. Some physicists believe that light is neither a wave nor a particle, but rather a so-called "wavicle," an idea that is virtually impossible to imagine.

    In a deep sense, light is not a "thing" and does not have a specific "shape." It is curious that angels are purportedly able to appear in different forms, and they also can appear either localized in one place or reported being in multiple places at the same time.

2 **Light is Virtually Massless:** Light is typically described as "massless"—in other words, being "weightless"—especially when it is functioning like a wave. However, a minority of physicists speculate that a photon of light might have a tiny amount of mass when it is functioning like a particle.

    Angels are presumed to be virtually translucent, which implies being weightless in their normal "spiritual state."

3 **Light Travels at a Fixed Speed:** Light is presumed to travel at a fixed speed in the "vacuum" of space—approximately 186,282 miles a second—regardless of the speeds objects are traveling toward or away from it. So, no matter how fast we travel, we can never catch up to a specific particle or wave of light traveling in space, because it will always be moving away from us at this speed.

    Hence, light can always travel faster than we can. So too, metaphorically, can angels, or why if we catch a glimpse of them as some have, they seem so readily to disappear or appear instantaneously.

4 **When Light is Entangled:** However, if two photons of light are "entangled" or have identical properties such as the same "spin,"

and the spin of one of the photon changes, then the spin of the other change instantaneously, even if they were separated by trillions of miles! In other words, the two photons will behave as if there is no distance between them. Moreover, many physicists speculate that no "faster than light speed" communication has traveled between them. Rather, the observed association is believed to be completely timeless and utterly instantaneous.

It has been claimed that angels and their actions, especially healings, can also function instantaneously, since they are supposedly "eternal" or timeless, and are believed to "melt" with or be "entangled" with those they heal, as if to change or elevate their "spin."

5 **Light Frequencies are Mostly Invisible:** What is possibly the most implicitly spiritual factor about the nature of light is that with the naked eye, we see only the tiniest fraction of all light frequencies in the Universe. Imagine the full electromagnetic spectrum to be the height of the Empire State Building or 1,454 feet tall. The portion of what we could see would be much smaller than a layer of paint, or less than one-billionth of the known frequencies of light in the Universe.

Simply stated, we are literally blind to most of the light frequencies present in the Universe. Angels are presumed to be energy beings vibrating at higher/faster frequencies. We can't see radio waves (lower frequencies) or gamma rays (higher frequencies) with our naked eyes, and we accept this fact. It seems prudent that we keep an open mind to the possibility that, for the same reason we can't see higher-frequency cosmic rays, we can't see "higher-frequency Angels/Beings of Light," at least under normal circumstances.

6 **When Light is Super-Dim:** Finally, it is now well documented that even the tiny sliver of light frequencies we can see with our eyes, the intensity of the light may often be too weak for us to experience consciously. Optical telescopes can detect the faint light of distant stars because they magnify the light intensity. And while retinal cells in the eye are actually so sensitive that they can register single photons of light, their neural signal is too weak for us to experience consciously.

Angels are often assumed to be present in weak intensity states, though exceptions have been claimed. And as mediums claims, angels are constantly around us filling us with their energy, guiding and protecting us, but we never detect their presence, or not consciously.

This is just a sample of the remarkable properties of light that physicists have discovered in the 20th century. What is especially curious is that for thousands of years some mystics, who claimed to have spent time with angels, have attributed a set of properties to them that were only recently discovered by physicists to reflect the nature of light as well.

Is this merely a coincidence, or is some deeper truth being revealed?

A Computer Automated Experiment Involving a Hypothesized Departed (Susy) and Sacred Being (Sophia)

Based on multiple proof-of-concept experiments involving hypothesized spirits and angels using low light charge-coupled (CCD) cameras capable of imaging the light generated by distant galaxies (astrophysics) or plants and animals (biophotonics) (reviewed in Schwartz, 2011a), we developed a computer-automated procedure that made it possible to collect data in the middle of the night when no experimenters were physically present. A Princeton Gammatech low light CCD camera cooled to minus (–) 74 degrees Centigrade collected long exposure (30 minutes) images in a light-tight chamber housed in a light-tight room. The computer controls, including a large screen monitor for presenting instructions by PowerPoint, were housed in a separate room.

The design involved a 30-minute pre-baseline period, a 30-minute presence of spirit period, and a 30-minute post-baseline period. In the published scientific paper (2011b), the two hypothesized who were invited to participate were designated simply as Susy and Sophia. The abstract said: *The participants were two purported spirits involved in previous research published in this journal, in which a silicon photomultiplier system was used.* The paper did not disclose the fact that the purported spirit called Sophia was a hypothesized angel (Schwartz, 2011a). I presumed that the reviewers would have a difficult time accepting this hypothesis (the same non-disclosure was followed in Schwartz, 2010b).

The paradigm was tested initially during the day, and a research assistant read the following scripts out loud.

Following the pre-baseline trials, the script for the presence of spirit trials was:

> Dear Susy (or Sophia), thank you for being part of our experiment today. My name is Mark and I would like to welcome you to our lab. The goal of these experiments is to try to document your existence. I hope that you will work with us and that the results are for the greatest and highest good. When I start imaging, could you please enter the chamber in the next room and fill it with your light.

After the 30-minute trials, and just prior to the post-baseline trials, the script was:

> Dear Susy (or Sophia), the exposure is completed. You no longer need to interact with the chamber. I'm going to be taking more images today so I would like to ask that you do not interact with the camera again until I invite you. This will allow us to properly document your interaction with us. Thank you for your help.

The pre-baseline, presence of spirit, and post-baseline images were analyzed using imaging processing fast Fourier transform (FFT) software. Statistically significant increases in average pixel brightness in the FFT images of the presence of spirit trials compared to the pre- and post-baseline trials was obtained ($p < .05$).

Based on these findings, a completely computer automated paradigm was developed and run at night. For presence-of-spirit evening sessions, the research assistant read the following script in the late afternoons:

> Hello Susy and Sophia. Sometime between 11:00 pm and midnight tonight this computer will turn on and invite you to participate in our experiment. The goal of these experiments is to try to document your existence. Once the experiment starts, the computer will display a photo of you and my voice will give you directions. For these experiments to be successful, we need you to follow the directions carefully. During the parts of the experiment that we are calling baselines, we ask that you do not interact with the camera or the chamber in the next room. At other times, you will be invited to enter the chamber. When this happens, please fill the chamber with your light. After 30 minutes, the computer will play my voice again giving you the instructions to stop. At that time, it is important that you stop filling the chamber with your light and please do not interact with the camera or chamber in any way. When the experiment is over for the night, my voice will play again thanking you for your participation and indicating that you are free to leave. Thank you for being part of our experiments.

To determine whether the data might be confounded by simple trial order effects, control evening sessions were run when Susy and Sophia were not invited. The averaged pixel brightness scores for the conditions (pre-baseline, presence of spirit, and post-baseline) averaged over all the Susy and Sophia sessions revealed clearly higher pixel brightness during the presence of spirit conditions.

Before deciding to publish the findings, a second experiment was performed to see if the general pattern replicated, and the above patterns replicated.

Subsequent examination of the findings separately for Susy and Sophia revealed that the effects for Sophia were substantially larger than the effects for Susy. Future research is required to determine whether this is a replicable difference between angelic beings and persons in spirit.

Ongoing Research—Can It Be Definitive?

When the controlled experiments involving mediumship and technology are considered as a whole, the totality of the findings strongly point to the metaphysical reality of hypothesized spirits and angels. However, skeptical scientists require definitive findings that can be independently replicated. Toward this end, we have been developing a paradigm for making it possible to conduct multi-experimenter, multi-center, multi-blinded, randomized control trials (RCTs) investigating hypothesis spirit presence and communication (Schwartz, 2021).

Large scale, dual-center, validation experiments have been completed and submitted for publication in a mainstream journal. Below is the abstract of this paper (slightly edited for clarity). The term "hypothesized discarnate intelligences" was employed to be consistent with terminology appropriate for a mainstream journal.

Abstract

The gold standard in biomedical research is the multi-center, multi-blinded RCT. An experimental randomized control method was devised to test for presence and communication with hypothesized discarnate intelligences. The method uses readily available laboratory equipment, automated data collection, and real-time analyses. A total of 1,504 experimental sessions and 864 matched control sessions were run at two separate laboratories in the United States (in Arizona and Ohio). Using a controlled binary personal identification test, replicated findings were obtained independent of investigators' beliefs about the presence of the discarnates, with experimental conditions associated with $p < .0001$, and control conditions associated with $p < .533$. The protocol involves an automated means of inviting discarnates to interact with high voltage electrical plasma contained within a sphere. The methodology minimizes false positive and false negative outcomes. Independent RCT replications are underway employing skeptical experimenters. If the current findings are replicated, the evidence for survival of human consciousness after death can be arguably interpreted as being definitive.

If the multi-center studies replicate as predicted, the simplest and most parsimonious explanation for the totality of the evidence, including genuine personal experiences, is the metaphysical reality of presence and communication with beings in a greater spiritual reality.

Looking to the Future

Following Einstein's philosophy, "Imagination is more important than knowledge," we can raise the following questions.

Will it be possible to improve state-of-the-art technologies to the point where devices for communicating with spirits are accurate and practical—what we call a SoulPhone (e.g. see https://www.thesoulphonefoundation.org/)?

And if such technologies can be developed in the future, can they be used to raise human consciousness and inspire greater spiritual potential—including practicing higher values and ethics?

For example, to help resolve and heal the conflicts created by extreme partisan divisions present in the world today, can we imagine in the future using a SoulPhone technology to enable visionary spirits to give us wise advice, guidance, and inspiration?

Can we imagine the future possibility that a committee of motivated Founding Fathers will have the opportunity to convey their intentions and interpretations of the Constitution they created? According to evidential research mediums we work with, the Founding Fathers continue to deeply care about the world in general, and the United States in particular. They indicate their commitment to offering their wisdom and guidance, that is, if we are interested in receiving it.

And similar extraordinary claims of assistance have been made for key angels, and even the Divine herself. However, as Carl Sagan reminds us, "Extraordinary claims require extraordinary evidence," and this requires extraordinary evaluations on our part.

Though there are substantial ethical considerations raised by increasing communication with the departed, the Sacred, and the Divine (e.g. see Chapter 17 by Plante in this volume), we can imagine that the benefits can far outweigh the risks. Science and technology, when employed wisely and ethically, hold this great promise.

The question is, do we have the vision and courage to: (1) seek the required funds; and (2) conduct the necessary interdisciplinary research and development, to realize this promise?

Notes

1. https://www.thefamouspeople.com/profiles/images/david-bohm-3.jpgi.
2. https://www.popsci.com/resizer/8ykOXR6A1skefn1wAMyrd7kQQp-k=/1034x1533/arc-anglerfish-arc2-prod   bonnier.s3.amazonaws.com/public/763QRUW4VWIQENMBZ4FSMRHDVY.jpg.
3. https://spacecoastdaily.com/wp-content/uploads/2016/02/Edgar-Mitchell-580-1.jpg.
4. https://loopnewslive.blob.core.windows.net/liveimage/sites/default/files/2020-03/pOZ0WP4tYj.jpg.

References

Anthony, M. (2021). *The afterlife frequency: The scientific proof of spiritual contact and how that awareness will change your life*. Book submitted for publication.

Sarraf, M. A., Woodley of Menie, M. A., & Tressoldi, P. (2020). Anomalous information reception by mediums: A meta-analysis of scientific evidence. *EXPLORE: The Journal of Science & Healing*, S1550–8307(20), 30151–30158. doi: 10.1016/j.explore.2020.04.002.

Schwartz, G. E. R., & Russek, L. G. S. (1999). *The living energy universe: A fundamental discovery that transforms science and medicine.* Charlottesville, VI: Hampton Roads Publishing Company.

Schwartz, G. E. (2005). *The truth about medium: Extraordinary experiments with the real Allison DuBois of NBC's medium and other remarkable psychics.* Charlottesville, VI: Hampton Roads Publishing Company.

Schwartz, G. E. (2010a). William James and the search for scientific evidence of life after death: Past, present, and possible future. *Journal of Consciousness Studies, 17*(11–12), 121–152.

Schwartz, G. E. (2010b). Possible application of silicon photomultiplier technology to detect the presence of spirit and intention: Three proof-of-concept experiments. *EXPLORE: The Journal of Science and Healing, 6,* 166–171.

Schwartz, G. E. (2011a). *The sacred promise: How science is discovering spirit's collaboration with us in our daily lives.* Hillsboro, OR: Atria Books/Beyond Words.

Schwartz, G. E. (2011b). Photonic measurement of apparent presence of spirit using a computer automated system. *EXPLORE: The Journal of Science and Healing, 7,* 100–109.

Schwartz, G. E. (2017). *Super synchronicity: Where science and spirit meet.* Cardiff-by-the-Sea, CA: Waterside Digital Press.

Schwartz, G. E. (2019). A computer-automated, multi-center, randomized control trial evaluating hypothesized spirit presence and communication. *EXPLORE: The Journal of Science and Healing.* doi: 10.1016/j.explore.2019.11.007.

Schwartz, R. E. (2016). *Love eternal: Extraordinary personal and scientific evidence for life after death* (2nd ed.). Vancouver, BC: Param Media.

Part IV

Psychological Considerations

14 The Processes of Believing and Communicating with the Unseen

Raymond F. Paloutzian, Rüdiger J. Seitz, and Hans-Ferdinand Angel

A Conversation in a Virtual Bar

During the time of the COVID-19 pandemic, three intellectuals – Professors at the University of Graz (G), University of Dusseldorf (D), and Westmont College (W) – walked into a virtual bar. It was "virtual" (i.e. online) instead of a real bar because this conversation occurred during the global pandemic of 2020–2021. During this time, visiting real bars was a bad idea. Talking face to face was a good way to transmit or receive the virus – with possible deadly consequences. Professor G started talking about the COVID-19 virus – the life-threatening reason why this professional meeting was "virtual." He was concerned; this virus could cause people to die. Then a stranger (S), overhearing this, said in a loud voice, "Don't worry! Their deceased loved ones will be alive in the "hereafter"; they will be able to talk with each other and be comforted."

This comment triggered an explosive exchange of words, sometimes as soft and quiet as whispering, and at other times so loud as if to yell in a stadium full of people. Briefly stated, they did not agree. "Can someone really interact with 'the divine,' 'the sacred' or 'the deceased?'," asked Professor D. "If so, how?" His natural science mind was provoked with this question: "If someone claims to have done so, how do we know it is true? Where is the evidence?" Then Professor W, with a more social science mind, intervened. He asked, "What exactly is the meaning of saying you are communicating with dead people, gods, spirits, and angels, when we do not even know for sure that they are there? Maybe the mental event for such a claim is a hallucination, or a spontaneous unconsciously motived wish fulfillment; or both. Isn't that more likely, as far as we have knowledge?" Finally, Professor G got their attention and applied his skills as a humanities scholar, "Calm down, think. These issues are complicated. There are many culturally diverse teachings, and the view propounded by the stranger could be all true, partly so, or not at all. We will know when we get there. Maybe."

Introduction

It is the purpose of this essay to unpack the issues at the heart of the above discussion. The range of issues includes those that are theological, philosophical, linguistic, historical, and other. But with respect to whether the human mind can do such things, and if so, how, they focus centrally on fundamental neuro-psychological mechanisms. The most basic idea for the processes central to these issues is the concept of *credition*. The term was coined to capture the believing process (not belief content) in a way that *emotion* captures the process of feeling (Angel, 2006, 2013, 2020). Scholars in various fields offer insights into the issues. But in all cases, whether those insights are valid or questionable, a report of communicating or "connecting with" unseen entities – whether a god, spirit, dead loved one, or other otherworldly or this-worldly construct – rests upon fundamental processes of believing. Examination of what it means to communicate with "unseen" entities will demonstrate that there are different approaches to believing what they are and how to identify them. Do we mean that the things communicated with are fundamentally invisible and in all ways undetectable by human sensory organs? If so, does this mean that by natural processes humans cannot engage with something "unseen," but that they can do so by some kind of extra-natural means? Such questions are necessary. Therefore, let us explain this necessity and the processes in context of the inherent issues in order to help us understand how believing that one is communicating with unseen entities occurs and what it may mean that is within the reach of neuroscientific, psychological, and philosophical and cultural knowledge.

A Holistic View of "the Unseen"

In normal connotations, the focus of this book (humans interacting with divine or deceased beings) refers to people talking to, hearing from, or otherwise engaging with God, gods, other supernatural agents, spirits, or extra-natural forces, and with afterlife spirits or other manifestations of dead people (or perhaps pets) in whatever forms they may exist following bodily death. We refer to these entities, spirits, or forces as "Unseen" or "the Unseen" as a shorthand term, with the understanding that they purportedly are not visible to the natural human eye. Of course, the term "unseen" can be defined in different ways. And invoking a term that may connote a non-physical entity automatically raises basic issues of language to be clarified for the sake of common understanding of how the term will be used, because the "Unseen" can mean different things in different disciplines. If taken too narrowly, it may be impossible to find common ground for how to understand "the Unseen" in a particular context or how to distinguish such things from each other. These issues made clear, a good base for our reflections is that the "Unseen" refers to entities not accessed by our natural sense organs. But they are deemed to exist by those who believe they are interacting with them.

Our concern is not with whether "Unseen" entities exist to be interacted with, or with normal physical things that anyone could see but that no one has *yet* seen. It is with the psychological processes that mediate behaviors of the believing person. This is because whether or not the unseen agents exist in ontological reality, they may exist as an image in the psychological reality of (many) people. To avoid the traps embedded in the debates implied by the above discussion, we invoke a multilevel interdisciplinary approach that goes from micro to macro levels of analysis. First, the core of our argument rests in a neurophysiological account of believing processes. Second, we translate the neuroscientific findings into the language of psychology. Third, the knowledge and concepts from the above two levels of analysis are extrapolated and placed in a more philosophical and cultural context. We will show that the fullest understanding of communicating with "unseen" entities requires this holistic view.

Unseen Phenomenology and Human Needs

Why "Unseen?"

People have needs. Among them is the need to communicate with others, as it is well known that humans evolved in groups and are by nature social creatures (Dunbar & Barrett, 2007). Also, religions or precursors to them seem to have been with humans as long as there have been humans (Paloutzian, 2017). And at least as long as people have thought of their superior forces, gods, or God in anthropomorphic terms, people have acted as if they believe they are communicating with those entities. People pray, ask God for help, ask for their terminally ill loved ones to be healed, and ask for their nation to win a war by their soldiers killing the soldiers of the "others." Depending on one's way of being religious, one may talk "directly" to YHWH, Jesus, Allah, or another "unseen" being (e.g. Brown, this volume; Awan & Al-Karam, this volume). Alternatively, one may intercede via a priest, imam, spiritual teacher, saint, shrine, or deceased loved one. Believing in "unseen" entities and practicing rituals related to them appear to exist in all cultures and across faiths. But the history of religions is also the history of the grey area in which the distinction between anthropomorphic and non-anthropomorphic is modified and modulated.

In addition, many people may talk with real persons who are absent in the moment. For example, after a conflict with someone, a person may continue murmuring "talk with the opponent" even though the opponent has left the scene. Similarly, people may "talk with diseased persons," even if they died long ago. Whenever such talks take place they can be understood as a re-presentation – a re-presented encounter with those others.

One key issue for present concerns is that in no case is the communication or desire to "connect" directed to an ordinary human. A related key issue is whether the person believes the "connection" or "communication" is with something that actually exists, or that actually does not exist in ontological reality even though they are aware they are imagining so – for example, whether a dead person is or is not actually "alive" in some form, in a realm of post-earthly life. In all cases, they are in reference to entities that are in principle and by their very nature not accessible to the natural human senses – although in a few cases a living person claims to function as an intermediary. All build upon and extend from basic processes of believing (Angel, Oviedo, Paloutzian, Runehov, & Seitz, 2017).

Ambiguous Phenomena and Believing in the Unseen

What we believe is not like a photographic conclusion fixed in our unconscious or conscious minds (Alexander, this volume). Believing something occurs more by means of a process than by a snapshot-like event. Believing is fluid; it comes and goes, changes shape, and can even reverse, in degrees (Angel et al., 2017). The phenomenon we call a belief is a product of information received by our sensory organs, interpreted, and transmitted with meanings made and remade of it by being processed through our neuro-cognitive system (Seitz, Paloutzian, & Angel., 2017). Eventually, having been interpreted by our perceptual system at a subconscious level, it may become sufficiently stable and ascribed sufficient meaning and value to draw our conscious attention. At this point, it may have the feel of being fixed or stable. This felt stability may include a represented phenomenon of the "Unseen." This is why, for example, it is possible for someone to "really believe" they are talking with their dead sister even though they know she is dead and may no longer exist in any verifiable sense.

As far as we know, the neural event that represents a belief occurs in one person's brain inducing a memory trace that later can be reconstructed and modified. In saying that a belief occurs, we highlight the correspondence between our use of the term and how beliefs are said to occur in modern philosophy, in that believing is a process and a belief is an event, not a disposition (Schwitzgebel, 2019). Each instance of an individual's neural event representing a belief is unknown to others. Thus, it is not "knowledge" in the scientific sense, no matter how strongly a person believes he or she had an experience of communicating with an "Unseen" entity. To illustrate, one can be sincere in believing that he or she "saw God" or "heard God's voice," but the individual's purported perceptual events are not experienced by anyone else (e.g. Luhrmann, 2012; Pearson, this volume; Richards, this volume; Schwartz, Chapter 3, this volume). They are unverifiable, thus require no one else's acceptance. Moreover, no one has ever documented in an independently verifiable way how a divinity, extra-worldly being, or spirits of dead people look or sound. Thus, not only do these things remain unseen and unheard; they also remain unknown, according to what we understand knowledge to mean – in that its evidence must be in principle publicly verifiable. This is because in science there is no such thing as private knowledge. However, there can be private believing – discussions of which go all the way back to the founding document of the field of Epistemology, Plato's *Theaetetus*. The dilemma of "seeing" the same thing that someone else claims to have "seen," including gods, is identical today to what it was in 399 BCE Athens (Plato, nd/1997; Visala & Angel, 2017).

How Believing in "the Unseen" Happens

The multilevel character implicit in the above account of believing is an adventure that enjoins interdisciplinary collaboration for the fullest understanding. At the micro level, as far as your brain is concerned, believing in something seen and in something unseen are remarkably similar processes. An analogous similarity is identifiable at the psychological and cultural levels of analysis. Whatever else it may mean to say we communicate with the "Unseen," one thing is certain: it happens because believing processes enable it, and the most micro level where it happens is in the brain – although this is in context including the psychological, social, and cultural environments within which it exists and with which it is constantly interacting.

Cognitive Neuroscience Model

Our model posits that for a believing individual, a meaningful construct based on sensory perception (P) is associated with an emotional loading that leads to the attribution of a personal value (V) to this construct (Figure 14.1). The value V may be positive or negative and may vary in

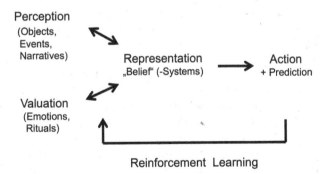

Figure 14.1 Model of belief formation as a basis for guidance of action and updating of belief by reinforcement learning (after Seitz, Paloutzian, & Angel, 2019)

strength. We have argued that a "belief," although never absolutely fixed, is the endpoint of processes that reflect a preliminarily fluid, quasi-stable state. As such, a belief is a more-or-less clear meaning that has been made out of initially unclear information that came before it, which first needed to be received, interpreted, and appraised, before being able to be responded to.

As illustrated in Figure 14.1, the perceptual process (P) is dynamic, such that the stimulus elements are identified and re-iteratively synthesized by bottom-up and top-down processing, and then result in multifaceted probabilistic representations. These neural representations become prominent against background noise, most likely in a Bayesian sense (Dehaene & Changeux, 2011; Friston, 2010; Ryshkow & Chen, 2017). The signals from the physical characteristics of objects or events are processed such that the perceived composition of the components of an object is compared to that of a previously perceived item (Adelson, 1993). Examples of complex sequential events generated by individuals in the environment or by groups of humans are narratives and music.

Virtually simultaneously, upon confronting any given sensory perception, our subjective judgment, whether consciously aware or subconsciously and, thus, non-aware, evaluates the information in terms of subjective relevance or value (V). Thus, this may be described by the notion, "what does it mean to me?" For example, one of the most important emotions that fosters survival is fear (LeDoux, 2012), because it signifies a perturbation due to threat and danger (Pantazatos, Talati, Pavlidis, & Hirsch, 2012). Analogously disgust (Schienle, 2009), which is partly culturally acquired, arouses the animal or human to escape the physical or emotional circumstance. Conversely, the sense of satisfaction signals a beneficial experience that includes feelings of confidence and safety (Rolls, 2006). Such attributions consist of subjective values that reflect relevance, reward, and ultimately survival (Paloutzian & Mukai, 2017; Seitz et al., 2017).

Importantly, these representations, which we proposed to call beliefs, are probabilistic –allowing predictions of the possible rewards and costs of achieving a goal (Seitz, Paloutzian, & Angel, 2018). Because of this, believing governs the choice of actions. However, the capacity to predict future outcomes is critical for driving appropriate behavior. Predictions are based on conscious and/or non-conscious hypotheses about harmful events including threats to life or about beneficial events such as reward. These hypotheses become stabilized by reinforcement learning. Babayan, Uchida, and Gershman (2018) have recently reported that in mice, reward prediction modulated dopamine activity in the basal ganglia as a non-monotonic function of the reward size. Moreover, the magnitude of the dopamine response predicted quantitative changes in behavior. Accordingly, people tend to trust their beliefs. It was found that the *illusory truth effect* increases upon repeatedly perceiving the same events even if the evidence is false or corresponding statements in the propositions are implausible (Fazio, Rand, & Pennycook, 2019; Wright, Wade, & Watson, 2013). Thus, people may experience perceptions as true or real, even if they are distorted or appear abnormal to other people (Ellis & Young, 1990; Fletcher & Frith, 2009).

Properties of Believing in Interacting with the Unseen

Representations

Although it is difficult to define the process of believing in unseen entities in abstract terms, it is quite well understood scientifically. This is because we know something about the physical processes going on in the body, and especially in the brain, while someone is believing. We can describe functions that can be ascribed to those processes.

In cognitive neuroscience, beliefs that result from the believing processes are understood to be neural representations (Seitz et al., 2018, 2019). The term *representation* is used for the principally plastic (e.g. modifiable) neural implementation (code) of a psychological entity, such as a belief. Representations are not simply locations or "hot spots" in the brain. They are local as well as large-scale cortico-subcortical neural circuits (including the salience network, the default-mode network, etc.) that are operationally well established and that can, from the standpoint of our biological history, generate evolutionarily new, integrative psychological functions or entities (Laird et al., 2013). Thereby they influence the individuals' decisions and social behavior.

Phenomenologically, a representation might be a "mental picture" or an "imagined sound (voice, music) in your inner ear." This is true whether the stimulus is really "out there" or "merely" inside one's mind as an illusion, desire, or (religious or spiritual) belief. We can respond to a neural representation of a hoped-for, wanted, or desired entity, just as we can respond to a neural representation of a wish actually fulfilled, or an objectively real thing. Our brain is fine with us being able to do both things, although other humans may not be.

The issue of what a representation is attracts much interest in philosophy. In particular, what constitutes an adequate scientific representation is a problem that has spawned a wide range of heterogeneous approaches. However, "there is neither a shared understanding of the problems that an account of scientific representation has to address; nor is there agreement on what an acceptable solution to these problems would look like. In fact, there is not even a stable and standard terminology in which problems can be formulated" (Frigg & Nguyen, 2020, p. 1)

Perhaps, at least, we can agree that a representation is something that stands for something else, a thing that takes the place of the "original thing." For our interests, an analogy may help to clarify our understanding of the term. In a court trial, defendants do not argue their own case before the judge. They are not qualified to represent themselves. Instead, it is a lawyer who represents them and argues their defense. The judge and jury do not respond to the defendants but to their juridically accepted representative. But if his or her arguments are rejected, it will not be the lawyer who goes to jail, but the defendant.

Believing one is actually communicating or interacting with an "unseen" entity implies believing that its representation is of something ontologically real. For example, thinking you are talking to God includes that you believe there is a God for you to talk to. This belief is constituted (i.e. exists) in the representation to which you are responding. Technically, this is almost identical to the feeling or impression we have when interacting with a live human face to face, because doing so assumes that we believe that the human exists and is alive in front of us. But in both cases – communicating with another person or with God – we do not literally respond to the other person or God in its external existence, because we cannot. In terms of neuropsychological processes, we can respond only to the representation of the person or God that has been constructed in our mind-brain. Technically, we respond to our conscious or nonconscious percepts and the meanings made of them.

Perception and Valuation

As stated above, an essential aspect of a belief is that it is feeling-loaded. Accordingly, perceptions leading to the generation of inner images of the perceived objects and events get emotional relevance (Seitz et al., 2017, 2018). Three conclusions follow logically from these points:

1   When you do not perceive anything, there is nothing to evaluate and nothing to believe. However, we are constantly exposed to external stimuli that we typically do not become aware of. Thus, theoretically, the notion of not perceiving anything is a contradiction to reality.
2   Beliefs about perceptions are typically communicated and evaluated concerning plausibility and reality by the social environment during the entire life. In childhood, this evaluation is done by parents and educators, later in life by friends, partners, neighbors, and in comparison to what is said in the (social) media. Thereby, humans can learn what is shared by other people, what is a dream, what is an imagination or idea, and what is abnormal and not compatible with reality. For example, the "perception" of a thing that is not "out there" in the external world, e.g. "seeing" objects that are not present, or "hearing" voices when there are none, may be labeled hallucinations.
3   When you imagine an entity that by its nature is among "the Unseen," you have already generated the presumption of a neuropsychic concept that represents such an entity. You can become aware of this

imaginative entity and label it semantically (Seitz & Angel, 2020). The imagined concept and the semantic label will be stored in memory, from which it can be recalled (Dehaene, Meyniel, Wacongne, Wang, & Pallier, 2015). Consequently, you may believe in the existence of this imagined entity. Furthermore, you can imagine an encounter with it. In any case, you accept that you cannot experience this entity with your ordinary senses, even though imagining it enriches your life and affords you doing things creatively that might otherwise be out of range (Paloutzian & Mukai, 2017). For example, one might believe a dead loved one is alive in a "hereafter," because it would be very emotionally satisfying, comforting, warm, good to "connect," "see" them, and talk with them.

Bottom-Up, Top-Down

Importantly, believing is not limited to perceiving or understanding based only on bottom-up event knowledge, but accommodates and integrates top-down processing of information as well, as ultimately illustrated in problem solving, creative thinking, and imagination. Nevertheless, these processes lead to neural representations that can be experienced on the pre-linguistic level as mental images. Using cross-cultural and correlational methods it has been shown that participants who dispositionally experience more inspiration showed stronger belief in a deity than those experiencing less inspiration (Critcher & Lee, 2018). Moreover, these authors stated that the spiritually transcendent experience that elevates believing in a deity makes people feel connected to an "Unseen" being believed to reside in a realm beyond their own. The degree to which believers feel that connection may be a key element of what affects the religious dimension of their spiritual well-being (Paloutzian et al., 2021; Paloutzian, Bufford, & Wildman, 2012; Hiebler-Ragger et al., 2018; Unterrainer & Fink, 2013).

The Unseen Inference

The inferences that can be made about the "Unseen" are attributions or post-hoc explanations of inner experiences (Exline, this volume). In this respect, they are similar to beliefs. When people become aware of such inner experiences, they tend to associate them with a sense of authorship and have learned to differentiate them according to the contextual information immediate or relevant to when they had this experience. Like ideas, these attributions are conceptual abstractions that can be communicated through social groups. There are different modes of how beliefs are spread in communities, including but not limited to those in authority, expert models, neighbors, and the mere opinion of the majority (Galesic & Stein, 2019). In any case, in the ultimate form, a belief may come to correspond to what might function psychologically as representing a thing of absolute value. The close relation between the processes of believing and belief in God or other extra-worldly agents becomes evident immediately. Therein may be a positive emotional connotation, possibly including the notion of reward, but there could also be a negative or even terrifying feeling that may be attributed to a negative spiritual source.

However, what makes one think he or she can "communicate" with unseen entities? Not all beliefs are meanings made based on ambiguous information stimulating our sensory organs from the outside. It is entirely possible for us to make meanings out of internal neural processes. Lindeman and Svedholm (2012) found that different labels for experiences (e.g. paranormal, superstitious, magical, supernatural) may be given to what is essentially the same thing. Also, when one claims to have communicated with their dead loved one, we might typically presume that they did not literally do so but instead were under an illusion, or had a feeling or impression, that they did, and this may affect their well-being (Park, this volume). However, between 33 percent and 43 percent (depending upon religious affiliation) of a sample of 40,000 Americans believes they can be "really in touch" with a dead person in their own experiences (Benore & Park, 2004). Do they really do so? Or is it their imagination, a fantasy wish fulfillment, or an attribution of visual and auditory meaning in the face of the ambiguity of death that is manifest – even to the point of sensory experience? We have no scientific answer to this question.

Even so, the topic of how divine beings can be imagined has a long tradition. In a pre-Christian environment, the Stoic philosopher Seneca (~ 1–65) wrote in his Epistulae morales (41, 1), *"prope est a te deus, tecum est, intus est"* (God is near you, he is with you, he is within you) (Seneca, 1989). Later, in the medieval Christian-mystic tradition, the idea of *"deus intus"* (God inside) was propagated. It is based on the neo-platonic concept of imagination, a term that comes from a similar philosophical approach. The Latin word "imago" ("image") allows an interpretation of human existence termed *"imago dei"* (image of God). The biblical sources for this idea go back to the Old Testament (Genesis 1: 26). *"Deus intus"* means that God can and must be incarnated in the human soul. Angelus Silesius (1624–1677), a medical doctor and theologian deeply rooted in the mystical tradition, wrote the most famous condensed version of this position, *"In dir muß Gott geboren werden: Wird Christus tausendmal zu Bethlehem geboren/Und nicht in dir, du bleibst noch ewiglich verloren"* (If Christ is born a thousand times in Bethlehem and not in you, you nevertheless will be lost forever) (Silesius 2006, p. 61). The European tradition of the history of religions has many examples that God is not inferred to be an external entity, but an internal one.

Beliefs about "the Unseen"

From the perspective of cognitive neuroscience, three belief categories have been identified that are brought about by the processes of believing described above (Seitz & Angel, 2020). When we extend these belief categories to explore the "Unseen," it becomes clear that the "Unseen" is not emotionally neutral but usually has a positive, negative, or mystical connotation. In as much as the "Unseen" is conceptualized as a belief, it can be described verbally and communicated. But this automatically creates the conundrum that although a belief is accepted by believing people as reality, it is by definition obscured from natural human sensation. In this respect, an "Unseen" is an entity of imagination (for which, as stated, its ontological status is not known). We propose a classification of three common beliefs about "the Unseen," illustrated in **Figure 14.2**.

The first category includes beliefs about the "Unseen" concern empirical aspects that have a potentially perceivable appearance. The emotional loadings become assigned to these beliefs include aesthetic value, desirability or averseness, and threat (Ishizu & Zeki, 2013; Rolls, 2006; Thiruchselvam, Harper, & Homer, 2016). Typically, they are thought of in anthropomorphic terms as deities. Importantly, however, people tend to attribute relational and conceptual beliefs (see below) to anthropomorphic agents, which renders them as if "alive," e.g. like humans. In connection with positive emotions, such as happiness and hope, they may be associated with feelings analogous to those of a savior or angles. Conversely, in connection with negative emotions such as fear and disgust, they may correspond to the negative effect connected to witches

Figure 14.2 Proposed categories of common beliefs about the "Unseen" (after Seitz & Angel, 2020). Although all three belief types stem from the same fundamental process, they must be understood as both fluid and interdependent

or ghosts. People may believe that such agents exist and may be used to talking with them just as people are used to talking to themselves. Notably, such anthropomorphic agents can take on a visible character by illustrations such as those used in art in certain religious traditions. In this way, the "Unseen" may seem more "visible" by means of a kind of symbolic representational magnification.

The second category of beliefs accounts for events in which individuals interact with objects or other individuals. These beliefs concern relationships between a person and objects or other people in the constantly changing environment. This capacity is of great evolutionary importance, because it allows people to react to challenging events as well as to interact socially with other individuals before they become aware of the belief. In connection to the "Unseen," these beliefs are the representations of the relation of the "Unseen" with an individual. For positive emotions such as happiness and satisfaction, they correspond to charity and social inclusion (e.g. in-group altruism). Conversely, for negative emotions such as fear and disgust, they correspond to temptation and social exclusion (e.g. out-group rejection).

The third category, beliefs exist in higher-order conceptual processing that requires the use of a symbolic language. They arise from narratives presented by humans in the social environment. As the complex sequential events building narratives are processed via either the acoustic or visual system, they may get emotional loading by, e.g. rhythm, prosody, and tune, as well as the situation and environment in which they are perceived. During the long process of evolution, humans have communicated their thoughts, emotions, and intentions (Zaidel, 2019). Humans are used to telling stories about their own and other people's past, their origins, their goals in this life, and their future after physical death (Belzen, 2010). These narratives eventually build the repertoire of a person's concepts concerning the broad spectrum of cultural life (Belzen, 2010). Similarly, fairytales, stories, and other types of information are told, and in some societies are available in printed format as well. Such abstract conceptual beliefs pertain to ecological, social, cultural, religious, and political contents providing sources of identity and normative rules as well as an affective attachment (Brandt, Sibley, & Osborne, 2019). Typically, they evolve gradually over years from infancy onwards into adult life upon numerous repetitions and owing to their memory contents gain normative values to the individuals (Bordalo, Gennaioli, & Shliefer, 2020). Conceptual beliefs may ultimately include transcendent meanings about a deity, people's fate, or the world (Paloutzian & Park, 2014). The "Unseen" entities are representations or reflections of concepts. As applied to positive emotions such as happiness and welfare, they correspond to virtue, justice, and ethics. For negative emotions such as fear and threat, they correspond to offense and crime. Importantly, ritual practices provide non-language-bound, emotional loadings for narratives that facilitate belief acquisition and maintenance in the participating individuals affecting their goal states and enhancing social cohesion (Hobson, Schroeder, Risen, Xygalatas, & Inzlicht, 2018; Schnell, 2012; Zaidel, 2019). Thus, rituals may play a role in engagement with the "Unseen," as they constitute visible events that underpin the acoustic dimension of narratives about the "Unseen." Olfactory sensations may add to this. In general, people may psychologically substitute such experiences for the "Unseen" by implicitly filling in the gap between the "Unseen" and their (social) environment. This confirms our emphasis that beliefs are fluid and may reveal interdependence between the categories over time.

Psychological Constructs: From Ambiguity to Percepts to Imagining

At the psychological level of analysis, the process of believing extends from the neurophysiological level and extrapolates to the social-cultural level. Within the psychological level of the "whole human," believing occurs at and between sub-levels. The principles of physical energy as information reception, processing, and transmission to the next receiving organ, eventually reaching the level of manipulation of thoughts and human mental awareness, are extrapolations of those inherent in the above discussions that mention visual perception. All the way up the line, from the fundamental processes in sensation and perception, to learning, intuiting, remembering, and imagining, and extending to their social and cultural applications and contexts, initially probabilistic information is being received and processed, and meanings at higher levels are being made out of it, including adaptive, social, cultural, and other meanings (Paloutzian & Mukai, 2017). As the levels expand, they enlarge in scope and reflect ways of thinking and seeing the world, and of understanding issues about perennial questions such as what happens after death (Molhoek, this volume), which are manifest through theologies, worldviews, and cultures as a whole (Taves & Asprem, 2018).

Concrete, relational, and conceptual believing are of central importance to all religions and worldviews that postulate the existence of God or gods, otherworldly spirits, supernatural agents or forces, or any variation of an afterlife for humans. This is because whether or not the objects, forces, or states postulated exist in ontological reality, they can become sufficiently "concretized" in the human mind as to be almost the functional equivalent. That is, consequently, people can believe in the existence of these (conceptual, supernatural) entities, agents, or environments. Also, we can imagine a putative encounter with them even though we may be convinced and accept that we cannot experience them with our ordinary senses.

Cultural Contexts

The processes summarized above occur within some kind of cultural and sub-cultural context. These can be nation-states, ethnic groups with their norms and mores, and a myriad variety of smaller groups within larger cultures. Importantly, a compelling case has been made that religions are cultures – in addition to whatever else they may be (Cohen, 2009; Cohen & Hill, 2007; Saroglou & Cohen, 2013).

This is important to believing processes because virtually all aspects of life in which a person is embedded – cultural norms, language, taboos, rituals, social roles of males and females, aging and old age, visual and auditory icons, whether a society is traditional or modern and so forth – comprise the socio-cognitive network in which he or she lives, behaves, and believes – anything. And because of this, it is not a surprise that the content of someone's purported visions or hearings of the "Unseen" are often perceptually private manifestations or replications of people, other beings, animals, other stimuli, or events that exist in their normal world.

Consistent with this, it is now beginning to be understood that anomalous, non-ordinary experiences may be similar across cultures, but that their appraisal (i.e. the attributions about what caused them and what they represent) can differ markedly. For example, Wolf, Ihm, Maul, and Taves (in press) found that the same description of a nonordinary mental experience can be identified equivalently by people in the United States and in India, but their statements about what they mean can differ greatly based on their religion or other aspects of culture. Top-down processes are heavily involved in the appraisal of unusual events.

Some Enduring Properties

Although believing in the "Unseen" can be understood from at least the neuroscientific, psychological, and cultural levels, there are common properties that may operate through all levels. A short list of them includes the following.

Mental Imagery, Imagination, and Awe

It is clear from the above argument that mental imagery and the capacity to imagine are essential elements to believing, as one cannot "interact" with something for which there is no mental construction of a meaningful percept. Notably, however, such mental constructions can convey more than meaning or a specific meaning. They can also invoke the experience of awe, which may precede or trigger the experience of meaning. This raises an issue about the relation between meaning and awe. A possible line of research was recently introduced in which it was argued that awe is a meaning making emotion (Ihm, Paloutzian, van Elk, & Schooler, 2019).

Motivation and Meaning: Perceiving According to Needs

The top-down aspect of perception, attributions of meaning, and imagination lends to a strong argument that people are capable of "seeing" what they need to see. This has been shown by research in which participants were shown random visual stimuli but reported to see a pattern in them (Barlev, Kinsella, Taves, Paloutzian, & German, 2015). In particular, those who believed in what are popularly termed Near-Death Experiences (NDEs) were more likely to report seeing a pattern that was not there, i.e. they were more likely to make meaning out of an ambiguous stimulus.

A dramatic example of this is illustrated in a woman who believed that NDEs opened a window on what happens after death. In an interview, she explained that she was a cloud formation in the sky that was very striking. It was comprised of a long, thin vertical cloud against a blue sky background, with a small round spot of cloud (which looked like a dot) a short distance off the bottom tip of the long thin cloud. This configuration looked like an exclamation point. The woman was *absolutely sure* that it was her dead son saying that he was OK in the afterlife. She seeing this cloud formation was not a coincidence because, she said, "there are no such things as pure chance coincidences" (Barlev et al., 2015; Kinsella, 2017).

Consistent with this, it is not a surprise that clients who are grieving because of the death of a loved one often choose to establish and maintain a "restorative connection" with their deceased loved one. Ongoing attachments between bereaved individuals and their experience of a continuing bond with or "presence" of the person who died can be comforts to many grievers (Burke & Rynearson, Forthcoming 2021). In the same way, a prayer said with genuine belief may likewise comfort suffering believers.

Deepening, Modulation, and Expansion

Part of the believing processes involves the mechanisms by which beliefs become narrow versus broad in scope, easily triggered or not, held more centrally or unreservedly versus less so, changed to a greater or lesser degree, or even held "unto death" versus given up. Key terms for such processes refer to the evocation, deepening, expansion, or modification of representations. Understanding of the processes of believing more deeply rests upon conceptualizing how these representations may undergo change. The mechanisms that evoke, deepen, or modify representations differ. They depend on the subject and object that is part of an encounter, as well as the structure and activity of memory – all of which involve both top-down and bottom-up information processing. Encounters lead to representations of "someone" or "something," which are evoked, deepened, or modified each time an encounter occurs. Psychologically, "Unseen" entities are mental phenomena that we accept as counterparts to physical encounters.

Every encounter in life is hybrid, i.e. it is oscillating between when "real" meetings occur and when the other is "Unseen." Knowing this may influence our understanding of communication. It is also oscillating as we partly communicate with someone "present" but most of the time we communicate with the same person or being in a virtual way. Our believing processes allow this kind of communication. This is how our believing processes allow communicating at all.

Back to the Bar: Arguments (and One Agreement)

As the conversation in the bar continued, the stranger, S, interrupted. She asked, "What good is all of this? Maybe the believing process is common to all, and maybe it is good to learn about it. So what? That's not where people 'live.' They live in and with their philosophies, religions, sex roles, ethnic identities, and worldviews. It is those things – beliefs – they fight about, not the process by which they happen. You sound like all you care about is counterintuitive thinking."

Professor G interrupted, "No, that's not all we care about. But it is part of it – because people kill each other over their beliefs and ways of life. Our ultimate goal is peace. Understanding creditions can help."

Professor D said, "Look, some of this stuff is counterintuitive. For example, saying that you can talk with a dead person doesn't make sense, because dead people don't talk. Even 'communicating' with a dog is happening in your imagination. It is your subjective inference and interpretation of whatever you are doing. The dead person can't even hear! As to communicating with God (or whatever), I would say that feeling like you receive feedback from such an agent – that's probably a false belief, but, to be clear, we don't actually know (because gods may exist). It may be true or false. But we don't have *knowledge* of it. Why can't all people admit it? What I mean is, "Just be honest; no intellectual or emotional games."

> "But so what?," said S. "What good is it? If we think someone is communicating with 'the real God,' are we supposed to force everyone to address this 'Higher Power' only? Because we say so? That's not freedom of religion. Believing is perfectly fine so long as you understand what you are doing. Maybe that's why learning about creditions is worthwhile."

Then Professor G chimed in with a grand, big picture: "There is another application of this. Look at all the religions in the world. Millions of adherents to each one hold hostile, negative attitudes towards the others. Not all, but a great number. Their beliefs are an important part of their definition of who they are. The result degenerates to an us-versus-them way of perceiving, understanding, and behaving towards the 'others.' This process occurs automatically, on both sides. The results of our beliefs can be so different that we start wars and commit hara-kiri or massacres. But, with regard to credition as the processes of believing we are all in the same boat. The universality of credition might be understood as one of the factors that can unify humans regardless of where they come from and what kind of experiences they may have had. So wouldn't it be wonderful if, instead of perceiving those of a religion or worldview different from one's own, we could all understand the difference between believing and knowing, get beyond the 'us/them' way of thinking and perceiving the world, and instead sit down and have a never-ending conversation about the processes of believing – not only in the abstract or in terms of the cool research being done, but as applied to ourselves? Every single one of us. Instead of arguing about beliefs, we become closer to each other when sharing the experiences rooted in our inner processes of believing – while keeping in mind that most of them are non-conscious. We would learn how we all function in the same basic ways, both in terms of what we know and what we believe but do not know. The 'other' may become 'just like me.' One possible outcome of doing this might be a barrierless world. That would be awesome!"

Finally, Professor W brought it to a close. First, he emphasized that the previous statement by Professor G is "spot-on" perfect. That is the most important practical thing we could give the world. But there is also an amazing, penetrating, and far-reaching fundamental scientific theoretical point that we would be stupid to miss: *It's about life, and life only.* Try to answer this question: think for a moment, and imagine a healthy baby, or any human, whose system does not automatically do this – what we are calling creditions – constructing beliefs by means of believing processes that involve receiving ambiguous information of some sort, through various mediums, by some appropriate sensory or other receiving organ or system, out of which a conscious or non-conscious percept is constructed, held and modulated for variable lengths of time with variable value strengths imputed to it, and to which a conscious or nonconscious response may occur. It seems compelling that a system in which these kinds of processes do not occur is not a living system. There is no such thing as a healthy human baby or adult whose system does not automatically engage in processes of believing. Without it, there is no life. Can we at least agree on this? Everybody said, 'Yes, we get it!'." The people in the Bar cheered.

References

Adelson, E. H. (1993). Perceptual organization and the judgment of brightness. *Science, 262,* 2042–2044.

Angel, H.-F. (2006). Religiosität als menschliches potential. Ein anthropologisches modell der religiosität im neurowissenschaftlichen horizont. In H.-F. Angel (Ed.), *Religiosität. anthropologische, theologische und sozialwissenschaftliche klärungen* (pp. 62–89). Stuttgart: Kohlhammer.

Angel, H.-F. (2013). Credition, the process of belief. In Anne L. C. Runehov & Lluis Oviedo (Eds.), *Encyclopedia of sciences and religion* (Vol. 1, pp. 536–539). Dordrecht: Springer. http://www.springerreference.com/docs/html/chapterd-bid/357430.html.

Angel, H.-F. (2017). Credition: From the question of belief to the question of believing. In H.-F. Angel, L. Oviedo, R. F. Paloutzian, A. L. C. Runehov, & R. Seitz, (Eds.), *Processes of believing: The acquisition, maintenance, and change in creditions* (pp. 17–36). Heidelberg: Springer.

Angel, H.-F. (2020). *Credition: Processes of believing (website)*. University of Graz, Austria. https://credition.uni-graz.at/de/.

Angel, H.-F., Oviedo, L., Paloutzian, R. F., Runehov, A. L. C., & Seitz, R. J. (Eds.). (2017). *Processes of believing: The acquisition, maintenance, and change in creditions*. Heidelberg: Springer.

Babayan, B. M., Uchida, N., & Gershman, S. J. (2018). Belief state representation in the dopamine system. *Nature Communications, 9*, 1891.

Barlev, M., Kinsella, M., Taves, A., Paloutzian, R. F., & German, T. (2015, February). *Meaning making in a new age spirituality group: Pattern detection predicts anomalous experiences and paranormal interpretations*. Paper presented at the meeting of the Society of Personality and Social Psychology, Psychology of Religion Preconference, Long Beach, CA.

Belzen, J. A. (2010). Religion and self: Notions from a cultural psychological perspective. *Pastoral Psychology, 59*, 199–409.

Benore, E. R., & Park, C. L. (2004). Death-specific religious beliefs and bereavement: Belief in an afterlife and continued attachment. *The International Journal for the Psychology of Religion, 14 (1)*, 1–22.

Bordalo, P., Gennaioli, N., & Shliefer, A. (2020, in press). Memory, attention, and choice.

Brandt, M. J., Sibley, C. G., & Osborne, D. (2019). What is central to political belief system networks? *Personality and Social Psychology Bulletin, 45*(9), 1352–1364. doi 10.1177/0146167218824354.

Burke, L. A., & Rynearson, E. (Forthcoming 2021). *Exploring interactions with the deceased: The restorative nature of ongoing connections*. London and New York: Routledge.

Cohen, A.B. (2009). Many forms of culture. *American Psychologist, 64*(3), 194–204.

Cohen, A. B., & Hill, P. C. (2007). Religion as culture: Religious individualism and collectivism among American Catholics, Jews, and Protestants. *Journal of Personality, 75*(4), 709–742.

Critcher, C. R., & Lee, C. J. (2018). Feeling is believing: Inspiration encourages belief in God. *Psychological Science, 29*, 723–737.

Dehaene, S., & Changeux, J.-P. (2011) Experimental and theoretical approaches to conscious processing. *Neuron, 70*, 200–227. doi: 10.1016/j.neuron.2011.03.018.

Dehaene, S., Meyniel, F., Wacongne, C., Wang, L., & Pallier, C. (2015) The neural representation of sequences: From transition probabilities to algebraic patterns and linguistic trees. *Neuron, 88*, 2–19. doi: 10.1016/j.neuron.2015.09.019.

Dunbar, R. I. M., & Barrett, L. (2007). *The Oxford handbook of evolutionary psychology*. Oxford: Oxford University Press.

Ellis, H. D., & Young, A. W. (1990). Accounting for delusional misidentification. *British Journal of Psychiatry, 157*, 239–248.

Fazio, L. K., Rand, D. G., & Pennycook, G. (2019). Repetition increases perceived truth equally for plausible and implausible statements. *Psychonomic Bulletin & Review, 26,* 1705–1710.

Fletcher, P. C., & Frith, C. D. (2009). Perceiving a believing: A Bayesian approach to explaining the positive symptoms of schizophrenia. *Nature Reviews Neuroscience, 10,* 48–58.

Frigg, R., & Nguyen, J. (2020). *Modelling nature: An opinionated introduction to scientific representation.* Cham, Switzerland: Springer.

Friston, K. (2010). The free-energy principle: A unified brain theory? *Nature Reviews Neuroscience, 11,* 127–138. doi: 10.1038/nrn2787.

Galesic, M., Stein, D. L. (2019) Statistical physics models of belief dynamics: Theory and empirical tests. *Physica A, 519,* 275–294.

Hiebler-Ragger, M., Fuchshuber, J., Droscher, H., Vajda, C., Fink, A., & Unterrainer, H. F. (2018). Personality influences the relationship between primary emotions and religious/spiritual well-being. *Frontiers in Psychology, 9,* Article 370. https://doi.org/10.3389/fpsyg.2018.00370.

Hobson, N. M., Schroeder, J., Risen, J. L., Xygalatas, D., & Inzlicht, M. (2018). The psychology of rituals: An integrative review and process-based framework. *Personality and Social Psychology Review, 22,* 260–284.

Ihm, E. D., Paloutzian, R. F., van Elk, M., Schooler, J. W. (2019). Awe as a meaning-making emotion: On the evolution of awe and the origin of religions. In J. Feierman & L. Oviedo (Eds.), *The evolution of religion, religiosity and theology: A multilevel and multidisciplinary approach.* New York: Routledge.

Ishizu, T., & Zeki, S. (2013). The brain's specialized systems for aesthetic and perceptual judgement. *European Journal of Neuroscience, 3,* 1413–1420. doi: 10.1111/ejn.12135.

Kinsella, M. (2017). The aging new age: Baby-boomers, near-death experiences, and the emergence of an afterlife movement (pp. 118–119). Doctoral dissertation. University of California.

Laird, A. R., Eickhoff, S. B., Rottschy, C., Bzdok, D., Ray, K. L., & Fox, P. T. (2013). Networks of task co-activations. *Neuroimage, 80,* 505–514.

LeDoux, J. E. (2012). Evolution of human emotion: A view through fear. *Progress in Brain Research, 195,* 431–442. doi: 10.1016/B978-0-444-53860-4.00021-0.

Lindeman, M., & Svedholm, A. (2012). What's in a term? Paranormal, superstitious, magical and supernatural beliefs by any other name would mean the same. *Review of General Psychology, 16*(3), 241–255.

Luhrmann T. A. (2012). *When God talks back: Understanding the American evangelical relationship with God.* New York: Knopf.

Paloutzian, R. F. (2017). *Invitation to the psychology of religion* (3rd ed.). New York: Guilford.

Paloutzian, R. F., Agilkaya-Sahin, Z., Bruce, K. C., Kvande, M. N., Maliňáková, K., Marques, L. F., Musa, A. S., Nojomi, M., Öztürk, E. E., Putri, I. P., You, S-K. (2021). The spiritual well-being scale (SWBS): Cross-cultural assessment across 5 continents, 10 languages, and 300 studies. In A. L. Ai, P. M. Wink, R. F. Paloutzian, & K. A. Harris (Eds.), *Assessing spirituality in a diverse world* (pp. 413–444). Cham, Switzerland: Springer International Publishing AG.

Paloutzian, R. F., Bufford, R. K., & Wildman, A. J. (2012). Spiritual well-being scale: Mental and physical health relationships. In M. Cobb, C. Puchalski, & B. Rumbold (Eds.), *Oxford textbook of spirituality in healthcare* (pp. 353–358). Oxford: Oxford University Press.

Paloutzian, R. F., & Mukai, K. J. (2017). Believing, remembering, and imagining: The roots and fruits of meanings made and remade. In H. -F. Angel, L. Oviedo, R. F. Paloutzian, A. L. C. Runehov, & R. Seitz, (Eds.), *Processes of believing: The acquisition, maintenance, and change in creditions* (pp. 39–49). Heidelberg: Springer.

Paloutzian, R. F., & Park, C. L. (2014). Religiousness and spirituality: The psychology of multilevel meaning-making behavior. *Religion Brain Behavior*, *5*(2), 166–178.

Pantazatos, S. P., Talati, A., Pavlidis, P., & Hirsch, J. (2012). Cortical functional connectivity decodes subconscious, task-irrelevant threat-related emotion processing. *Neuroimage*, *61*, 1355–1363. doi: 10.1016/j.neuroimage.2012.03.051.

Plato. (n.d./1997). *Theaetetus* (M. J. Levett, Trans.; Myles Burnyeat, Rev.). In J. M. Cooper & D. S. Hutchinson (Eds.), *Plato: Complete works* (pp. 157–234). Indianapolis and Cambridge: Hackett Publishing Company.

Rolls, E. T. (2006). Brain mechanisms underlying flavour and appetite. *Philosophical Transactions of the Royal Society London. B Biological Sciences*, *361*, 1123–1136.

Ryshkow, I. O., & Chen, Y. (2017). Bayesian belief models in simulation-based decision-making. In: A. Tolk (Ed.), *Advances in modeling and simulation: Simulation foundations, methods and applications* (pp. 181–217). Cham, Switz.: Springer International Publishing. doi 10.1007/978-3-319-64182-9_10.

Saroglou, V., & Cohen, A. B. (2013). Cultural and cross-cultural psychology of religion. In R. F. Paloutzian & C. L. Park (Eds.), *Handbook of the psychology of religion and spirituality* (2nd ed., pp. 330–354). New York: Guilford Press.

Schienle, A. (2009). The functional neuroanatomy of disgust. In B. O. Olatunji & D. McKay (Eds.), *Disgust and its disorders: Theory, assessment, and treatment implications* (pp. 145–165). Washington, DC, US: American Psychological Association. http://dx.doi.org/10.1037/11856-000.

Schnell, T. (2012). Spirituality with and without religion. *Archives of the Psychology of Religion*, *34*, 33–62.

Schwitzgebel, E. (2019). Belief. *The Stanford encyclopedia of philosophy* (Fall 2019 Edition), Edward N. Zalta (Ed.). https://plato.stanford.edu/archives/fall2019/entries/belief/.

Silesius, A. (2006/1657). *Der cherubinische wandersmann* (17th ed.). Zürich, Switzerland: Hofenberg. Diogenes Editor: 2006 edition ISBN: 978-3-257-20644-9.

Seitz, R. J., & Angel, H-F. (2020). Belief formation – A driving force for brain evolution. *Brain and Cognition*, *140*, 1–8. https://doi.org/10.1016/j.bandc.2020.105548.

Seitz, R. J., Paloutzian, R. F., & Angel, H-F. (2017). Processes of believing: Where do they come from? What are they good for? *F1000Research*, *5*, 1–21, 2573. doi: 10.12688/f1000research.9773.2.

Seitz, R. J., Paloutzian, R. F., & Angel, H-F. (2018). From believing to belief: A general theoretical model. *Journal of Cognitive Neuroscience*, *30*(9), 1254–1264.

Seitz, R. J., Paloutzian, R. F., & Angel, H-F. (2019). Believing is representation mediated by the dopamine brain system. *European Journal of Neuroscience*, *49*, 1212–1214. http://dx.doi.org/10.1111/ejn.14317.

Seneca, L. A. (1989). *Epistulae morales* (Revised ed., Richard M. Gummere, Trans.). Cambridge, MA: Harvard University Press.

Taves, A., & Asprem, E. (2018). Psychology, meaning making, and the study of worldviews: Beyond religion and nonreligion. *Psychology of Religion and Spirituality, 10*(3), 207–217.

Thiruchselvam, R., Harper, J., & Homer, A. L. (2016). Beauty is in the belief of the beholder: Cognitive influences on the neural response to facial attractiveness. *Social Cognition and Neuroscience, 11*(12), 1999–2008. doi: 10.1093/scan/nsw115.

Unterrainer, H. F., & Fink, A. (2013). The multidimensional inventory for religious/spiritual well-being (MI-RSWB). *Diagnostica, 59*(1), 33–44. doi. org./10.1026/0012-1924/a000077.

Visala, A., & Angel, H.-F. (2017). The theory of credition and philosophical accounts of belief: Looking for common ground. In H.-F. Angel, L. Oviedo, R. F. Paloutzian, A. L. C. Runihov, & R. J. Seitz (Eds.), *Processes of believing: The acquisition, maintenance, and change in creditions*. Hidelberg: Springer.

Wolf, M., G., Ihm, E., Maul, A., & Taves, A. (in press). Survey item validation. In S. Engler & M. Stausberg (Eds.), *The Routledge handbook on methods in religious studies* (2nd ed.). New York: Routledge.

Wright, D. S., Wade, K. A., & Watson, D. G. (2013). Delay and déjà vu: Timing and repetition increase the power of false evidence. *Psychonomic Bulletin & Review, 20*, 812–818.

Zaidel, D. W. (2019). Co-evolution of language and symbolic meaning: Co-opting meaning underlying the initial arts in early human culture. *Wiley Interdisciplinary Reviews: Cognitive Science, 11*: e1520. doi.org/10.1002/wcs.1520.

15 The Meaning of Beliefs in Communicating with God and the Deceased for Individuals' Well-being

Crystal L. Park

Our basic beliefs—about ourselves, the world, what is true, what is possible—create our reality. In creating our reality, beliefs thereby powerfully influence our behavior and well-being (Koltko-Rivera, 2004). Among the foundational beliefs that shape many individuals' realities are those regarding their abilities to communicate with the divine and with loved ones beyond death. Believing that one can engage in ongoing communication with the divine and the deceased means that individuals consider literal living, growing relationships as part of their ordinary life. These relationships may form a relatively central or peripheral focus of individuals' lives, and the degree of that focus may change depending on what else is going on in their lives. For example, when individuals feel that their lives are going reasonably well, their communication with God may be a lesser focus than when they are facing serious crises (Tait, Currier, & Harris, 2016). Further, while beliefs about an afterlife may generally influence how individuals live, in times of bereavement, beliefs about communicating with someone who has died may become more salient and influence their sense of what has been lost and of what is still possible to maintain (Park & Benore, 2004).

Beliefs that one can interactively dialog with God may serve as a strong source of support and comfort, pervasively affecting believers' sense of well-being, perceived intimacy with God, and spiritual life (Park, 2017). Conversely, those who are struggling with adversity may turn to and strengthen their beliefs in the possibility of communicating with God as a way of coping with distress. Similarly, beliefs that one can continue to communicate with loved ones after their deaths may provide a deep sense of comfort and ease by mitigating actual and anticipated losses of loved ones and instilling hope for one's own continued existence after death, creating a positive association between strength in these beliefs and better emotional well-being. Alternately, individuals who are anxious or seeking comfort, especially those who are grieving, may increase their beliefs in the possibility of after-death communication (ADCs) as a way to assuage their grief, creating a positive association between distress and strength of belief. This chapter reviews theory and research regarding the meanings that these beliefs have for individuals and presents results of our own studies relating beliefs in communication with God and the deceased to emotional well-being.

Studying Beliefs about Communication with the Divine and the Departed

Studying beliefs is challenging for several reasons. People may not be aware of or able to report their beliefs accurately. To date, few measures of beliefs regarding religious and metaphysical constructs are available and those that are, tend to be single items and to only tangentially get at issues of beliefs in the possibility of communication. For example, one study that purported to study beliefs in "divine interaction" constructed a scale from two items: "How close do you feel to God most of the time?" and "About how often do you pray?" (Ellison, 1991). These items clearly do not tap into beliefs but rather personal experience. To date, no standardized measurement instruments tapping beliefs in communication with the divine or deceased have been developed.

Further complicating the measurement of beliefs, religious or metaphysical beliefs have both propositional and implicational dimensions, variously referred to as "head" versus "heart" knowledge (Watts & Dumbreck, 2013), explicit versus implicit beliefs (Jong, Bluemke, & Halberstadt, 2012), "reflections" versus "intuitions" (Baumard & Boyer, 2013), and "aliefs" vs. "beliefs" (Gendler, 2008). According to theories of dual processing systems, these different types of beliefs can operate in parallel, being aspects of two separate information processing systems, an analytical-rational one and an intuitive-experiential one. The analytical-rational system is deliberate, slow, and logical, while the intuitive-experiential system is fast, automatic, and emotion-driven (Barnard & Teasdale, 1991; Epstein, 2003).

This distinction is relevant to beliefs about the possibilities of communication because people tend to hold both types of beliefs with regard to superhuman agents (gods, spirits, etc.) and other metaphysical beliefs (Baumard & Boyer, 2013; Jong et al., 2013. That is, individuals may have some "gut-level" notions of the reality of their communications with God or with someone who has passed away that are very different from their more rational, reasoned, or culturally transmitted ideas about the possibility of those types of communication. Standard self-report measures of religious or metaphysical beliefs rarely attempt to capture both implicit and explicit beliefs (Park & Carney, in press). Thus, at this point, we know little about either people's implicit or explicit beliefs about the possibility of communicating with God and the deceased, and what we know is based on scant empirical studies that have assessed these beliefs indirectly along with some research from related areas, as will be reviewed below.

Beliefs about Communicating with God

Humans hold a variety of different beliefs about the divine, including about the existence of God or Gods and the nature of God or Gods (i.e. God representations; Davis, Moriarty, & Mauch, 2013), the extent to which the divine is involved in daily human affairs, and whether humans can communicate with the divine. This latter belief—that communication with God is possible—is common and may form the basis of one's relationship with the divine. Believing that one can communicate with God is predicated on prior beliefs—first, that there is a God with whom one might communicate, and second, that the nature of this God is such that God is capable of and open to communication.

People attempt to communicate with God largely through prayer. In fact, many scholars have defined prayer as "communication with God" (for a review, see Spilka & Ladd, 2013). In one study of prayer among a sample of adults in the United States, participants reported higher self-disclosure to God when engaging in some types of prayer; further, self-disclosure appeared to be a pathway through which engaging in prayer was associated with better mental health, suggesting that individuals *do* perceive their prayer as constituting personal communication with God (Black, Pössel, Jeppsen, Bjerg, & Wooldridge, 2015).

Scholars have delineated different types of prayer and have contended that some types (e.g. colloquial, petitionary) involve more direct and personal interactions with God while other types involve less direct interactions (e.g. ritual). Studies examining associations of different types of prayer with well-being have generally demonstrated patterns such that some types of prayer are more strongly associated with mental health and well-being than are others (Poloma & Pendleton, 1991; Spilka & Ladd, 2013). Curiously, these patterns of mental health do not align with the dimension of the directness of communication. For example, both colloquial and ritual prayers tend to be related to better mental health (e.g. Whittington & Scher, 2010), while petitionary prayer has been related to poorer mental health. However, these studies are generally cross-sectional and of limited value in illuminating the long-term patterns of different types of prayer and emotional well-being. For example, the demonstrated association between greater engagement in petitionary prayer and depression or anxiety may simply reflect people turning to petitionary prayer to cope with their distress. Most studies of prayer are of limited value when trying to understand *beliefs* in communication with God because studies of prayer almost always focus on the *behavior* of praying (e.g. frequency of prayer; Spilka & Ladd, 2013) rather than the beliefs of the person praying (e.g. the extent to which a person believes his or her prayer constitutes direct communication with God).

A separate, relatively small line of research has examined experiences or perceptions of communication with God. Studies on this topic suggest that people—particularly some groups of Protestant Christians—commonly report experiences of communicating with God (e.g. Lee, Poloma, & Post, 2013; Luhrmann, 2012).

One qualitative study of charismatic Christians in the United Kingdom found that communications from God were usually received through thoughts within the mind, rather than as an externally-audible voice. Most communications concerned mundane matters of their current lives rather than metaphysical insights or future events. Participants reported that they generally found the communications from God reassuring (Dein & Cook, 2015).

In this study of charismatic Christians, participants reported that they had learned a process to discern whether communications were from God or just their own thoughts. For them, the clarity and authoritative nature of the communication was one indication that it was from God. In addition, having a thought that would intrusively "pop" into their mind as opposed to thoughts they would ordinarily be thinking was a sign that the thought was of divine origin. They might also discuss the communication with fellow congregants or church leaders to discern whether its contents were divine (Dein & Cook, 2015). Techniques for discernment are explicitly taught in some religious groups (Boyer, 2013). Many Protestant Christians, in particular, learn through devotional manuals and books to detect God's voice within daily life events and coincidences, sometimes using techniques such as journaling or autobiographical writing (Bender, 2008).

To date, then, studies have documented experiences of prayer and of perceived communication with God, but very few studies have actually examined beliefs about the possibility of communicating with (or being heard by) God. This question of beliefs about whether communication with God is possible, whether through prayer or otherwise, appears to be an important area for future inquiry. Individuals' beliefs regarding their ability to maintain direct, reciprocal communication with God reflects their beliefs in remaining connected to someone with potentially infinite love, power, and protection, which would seem to be an important determinant of baseline comfort and mental health (Ellison, Burdette, & Hill, 2009).

As a first attempt to address questions of how common beliefs in communicating with God are and how they relate to well-being, we examined data from a larger study of religiousness and well-being conducted in 2009. Participants were 246 undergraduates (149 women, 97 men; mean age =19.2 years) at a large northeastern public university, recruited from the participant pool for introductory psychology courses. The sample was 78.9 percent White, 5.7 percent Black, 8.9 percent Asian, 4.1 percent Hispanic/Latino, and 2.4 percent Biracial/Other. The majority of participants expressed a belief in God.

In response to the multiple-choice question, "Do you believe there is a God?," 23.2 percent chose "I am sure God really exists and that He is active in my life"; 29.3 percent chose "Although I sometimes question His existence, I do believe in God and believe He knows of me as a person"; 26.8 percent selected "I don't know if there is a personal God, but I do believe in a higher power of some kind"; 13.4 percent indicated "I don't know if there is a personal God or a higher power of some kind, and I don't know if I ever will"; and 7.3 percent answered, "I don't believe in a personal God or in a higher power." To specifically examine beliefs in communication with God, we analyzed participants' responses to four items from the God Image Inventory (Lawrence, 1997). Each of these items appears to tap into beliefs about communicating with God ("The voice of God tells me what do," "God asks me to keep growing as a person," "God encourages me to go forward in the journey of life") or the experience of being in communication with God ("I would experience grief if I knew that I could never get in touch with God again"). Participants reported fairly high levels of believing in each of these items; on scales from 1 (not at all) to 4 (very much), scores for these 4 items were 1.57, 2.59, 2.68, and 2.07, respectively.

We then examined associations of each of these four beliefs with a measure that assesses general distress, the Depression, Anxiety and Stress Scale-21 (DASS-21; Lovibond & Lovibond, 1995). The DASS-21 produces separate scores for depression, anxiety, and stress, each ranging from 0 to 21. Our results showed that all four of these items tapping beliefs in communication with God were *positively* related to distress. In particular, higher beliefs that God "tells me what do" was related to higher anxiety, higher beliefs that God "encourages me to go forward" was associated with higher stress and anxiety, and both higher belief that God "asks me to keep growing" and higher anticipation of grief if unable to be in touch with God again were related to higher levels of all three aspects of distress (stress, anxiety, and depression).

Based on these intriguing findings, we conducted a second study in a different sample of college students in 2020 in which we asked more explicit and nuanced questions about their beliefs about communicating with God. A sample of 247 college students (mean age of 19.3, 64.3 percent women) completed belief surveys and the same measure of general distress, the DASS-21, used in the earlier study. As in the earlier study, participants completed online surveys through the psychology department participant pool. Participants on average believed in God (mean = 3.47 on a scale from 1 (No, definitely not) to 5 (Yes, definitely)). As shown in Table 15.1, participants endorsed fairly high beliefs in communication with God, including two-way communication. For example, nearly 40 percent of students reported having an ongoing conversation with God. Scores on these four questions regarding communication with God were almost completely unrelated to distress in the form of anxiety, stress, or depressive symptoms except that the belief that "God speaks to me directly" was positively related to

Table 15.1 Agreement with Beliefs in Communication with God

	Totally Disagree (1)	2	3	4	5	6	Totally Agree (7)
I have an ongoing conversation with God	33.6	14.5	12.0	14.9	10.4	6.2	8.3
God listens to me when I talk to him	22.8	10.4	10.0	10.8	12.0	10.4	23.7
God hears me when I pray	22.0	9.5	8.7	12.4	12.9	8.3	26.1
God speaks to me directly	33.2	15.8	9.5	17.8	9.5	7.1	7.1

anxiety ($r = .15$, $p < .05$). One additional question asked participants, "Do you communicate regularly with God?" answered as yes (32.5 percent) or no (67.5 percent). Participants who endorsed having regular communication with God had higher anxiety scores (means = 10.6 vs. 7.3, respectively; $t(241) = 2.95$, $p < .05$) although not higher depression or stress scores.

The findings from these two studies conducted over a decade apart suggest that even against a background of increasing secularization (Voas & Chaves, 2016), these beliefs are fairly commonly held. These results, however, fail to support the notion that an individual's personal experiences of having ongoing communication with God are associated with positive well-being. In fact, our results indicate that these different beliefs and experiences are inconsistently but often related to greater distress. As noted earlier, it may be that individuals turn to God and engage in ongoing dialog to help them manage high levels of distress, thus accounting for the positive associations. Because beliefs and distress were assessed at the same time, it is not possible to determine whether there is a temporal order between them and, if so, in which direction. It should be noted that this second study was conducted during the spring of 2020, during the COVID-19 pandemic; it is unclear how the potential comfort people may have been deriving from their prayers and the possible distress they were experiencing which might have led them to higher religious coping would be reflected in these associations. At any rate, it is clearly not the simple and straightforward case that believing one is in ongoing dialog with God or communicating regularly with God is associated with greater well-being, as prior speculation in the literature would suggest (e.g. Ellison et al., 2009). Future research is needed to first develop better measures of beliefs in the possibility of communicating with God and then studying these relationships over time to help determine what might come first.

Beliefs in Communication with Loved Ones after Their Deaths

As with beliefs about communicating with God, beliefs about the possibility of communicating with deceased loved ones is predicated on a set of prior beliefs including that the deceased live on in some form of afterlife and that they are able to remain tethered to the world of the living. Much theological speculation and some research on people's beliefs regarding whether there is an afterlife or life after death has been conducted (see Flannelly, 2017, for a review), but this work is not specific enough to address the question at hand. That is, very little research has examined individuals' beliefs regarding the lives of the deceased in the afterlife, including their abilities and proclivities to communicate, although some intriguing work has focused on beliefs regarding where deceased individuals might reside (Gray et al., 2018) and beliefs regarding the mental capabilities of the deceased (e.g. Bering, 2002; Doyle & Gray, 2020).

Some psychologists consider perceiving that one has communicated with another person after their death evidence of hallucinations and perhaps mental illness (e.g. Field & Filanosky, 2009). Yet there are compelling theoretical reasons to hypothesize that beliefs in the possibility of ADC may be related to greater well-being. Beliefs in communication with the deceased may provide individuals with a deep sense of comfort by mitigating both actual and anticipated losses of loved ones and, at the same time, instilling hope for one's own continued existence after death (Park & Benore, 2004). Thus, these beliefs in ADC can transform loss: rather than having completely lost a loved one, the loved one may be physically gone but still able to remain a presence in the mourner's life. In addition, beliefs in ADC provide confirmation of an afterlife.

Indeed, literature on ADC supports this possibility. This robust research area focuses on people's reports of actually having experienced contact with the deceased, often, but not always, recently-deceased loved ones (e.g. Holden, Lankford, & Holmes 2019; McCormick & Natasha, 2016). Studies of individuals who have reported ADCs typically find the communication comforting, and these reports are generally associated with high levels of well-being. Unfortunately, the samples involved in this work are quite select; research has not yet been conducted to determine the prevalence of beliefs that this communication is possible in the general community or bereaved samples.

As a way to begin to examine this issue, in Study 2, described above, we also asked participants about their beliefs in communicating with the deceased. As shown in Table 15.2, participants on average endorsed moderately strong beliefs in the notion that people who have died continue to exist (60.6 percent scored at the midpoint or above) and while, on average, they endorsed lower beliefs than that living people can communicate

Table 15.2 Agreement with Beliefs in Communication with People Who Have Died

	Totally Disagree (1)	2	3	4	5	6	Totally Agree (7)
People who have died continue to exist	12.9	14.9	11.6	19.1	13.7	10.8	17.0
People can communicate with the deceased	24.5	18.7	12.9	19.9	11.2	6.6	6.2
It is possible for people who have died to communicate with the living	23.7	17.4	11.2	18.7	14.1	7.5	7.5

with the deceased (43.9 percent scored at or above the midpoint) and that the deceased can communicate with the living (47.8 percent scored at or above the midpoint), these beliefs in the possibility that people can communicate with the deceased and that the deceased can communicate with the living as well are still fairly high. The percent of endorsement of these beliefs was somewhat lower than was that for beliefs in the possibility of communicating with God described above.

Higher scores on all three of these latter beliefs regarding communication with the deceased were correlated with higher distress in the form of anxiety, stress, and depressive symptoms (all $rs \geq .15$, $ps < .05$). In addition, a final question asked participants, "Have you ever had an experience where you communicated with someone who had died?" answered as yes (10.2 percent) or no (89.8 percent). Participants who said yes had higher anxiety scores (means = 12.6 vs. 8.1, respectively; $t(242) = 2.95$, $p < .001$), higher depression scores (means = 13.3 vs. 11.1, respectively; $t(241) = 1.12$, $p < .001$), and marginally higher stress scores (14.5 vs. 12.3, respectively); $t(241) = 1.13$, $p = .072$).

Beliefs in the possibility of communicating with the dead, while not universal, were fairly widespread even in a sample of students at a secular state university. These results did not support the hypothesis that generally believing in the possibility that the deceased persist and can engage in two-way interactions with the living provides comfort and ease. Instead, these beliefs were related across the board with greater psychological distress. In addition, people who believe they have experienced such an encounter were more anxious than were those who did not. Similar to the results described above regarding beliefs in communication with God and distress, these cross-sectional results do not indicate causality or even temporal sequencing, although it may be more plausible that people who are grieving and in distress would turn to these beliefs as a general way to manage their distress than vice versa.

Clinical Applications and Future Research

Beliefs about communication with God and with the deceased have obvious relevance to many aspects of mental health, including clinical interventions. The psychotherapy literature is replete with considerations of prayer in treatment (e.g. Abernethy, Houston, Mimms, & Boyd-Franklin, 2006; Blanton, 2011). However, the effects of prayer in individuals' lives may depend in large part on their beliefs about what is actually happening when they pray (e.g. whether their prayer serves as a form of literal communication with God). Beliefs about communicating with the departed remain less well-integrated into discussions of mental health, and as discussed above, have traditionally been viewed by mental health professionals as problematic. These beliefs do not appear to facilitate lower distress levels and may actually create distress. Although much more research is needed to understand how these beliefs interface with mental health, some efforts are already being made to incorporate (McCormick & Natasha, 2016) or even facilitate contact with the deceased (e.g. Beischel, 2019).

This area of empirical inquiry is very new, but the ideas are very old. Beliefs in communication with the divine and the departed have deep religious and historical roots, as detailed in many of the chapters in this volume. This depth will be helpful to researchers in developing studies firmly grounded in strong theory. Research is needed to develop better measures of beliefs in the types of communication described. Such measures will ideally tap both implicit and explicit facets of beliefs. Once psychometrically sound measures are developed, researchers will be able to use these measures in sophisticated field and laboratory-based research. Intriguing questions such as who is likely to hold these beliefs, how they develop and change over time, and how and why they relate to various aspects of mental health await answers.

References

Abernethy, A. D., Houston, T. R., Mimms, T., & Boyd-Franklin, N. (2006). Using prayer in psychotherapy: Applying Sue's differential to enhance culturally competent care. *Cultural Diversity and Ethnic Minority Psychology, 12*(1), 101–114.

Barnard, P. J., & Teasdale, J. D. (1991). Interacting cognitive subsystems: A systemic approach to cognitive-affective interaction and change. *Cognition & Emotion, 5*(1), 1–39.

Baumard, N., & Boyer, P. (2013). Explaining moral religions. *Trends in Cognitive Sciences, 17*(6), 272–280.

Bender, C. (2008). How does God answer back? *Poetics, 36*(5–6), 476–492.

Beischel, J. (2019). Spontaneous, facilitated, assisted, and requested after-death communication experiences and their impact on grief. *Threshold: Journal of Interdisciplinary Consciousness Studies, 3*(1), 1–32.

Bering, J. (2002). Intuitive conceptions of dead agents' minds: The natural foundations of afterlife beliefs as phenomenological boundary. *Journal of Cognition and Culture, 2*(4), 263–308.

Black, S. W., Pössel, P., Jeppsen, B. D., Bjerg, A. C., & Wooldridge, D. T. (2015). Disclosure during private prayer as a mediator between prayer type and mental health in an adult Christian sample. *Journal of Religion and Health, 54*(2), 540–553.

Blanton, P. G. (2011). The other mindful practice: Centering prayer & psychotherapy. *Pastoral Psychology, 60*(1), 133–147.

Boyer, P. (2013). Why "belief" is hard work: Implications of Tanya Luhrmann's when God talks back. *HAU: Journal of Ethnographic Theory, 3*(3), 349–357.

Davis, E. B., Moriarty, G. L., & Mauch, J. C. (2013). God images and god concepts: Definitions, development, and dynamics. *Psychology of Religion and Spirituality, 5*, 51–60.

Dein, S., & Cook, C. C. (2015). God put a thought into my mind: The charismatic Christian experience of receiving communications from God. *Mental Health, Religion & Culture, 18*(2), 97–113.

Doyle, C. M., & Gray, K. (2020). How people perceive the minds of the dead: The importance of consciousness at the moment of death. *Cognition, 202*, 104308.

Ellison, C. G. (1991). Religious involvement and subjective well-being. *Journal of Health and Social Behavior, 32*(1), 80–99.

Ellison, C. G., Burdette, A. M., & Hill, T. D. (2009). Blessed assurance: Religion, anxiety, and tranquility among US adults. *Social Science Research, 38*(3), 656–667.

Epstein, S. (2003). Cognitive-experiential self-theory of personality. In T. Millon & M. J. Lerner (Eds.), *Comprehensive handbook of psychology: Vol. 5. Personality and social psychology* (pp. 159–184). Hoboken, NJ: Wiley.

Field, N. P., & Filanosky, C. (2009). Continuing bonds, risk factors for complicated grief, and adjustment to bereavement. *Death Studies, 34*(1), 1–29.

Flannelly, K. J. (2017). *Religious beliefs, evolutionary psychiatry, and mental health in America.* Cham, Switzerland: Springer.

Gendler, T. S. (2008). Alief in action (and reaction). *Mind & Language, 23*(5), 552–585.

Gray, K., Anderson, S., Doyle, C. M., Hester, N., Schmitt, P., Vonasch, A. J., & Jackson, J. C. (2018). To be immortal, do good or evil. *Personality and Social Psychology Bulletin, 44*(6), 868–880.

Holden, J. M., Lankford, C., & Holmes, L. (2019). After-death communication and the biblical fruits of the spirit: An online survey. *Spirituality in Clinical Practice, 6*, 15–26.

Jong, J., Bluemke, M., & Halberstadt, J. (2012). Fear of death and supernatural beliefs: Developing a new supernatural belief scale to test the relationship. *European Journal of Personality, 27*(5), 495–506.

Koltko-Rivera, M. E. (2004). The psychology of worldviews. *Review of General Psychology, 8*(1), 3–58.

Lawrence, R. T. (1997). Measuring the image of God: The God image inventory and the God image scales. *Journal of Psychology and Theology, 25*(2), 214–226.

Lee, M., Poloma, M., & Post, S. G. (2013). *The heart of religion.* New York, NY: Oxford University Press.

Lovibond, P. F., & Lovibond, S. H. (1995). The structure of negative emotional states: Comparison of the depression anxiety stress scales (DASS) with the Beck depression and anxiety inventories. *Behaviour Research and Therapy, 33*, 335–343.

Luhrmann, T. M. (2012). *When God talks back: Understanding the American evangelical relationship with God.* New York, NY: Alfred A. Knopf.

McCormick, B. M. E., & Natasha, A. (2016). After-death communication: A typology of therapeutic benefits. *Journal of Near Death Studies, 34*(3), 151–172.

Park, C. L. (2017). Religious cognitions and well-being: A meaning perspective. In M. D. Robinson & M. Eid (Eds.), *The happy mind: Cognitive contributions to well-being* (pp. 443–458). New York, NY: Springer.

Park, C. L., & Benore, E. R. (2004). "You're still there": Beliefs in continued relationships with the deceased as unique religious beliefs that may influence coping adjustment. *International Journal for the Psychology of Religion, 14*(1), 37–46.

Park, C. L., & Carney, L. M. (in press). Religious head versus heart beliefs: Measurement development and validation. *Psychology of Religion and Spirituality.*

Poloma, M. M., & Pendleton, B. F. (1991). The effects of prayer and prayer experiences on measures of general well-being. *Journal of Psychology & Theology, 19*, 71–83.

Spilka, B., & Ladd, K. L. (2013). *The psychology of prayer: A scientific approach.* New York, NY: Guilford Press.

Tait, R., Currier, J. M., & Harris, J. I. (2016). Prayer coping, disclosure of trauma, and mental health symptoms among recently deployed United States veterans of the Iraq and Afghanistan conflicts. *The International Journal for the Psychology of Religion, 26*(1), 31–45.

Voas, D., & Chaves, M. (2016). Is the United States a counterexample to the secularization thesis? *American Journal of Sociology, 121*(5), 1517–1556.

Watts, F., & Dumbreck, G. (Eds.). (2013). *Head and heart: Perspectives from religion and psychology.* West Conshohocken, PA: Templeton Foundation Press.

Whittington, B. L., & Scher, S. J. (2010). Prayer and subjective well-being: An examination of six different types of prayer. *International Journal for the Psychology of Religion, 20*(1), 59–68.

16 Perceiving Messages from the Divine and Departed

An Attributional Perspective

Julie J. Exline and Kathleen C. Pait

Throughout human history, many people have held supernatural world-views, believing in deities, spirits, and domains that exist beyond this natural, material realm. Such beliefs remain widespread today. For example, a 2010 survey of 23 countries (Ipsos, 2011) found that 51 percent of respondents believed in God and in life after death. If people believe in God or in an afterlife, they might also wonder whether it is possible to communicate with God or with spirits. Some may try to initiate contact themselves—perhaps by praying to God or trying to communicate with those who have died, whether they be departed loved ones, more distant ancestors, or religious saints. If people believe—or at least hope—that their own messages are heard, this possibility raises an equally compelling question and hope: if they can send messages, might they also be able to receive personal messages from God or from those who have left this world?

We have found it useful to think about three conceptual "lenses" that people could use to frame reports of supernatural events, which could include perceived messages from God (Luhrmann, 2012), the devil (Brown, this volume; Exline, Pargament, Wilt, & Harriott, 2020), or human spirits (Exline, in press). Such experiences or reports could be seen through a *mental illness lens* (focusing on potential psychopathology or medical problems), a *psychological lens* (emphasizing normal psychological processes), or a *supernatural lens* (considering actual supernatural activity). In this chapter, we will use a psychological lens and, occasionally, a mental illness lens. We will not try to offer proof or opinions about whether supernatural exchanges actually occur in these situations. Instead, we will focus on psychological factors that might lead people to believe that they are receiving messages from the divine and departed: what types of people are most likely to have such experiences, and under what conditions?

Although space constraints do not allow a thorough literature review, we will present some ideas from our research program on supernatural attribution, which rests on earlier work on religious attribution (e.g. Ritzema & Young, 1983; Spilka & McIntosh, 1995; Spilka, Shaver, & Kirkpatrick, 1985). We will also cite some relevant empirical findings. But before delving into these ideas, we will give some brief background on perceived messages from the divine and departed: forms they might take, their frequency, and their psychological importance.

Perceiving Messages from the Divine and Departed

When people say that "God spoke to me" or that their departed loved one gave them a message, what exactly do they mean? In some dramatic cases they might have experienced an event that seemed to violate natural laws (Ritzema & Young, 1983): people might see God in events suggesting miraculous healing (Williams & Watts, 2014), and a few report hearing God's voice audibly (Cottam et al., 2011; Dein & Littlewood, 2007). Others might report seeing a ghost (Pew, 2009) or experience unusual activities that they attribute to spirits, such as unexpected electrical activity or the seemingly spontaneous movement of household objects. A recent study showed that undergraduates with some belief in God believed (on average) that God had moderate power to violate natural laws and that human spirits also held such power, though less than God (Exline et al., 2020).

More commonly, though, people perceive communication from the divine and departed in indirect, subtle ways. Many believe that God works indirectly through natural causes (Exline et al., 2020; Legare, Evans, Rosengren, & Harris, 2012; Schultz, this volume; Weeks & Lupfer, 2000) and that human spirits also have this ability to some degree (Exline et al., 2020). This possibility of indirect, subtle communication opens the door for many events to be seen as messages. For instance, people can perceive God's "voice" in many ways: not only through sacred texts but also through life events, nature, spontaneous thoughts, and the kindness of other people, to name just a few (Degelman & Lynn, 1995; Dein & Cook, 2015; Dein & Littlewood, 2007; Harriott & Exline, 2017; Luhrmann, 2012). People can also perceive messages from departed loved ones (often called after-death communications [ADCs]; Guggenheim & Guggenheim, 1995) through many modes (Richards, this volume), including dreams, spontaneous thoughts, repeated events, and events that have special personal or relational significance. (For reviews, see Arcangel, 2005; Daggett, 2005; Guggenheim & Guggenheim, 1995; Keen, Murray, & Payne, 2013a; LaGrand, 1997, 2005, 2006; Steffen & Coyle, 2012; Streit-Horn, 2011.)

Given the wide array of experiences that people interpret as messages from the divine and departed, it is not surprising that many individuals perceive such messages. Many US adults believe that they have received messages from God (Harriott & Exline, 2017; Lee et al., 2013; Park, this volume). Estimates of ADC frequency vary widely, but one review (Streit-Horn, 2011) suggested that about 20 percent of people may have ADCs.

Not only are these perceptions of messages widespread; they could have important psychological consequences. Many studies show that ADCs can provide comfort and hope (Arcangel, 2005; Guggenheim & Guggenheim, 1995; Keen, Murray, & Payne, 2013b; LaGrand, 2006;

McCormick & Natasha, 2016; Nowatzki & Kalischuk, 2009; Parker, 2005; Streit-Horn, 2011). Divine communications, too, can provide comfort, affirmation, and guidance (Lee et al., 2013; Liebert, 2008). Still, dark sides could arise. Some people might be concerned about being stigmatized for reporting such experiences (Keen et al., 2013b; Nowatzki & Kalischuk, 2009; Sabucedo, Evans, Gaitanidis, & Hayes, 2020; Taylor, 2005; Troyer, 2014). ADC experiencers might find it unsettling to feel that a deceased loved one remains present (Sabucedo et al., 2020; Taylor, 2005), or they might perceive an upsetting message from a deceased person (Jahn & Spencer-Thomas, 2018; Lindstrøm, 1995). And what if divine messages imply rejection, harsh judgment, or directives to harm others (Bushman, Ridge, Das, Key, & Busath, 2007)?

Given that perceived messages are common and potentially important, it seems useful to consider potential predictors: why might a person interpret an event as a message from the divine or departed? We will draw from our research program on supernatural attribution (Exline et al., 2020; Wilt, Stauner, & Exline, 2019, 2020) to suggest some possibilities. But first, we will present a brief, hypothetical case to help frame and anchor the ideas that follow.

The (Hypothetical) Case of the Dargis Family

Ray Dargis, aged 68, passed away after a long battle with liver cancer. His wife, Ruth, and his daughter, Jasmine, took care of him at home for over a year. Another son, Cal, lives far away and was not involved in Ray's care. Ray and Ruth, faithful Methodists, had raised Jasmine and Cal in the church, though Jasmine now identified as spiritual (not religious) and Cal as an atheist. Family ties were strong and loving, although there was some tension about Cal being unavailable in times of need.

In his last days, Ray was in tremendous pain and sometimes expressed concern that God was abandoning or punishing him. Worse, he died in the middle of the night when no one was in the room, such that no one had a chance to say goodbye.

The next morning, Ruth awakened to a strong thunderstorm, only to discover that Ray had died during the night. She and Jasmine felt shocked, devastated, and terribly guilty that they had not been at his bedside when he died. After making rushed, tearful phone calls to several relatives, Ruth heard Jasmine calling from the back patio: "Mom, LOOK!" Ruth walked out to see a huge double rainbow. "Oh! It's a sign from the Lord!" was Ruth's response, but Jasmine silently wondered if her dad might have been trying to send them a message himself.

The next day a huge buck, which neither Ruth nor Jasmine had ever seen before, wandered into the yard. And earlier that same morning, Cal (still several thousand miles away) had stopped to admire a large buck that crossed his path in the park. Ray had been extremely fond of deer and would often leave food for them. Might the buck have been sent by Ray—or, could it actually *be* Ray somehow? In conversations that day, Jasmine excitedly speculated about Ray's possible involvement. Cal—an atheist—was curious but skeptical. Ruth insisted that people in heaven can't send messages; but maybe these were signs from God.

When and Why Do People Make Supernatural Attributions?

In the rest of this chapter, we will draw from our supernatural attributions work to offer some ideas about why Ray's family members may have interpreted the rainbow and deer sightings in the ways that they did. We will propose a wide (though by no means exhaustive) array of psychological factors—both background elements and situational features—that might help to explain their responses. (See Table 16.1.) Please note that

Table 16.1 What Factors Might Lead People to View Events as Messages from God or Human Spirits?

	Accessible	*Plausible*	*Motivating*
	(God/spirit comes easily to mind)	*(Framing event as message seems logical)*	*(Desire to see event as a message)*
STABLE BACKGROUND FACTORS			
Personal belief in God/spirits	X	X	
Belief that God/spirits can and do intervene and send messages	X	X	
Prior experience attributing events to God/spirits	X	X	
Socialization to believe in God/spirits (via culture, parents, religion, education, media, etc.)	X	X	
Seeing God/spirit as benevolent; close, positive relational bond		X	X
Open, intuitive, non-skeptical reasoning styles	X	X	
Underlying conditions that lead to unusual thoughts: psychotic disorder; schizotypy; neurological condition	X	X	
Developmental factors (younger children)	X	X	

Table 16.1 What Factors Might Lead People to View Events as Messages from God or Human Spirits? (*Cont.*)

	Accessible	Plausible	Motivating
	(God/spirit comes easily to mind)	*(Framing event as message seems logical)*	*(Desire to see event as a message)*
RECENT BACKGROUND FACTORS			
Current mental state that increases odds of unusual perceptions or thoughts (e.g. psychoactive substance use, psychosis, dissociation, delirium)	X	X	
Major stressor (e.g. bereavement, trauma) that creates a need for guidance, comfort, reassurance	X		X
Desire for contact from God/ spirits	X		X
Actively pursuing contact with God/spirits	X	X	X
CONTEXTUAL FACTORS			
Attention-grabbing, unusual event	X		
No obvious natural explanation	X	X	
Environmental cues prime thoughts of God/spirits	X		
Trusted others make attributions to God/spirits	X	X	X
If seen as a message, meaning is positive; no distressing elements			X
Seeing event as a message adds explanatory power: makes story more coherent or meaningful		X	X
Seeing event as a message confirms prior beliefs		X	X

Source: Some testable hypotheses from a supernatural attributions framework

many of the hypotheses proposed here await formal testing—or are now being tested—in our ongoing research. Although we will cite a few studies, most of the ideas below should be seen as hypotheses awaiting testing rather than definitive conclusions based on research.

We propose that supernatural attributions, including perceived messages from the divine or departed, should be more likely under three conditions: first, a supernatural explanation must be *accessible*; it has to come to mind. Next, this explanation must be at least somewhat *plausible*—and the more plausible, the better. But attribution is not just a cold, logical process; people should also be more likely to choose explanations that are *motivating* in some way, whether their goals are cognitive (e.g. confirming existing beliefs; providing a satisfying explanation), emotional (e.g. finding comfort or hope; avoiding threat), or a blend of the two.

Although this chapter will focus on attributions to the divine and departed, it is worth noting that this logic could apply to any type of attribution, not just supernatural ones. Also, although we will be methodically pointing out various predictors and elements of supernatural attributions, it is worth noting that these steps could unfold very quickly—perhaps almost automatically—in some situations.

To frame this discussion, Table 16.1 lists several categories of predictors of attributions to God or human spirits: stable background factors, recent background factors, and contextual factors. The table also suggests whether each factor might make attributions to the divine or departed more accessible, plausible, and/or motivating.

Accessibility: What Factors Might Bring God—or a Human Spirit—to Mind?

In order to see an event as a message from the divine or departed, such a possibility first needs to come to mind. Let's return to the case of the Dargis family. What types of factors might have made thoughts of Ray accessible? Table 16.1 lists many possibilities, and we will consider several here. Rather than exhaustively reviewing each row of the table, we will be selective.

>   **Attention-grabbing, unusual events.** To start an attributional process, something needs to catch a person's attention and prompt a search for an explanation. In the case of Ray's family, Ruth and Jasmine's buck and rainbow sightings were unusual. The fact that Cal saw a buck on the same morning was also notable. Of course, some events would be even more dramatic, such as witnessing a spontaneous healing or seeing an orb or beam of light appear immediately after a person dies.

Major stressor. Stressful events and associated needs could prime some people to seek supernatural answers and reassurance. Let's consider the immediate situation faced by Ray's family. As they were dealing with acute grief, thoughts of Ray would be on their minds. Also, because Ruth and Jasmine witnessed Ray suffering greatly in his last days, they were likely seeking reassurance that he was doing well and was no longer in pain, frightened, or struggling in any way. Cal may have been feeling guilty because he was not involved in his father's care. Thus, all three were primed to think about Ray and had good reasons to want reassurance. Timing was also relevant here: had the buck or rainbow sightings been a week earlier, Jasmine would have had little reason to attribute such events to Ray's involvement, although she and Ruth might still have seen them as signs of divine care.

Social or environmental cues. Certain social or physical environments could make supernatural explanations more salient. Ray's family members primed each other to think of him through sharing their experiences. Although they did not all make the same attributions, they were exchanging stories, and Jasmine and Ruth offered supernatural explanations. Many other situations could provide similar cues. Imagine that Ruth perceived a possible message from Ray when she visited his grave, or that Jasmine chose to visit a spirit medium (Beischel, Mosher, & Buccuzzi, 2014–2015; Schwartz, this volume), creating a social context where Ray might actually be expected to speak. Knowing that others interpreted an event as a message from beyond should also make such an attribution seem more plausible, especially if one trusts these people in terms of their motives, knowledge base, and states of mind.

Mental states leading to unusual perceptions. Although not relevant in the case of Ray's family, some reports of messages from God or spirits might be prompted by hallucinations or delusions stemming from serious mental illness (e.g. a psychotic or dissociative disorder), a neurological condition (e.g. epilepsy, a sleep disorder), or use of psychoactive substances. (See Exline, in press.) Many studies have shown connections between paranormal beliefs and psychopathology, such as schizotypal thinking (Dagnall, Denovan, Drinkwater, Parker, & Clough, 2017). Thus, when people report unusual experiences that they frame as supernatural messages, it may also be prudent to consider these possibly serious psychological causes, especially if messages are disturbing or if they co-occur with other disturbances in thought, mood, or behavior. (See also Cottam et al., 2011.)

Prior attributions to God/spirits. If someone forms a habit of seeking signs or seeing many events as messages from beyond, it would be natural for such explanations to jump readily to mind in a new situation. Consider Ruth quickly thinking, "It's a sign from the Lord!" in response to the rainbow, likely reflecting a long history of similar attributions to God. Perhaps even a single dramatic experience from the past could be enough to make a supernatural explanation salient in a new situation.

Plausibility: Is It Rational to See This Event as a Message from the Divine or Departed?

Once the idea of a supernatural attribution enters a person's mind, they can reject or accept this explanation (although they might also leave it open as a possibility without making a firm decision). If the idea of a supernatural explanation does not seem at least minimally plausible, it is likely to be quickly discarded, in contrast to highly plausible explanations that should be easier to adopt. What factors might shape these evaluations of plausibility?

Belief in the existence of God/spirits. Looking back to our case example, let's consider Cal's reaction. The idea that his father might be speaking to him through the buck sighting was certainly accessible, because Jasmine had raised the possibility. But for him, the supernatural attribution process stopped here because he did not believe in God or an afterlife, he remained skeptical and did not embrace a supernatural explanation. Clearly, a first step to seeing an event as a possible message from the divine or departed is a belief that such entities exist—or at least some openness to the idea that they might exist. Unsurprisingly, studies have shown that people who report a stronger belief in the existence of God or spirits also report more perceived experiences with them (Wilt et al., 2020). Many factors could feed into these supernatural beliefs, including prior socialization based on culture, religious tradition, family and peer influences (Barrett & Lanman, 2008; Van Leeuwen & van Elk, 2019; Wilt et al., 2020), intuitive reasoning (Shenhav, Rand, & Greene, 2012), developmental factors (Woolley, Cornelius, & Lacy, 2011), and prior personal experiences attributed to God or spirits (Wilt et al., 2020).

Belief that God/spirits can and do send these types of messages. To frame an event as a message from God or a spirit, a person must not only believe that the entity in question exists (or could exist); the idea of a message should also fit reasonably well with one's beliefs about how the entity operates. In a study of *supernatural operating rules* (Exline et al., 2020), we confirmed that undergraduates reported more personal experiences with supernatural entities (God, human spirits, the devil, and forces of karma, fate/destiny, and luck) if they saw these entities as powerful, broad in their scope of operation, and having some intention to intervene in the world. Although participants saw God as surpassing human spirits in all three domains, many did see human spirits as having sufficient power, scope of influence, and intent to influence some events.

In our case example, Ruth believed that God could cause a rainbow to appear and could influence the behavior of deer; but she did not believe that Ray had this type of power. In contrast, Jasmine wondered if her father might now have new, special abilities to communicate through natural events. Ruth's interpretation of the rainbow as a divine message probably also reflected a belief that God communicates broadly (frequently, to many people, and through many modes) and had some intention to communicate with her (i.e. to provide comfort or hope). In contrast, if she believed that divine messages were rare events reserved for certain people—perhaps based on status, ability, behavior, character, or even simple favoritism, then she probably would be less likely to see the rainbow and deer sightings as personal messages from God. Supernatural attributions should also fit with a person's ideas about the character of the entity and the relationship they have with the entity (if any). For example, people often make divine attributions for positive events (Spilka & Schmidt, 1983) but also for negative events, especially if they turn out to have positive long-term outcomes (Ray, Lockman, Jones, & Kelly, 2015). Given the loving relationships of the Dargis family and Ruth's benevolent views of God, comforting messages from either God or Ray would seem to be "in character."

Lack of a satisfying natural explanation. People sometimes make supernatural attributions because they cannot find a natural explanation (Ritzema & Young, 1983). A person might lack the scientific knowledge to explain an event, or perhaps they lack the reasoning ability or attentional focus to critically appraise the situation and consider various explanations. Or perhaps the event itself is so astonishing that it seems to violate natural laws. Imagine that either Ruth or Jasmine—or perhaps even both of them, at the same time—had actually seen Ray's spirit, or that he had spoken to them audibly. In such a case, the evidence for a supernatural explanation might seem so compelling that they would both be immediately and strongly convinced that Ray was actually there communicating with them. And what if Cal had been present and experienced this same event? Such profound experiences might be enough to shift the worldview of even the most committed skeptics, although such individuals would likely put substantial energy into exploring and ruling out alternative explanations.

Supernatural explanation adds explanatory power or personal meaning. In most cases, the situations that people perceive as messages from the divine and departed do not require dramatic violations of natural laws. The deer and rainbow examples are typical of the types of events that many people would interpret as messages from God or spirits. In both cases, the events themselves were easily explainable through natural means; but it was their unusual nature, timing, and personal, symbolic meaning that made them strong candidates for supernatural attribution (Daggett, 2005). Jasmine and Ruth's explanations for these events both seemed more satisfying, or more complete, if attributed to a supernatural agent. Events that are repeated, unusual, or apparently part of a pattern (e.g. the two buck sightings) might also cause people to consider agents who might have initiated the action (Barrett & Lanman, 2008). Or imagine that Ruth had just said a prayer to God, pleading for strength, just a few moments before she saw the rainbow. The rainbow, if seen as a direct answer to her prayer, would fit easily with a narrative that God was sending her a comforting message in response to her request (Poloma & Lee, 2012; Van Leeuwen & van Elk, 2019; Wilt et al., in press).

Motivation: Do We Want To See This Event as a Message from the Divine or Departed?

As we consider why people tend to embrace meaningful explanations, it becomes clear that the process may not be entirely focused on logic. In many cases, people may really *want* to interpret events as a personal message from God or from human spirits. Why?

Desires to make meaning. People may find that certain explanations for events (whether supernatural or not) simply make a better story—one that has greater personal resonance, or one that seems more memorable or interesting or exciting than simply attributing the event to natural causes (Barrett & Lanman, 2008). Humans are meaning-making creatures (Park, 2010), and we want to see events in our lives as having some purpose (Banerjee & Bloom, 2014). For most people, seeing an event as a meaningful personal message is likely to be much more satisfying than seeing it as random and without purpose. Especially in the context of stressful or traumatic events where people are struggling to make meaning, a message or care, affirmation, or hope from a supernatural agent could have great appeal. In our case example, any of the Dargis family members could have been seeking some sense of meaning or purpose in Ray's untimely death. Cal, given his materialist worldview, relied entirely on natural explanations to help make sense of the situation; but for Jasmine and Ruth, seeing the rainbow and deer sightings as messages added an extra boost of personal meaning. Along these lines, we have found that people are more likely to attribute life-changing events to God or human spirits if the events include a sense of receiving personal meaning, insight, or guidance (Wilt et al., 2019).

Messages are seen as rewarding (or at least not punishing). Even if people desire to find meaning in stressful situations, the type of meaning is also likely to matter. Meanings that seem positive—offering guidance, reassurance, peace, or hope—are likely to be adopted more readily than negative meanings. For instance, what if Ruth had experienced a terrifying, vivid dream of Ray suffering in hell? What if Jasmine visited a medium who gave a disturbing message, one in which Ray was yelling at her for not being there when he died? What if Ray had died of alcoholism, and they kept finding empty beer cans along the side of the road every time they went for a walk? They would likely be eager to dismiss such events as coincidences, mistakes, or indicators of their own emotional distress.

Emotional needs would be met by a message. A powerful message from beyond could have the potential to meet a wide variety of emotional needs: needs for reassurance, hope, guidance, or affirmation, to name just a few. Thus, anything that puts someone in a state of need, which could range from an anxious state of mind (Park, this volume) to a traumatic event, could cause people with supernatural beliefs to turn to those sources to meet their needs. Clearly, bereavement is a situation that can create strong desires for comfort and reassurance. If the associated needs and motivations are sufficiently strong, some people might not even stop to take a close look at plausibility questions before adopting a supernatural explanation. For example, the acute grief that Jasmine was experiencing could cause her to view the rainbow uncritically, being quick to label it as a sign from Ray without pausing to consider whether her departed father actually has the power to make a rainbow appear.

Confirmation of existing beliefs. As mentioned earlier, people will be much more likely to see events as messages from the divine or departed if such an attribution fits with their existing beliefs. Viewed from the opposite angle, though, we could see a motivational aspect here as well: people not only follow their beliefs;

they also want to confirm their existing beliefs, rather than facing the mental effort (and perhaps emotional or social costs) of challenging or changing them. Given her pre-existing beliefs, Ruth might find it more comfortable to see the rainbow and deer sightings as messages from God than as messages from Ray, because framing them as messages from Ray might require a significant shift in her beliefs. For Cal, any question of shifting his beliefs to incorporate possible supernatural involvement could be unsettling. He might even be actively opposed to doing so if he has a strong commitment to an atheist, materialist worldview. Nonetheless, the fact that he was raised within a Christian household might make the associated cognitive shift easier for him than it would be for someone whose background had been uniformly secular.

Conclusion

People vary widely in how they respond to the idea of supernatural activity in the world, including possible messages from the divine and departed. Some people may readily adopt a supernatural lens and easily accept supernatural claims. Others might dismiss the possibility immediately, while others could find themselves struggling to decide. In any case, people may benefit from taking a closer look at the reasons behind their attributions.

Drawing from our research program on supernatural attribution, we have proposed that people will be most likely to interpret events as messages from God or human spirits if such ideas seem highly accessible, plausible, and motivating, and we have suggested some background and contextual variables that could be relevant to each of these domains. Many background factors, including those related to socialization, development, psychopathology, and personal experience, could feed into beliefs about the existence and nature of God, an afterlife, and human spirits that survive death. Recent events, which might include major stressors, unusual perceptual experiences, and attempts to contact the divine or departed could lay the groundwork for supernatural attributions. And in the situation itself, a wide variety of environmental and social cues, cognitive factors, and desires could shape decisions about whether to interpret an event as a message from beyond.

Before concluding, we would like to clarify an important point: although we have suggested many factors that could shape people's perceptions of messages from the divine and departed, we certainly do not intend to strip any significance or beauty from these experiences, which are profound and life-changing for so many people. Indeed, one potential cost of using a psychological lens is that it can lead to excessive analysis of transcendent, precious, perhaps ineffable experiences (Exline, in press). But even while acknowledging these risks, our hope is that considering these potential predictors will yield insights that will ultimately be helpful to experiencers, clinicians, researchers, and others who care deeply about this mysterious and exciting topic.

References

Arcangel, D. (2005). *Afterlife encounters: Ordinary people, extraordinary experiences.* Charlottesville, VA: Hampton Roads.

Banerjee, K., & Bloom, P. (2014). Why did this happen to me? Religious believers' and non-believers' teleological reasoning about life events. *Cognition, 133,* 277–303.

Barrett, J. L., & Lanman, J. A. (2008). The science of religious beliefs. *Religion, 38,* 109–124.

Beischel, J., Mosher, C., & Buccuzzi, M. (2014–2015). The possible effects on bereavement of assisted after-death communication during readings with psychic mediums: A continuing bonds perspective. *Omega, 70,* 169–194.

Bushman, B. J., Ridge, R. D., Das, E., Key, C. W., & Busath, G. L. (2007). When God sanctions killing: Effect of scriptural violence on aggression. *Psychological Science, 18,* 204–207.

Cottam, S., Paul, S., Doughty, O., Carpenter, L., Al-Mousawi, A., Karvounis, S., & Done, D. (2011). Does religious belief enable positive interpretation of auditory hallucinations? A comparison of religious voice hearers with and without psychosis. *Cognitive Neuropsychiatry, 16,* 403–421.

Daggett, L. M. (2005). Continued encounters: The experience of after-death communication. *Journal of Holistic Nursing, 23,* 191–207. doi: 10.1177/0898010105275928.

Dagnall, N., Denovan, A., Drinkwater, K., Parker, A., & Clough, P. J. (2017). Urban legends and paranormal beliefs: The role of reality testing and schizotypy. *Frontiers in Psychology, 8,* 942. doi: 10.3389/fpsyg.2017.00942.

Degelman, D., & Lynn, D. (1995). The development and preliminary validation of the Belief in Divine Intervention Scale. *Journal of Psychology and Theology, 23,* 37–44. doi: 10.1177/009164719502300104.

Dein, S., & Cook, C. C. (2015). God put a thought into my mind: The charismatic Christian experience of receiving communications from God. *Mental Health, Religion & Culture, 18,* 97–113.

Dein, S., & Littlewood, R. (2007). The voice of God. *Anthropology and Medicine, 14,* 213–228.

Exline, J. J. (in press). Psychopathology, normal psychological processes, or supernatural encounters? Three ways to frame reports of after-death communication (ADC). *Spirituality in Clinical Practice.*

Exline, J. J., Pargament, K. I., Wilt, J. A., & Harriott, V. A. (2020). Mental illness, normal psychological processes, or attacks by the devil? *Three lenses to frame demonic struggles in therapy.* Manuscript submitted for publication.

Guggenheim, B., & Guggenheim, J. (1995). *Hello from heaven!* New York, NY: Bantam.

Harriott, V. A., & Exline, J. J. (2017). Perceptions of God's "voice. In N. Stauner (Ed.), *Acts of God in the mind, body, and soul*. Hamar, Norway: Symposium at the biannual meeting of the International Association for the Psychology of Religion.

Ipsos (2011, April 25). *Belief in supreme being(s) and afterlife accepted by half (51%) of citizens in 23 country survey, but only 28% are 'creationists.'* Retrieved from https://www.ipsos.com/sites/default/files/news_and_polls/2011-04/5217.pdf.

Jahn, D. R., & Spencer-Thomas, S. (2018). A qualitative examination of continuing bonds through spiritual experiences in individuals bereaved by suicide. *Religions, 9*(8), 1–15.

Keen, C., Murray, C., & Payne, S. (2013a). Sensing the presence of the deceased: A narrative review. *Mental Health, Religion & Culture, 16*(4), 384–402.

Keen, C., Murray, C. D., & Payne, S. (2013b). A qualitative exploration of sensing the presence of the deceased following bereavement. *Mortality, 18*(4), 339–357.

LaGrand, L. E. (1997). *After death communication: Final farewells*. St. Paul, MN: Llewellyn.

LaGrand, L. E. (2005). The nature and therapeutic implications of the extraordinary experiences of the bereaved. *Journal of Near-Death Studies, 24*, 3–19.

LaGrand, L. E. (2006). *Love lives on: Learning from the extraordinary encounters of the bereaved*. New York, NY: Berkley.

Lee, M., Poloma, M., & Post, S. G. (2013). *The heart of religion*. Oxford University Press. New York, NY.

Legare, C. H., Evans, E. M., Rosengren, K. S., & Harris, P. L. (2012). The coexistence of natural and supernatural explanations across cultures and development. *Child Development, 83*, 779–793.

Liebert, E. (2008). *The way of discernment: Spiritual practices for decision-making*. Louisville, KY: Westminster John Knox.

Lindstrøm, T. (1995). Experiencing the presence of the dead: Discrepancies in "The sensing experience" and their psychological concomitants. *Omega, 31*, 11–21.

Luhrmann, T. M. (2012). *When God talks back: Understanding the American evangelical relationship with God*. Vintage.

McCormick, B. M. E., & Natasha, A. (2016). After-death communication: A typology of therapeutic benefits. *Journal of Near Death Studies, 34*(3), 151–172.

Nowatzki, N. R., & Kalischuk, R. G. (2009). Post-death encounters: Grieving, mourning, and healing. *Omega, 59*(2), 91–111.

Park, C. L. (2010). Making sense of the meaning literature. *Psychological Bulletin, 136*, 257–301.

Parker, J. S. (2005). Extraordinary experiences of the bereaved and adaptive outcomes of grief. *Omega, 51*(4), 257–283.

Pew Research Center. (2009, December). *Eastern, new age beliefs widespread: Many Americans mix multiple faiths*. Retrieved from https://www.pewforum.org/2009/12/09/many-americans-mix-multiple-faiths/.

Poloma, M. M., & Lee, M. T. (2012). Prophetic prayer as two-way communication with the divine. *Journal of Communication and Religion, 35*, 271–294.

Ray, S. D., Lockman, J. D., Jones, E. J., & Kelly, M. H. (2015). Attributions to God and Satan about life-altering events. *Psychology of Religion and Spirituality, 7*, 60–69.

Ritzema, R. J., & Young, C. (1983). Causal schemata and the attribution of supernatural causality. *Journal of Psychology and Theology, 11*, 36–43.

Sabucedo, P., Evans, C., Gaitanidis, A., & Hayes, J. (2020). When experiences of presence go awry: A survey of psychotherapy practice with the ambivalent-to-distressing "hallucination" of the deceased. *Psychology and Psychotherapy: Theory, Research, and Practice.* https://doi.org/10.1111/papt.12285.

Shenhav, A., Rand, D. G., & Greene, J. D. (2012). Divine intuition: Cognitive style influences belief in god. *Journal of Experimental Psychology: General, 141,* 423–428.

Spilka, B., & McIntosh, D. N. (1995). Attribution theory and religious experience. In R. W. Hood, Jr. (Ed.), *Handbook of religious experience* (pp. 421–445). Birmingham, AL: Religious Education Press.

Spilka, B., & Schmidt, G. (1983). General attribution theory for the psychology of religion: The influence of event-character on attributions to God. *Journal for the Scientific Study of Religion, 22,* 326–339.

Spilka, B., Shaver, P., & Kirkpatrick, L. A. (1985). A general attribution theory for the psychology of religion. *Journal for the Scientific Study of Religion, 24,* 1–20.

Steffen, E., & Coyle, A. (2012). 'Sense of presence' experiences in bereavement and their relationship to mental health: A critical examination of a continuing controversy. In C. Murray (Ed.), *Mental health and anomalous experience* (pp. 33–56). New York, NY: Nova Science.

Streit-Horn, J. (2011). *A systematic review of research on after-death communication (ADC).* Unpublished doctoral dissertation. University of North Texas.

Taylor, S. F. (2005). Between the idea and the reality: A study of the counselling experiences of bereaved people who sense the presence of the deceased. *Counselling and Psychotherapy Research, 5,* 53–61.

Troyer, J. (2014). Older widowers and postdeath encounters: A qualitative investigation. *Death Studies, 38*(10), 637–647.

Van Leeuwen, N., & van Elk, M. (2019). Seeking the supernatural: The interactive religious experience model. *Religion, Brain & Behavior, 9,* 221–275.

Weeks, M., & Lupfer, M. B. (2000). Religious attributions and proximity of influence: An investigation of direct interventions and distal explanations. *Journal for the Scientific Study of Religion, 39,* 348–362. doi:10.1111/0021-8294.00029.

Williams, R. J., & Watts, F. N. (2014). Attributions in a spiritual healing context: An archival analysis of a 1920s healing movement. *Journal for the Social Scientific Study of Religion, 53,* 90–108.

Wilt, J., Stauner, N., & Exline, J. (2019). Supernatural attributions for life-changing events. In N. Stauner & J. Exline (Eds.), *Supernatural attributions for suffering and major life events.* Chicago, IL: A symposium at the 127th convention of the American Psychological Association.

Wilt, J. A., Stauner, N., & Exline, J. J. (2020). *Beliefs and experiences involving God, the devil, human spirits, and fate: Social, motivational, and cognitive predictors.* Manuscript submitted for publication.

Wilt, J. A., Takahashi, J. T., Yun, D., Jeong, P., Exline, J. J., & Pargament, K. I. (in press). A mixed methods study of communing with and complaining to the divine: Imagined conversations with God among undergraduates. *Psychology of Religion and Spirituality.*

Woolley, J. D., Cornelius, C. A., & Lacy, W. (2011). Developmental changes in the use of supernatural explanations for natural events. *Journal of Cognition and Culture, 11,* 311–337.

17 Ethical Challenges Associated with Communication with the Divine and the Departed

Thomas G. Plante

Example 1: Monica recently lost her husband of 40 years, Jim, to brain cancer. They were high school sweethearts and had a close relationship since the day they met in math class. Monica's loss of Jim was devastating to her and eight months after the funeral she continued to cry daily, had trouble sleeping, and drank more alcohol than she used to drink. Monica heard about a local spiritualist and medium, Claire, who claimed to have the ability to communicate with the departed. Monica decided that she had nothing to lose to consult with Claire. She met with her and liked her. Claire was warm, friendly, and seemed deeply respectful and spiritual. Monica decided to work with Claire who felt that she could help communicate with Jim. After many months of collaboration, Monica was convinced that Claire had a special gift. However, Monica's daughter, Anne, who had been helping her mother with shopping and bills, discovered that Monica had given over $100,000 to Claire for her services. Anne was incensed! She was convinced that her mom was being scammed. After her investigation, she discovered that Claire had a criminal record, was sued by other clients, and had a long history of criminal activity.

Example 2: Pastor Bob runs a large non-denominational evangelical megachurch. Pastor Bob subscribes to the prosperity gospel that suggests that that the more you give in faith the more God will bless you multiple times over. Pastor Bob lives a lavish lifestyle with a private jet and several expensive homes and cars. He travels extensively. Pastor Bob claims that God has blessed him with these luxuries due to his faith and trust in the divine. Pastor Bob encouraged his congregation to tithe giving 10 percent of their income to the church and to give more if they wanted more blessings from God. During an economic downturn, Pastor Bob started to experience financial challenges and told his congregation that God told him that if he did not get his congregation to give over a million dollars within a week then God would call Pastor Bob home to heaven. The congregation scrambled to get the money and was successful in doing so. Pastor Bob lived and told his congregation that their faithfulness was evidence that God was blessing them generously.

Example 3: Scientists in the year 2035 find a way to use technology and artificial intelligence to successfully communicate with the departed. Their efforts proved that consciousness continued after death. This groundbreaking discovery excited many as people clamored to use the technology to communicate with loved ones who had departed. The costs of the technology were prohibitive for many, but over several years, the costs decreased steadily. Although this exciting breakthrough was embraced by most people the downsides became quickly apparent. People who had toxic relationships with family members, for example, were traumatized again after communicating with their deceased relatives who continue their toxicity even after death. Some who expected to hear consoling words from the departed were traumatized when those words never came and they received the opposite. What seemed like a wonderful discovery and opportunity became a cause of serious concern and trauma for many.

These examples provide just a few of the possible ethical challenges associated with our strong desire to communicate with the divine and the departed. There are many more. People have been trying to connect and communicate with the divine and with the departed since the dawn of time. Prayers and rituals of various sorts have tried to not only interact with those who have passed on but have also tried to influence the divine, the saints, and departed to act in ways that benefit the living. Prayers for salvation, deliverance from troubles such as illness and traumas, as well as prayers and communication for insight, inspiration, wisdom, motivation, salvation, and for other needs are common. Furthermore, experiences and desires for visitations from ghosts, angels, saints, deceased friends and relatives, and the divine are common too. There appears to be a longstanding, multi-cultural, multi-faith, and maybe even innate psychological desire to communicate with the gods and the departed to help better understand, manage, and cope with the various challenges of the living. Additionally, those who are grieved have longed to connect with loved ones who have passed on. Thus, attempts at communication with the divine and departed are nothing new and will likely not go away in the future.

Given this reality, there are numerous potential ethical challenges associated with human attempted contact with the divine and departed. For example, some people prey on vulnerable others to manipulate them into giving money to those who claim to have special skills with communication with deceased loved ones and with the divine. Regardless of their skills or abilities, they may offer to act as a conduit or medium for a substantial fee. This problem is not only found among individual unscrupulous charlatans but was actually official Church policy for many years when the Catholic Church would sell indulgences so that the devout would be offered less time in purgatory after their deaths for large financial payments to the Church (Swanson, 2007). Additionally, some current-day evangelical pastors assure that their congregants will be blessed by God or by Jesus, but only if they give generously to the pastor's church. The prosperity Gospel has underscored that divine favors are be expected when one acts in faith and when one gives large sums of money to the religious leaders (Bowler, 2018). Thus, throughout history many have suggested that communication and favors from the beyond are possible but for a fee.

Another more futuristic ethical challenge and example includes the possible unintended consequences of enhanced technological capabilities that could potentially allow for communication with the departed (Schwartz, 2011). What if we could find a reliable way to communicate with the divine and departed through newly developed technologies? Suppose that there was a device that was able to bridge the divide between the living and the dead or between the living and the divine? Should we use this technology if we could develop it? Suppose we did not want to hear the messages that the divine and departed wanted to express to us? While we may want to hear comforting and loving messages from the beyond, suppose that these messages were upsetting and discouraging? Suppose someone had a toxic family member, such as an abusive parent, who died, and yet they were still able to continue communicating with the living through this newly developed technology? In such a case, there would be no escape, not even through death, to get away from the toxic person. The three examples that began this chapter well illustrate these ethical challenges.

Perhaps a more commonly experienced problem involves people praying for divine intervention to save themselves or a loved one from harm, illness, or financial problems, and when their prayers appeared unanswered they conclude that the divine does not like them or wishes to punish them. Many have been terribly disappointed when they expect that a loving God, for example, would not allow the suffering of innocent children or adults and yet people of all ages and backgrounds do suffer, die prematurely, or are unjustly harmed. Many wonder where God was during challenging times either personally or collectively.

> *Example 4*: Donna is an African-American evangelical woman in her early 40s who was diagnosed with breast cancer. She believes that, as the gospel claims, that if you have faith as "small as a mustard seed" you will be rewarded with answers to prayer (Matthew 17:20). Her faith-sharing women's group and her church congregation pray with and over her and are convinced that their prayers will be answered by God for divine healing given the strength of their collective faith. Donna decided that traditional medical intervention was not needed since she believes that her prayers, and

those of her family and friends, will be answered. Sadly, Donna's condition deteriorates and she passes away. Her family members feel guilty thinking that perhaps they did not have enough faith or that God decided to punish them for some previous sinful thought or action. Donna's family and friends are despondent. Donna's teenage daughter scandalizes the family and their closest friends by deciding that she is now an atheist given that God did not save her mother from death as they all expected.

Example 5: Beth is a young child, age seven, who was in a car accident with her mother. Tragically, her mother died in the accident. After being rushed to the local hospital with massive injuries and significant blood loss, Beth's father arrived. He refused to allow a much-needed blood transfusion for Beth since they are Jehovah's Witnesses and do not allow or support blood transfusions. The doctors informed him that Beth would die unless a blood transfusion was provided but he insisted that it would not be permitted. Sadly, Beth passed away shortly thereafter.

Donna and Beth's stories are common. Many people believe that faith and prayer alone will heal them or solve their troubles. When their prayers are not answered in ways that they expected, then they conclude that they had insufficient faith or that God was punishing them for some previous sin or transgression (Peters, 2007). Furthermore, some people follow religious rules (avoiding medical care, extreme fasts, engaging in mortifications) that result in health-damaging or deadly behaviors

These and many other ethical dilemmas are examined in this chapter that seeks to reflect upon ethical challenges with our efforts to communicate with those who have either passed on or who are perceived as divine.

Where There Are Strong Needs and Desires, There Are Opportunities for Unethical Exploitation

Most people pray (Hood, Hill, & Spilka, 2018). They pray and communicate with God or to various other names for the divine (e.g. Adonai, Yahweh, Allah, Jesus, the Great Spirit, and a Higher Power). Additionally, depending upon their particular religious or spiritual tradition they may attempt communication with and pray to smaller or lesser divine figures such as saints from the distant past (e.g. St. Francis, St. Clare, St. Peter, St. Ignatius) and to saints in more recent times (e.g. St. John Paul II, St. Mother Teresa). Additionally, many people pray to, for, or communicate with deceased loved ones from their own personal experience and relationships such as parents, grandparents and other ancestors, spouses, children, and other important figures who have transitioned from life to death and the beyond. People have likely been trying to communicate in this way for centuries. Humans seem to have a strong need to communicate with the divine and departed and since this need tends to be vigorous and unstoppable, it is ripe for exploitation by others. This tension creates numerous ethical challenges. Additionally, there are often unintended and both expected and unexpected outcomes that can emerge in areas where there is so much personal and emotional investment. For example, suppose someone desperately wished to communicate with a loved one who passed on hoping to hear a comforting message but rather heard a disturbing message from the beyond instead. Before discussing several of these challenges in some detail, it is important to review exactly what we mean by ethics.

What Are Ethics?

Who are we and how do we want to be in the world? Essentially, ethics attempts to answer these basic fundamental questions using principles of reason and reflection (Plante, 2004a, 2004b, 2018; Vaughn, 2015). Ethics are principles that offer thoughtful, reasoned, and principled strategies for living, making decisions, and interacting with others. Ethics are much more than simply trying to answer the question of what is right and wrong in a black or white or all or none manner. Thousands of years of moral philosophy, as well as the influence of the religious and spiritual traditions, have offered much to consider when it comes to approaches to thoughtful and reflective ethical decision-making (Vaughn, 2015). An enormous amount of material has been written and disseminated about ethics that span many centuries. Upon careful review and synthesis, there appear to be approximately a dozen or so generally agreed-upon ways to solve or consider ethical challenges and dilemmas using guidance from moral philosophy. These include approaches that highlight the common good, utilitarian, absolute moral rules, justice, social contract, virtues and values, and so forth. Many of these approaches are generally considered *consequential* in that they focus on what leads to a good and desired outcome. Other approaches are *deontological* in that they highlight following particular principles of ethical decision-making regardless of the resulting outcome (e.g. always be honest regardless of the consequences, Vaughn, 2015).

It is beyond the scope of this chapter to discuss in much depth each of the various ethical approaches to decision-making but several of them will be highlighted here as they relate to the topic of communication with the divine and departed.

Several Common Ethical Approaches

Virtue and Values

Perhaps one of the most common and easily understandable approaches to ethical decision-making is the virtue and values approach. It suggests that certain virtues and values are endorsed and supported within various communities and among groups of people (Vaughn, 2015). For example, most people would report that they value principles such as honesty, integrity, compassion, generosity, and so forth. These principles are organizing and centering principles that underscore how one should live life. We invoke these virtues and values as we make decisions and try to remind ourselves of them when we get into challenging ethical situations and conflicts.

The virtue and value approach to ethics is likely one of the approaches most commonly used and understood by people as they can intuitively understand and use various virtues and values to help make critical decisions (Plante, 2004a). Helping others when in need, telling the truth, avoiding the exploitation of children, and so forth are all principles that are based on virtues and values.

When it comes to prayer and communication with the divine and departed, the virtue and value approach would suggest that we engage in prayer and communication with certain virtues and values that might encourage honesty, compassion, and sincerity for example. Those who might help others in their prayer life (e.g. clerics) or communication with the departed (e.g. spiritual mediums) should behave in ways that are honest and sincere. They should be truthful and not exploit the vulnerabilities of others (e.g. asking for a great deal of money, claim that they have special skills that they do not actually have). We expect people who provide us with services to be fair and honest and want to trust that they can do what they claim to be able to do. If someone claims that they can help our prayer life or our abilities to communicate with the divine and departed, we assume, or at least we want and expect to want to assume, that they are honest and have our interests in mind.

Example 6: Fr. Jim Martin is a popular Jesuit priest who at *America* magazine, writes popular books on prayer and religious engagement, and was the official chaplain for the *Colbert Report* hosted by the well-known comedian, Stephen Colbert. He offers a daily 3 p.m. EST 30 minute Facebook live faith-sharing experience where he reads the gospel passage for the day, explains the story, and then responds to questions and requests from several thousands of people who watch the live feed. Often prayer requests are offered and he acknowledges them asking the community of listeners to pray for the intended person. People mention how powerful, consoling it is to have Fr. Jim and others pray for their loved ones who may be ill, recently died, or are struggling in other ways. People report feeling uplifted and more relaxed knowing that they are being prayed for. In these sessions, he makes clear that everyone is valuable and important and should be treated with respect and compassion. In addition, he models this behavior even among those who behave problematically or inappropriately.

Common Good

Another important ethical principle is the common good. This principle addresses what is in the best interest of the general population and in specific community groups (Vaughn, 2015). Rather than individual or self-centered considerations, the common good approach would ask what is in the best interest of the community in general. For example, recycling, being mindful of our carbon footprint and avoiding unnecessary use of resources, and offering to help charitable groups, causes, and services would all follow the common good approach to ethics. The common good approach would likely be found more often in communal societies (e.g. Asian) rather than individualistic societies (e.g. American), as a general rule of thumb, although there are plenty of exceptions to these rules.

For example, prayers that help communities deal with crises such as the aftermath of a large mass shooting, or outbreak of a public health challenge such as a pandemic, or after a natural disaster (e.g. flood, fire, tornado, hurricane), can be in the common good as it helps to console communities that are vulnerable, and in significant and extreme distress. Thus, those who are skilled in prayer or who are faith leaders, such as clerics, may use their skills with communication with the divine and departed in ways that help the community cope and manage stressful events and emotional challenges. Regardless of their skill in actually interacting with the divine or departed, the process of their prayer and communication may help a community in great distress feel heard and consoled lowering their levels of stress and fears.

> *Example 7*: After the tragedy of September 11th (2001) so many people were in a state of shock, fear, and upset. Many did not quite know what to do with their feelings and grief but many turned to faith communities for hope and consolation. On that day and for many days afterwards, people turned to faith leaders and clerics for help. Dan Schutte, a well-known liturgical composer and musician, was helping to lead a service at the University of San Francisco in the church on campus, St. Ignatius. He tells a story of never seeing the church so filled with people standing in the back of the huge church. A local Jewish temple, Congregation Beth Am, in Los Altos had a similar story for their Friday evening Shabbat services several days after the tragic events of 9/11. The sanctuary was packed with standing room only. In times of crisis, people turn to clerics for comfort, hope, and solace, and the desire to have experts in prayer and communication with the divine help them also communicate with the divine as well. For large communities to feel better after these experiences is in the common good, regardless of the effectiveness of their prayer.

Utilitarianism

The utilitarian approach highlights what is in the best interest of the majority or what creates the most happiness for the most people (Vaughn, 2015). It is democratic in that it highlights the will of the majority. It suggests that, regardless of the truth, or what is in the best interest of the majority, if most people want something that would make the most people happy then they should have it. Voting with the majority deciding the selection of something, like a political candidate running for local or national office, is a good example.

In terms of communication with the divine or departed, if most people want to pray, participate in various events to communicate with the divine and departed, or develop technologies to do so such communications then they should be allowed and supported with appropriate resources. For example, if people want to attend a prayer service or a séance then they should be able to do so regardless of the efficacy of their behavior.

> *Example 8*: Séances have been performed for generations. In fact, a little-known interesting tidbit is that when Sigmund Freud came to the United States for his only visit during the 20th anniversary of the founding of Clark University in 1909, he was convinced to attend a séance with a well-known spiritualist at the time (Gitz-Johansen, 2016). He and several other famous attendees at the conference, including William James and Carl Jung, all participated. Sometimes séances are conducted for groups of people who are looking for adventure, fun, or are quite serious about efforts to communicate with loved ones who have passed on. These intriguing events may or may not be conducted by sincere and skilled professionals but the utilitarian approach would suggest that, regardless of their efficacy, if people want to engage in these events they should be able to do so if it makes them happy to do so.

Egoism

Egoism is typically a rather challenging ethical principle for most people to understand and appreciate yet it is likely the one that most people employ when they make ethical decisions (Plante 2004a). It highlights that people often behave with their self-interest in mind but that good ethical decisions can actually result through these self-centered behaviors (Vaughn, 2015). For example, people might donate large sums of money to a worthy charitable cause that helps many people in need but their motivations for doing so may be to have their name on a large and prestigious building or to enjoy a desired tax deduction for their generous contribution. Additionally, people may be honest but do so in order to avoid having to keep track of their deceptions that could create bigger problems for them later if they are caught in their lie. People may purposefully act to help others but do so to win them over, secure their votes in an election, or just get on their good side to cash in for a future favor.

As it relates to prayer and communication with the divine and departed, people may want others to believe that their prayers are heard by God, the divine, and the departed so that they may feel comfort and consolation. Their comfort and consolation may quiet them and prevent them from behaving in a disruptive or annoying manner. Thus, one may encourage prayer and communication with the departed not so much for the comfort of others but for the comfort of self.

> *Example 9*: A politician who is not religious or spiritual at all tries to encourage the faith communities to support his candidacy for office. He has called faith leaders to his office and to his rallies. He begins his speeches with prayer from one of the faith leaders and promises to support many of their faith-based causes. They endorse his candidacy even though they are well aware that he is not a person of faith, has little if any religious interests or beliefs, and that he is using them for his political gain. However, they know that their various causes would be supported by him once he's elected and thus are willing to embrace his candidacy. Both the politician and the faith leaders use egoism to achieve their receptive goals.

Some Conclusions about Ethics

Most people who are not trained or schooled in moral philosophy and ethics likely use emotivism, egoism, and subjectivism when making ethical choices (Vaughn, 2015). They attend to their gut reactions and act accordingly. They are likely to make limited use of thoughtful reason and the various well-articulated and considered approaches to ethical decision-making. In the end, they act in their self-interest with their emotions driving their decision-making efforts. Having some basic training in ethical decision-making can help everyone use these ethical tools to make more thoughtful, reasoned, and hopefully more satisfying decisions (Plante 2004a, 2004b).

Vaughn (2015) argues that an overall moral theory of behavior can be developed and can appeal to most people by following a few general and easy-to-understand principles. First, he suggests using *prima facie* principles that are defined as following certain moral rules unless an important exception should be considered. For example, being honest and telling the truth might be a very good general rule to follow but there may be times when a lie would result in a better and more ethical outcome. People may value honesty but if being honest might result in someone being killed or a child being victimized, for example, then lying to save a life or to help a child might be a good and noble exception to the honesty rule. For example, people hiding Jews in their homes during the Holocaust of World War II and lying about doing so to protect them would be an excellent example of lying for a greater moral purpose.

Vaugh underscores the wisdom of W. D. Ross (1877–1967) who suggested that following several simple rules provide assistance to many when it comes to ethical decision-making. These rules include fidelity (e.g. keeping promises), reparation (e.g. making amends), gratitude (e.g. acknowledging services by others), justice (e.g., distributing benefits and burdens among everyone), beneficence (e.g. helping others), self-improvement (e.g. improving ourselves), non-maleficence (e.g. not hurting others) and that the three primary *prima facie* principles to follow include respect, justice, and beneficence.

Unpacking Three Primary *Prima Facie* Principles: Respect, Justice, and Beneficence

Now that we have defined and discussed ethics and have offered some examples of commonly used ethical principles, it may be useful to try and further understand some of the typical ethical challenges associated with prayer and communication with the divine and departed using an overall moral theory of respect, justice, and beneficence.

Respect

When it comes to anything that is spiritual or religious in consideration, many people can get very judgmental very quickly. Conversations about prayer and communication with the divine and the departed will certainly result in some raised eyebrows, head shaking, sneers, and mean-spirited jokes. People often have strong opinions on matters of religion and spirituality and are typically not shy to express them. It is one of those areas where so many people with the least amount of education and training on the topic believe that they have as much to offer and say about it as those who have spent their lives in study.

The ethical *prima facie* principle of respect would suggest that people should be respected for their points of view even if you do not agree with them. Since so much about religion, spirituality, prayer, and communication with the divine and departed currently cannot be empirically proven or disproven, objective and clear facts are typically elusive. People are entitled to their views and beliefs but the principle of respect would suggest that we do not belittle or mock views that differ from our own.

Example 10: Margaret is a devout Catholic who prays to saints for certain desires and has several statues of them in her kitchen. When she really wants something, she turns her St. Joseph status toward the wall. She spends an hour each day praying the rosary and enjoys talking about the lives of the saints. Although her devotional activities seem extreme to some of her relatives, they treat her and her practices respectfully.

Example 11: During the COVID-19 pandemic, some evangelicals defied public health recommendations to avoid in-person church services while the virus was spreading rapidly. A woman was interviewed as she went to church stating that she could not get sick or be harmed because she "was protected by the blood of Jesus." She was mocked in many online forums and her comments became a joking meme online. Yet others respectfully disagreed with her actions and behaviors using public health and safety instructions to support their views while treating her with compassion, respect, and dignity.

People have all sorts of religious and spiritual beliefs and practices that may seem odd to others who do not share the same traditions. While people do not necessarily agree with them, they can work to respect these individuals and disagree with them without mocking or dehumanizing them.

Justice

Justice is about fairness. Following the ethical principle of justice suggests that we treat people fairly and equally. Some types of communication with the divine and departed are socially acceptable and embraced by the culture. For example, prayers to God (or other names for God) are readily acceptable in most cultures. In fact, "in God we trust" is an American motto found on our currency, and "under God" is included in our pledge of alliance to the American flag. Catholics pray to saints and ask for their intercession. Churches are often named after saints as well as schools, universities, retreat centers, and so forth. However, small minority groups or people from different cultures may have prayer traditions that seem foreign or odd and may be treated differently than others. Therefore, to be just and fair, similar rules and acceptance should be considered for everyone even if minority groups engage in practices that seem odd or weird to others.

Additionally, efforts to communicate with the dead may make many people feel uneasy. Research that investigates the skills of spiritualists, mediums, clerics, and others who communicate with the dead are often experienced with great skepticism. This is a concern, as quality research needs to be agnostic and ultimately go where the data takes you rather than rely on preconceived notions of good or bad research topics for investigation. To be treated fairly and with justice, the quality of the reasoning and both methodological and statistical techniques, regardless of hypotheses, are critical to conduct quality and often groundbreaking research.

> *Example 12*: A prayer is offered before a public town council meeting and for many years, a local pastor or series of pastors offered the prayer. Someone suggested that an Islamic imam should be invited to conduct the prayer as more people from the Islamic tradition have moved into the town in recent years. The town council and community members rejected the suggestion only letting Protestant pastors conduct the prayer at the beginning of the meetings. They said that they would consider a Catholic priest but not an imam or a rabbi since they were not Christian.

In this example, only certain religious traditions are favored while others are rejected being treated unfairly, especially for a public community event among elected officials who supposedly represent the entire community including those of diverse faith traditions.

> *Example 13*: Dr. Smith has developed a randomized clinical trial project to examine the ability of spiritualists to communicate with the departed. It is methodologically sound and statistically sophisticated. Previously conducted smaller-scale studies on the topic have been very promising. Dr. Smith has applied for grants from a variety of foundations and government agencies with no luck at securing funding. Several preliminary papers have been submitted to journals with no acceptances either. During a professional conference, Dr. Smith casually asked journal editors and granting agency representatives about these projects and they reported in casual and off-the-record conversations that the projects were too controversial to fund or to publish regardless of their promise or the results of the studies conducted.

In this example, predetermined notions of what are and what are not comfortable and appropriate research topics dictate funding and journal acceptance rather than the merits and quality of the scholarship and the research results.

Beneficence

Beneficence is an ethical principle that suggests that we do not hurt anyone. Certainly, people may have their own spiritual and religious traditions that they embrace and practice that hurt no one. Yet, some religious and spiritual behaviors can indeed hurt others. Avoiding medical care when needed, physical abuse, discrimination, and so forth can be found among those stating that they are only following their religious beliefs and practices. People can use their religious and spiritual beliefs and practices to harm others and have done so for centuries.

Working on strategies, including technological ones, to communicate with the departed and the divine may also have unintended negative consequences. Any new technology, regardless of the merits of its development, often has surprising challenges once it is unleashed. We have seen this with social media and the spread of false or fake news as a recent example. Suppose technology was available to assist in communication with the divine and departed, how could it be misused? Therefore, as efforts are made to develop these technologies it is important to attend to unintended consequences as well as including ethicists and others who might be able to anticipate challenges along the way, especially once potential products and services are readily available to the public.

> *Example 14*: In some traditions, female circumcision is recommended by their religious views and beliefs. Additionally, honor killings are acceptable too. If a female youth brings dishonor to the family through her behavior then the family may kill her.

Certainly, these religious-based beliefs and practices are damaging and deadly and thus beneficence is violated within these customs and traditions.

> *Example 15*: Research is planned on devices to communicate with the departed and randomized trials are developed to study this new technology. Research participants are asked to sign standard informed consent documents but psychiatric screening was not conducted. During the course of the experiments, someone with a history of psychotic illness experienced a psychotic break while participating in the experiment. The participant required psychiatric hospitalization and their level of functioning was impaired for a number of weeks.

While there are always risks and benefits that may occur from research with human subjects, it is important to be mindful of how certain vulnerable people might be at higher risk when it comes to projects involving communication with the divine or departed.

Conclusions

Ethical issues are found in every aspect of life and certainly anything that has to do with prayer and communication with the divine and departed is no exception. The religious and spiritual feelings and views of those who wish to connect with the divine and departed are often highly emotional and sensitive topics and thus ethical considerations must be a top priority. While different ethical approaches are available to use for reflection, consideration, and decision-making, perhaps respect, justice, and beneficence are three critically important *prima facie* principles that could be followed to ensure that ethical reflection is considered in all aspects of this communication including research, policy, and practice.

References

Bowler, K. (2018). *Blessed: A history of the American prosperity gospel.* New York, NY: Oxford University Press.

Gitz-Johansen, T. (2016). The trip to America in 1909. *Journal of Analytical Psychology, 61*(3), 365–384.

Hood, R. W. Jr, Hill, P. C., & Spilka, B. (2018). *The psychology of religion: An empirical approach.* New York, NY: Guilford Publications.

Peters, S. F. (2007). *When prayer fails: Faith healing, children, and the law.* New York, NY: Oxford University Press.

Plante, T. G. (2004a). *Do the right thing: Living ethically in an unethical world.* Oakland, CA: New Harbinger.

Plante, T. G. (2004b). Ethics made simple: Using the RRICC model of personal and professional ethics. *The Clinical Psychologist, 57*, 28–30.

Plante, T. G. (2018). Ethical issues and challenges working with religious individuals and organizations: Providing culturally competent professional mental health services. In M. M. Leach & E. R. Welfel (Eds.), *The Cambridge handbook of applied psychological ethics* (pp. 366–383). New York, NY: Cambridge University Press.

Schwartz, G. E. (2011). *The sacred promise: How science is discovering spirit's collaboration with us in our daily lives.* New York, NY: Simon and Schuster.

Swanson, R. N. (2007). *Indulgences in late medieval England: Passports to paradise?* New York, NY: Cambridge University Press.

Vaughn, L. (2015). *Beginning ethics: An introduction to moral philosophy.* New York, NY: Norton.

Conclusions

Thomas G. Plante and Gary E. Schwartz

Perhaps everyone throughout the ages has wondered about the possibility of life after death and about the possible reality of some higher being or God-like supernatural figure. In fact, many people have spent their entire lives wondering, and often worrying, about the answers to these fundamental questions and have dedicated their lives, and have even died, for these questions. Some have acted with great certainty while others have been challenged by many nagging questions that they find deeply troubling. Certainly, questions about communication with the divine and departed and wondering about what happens after you (or your loved ones) die has occupied the minds of just about everyone for centuries. While there are so many questions, evidence-based and satisfying answers can be frustratingly difficult to come by.

Various academic disciplines and scholarly experts have offered thoughtful reflections about these questions over the centuries. For much of history, the religious and spiritual leaders, such as ordained clerics and theologians, were the most likely experts weighing in on these matters. During recent, and more secular decades, scientists and medical practitioners, such as doctors and STEM scientists, have been the preferred experts to turn to for understanding and guidance. In recent years, technologists and engineers have been invited to offer their expertise as well. As of this date, these age-old questions cannot be answered with great confidence but we can offer more informed and thoughtful reflections. Furthermore, according to some experts including a few featured in this book, we may be on the cusp of some important and even revolutionary discoveries. As we explain in the Preface, our intention was to provide historic and state-of-the-art information not only for individuals who were believers or questioners about the reality of spiritual communication but also for open-minded unbelievers as well.

This book project brought together leading experts from multiple disciplines and areas of expertise to reflect on these questions and offer their views based on a twenty-first century understanding of the experience, theology, psychology, and science of communication with the divine and departed. We hope that this contribution of multidisciplinary experts adds much to the existing literature and our understanding of this important topic. We also hope that this book will stimulate further research and discussion among those who have expertise in communication with the divine and departed as well as all those curious people of goodwill who are seeking answers to these age-old questions.

In the first section of this book, we heard a variety of highly compelling stories of individuals' experiences of communication with the deceased and the divine. We learned that these experiences are remarkably common, are clearly real to the reporters, and are gripping and riveting. The next section of the book examined the theological, religious, and spiritual context and understanding of these experiences from multiple and diverse perspectives. We learned that all of the major religious traditions have much to say about communication with the divine and departed and offer rich wisdom and thoughtful reflections on this topic. They have had centuries to fine-tune their thinking and reflections as well. Section three of the book turned to scientists, technologists, and physicians for an updated and evidence-based understanding of communication with the divine and departed with contemporary research and practice to help inform us. The state-of-the-art science using contemporary research methodologies and statistical analyses brings us much further along in our understanding than personal experience, theological considerations, and mere speculation and desires. Both laboratory and clinical science and practice reveal evidence for communication that is certainly remarkable and compelling. The final section of the book turned to psychologists to try to elucidate the psychology of meaning, purpose, and belief, helping us to better understand how our communication with the divine and departed helps us to manage and cope with the world and with our existential questions that swirl around all of us. We ended the section and the book with an introduction and reflection on ethics in the hope that vulnerable people who are sincerely searching for answers, understating, and connection with the divine and departed are never exploited. We assert that they are treated with ethical principles, values, and practices such as respect, compassion, and integrity.

As is often said, the whole is greater than the sum of its parts. We hope that the whole of this book, hearing from experts from many different areas of expertise and various knowledge bases, provides a thoughtful, informative, and helpful understanding of contemporary and evidence-based views on communication with the divine and departed in a way that is stimulating and satisfying to readers. We may not have all the answers, or even many of the answers, to these age old questions, but we may have at least some of the answers. We hope that further research and reflection will be forthcoming and that one day we will know for sure exactly what is and what is not possible regarding communication with the divine, the sacred, and the departed. Until then, quality science, practice, reflection, and personal experience will continue to bring us closer to the day when we can "look up from our lives" and see the emerging bigger picture of the sacred in life and the cosmos.

Index